How to Keep Your Teenager Out *of* Trouble

AND

What to Do If You Can't

BY DR. NEIL I. BERNSTEIN

WORKMAN PUBLISHING • NEW YORK

Library of Congress Cataloging-in-Publication Data
Bernstein, Neil I.
How to keep your teenager out of trouble and what to do if you can't/
by Neil I. Bernstein.
p. cm.
"A survival guide for all parents. The do's and don'ts for successful
cohabitation with adolescents and teenagers."
Includes bibliographical references.
ISBN 0-7611-2591-4 (hardcover)
ISBN 0-7611-1570-6 (pbk. : alk. paper)
1. Parent and teenager. 2. Parenting. 3. Communication in the family.
4. Discipline of children. 5. Adolescent psychology.

HQ799.15 .B48 2001
649'.125—dc21   2001035978

Cover design by Janet Vicario
Book design by Lisa Hollander and Susan Macleod

Workman books are available at special discounts when purchased in bulk for
premiums and sales promotions as well as for fund-raising or educational use.
Special editions or book excerpts can also be created to specification. For
details, contact the Special Sales Director at the address below.

Workman Publishing Company, Inc.
708 Broadway
New York, NY 10003-9555
www.workman.com
Printed in the U.S.A.
First printing, October 2001
10 9 8 7 6 5 4 3 2 1

To my parents,

whose love

runs deep in my heart

....

To my own teenagers,

Daniel and Julie,

who make parenting a joy

ACKNOWLEDGMENTS

I am grateful to all the teenagers and families who shared their lives with me over the years. Their stories form the nucleus of this book and remind me that the problems facing today's youth are solvable. My children deserve credit for tolerating my countless hours at the computer and for offering their own twists on some of the issues presented in this book.

Special thanks to my literary agent, Jenny Bent, who walked me through the arduous process of writing this book. She was always there when I needed her, from computer glitches to unscrambling my embryonic manuscript. An agent is truly a writer's best friend. Wendy Hammond provided solid editing and creative suggestions in the early drafts of this book, and Lynn Whittaker picked up the editing baton and ran with it in the later drafts, working tirelessly and supporting my efforts. The people at Workman—Suzanne Rafer, Beth Doty, Jim Eber, and particularly Jennifer Griffin—have been a pleasure to work with, and I consider myself fortunate to be a member of their family. Finally, Dr. Susan Gordon, a special friend, listened to my interminable ruminations and lent her support and professional insights to the creation of this book.

CONTENTS

INTRODUCTION

As a small child, **Michael Burke** was the apple of his parents' eye—precocious, athletic, and a pleasure to be around. Sure, he was a little headstrong, but he seemed to be an all-around good kid. Consequently, when his parents heard minor complaints from his elementary-school teachers, they were not concerned, feeling confident their son was a creative child who just needed some understanding and leeway.

Then, in fourth grade, Michael was sent home for starting a fight with a classmate. When his parents met with the principal, his father was flippant. "Boys just do that sometimes," he said. "We're not going to let a little thing like that worry us." The principal, however, took a less charitable view. "Mr. Burke," he said, "we're starting to worry about your son. He has trouble accepting directions from his teachers and seems intent on having his own way. We'll have to keep a closer eye on him in the future." His parents discussed this a little but assured each other there was no real problem.

By the time Michael was in sixth grade, annoying behavior was taking over his life. He had become disruptive, defiant, and difficult to manage. The Burkes, once tolerant of and even amused by their son's stubbornness, were angry with him most of the time and occasionally scared by his outbursts. How had their active, charming little boy become so hostile and aggressive?

When I met Michael, he was in ninth grade and in conflict with nearly everyone around him. In addition to shoplifting and fighting frequently, he was contemptuous and defiant of authority figures like his teachers and even the police. He was oblivious to rules and unresponsive to punishment. He answered my questions with a combination of indifference and annoyance, complaining of people being "on my case." As we proceeded, he offered a long justification of his behavior. His parents, he said, always blamed him for things that weren't his fault and never cut him any slack. High school was boring; the teachers picked on him; and his drinking was no big deal—almost everyone at school was doing it. He really didn't think he had any problems.

The Burkes, on the other hand, felt completely overwhelmed by their son's situation. Michael's mother explained, "There's no peace or happiness in our house anymore. There are just endless arguments with Michael over every possible thing: his drinking, his volatile temper, his failing grades." Michael's father agreed with her and added sadly, "We still love him, but we can't handle this anymore. Nothing we've said or done has made any difference. I just don't know what else we can do." He went on to explain that after a particularly violent episode, he had even looked into changing the locks on the doors. It broke his heart to think about throwing Michael out of the house, but he knew they couldn't go on like this any longer.

Your family may be like the Burkes'. It may be better or it may be much worse. Whether your child has simply become difficult and willful or has really spiraled out of control, this book is for you.

As the parent of a teenager, you know what wonderful creatures teens can be. They are charming, funny, and kind—filled with curiosity, boundless energy, and ideas about how the world ought to be. When you look at your teen, you remember the adorable child he once was; at the same time you see an incredible adult emerging, full of humor and personality and seemingly limitless potential. Watching him develop makes your heart swell with pride, especially when you look at how treacherous the world around you has become.

That very same kid, however, can also be defiant, irritable, sullen, and reckless. He disagrees with whatever you say, considers you embarrassing, and thinks he knows everything. At times his behavior makes little sense, only to shift again before you can figure it out, and through it all he is adamant that you could not possibly understand his life. He may be impervious to authority, unfazed by punishment, infuriating, and nearly unlovable. His concerns may seem limited to his friends and his room—when he seems to have any interests at all—and he wants you to just stay out of the way, while assuming you'll be there when he needs you.

If you are reading this, you are probably nearing the end of your rope. You may feel that your teen's behavior has surpassed what can reasonably be expected from an adolescent. You may be worried about his or her safety, or about that of others. You are certainly concerned for your whole family's happiness. At times you may gaze in astonishment at this child of yours and feel he or she is no longer someone you even know, but has become a stranger in your house.

For more than twenty years in my practice as a psychologist, I have worked with teenagers in private practice, hospitals, outpatient clinics, and school settings. I have taught them, counseled them, and lived with them. I have seen teenagers alone, with their families, and in groups. I have dealt with family issues ranging from daily annoyances (sarcasm, dirty rooms, procrastinating over homework) to significant crises (antisocial behavior, substance abuse, flagrant defiance, running away). Regrettably, my business is booming.

My experience with adolescents is not limited to my office. I have coached sports teams and volunteered in classrooms, and I'm raising two teenagers of my own. I have worried about children coming home late, handling unfamiliar situations, and choosing friends who are headed in the wrong direction.

It is no exaggeration to say that the challenges of growing up are more daunting than ever. Adolescence will never be without awkwardness and uncertainty. Today's teenagers, like those of generations past, are concerned with asserting their independence, being accepted by others, and ultimately carving out a role for themselves in society, all of which can create confusion, rebellion, and experimentation. Today's teens, however, are also facing the complications of the times we live in—some may be coping with divorce, others with violence, and almost all are facing more pressures surrounding sex and drugs than you or I did at their age. The road to adulthood will be filled with many bumps and detours. It is your job to keep your family on track through the rough passages as well as the clear ones to ensure that your teen becomes a responsible, well-adjusted adult with strong values, self-esteem, and respect for others.

My approach to getting teens back on track and mending family fences has evolved gradually over years of practice with desperate parents and struggling kids. I've had numerous opportunities to observe effective parenting practices, as well as those that don't work or even backfire. I offer you only what I know has worked, and I present it in the way I have found most clear and effective. *First,* I remind you of what challenges and stresses your teen may be experiencing and how he or she may be feeling as a result. *Second,* I reinforce the parenting skills that are essential to raising all teenagers and keeping them out of trouble. And *third,* I tell you what you must know to address challenging, risky, defiant, and antisocial behaviors. My hope is that after reading this book you'll know how to detect problems before they blow up, and that if things have already gone too far, you will have the resources to regain control of your family.

I'm a firm believer in learning from others' experiences, so an important part of this book is the case histories of parents and teenagers I've gotten to know in the course of my practice. (All names have been changed for confidentiality.) Case studies offer examples of how misunderstandings can arise and trouble incubate in your own family, and they reveal a range of behavior from normal to distressing to imminently dangerous. While some may reflect behavior that is too tame or too extreme to be relevant to you, they all give you something to compare your experience against.

Tolstoy observed that all happy families are alike, while unhappy families are unhappy in their own ways. I hope this book will be a first step toward meeting whatever unique challenges you and your teen face, and that you will find here the knowledge, skills, and resources—not to mention some measure of strength and camaraderie—to ensure that your family becomes happy and whole again.

HOW TEENAGERS GET INTO TROUBLE

"Why has my teenager started doing such stupid things?"

"Did I completely miss the warning signs?"

"Is he acting out because of bad childhood experiences?"

"Why does my daughter have such a sleazy group of friends?"

"How did my son end up in this downward spiral?"

Unfortunately for frustrated parents, it is often difficult to figure out why a teenager has started getting into trouble. Troubled teens don't come only from dysfunctional or broken families, and they don't all live on the wrong side of the tracks. They come from a wide variety of families, with different values, cultures, ethnicities, and economic backgrounds. And they weren't necessarily "bad seeds" when they were growing up, either. Some were hard to manage from early on, but others drifted gradually (seemingly irretrievably) into problems. Still others seemed to become difficult all of a sudden.

Behavioral problems don't arise overnight, although it can seem that way. Teenagers who break rules, abuse drugs and alcohol, do poorly in school, and behave aggressively developed these difficulties (or the underlying problems that led to them) gradually, whether you noticed the warning signs or not. Typically, serious problems grow out of multiple frustrations, which often include weakened family connections and an inability to acquire the skills needed to negotiate adolescence. And behavior problems tend to run in clusters. If you catch your teen in some deviant or out-of-control behavior, chances are he's misbehaving in other ways as well, although not as noticeably. But not all teenagers who break a rule every now and then are headed for trouble. There are big differences between normal adolescent behavior, which is to be expected; risk-taking behavior, which exceeds normal expectations; and serious difficulties, which must be addressed immediately.

THE TEENAGE YEARS: A WORK IN PROGRESS

The teenage years pass relatively quickly when compared with later periods in life, but the changes that occur during them are enormous. Just think of the world of difference that exists between a thirteen-year-old and a nineteen-year-old. A thirteen-year old is barely out of childhood; he relies on his parents for meals, clean clothes, and transportation, and sometimes physically resembles an awkward child. A 19-year-old, on the other hand, usually has a driver's license, can vote, has probably graduated from high school, is physically mature, and may be living on his own, attending college or working full-time. There are profound developmental milestones that a teenager must reach during his or her journey to maturity: learning to be independent, developing an identity, and separating from parents in a healthy way. These often progress in sequence, although each young person will progress at his or her own pace.

The road to adulthood is made even bumpier by hormones, which send your teen careening on a chemical joyride. Criticism and rejection can trigger overwhelming feelings of inadequacy and anger, while a simple compliment can elate and inspire. Young teens lack experience, and therefore perspective. And because their moods are often so volatile and they feel things so extremely, they may exhibit an astonishing range of emotion. One moment your daughter is raging and screaming over whose turn it was to do the dishes; two minutes later she is laughing hysterically when a friend calls with funny news.

Your child's priorities may completely change as he enters adolescence. He may no longer enjoy his favorite childhood activities, and you may be surprised at what he does enjoy. Peer pressure, with its dictates of what's cool and what's not, often contributes to changes in a child's tastes. Parents may be astonished to notice their daughter buying the latest hit CD when she used to like listening to the oldies station, or their son pestering them for new, expensive clothes when just a year ago they couldn't get him out of his favorite ratty T-shirt. Teenagers' behavior may not always make sense to you, but it does follow its own logic as they grapple with changes that fuel their actions.

During the initial stage of adolescence, some teens must adjust to their rapidly developing bodies, while others worry at their lack of development. Magazines and TV provide plenty of images of the ideal appearance—usually based on models and actors—which most teens cannot (and in many cases should not) live up to. Physical differences from the norm are considered bad and sometimes attract teasing. It's difficult for many adults to remember how brutal adolescent society can be. Our adolescent children witness (or experience) a great deal of verbal abuse: the overweight, unattractive, and uncool are often reduced to tears. This leaves all teens feeling excessively concerned about their appearance and sensitive to any perceived criticism. The beginning of sexual feelings further complicates things as teens experience their first crushes and relationships.

Older teens begin to resolve some of these insecurities. As they become more comfortable with themselves, they develop a stronger sense of identity. They take on responsibilities such as driving, owning a car, holding a job, getting good grades, observing curfews, and looking to their future—and they encounter things they rarely share or discuss with their parents, like alcohol, drugs, and sex. The way they negotiate these new responsibilities and challenges powerfully contributes to their identity.

Alongside their search for a meaningful identity is their attempt to separate from their parents. Teenagers want to be thought of as individuals who can make their own decisions, and their struggles to be independent take many guises. They experiment with different clothing styles, language, music, and ideas, and they challenge their parents' taste and values. But they continually look over their shoulders to see what their peers are doing because they need reinforcement from others like them.

During the final stage of adolescence, young people are preparing for their role in the adult world. This stage, which can extend from the later high school years through college, remains a time of great uncertainty for teens as they begin to live on their own and take on responsibility for their future. They begin to think about what kind of people they are and how they affect those around them.

These typical teenage attitudes and behaviors do not usually suggest serious problems:

- Mood changes and occasional irritability (particularly with what they see as their parents' "dumb" questions)
- Locking themselves in their room for hours on end
- Self-consciousness about their appearance
- Concern about acceptance by their peers
- Being convinced that they know almost everything
- Pronounced need for independence and distance from their parents (usually combined with an expectation that those same parents will be there when needed!)
- Disagreeing just for the sake of disagreeing
- Taking their parents for granted
- Frequent shifts in beliefs and loyalties
- Expressing fear and uncertainty about their future

With all these changes, it's no wonder the teenage years are rough on both teens and their parents. Teenagers are often bewildered and overwhelmed by the changes taking place, internally and externally. And their confusion can inspire rebellion. They'll break your rules, experiment with risky behaviors, and allow themselves to be influenced by undesirable peers. And if you're not careful, before you know it, their behavior will exceed the normal expectations of adolescence.

The following behaviors should alert you to possible trouble:

- Marked isolation from family life and continual refusal to talk to you
- Ongoing extreme or suspicious behavior (being secretive, sullen, or constantly angry)
- Continually breaking rules and curfew
- Constantly sleeping beyond normal nighttime hours
- Spending most of their time with friends who get into trouble
- Across-the-board rejection of your values and protesting at every opportunity your attempts to uphold them
- Loss of interest in school and other constructive activities

- Irrational overprotectiveness regarding friends, especially in the face of clear evidence of their faults or wrongdoings
- Frequent aggressiveness toward family and other authority figures outside the home
- Consistently engaging in risky or criminal behavior (drinking, stealing, vandalizing, fighting)
- Dishonesty toward and manipulation of others, whether in the family or outside

BELOW THE SURFACE

Your daughter tells you that she's embarrassed to even be seen with you and that she hopes people can't tell the two of you are related, yet she's crushed when you can't make it to see her cameo role in the school production of *Oklahoma!* Your son angrily criticizes you and your spouse for being too materialistic and money oriented, but five minutes later he demands more money to buy CDs. What's going on?

It's hard to understand the paradoxical, contradictory behavior of teens until you begin to perceive the world as they do. Of course, you have your own memories of high school to refer to, but memories are selective; it's easy to remember the dramatic events, but not so easy to remember what it's like day to day. And times change; compared to some of the problems teens face today, your ideas about high school may be as quaint as *Leave It to Beaver*. So it's important that parents really pay attention to their adolescent children, because the sources of the anger and bad behavior you witness often lie far beneath the surface.

Teenagers are ingenious at devising ways to express their pain and anger, directly and indirectly, and many teens' explanations and justifications for their actions are enigmatic. It can be very difficult for a parent to get to the root of a problem. Some years ago a young man told me that anger was his friend. When I asked him to explain, his response was revealing. "Well, I guess having a bad temper helps me get what I want," he said. "You know, some people just give in when you create a hassle. The kids in school are a little afraid of me and I've got this reputation. To tell you the truth, I sort of like it."

Nearly every teen will complain regularly and openly about things parents do or say that bother them. A few will store their angry and painful feelings, but even if they aren't obvious, they influence how your child acts. For example, some teenagers will hide their most painful, hurt, angry feelings but will allow this anger to surface in other ways, such as aggressive behavior or fighting over comparatively minor issues. Despite teens' rebuffs of their parents, they still expect you to love them, set limits for them, be there when they need you, and treat them with respect. The absence of any of these essentials can fuel pain and anger and eventually lead to trouble.

If you want to deal effectively with teenagers, you must understand their logic and their sometimes roundabout ways of getting what they want and need. You may not agree with what your children say, but you must respect their right to say it. And you must also learn to look beyond the surface to see what's really going on.

TEENS' COMPLAINTS ABOUT PARENTS

So what are teenagers thinking? Listen carefully to what they say. Here is my top five list of the most popular teen complaints about parents. Typical teenagers occasionally make these comments, but those heading for trouble seem to dwell on them. The more intense the complaints, the greater the cause for concern. As you read them and think about how they apply to your own situation, keep in mind that there's often more to a complaint than meets the ear. Hearing the true message behind the complaint is crucial to an improved relationship that can help keep your teen out of trouble.

1. "If my parents would just leave me alone, everything would be fine." Almost all teenagers want greater independence from their parents. But teenagers in trouble strongly believe they'd be much better off without any parental help or supervision at all. Unfortunately, given the opportunity to prove it, most fail miserably, because they lack the basic skills they need to manage their own lives. The angry words that come so easily to them often express their frustration with their inability to cope. Does your child complain vehemently about your excessive nagging and yet seem to depend on you to manage her life? Think about how lost she might feel if you didn't say anything about her clothes, homework, chores, or bedtime for a whole day.

2. "My parents are so out of touch." It would surprise many teenagers to know that you often understand exactly what they're going through. Teens can barely believe that you were once an adolescent too and had the same feelings about your parents, so it never occurs to them that you might be able to offer them support and understanding. Usually, the angrier the teens are, the more strongly they believe you are clueless. Sometimes they withhold pertinent information and then complain that you don't know about it. As informed parents, you should know about drugs, fads, and other aspects of adolescent culture your children take for granted. They'll insist that their friends' parents let *them* stay out late, go to concerts you don't approve of, or wear outfits you find inappropriate. (These "cool parents" are often a fabrication or exaggeration, designed by your teen to manipulate you into being more accommodating.) It helps to remember that your teen's real anger is over his or her inability to communicate with you.

3. "My parents are control freaks." Teens frequently resort to this convenient expression whenever you take a firm stand about what you will or won't tolerate. Parents do sometimes have unreasonable expectations and impose unreasonable consequences, but even when this isn't the case, your teenager may feel she needs to justify her rebellion by placing the blame on somebody else: you. Be leery of excessive control, and be honest with yourself about how realistic your expectations are. Setting limits is an essential ingredient of effective parenting; we'll be talking about it throughout this book. Although many teenagers balk at limits and it seems almost routine for adolescents to complain about unfair rules, they're usually secretly relieved to have them, provided the limits are reasonable.

4. "All my parents care about is . . ."

Teenagers often attack their parents' values because they feel frustrated, hurt, and unable to please their parents. Many believe that nothing they do is ever good enough. So they abandon their efforts, and the family situation turns sour. They complain about your social networks, possessions, favoritism toward their siblings, or preoccupation with their school achievement. Unsure about her own values, your teenager defines herself in terms of what she doesn't like rather than what she does. This pattern of behavior usually occurs when young people feel misunderstood; angry at their inability to make their points through normal channels of communication, they attack and disparage, going out of their way to do things that make you cringe. Beware, though: sometimes their frustrations are a genuine response to unrealistic parental expectations (as when a struggling student's parents expect her to get straight A's).

Signs That Teenagers Are Feeling Frustrated and Hurt

- She continually tells you that it doesn't matter when you let her down.

- He overreacts to seemingly neutral comments.

- She goes out of her way to avoid you.

- He tells you about his friends' parents who are "so cool."

- She abandons any efforts to gain your approval.

- He insists that everything is fine when his appearance and actions suggest otherwise.

5. "They don't even know me." This may be the most compelling complaint teenagers level at their parents—because it's often true: you don't know them much of the time. How could you, when their world is so different from yours? Yet this, too, often comes down to communication. Teens usually feel misunderstood when they think they are being rejected or feel unable to communicate with you. Your daughter may allege that you show no interest in her except for her performance in a school recital, where she demonstrates the talent you've invested in. You don't know anything about her *real* interests, she wails—her important relationships or biggest concerns. Many teenagers complain that they want their parents to stay out of their business and at the same time lament that their parents don't care what interests them! You're damned if you do and damned if you don't. My advice is, always respond to your children's desire for you to know them, not to their wishes that you leave them alone, and even more so if the signals are implicit rather than explicit.

PARENTS' COMPLAINTS ABOUT TEENS

There are two sides to every story. Over the years I've heard parents voice many legitimate complaints about their teenagers. And sometimes, like their children's complaints, those voiced by parents can be exaggerated. But such statements are useful commentaries on how parents feel and what issues they are grappling with. Among other things, they demonstrate that teenagers don't have a monopoly on anger and hurt. No doubt, some of these complaints will sound very familiar.

"We don't get any respect." Like many parents, you may often feel your teen is insensitive to your feelings. He treats you with contempt and makes no effort to cooperate. You've tried to bite your tongue in the face of his criticism, his attacks on your integrity, his inconsiderate behavior. Years of bickering may even have eroded the natural affection and easy communication you once treasured. As one father put it to me, "They just turn on you." But respect in a relationship has to be earned, not demanded, by both children and parents. And without it there is little basis for productive dialogue. Fortunately, in most cases you can earn your children's respect by being caring, consistent, firm, and fair. And if your children regularly toss cruel remarks and insults your way, keep a cool temper but don't be shy about letting them know that their words can really hurt.

"They don't appreciate anything we do for them."

"How sharper than a serpent's tooth it is," said King Lear, "to have a thankless child." Most parents make great sacrifices for their children and feel they get no gratitude in return. The parents of one girl I was counseling went to great lengths to tell me all they had done for their daughter, who was in serious trouble for shoplifting. "When she was a child," her mother said, "we took her everywhere she wanted to go: her friends' houses, McDonald's, Disney World. We felt like chauffeurs. We went to as many of her games as we could. We spent our savings to buy her the things we never had: nice clothes, summer camp, and a house in the suburbs. When she was little she used to thank us and give us her big smile and a hug. Now all she says is, 'It's no big deal—all my friends get those things.' She has no idea how much we've done for her. Sometimes we ask ourselves if it's been worth it."

This complaint about feeling unappreciated is voiced by many parents, including those whose teenagers are not in trouble. Many teens are in such a hurry with their lives that they don't take time to stop and say thank you every now and then. It doesn't mean they don't notice and don't care. However, you can certainly teach your children to feel appreciation and say thank you when someone, even a parent, does something nice for them.

Parents who find themselves identifying with this complaint should pay special note to the dangers of overindulgence (page 23).

"Our child has turned out to be such a disappointment." No teen is ever perfect, and most parents suffer occasional mild feelings of disappointment over things they wish their children had done differently. But parents of teenagers who are continually in trouble find it hard to tolerate their feelings of frustration and helplessness, and sometimes they abandon hope. They ask themselves where they've failed and how they got to the point of writing off their child as a lost cause. One mother told me in anguish how during an angry tirade she'd told her son he was a real loser and should just leave the house. For once, the son cooperated, running away the next day and staying away for almost two weeks. Sometimes conditions get so bad that you're convinced your child is unsalvageable. But don't make the mistake of accepting this view, as this could turn into a self-fulfilling prophecy.

"We feel like we just don't know her anymore." Ironically, this may be just what your teenager is saying about you. Parents have often told me they don't feel connected with their child, that she's become secretive, spends much of her time in her room, and talks only to her friends. Despite their efforts, they can't bring her back into the family fold. The teenager, of course, is going out of her way to avoid them, maybe because she's involved in some kind of illicit activity or, worse, because she's convinced they don't care about her or won't try to understand her. Teenagers who feel alienated from their parents are at great risk for serious problems like substance abuse and antisocial behavior.

"He's just pulling the wool over your eyes." Over the years I've heard angry parents tell me their child is fooling everyone. If I say how cooperative she's been in my office, or mention a teacher's positive report, they laugh cynically. They worry that others don't see her as she really is and won't be able to believe the trouble she's causing at home. It's normal for teens to reserve their worst behavior for their family and to be perfectly well adjusted everywhere else. But if the behavior at home is really that of a troubled teen, there are two serious possibilities. It could be that their teen really does have behavioral problems and a terrible attitude that she is hiding behind a kind, polite mask. If that's the case, her polite façade will eventually crumble, even if it takes a while for something to provoke her, and other people will witness her unpleasant side for themselves. The other possibility is that their teenager actually is much worse at home than anywhere else. If that's really the case, parents will need to carefully assess their parenting practices to determine what changes are needed. And observing their child in other situations may reveal what fuels the difference in her behavior.

PROBLEMS THAT CAN LEAD TO TROUBLE

Of the most frequent reasons, listed below, why teenagers get into trouble, the first three are conditions nearly all young people have experienced—depression, alienation, and anger. They lead to real trouble only if they become extreme. The other four problems are experienced by only some teens and are generally related to ongoing harmful experiences or physiological problems.

Depression

Most teenagers feel sad every now and then. Their excessive concerns with their appearance and peer acceptance can lead to self-doubt. And they'll probably have to endure such disappointments as poor grades on tests, failing to make a team, and being ignored by their crush, all of which can lead them to question their own worth. But these feelings of sadness are usually short-lived and should not be confused with depression. Your child may mope around the house for a few days, complaining about what's wrong, but the negative feelings will pass.

Some teens, on the other hand, become clinically depressed,

a condition that differs from sadness and often accompanies behavior problems. These teens are genuinely and profoundly unhappy with their lives and prone to trouble. Some depressed teens engage in dangerous behaviors, abandon their school efforts, and pull away from their families. Others may become so depressed that they lack the emotional energy to get through their daily lives. They may spend most of their time locked in their rooms or turn to drugs for relief. These teens are more likely to harm themselves than others, and they desperately need help. Teenagers whose depression is combined with anger are at risk for especially potent problems.

How do you know when your teenager is depressed? Be on the lookout for these signs:

- Lack of energy
- Sleeping problems
- Marked change of appetite
- Decreased motivation at school or at home
- Increased agitation and irritability
- Showing interest in music, drawings, or writing with depressing themes
- Persistent sadness
- Expressing an interest in death or suicide

Some other signs that you may not realize reflect an underlying depression:

- Use of alcohol and marijuana
- Reckless driving
- Risky sexual behavior
- Extreme difficulty tolerating boredom
- Reduced interest in friends
- Radical change in appearance

If substance abuse, suicidal thoughts, and risky sexual behavior become a pattern, I strongly suggest that you seek professional help; this is not something you can handle on your own. You can contact your family physician, a school counselor, or the referral service of a professional association (psychologists, social workers, or psychiatrists). These experts will be happy to give you the names of qualified professionals who can be of help. You'll find a list of additional resources in the Appendix of this book.

Alienation

Most kids buck convention every now and then. They'll dye their hair, wear bizarre clothing, and listen to music that makes their parents' skin crawl. They're making a statement to the world around them that they are different, unique, or avant-garde. Fortunately, this kind of behavior will usually pass—it is merely a step in the journey toward adulthood and it should not be confused with alienation.

A small but significant group of teenagers, however, feel completely estranged from their peer group, school, and parents. Often from early in their lives, they were teased, picked on, or otherwise ostracized by classmates. Their parents were either unwilling or unable to support them, and they grew increasingly distant from their families, convinced that their parents were indifferent. Their teachers and counselors may have failed to notice their distress signals and respond to their needs as well, leaving them feeling further isolated. As a result, many of these kids failed to experience school as a safe place and withdrew from those around them.

The treatment they received may or may not have been motivated by their own behaviors, but the wounds linger long after they have been inflicted. These teenagers often speak about their contempt for those who have mistreated them, and in some cases about their wish to get back at those people. They carry around these grudges for years and seek dramatic ways to express their feelings: outrageous forms of dress, oppositional behavior, mockery and disrespect toward their peers, and at the most extreme, school violence.

Because these youth are angry and bitter about their experiences, they are drawn to like-minded peers who offer them solace and a feeling of belonging. Together, these alienated young people plot ways to make their presence known. Fortunately, not all these teens get in trouble, but they are more likely to because of their need to rebel against those they see as the typical teenagers who have rejected them.

Signs of alienation include:

- He complains bitterly that the other kids in his grade are all jerks.
- She is extensively involved with interests that clearly fall outside the realm of typical teen pursuits (for example, music with occult or Satanic lyrics, collecting weapons, subversive political groups, cults).
- He has relinquished his identification with family members and rejects their values.
- She rejects the value of school, claiming the classes are irrelevant to her life, and her grades reflect this attitude.
- He makes angry references to getting back at those teenagers who have given him a hard time.
- She admires those who openly rebel against society's conventions.
- His dress is intentionally and conspicuously different from his peers' for an extended period of time (in combination with the above signs).

Anger

Almost all teens get angry at their parents every now and then. They'll scream at you for forgetting to give them a message, intruding into their room, or making them go on a family outing. But this anger is usually short-lived. They'll vent their feelings and then return to business as usual. What seemed to be a mortal wound one day is history the next. In fact, sometimes they seem compelled to disagree with everything you say, to get some perverse pleasure out of upsetting you. One mother swore that if she remarked that the sun was shining, her daughter would say it was raining. While this compulsion to contradict may seem extreme to you, it's normal to teenagers. And in fact, there is something therapeutic to them about complaining.

But while some teenagers stop at that, others carry around a heavy load of anger and often vent it, usually at their parents. These teenagers who are angry most of the time are more prone to trouble than those who experience anger only occasionally. Recurrent, powerful feelings of anger can often cause teens to defy adults and to engage in risky behavior that contradicts good judgment. Often their anger has accumulated over the years and underlies many of their actions.

In my experience, the following feelings most often underlie teenagers' anger:

- They believe their parents are selfish and don't have time for them.
- They feel criticized and rejected.
- They need more attention and caring but are unable to ask for it directly.
- Deep down they want limits set on their behavior, and they are not getting any.
- They want to feel understood by their parents, but they aren't.
- They feel burdened by their parents' inappropriate and excessive worries.
- They're unhappy with their own lives and take it out on their parents.

It's critical that you develop an understanding of what these angry teens are so worked up about, for only then can you judge the legitimacy of their gripes and respond accordingly. Although sometimes you'll recognize expressions of anger as self-serving manipulations, at other times you may have to take a close look in the mirror. When you do, what you'll see is an audience—which is

An Angry Young Man

Angry adolescents are skilled in finding the most offensive ways to express themselves to their parents. If you value neatness, your daughter keeps her room messy. If you're proud of your house, your son kicks holes in the wall when he loses his temper. If foul language makes you uncomfortable, your angry teen perfects his vocabulary of obscenities. Turning up the volume of the stereo is another simple way to annoy parents. And one of the most far-reaching angry protests is deliberately failing school in response to parents' demands for academic excellence.

Several years ago, I worked with David, a fifteen-year-old who his parents felt devoted his entire existence to upsetting their equilibrium. As we got to know each other better, David told me that he felt his parents put him down, and he was certain he could never get their approval. Since he didn't care about their feelings, what difference did it make how he behaved? In fact, David acknowledged that he often calculated his actions to be the opposite of what his parents valued. They were ardent churchgoers—he refused to attend. His mother dressed conservatively—he wore all black clothing like his rock idols. His father voted against a local initiative to legalize marijuana—David was strongly in favor of it. This type of protest felt like a statement of independence to David. However, David's actions and opinions were all completely dependent upon what his parents thought or did. He hadn't spent any time figuring out who he really was or what he believed in; he was too busy focusing all of his energy in being his parents' opposite.

I told David during one of our meetings that he would really be independent when he could do what he wanted even if his parents were in favor of it. At first David could not grasp this. "There's no way I'll act the way they want me to. They want me to be a geek." David was so consumed with his anger and contempt that he was a prisoner of it. It took time for him to learn how to effectively convey his intended message— that he needed ways to express his own personality apart from the preferences of his parents.

exactly what angry teens need most. When they think they've gotten their point across, they're less likely to remain at odds with you.

As you try to understand the sources of your teen's anger, remember that no matter how unjustified their actions may seem to you, from their point of view such actions are perfectly defensible. In fact, teens don't always *realize* why they're so unhappy, frustrated, or angry—they simply react. To their way of thinking, other people just don't understand them, so they have every right to be angry.

Experience of Abuse and Neglect

I can't think of anything more harmful to a child's development than abuse and neglect. Often this problem begins well before adolescence, but may continue throughout it. The effects are far-reaching. Youth who have been either physically or emotionally abused in any way are likely to have difficulty trusting others. They harbor considerable anger over the way they have been treated, and they may not express this anger directly. The results of their mistreatment are disastrous.

Some of these abused youth withdraw from society, while others lash out at the world around them. In either case, kids who have been abused are far more likely to get into trouble than those who have not. And worse yet, teenage violence is frequently associated with a history of early abuse. This issue is especially difficult for parents to face, but there's no avoiding it. If you or a loved one are behaving abusively toward your child, seek help immediately. Further, if you know of a situation where a young person is being abused, you owe it to yourself and the child to report it. You'll find information and referral sources at the end of this book.

Neglected children do not receive messages that they are loved and important, and they do not receive adequate parental care. At too young an age they are left alone to struggle with tasks like homework, eating, and bedtime without the help they need from their parents. They receive little or no validation or support from their parents.

Such children experience all sorts of difficulties later in life. As teens they may fill the empty, unsupervised hours with friends whose influence, good or bad, will go unchecked, or they may choose to watch excessive amounts of TV or use alcohol or drugs. They may suffer from a poor diet of junk food since they eat unsupervised, and their appearance and hygiene can be bad since they must take care of themselves. They are often solitary, mistrustful figures who weren't given the opportunity to make real connections at home and thus have a hard time making real connections with people outside the home. They may suffer from depression and lack a sense of self-worth. As with abuse, you should report any cases of severe neglect that you encounter, using the information and referral sources at the end of the book.

School Difficulties

Academic deficiencies are highly correlated with behavior problems. Teenagers who fail to adjust to school and to negotiate academic demands have difficulties in many aspects of their lives. They are likely to have problems with their peers and family members as well. Naturally, poor school performance weakens self-esteem and spills over into other areas of their lives. Often the result is an increased susceptibility to trouble. There are many reasons why kids have academic problems, and once you have determined the cause, there are steps that you can take to help them. (Chapter 9, which begins on page 369, goes into school-related problems in more depth.)

Neurological Problems

Although you're probably aware of attention deficit disorder (ADD), you may not know that about 50 percent of teenagers who get in trouble have it. That's an alarming statistic, underscoring the role that neurological problems can play. Teenagers with ADD (with or without a hyperactive component) have difficulty with attention and concentration, impulsive behavior, and a high activity level. This puts them at much greater risk of getting into trouble than the average teenager. There are also other, less common neurological disorders, both major and minor, that may lead to negative behavior in your teen. If you suspect this may be the case, you will all benefit from identifying and treating these problems as quickly as possible.

Experience of Criticism and Rejection

Teenagers who feel they belong nowhere as a result of having been frequently criticized and rejected may respond in several different ways. Beneath their façade of indifference, they are profoundly sad and negative about themselves. They genuinely don't believe life could be different. *I don't deserve to be happy,* they think, and with no hope they show no incentive to change. Their pessimism prevents them from setting realistic goals and seeking healthy challenges.

Many of these teens strike out angrily at the world. They devote their energy to covering up their perceived inadequacies, protesting against parents' encouragement, and looking for shortcuts (like drinking, using illegal drugs, violating rules, cutting school, becoming sexually promiscuous, and behaving aggressively) to make themselves feel better. Other teens retreat from the society that has caused them such pain and exist in isolation. They are afraid to reach out to someone else for fear that they will be rejected again, so they try to be as unobtrusive as possible. They may also turn to drinking and drugs, may indiscriminately befriend anyone who will tolerate them, or may turn to promiscuity as a way to gain acceptance. The bottom line is that whether they are lashing out or turning inward, these rejected teens are in a great deal of trouble.

HOW PARENTS' BEHAVIOR CAN MAKE PROBLEMS WORSE

Even though you want the best for your children, sometimes you can lose perspective when faced with a difficult situation and instinctively behave in whatever way is familiar to you. This reaction may have evolved from your own upbringing and usually reflects your personality. Sometimes you may take the path of least resistance and give in to whatever your teen wants;

The Effects of Criticism and Rejection

When fourteen-year-old Cathy was brought to my office by her desperate parents, they said everything was a hassle with her. When they asked her to clean her room, come to dinner, or do her homework, she refused. Sometimes she didn't answer at all. "She does whatever she wants," her parents lamented.

Cathy had been angry for years by the time she came to see me. On the surface, she seemed obstinate and unaffected by her parents' attempts at discipline. Her trademarks were angry outbursts and self-righteous indignation. Yet beneath the bravado was a very different young woman.

Childhood hadn't been easy for Cathy, partly because she was awkward and uncoordinated. When her father tried to teach her to ride a bicycle, she cried and insisted she couldn't do it. He encouraged her to keep trying and spent hours running alongside the bike, holding it up while she struggled to keep her balance. But no matter how patient he tried to be, nothing seemed to work. Finally he lost his temper and shouted that he knew she could do it because her brother had learned the same

way. This outburst, of course, only made a bad situation worse, and Cathy never did learn to ride a bicycle.

While Cathy's father remembered this incident as an example of her noncompliance, her memory of the experience was different. "All I can remember," she said, angry and tearful, "is my dad yelling and screaming at me. I thought it would never stop. God, I used to dread it when he'd say we were going out to ride that bike. It was like that with a lot of other things when I was a kid. I'd try my best and just couldn't do it. And my parents didn't believe me! They would keep telling me to try harder and compare me to my brother. When I got older they would criticize me and I would yell back or take off to my room. Now I'm through taking their shit."

Not surprisingly, Cathy felt just as discouraged at school. She struggled with academic subjects and was described by her teachers as an underachiever with a negative attitude. When they leaned on her to try harder, she resisted. Her parents' support of the school's efforts only led to more arguments. Her social experi-

at other times you may take an extreme position and create a situation that will harm both you and your child. What you hope is to foster compliance and head off problems, but certain child-rearing approaches, however well intentioned, appear to add fuel to the fire. Beware of these practices and their accompanying dangers.

ences weren't very successful either. She wanted desperately to fit in with her peers but she was overweight, boisterous, and socially awkward, and other girls kept their distance. Cathy pressed harder, and sensing her desperation, they responded by teasing her. Over the years, she became isolated, irritable, and bitter. "The other kids can go to hell," she spat out during one meeting with me.

Cathy is one of many teenagers who have known disappointment, rejection, and criticism all their lives. Cathy was angry at her parents because she felt they always found fault with her actions and never accepted her as she was. Young people like her become cynical and defiant toward a world they see as full of enemies. They're no longer willing to talk—certainly not to their parents—about their frustration and sadness. Home doesn't feel like a safe haven to them. Cathy drifted further and further away from the people who could offer her solace: school counselors, relatives, and her minister. Like other troubled teenagers, she compensated by seeking out like-minded peers who would make her feel like she belonged. She was at great risk. Was there a happy ending for Cathy?

Unfortunately, high school remained an unhappy place for her. When she was an upperclassman, the teasing slacked off somewhat, but Cathy still found herself lonely and frustrated. She would hear other students talk about parties and the prom and know that she would never be included in these activities. But because she wanted to earn her high school diploma, she made an effort to stick it out and worked hard for her mostly C grades. On graduation day she was proud of herself, as were her parents.

Despite her parents' pressure to enroll at the local community college, Cathy decided to skip college. Instead she took a job as an administrative assistant at a big company. There she found coworkers who were friendly and supportive. There was a strong sense of camaraderie, and they helped her to figure things out during her first few months. She made a few good work friends with whom she would eat lunch and go for drinks after work. Cathy had finally found a place where people liked her as she was, and she slowly began to bloom in her new surroundings. However, her low self-esteem and frustration would take a long, long time to get past.

Overindulgence

Some children are raised with everything they want and still find their way into trouble. There is such a thing as having too much. Children who never learn to appreciate what they're given become selfish and difficult to live with. Although your behavior may spring from a simple desire for the best for your children, parents who overindulge their kids may create a serious risk to their healthy emotional development.

Italian actor Roberto Benigni, in his Oscar acceptance speech for *Life Is Beautiful*, made a touching and profound observation. He thanked his parents for giving him the gift of poverty, because it made the rest of his life seem so precious. Some parents, particularly if they felt deprived rather than enriched by their childhood, think their children should have everything they didn't. If this is your case, you may pamper your children deliberately or compensate unconsciously for your own disadvantaged past. As a result, though, your children may grow up feeling entitled to whatever they want. These wants may be limited to material possessions but are usually extended to special privileges, late curfews, or extravagant allowances. Being denied what they want at any time may then lead to anger and defiance.

How do well-intentioned parents fuel such anger and defiance in their children? The problem with teenagers always getting their own way with their parents is that they then expect everyone else to accommodate them. And since the world isn't designed for their benefit, they frequently find themselves at odds with others. They not only get angry with people who get in their way, but can also be extremely hard on themselves. As trite as it sounds, life's little adversities do build character and can inspire children to greatness.

Overpermissiveness

Most parents give in at some point when their children are so draining that they wear them down. My patient Melanie, for instance, had always been demanding and argumentative. Despite her parents' assurances, she was sure they loved her little brother better than her, and she was quick to bring up past grievances to prove it. When her parents tried to discipline her, she claimed she was treated unfairly and blamed someone else.

Melanie was a tireless fighter and never gave in. Unfortunately, her parents did. They began to let her have her own way just to keep the peace. Trying to follow the advice they'd heard about "picking their battles," they kept backing off and eventually abdicated their authority.

When you fail to set limits, your children develop an inflated sense of their own power. Permissive parents are not effective at protecting children at risk for trouble. Most teenagers need at least some constraints, with clear consequences for breaking rules. You must learn to stand firm despite their incessant demands for freedom.

Overcontrol

The flip side of the overpermissive approach is the overcontrolled teenager. If you're a repressive parent with an angry adolescent, you're in for a rough ride. You demand respect and your teenager feels compelled to rebel. You tell yourself that you have to keep your child from doing something dangerous or destructive. What good parent wouldn't? Unfortunately, your demands usually backfire.

Consider the case of Bill's father, a hard-liner who'd had a strict upbringing and wouldn't tolerate insubordination from his children. He held his family to high standards and tried to instill in them his own values: no swearing, no disrespect for adults, chores done promptly, and church every Sunday. This seemed to work nicely until Bill entered adolescence and he began to question the wisdom of his father's beliefs.

Going to church was okay, but Bill resented having to go every week. Occasionally he asked if he could sleep in on Sundays and miss the service, but his father wouldn't hear of it. He told Bill, "If you want to stay out late with your friends on Saturday nights, that's your business, but I expect you to be up in the morning." As his peers became more important to him, Bill asked now and then to be excused from family dinners, chores, or visits to relatives. His father resolutely refused

every request, thinking he was doing his son a favor by standing firm on his principles. Bill began to feel there was no room
for negotiation.

You may be thinking, Well, this seems perfectly reasonable;
Bill's parents just expected their children to be involved in family activities they thought were worthwhile. Most teenagers,
though, feel a need for more independence and begin to pull
away from the family. Instead of understanding Bill's need and
giving him some leeway—after all, he willingly did what they
expected most of the time—his father simply wouldn't tolerate
any variation. Bill came to feel his perspective didn't matter, and
this made him angry. Unable to question his father's authority, he
was left with only two options: he could give in or find other
ways to protest.

Not surprisingly, Bill chose the latter. He began to stay out
past his curfew and disappear when special events were scheduled. While he rarely argued directly with his father, he continued to be disobedient. Whatever punishment his father imposed,
Bill would violate. He had chosen an unhealthy way to assert his
independence. Bill's parents weren't willing to relinquish control,
and Bill couldn't tolerate their constraints. This tug-of-war went
on until the parents sought help.

Parents who favor strict controls may find particular difficulty with children who routinely try their patience, seeming to
bring out the worst in their parents with their annoying behavior, whining, and noncompliance. Well-meaning parents may be
shocked to find themselves screaming, threatening, and resorting to punishment. The child feels picked on and resents it; the
parents feel frustrated, helpless, and exhausted. They hope coercion will somehow make the child obey. But children usually
rebel against this overly controlling approach, and the cycle of
rebellion followed by control perpetuates itself. (And children
who give in to these overbearing parents may find themselves in
trouble later in life, when they indulge in silly, rebellious behavior in their adult years, or when they are unable to stand up for
themselves.)

Inconsistency

You probably remember being a teenager and sneering at adults who warned you not to drink but were known to enjoy a raucous, alcohol-filled night on the town. Or you joked about so-called pillars of the community who ran around on their spouses. Teens have always really resented adults, especially parents, who live by the motto "Do as I say, not as I do."

You naturally want the best for your children and mean well when you try to steer them in the right direction. The problem is that teens are keen observers of your behavior and quick to point out any sign of hypocrisy. At such a time, if you can swallow your pride and embarrassment and admit they've caught you doing something you shouldn't, you can open the door for a productive discussion. "I know I told you not to use that word," you might say. "I lost my temper and wasn't thinking. I feel bad about it and bad about disappointing you." But if you say, instead, "That's none of your business. You have no right to use that language in this house," your teenagers will lose respect for you and slam the door on any communication.

> **Teens are keen observers of your behavior and quick to point out any sign of hypocrisy.**

Susan, for instance, had been smoking cigarettes for about six months when her mother pointed out the dangers of smoking and insisted that she stop. Susan didn't dispute the fact that cigarettes were bad for her health. She took a different tack. "Mom," she said, "you've been smoking a pack a day for almost twenty years. How can you sit there and tell me it's bad for me?" Her mother evaded Susan's question and countered by saying that she was an adult and could make her own choices. If her daughter didn't stop smoking, she continued, there would be consequences. This response angered Susan, and neither mother nor daughter would give any ground. They were likely to continue arguing for some time and the stage was set for further problems, as this mother's "Do as I say, not as I do" approach would only encourage rebellion.

Because of its tendency to result in anger on both sides and a breakdown in communication, inconsistency may be the most troublesome parenting approach of all. Sometimes parents alternate between firmness and permissiveness on an apparently random basis. You may be preoccupied with your own issues or simply lack the energy to be consistent on follow-through. One effect of inconsistency can be that your teenager, sensing this, begins to play one parent against the other. This kind of manipulation usually happens when the child feels you don't communicate with your spouse. "Mom," she says, "*Dad* says it's okay if I go to the movies on a school night." If one parent doesn't check with the other, her will prevails.

Approaches to parenting that involve overindulgence, overpermissiveness, overcontrol, or inconsistency rarely work.

When to Involve a Professional

■ School officials express concern about your child's behavior and academic performance.

■ Your teenager's behavior has changed suddenly and drastically for the worse, and the change has persisted for at least a month.

■ You no longer feel that you can exercise control over what he does and whom he associates with.

■ Your teenager's mood is now sullen, and she has grown increasingly withdrawn and uncommunicative.

■ There are frequent extreme angry outbursts that scare you.

■ You no longer trust your child and are unable to relax when he is out at night.

■ Your son or daughter has run away or disappeared from the house for lengthy periods of time with no apparent explanation.

■ You suspect that your child is involved in illegal activities (such as alcohol, drugs, or theft).

■ Despite your best efforts, there is no change in the above situations.

Balance is the key. If your teenager sees you as predictable, even-handed, and caring, he's more likely to be cooperative, but if he feels misunderstood, arbitrarily controlled, or neglected, he's probably going to rebel. You should never underestimate the influence you have on your children. The challenge, of course, is to exercise that influence wisely.

WHEN YOUR PROBLEMS BECOME THEIRS

Tension at home can also fuel your children's anger and rebellion. No matter how uninterested they pretend to be about what goes on within the home, teenagers have sophisticated radar systems and are quick to jump to their own conclusions. When fourteen-year-old Jana noticed that "Mom and Dad looked uptight when I got home," she concluded that "they must have been arguing again about money. I bet we're going to have to move to a cheaper place." Teens with stressful homes often seek relief from the tension elsewhere. If they're resourceful, they'll channel their frustration into adaptive pursuits like academics or sports. If not, they'll block out their feelings by getting high or putting themselves in other kinds of danger. Parents must always be on the lookout for fallout from their own issues, the two most common of which are marital discord and unavailability.

Marital Discord

A troubled marriage is a burden for teenagers. A young person hears his parents arguing and blaming each other. He tries to stay out of it but notices that they are drifting further apart and communication is deteriorating. As he senses the growing tension, he is likely to spend less time at home. Sometimes children provide a catalyst for their parents' arguments, and the children blame themselves for their parents' discord. Perhaps unconsciously each parent would like their children to believe the other parent is at fault. The children's natural response is to feel angry and helpless and to distance themselves from both parents. Sometimes they feel caught in the middle.

Unavailable Parents

Although teenagers would rather be caught dead than ask for it, they need and want parenting. Sometimes one parent can pick up the slack for the other, but if this imbalance goes on indefinitely, the child's resentment builds. Many parents are too busy to spend the time they'd like with their children. They may rationalize their absence by saying they have to work hard to give the kids a better life, forgetting that losing them is too high a price to pay.

Teenagers have an expression for parents who are too busy with work or other pressing issues to be there when they need them. They call them "twenty-four/sevens": busy twenty-four hours a day, seven days a week. This is no term of endearment; these parents are neither physically nor emotionally available for their children. When I ask teenagers about their twenty-four/seven parents, many feign indifference or insist that it's cool because they have a lot of freedom. Don't believe it. This kind of absence on the part of their parents causes a lot of distress for their children.

There are several detrimental effects on children of absent and unavailable parents. First, it is impossible to provide adequate supervision when you are not around. Your absence leaves teens free to engage in risky behaviors for which they are not accountable. Although some kids can handle the increased freedom and responsibility, others fall prey to negative influences. Second, unavailable parents often fail to establish meaningful connections with their children. This lack of closeness makes teens more prone to trouble because they don't communicate with their parents. Finally, when parents are always busy, their children are left feeling that they are not very important. This impression can fuel poor self-esteem, which leaves young people more vulnerable to peer pressure.

Workaholic parents don't have a monopoly on emotional and physical distance. Those who drink frequently or are self-absorbed can be functionally absent even if they're physically on the premises. This kind of absence often generates considerable anger and resentment in their children. A child whose parents are consumed by their own issues may react by withdrawing from them or compensating in some way.

Blake grew up in a big house in an upscale neighborhood with a pool in the backyard and nice cars in the driveway. His parents were both hardworking and career oriented: his father was a lawyer and his mother was a local reporter. Whenever his parents were together they fought, and when Blake was in seventh grade they got a divorce. Blake's father moved across town to a deluxe apartment next to his law office. He buried himself even further in his work and made few efforts to spend time with Blake. Blake's mother decided to make up for lost time; she started paying a lot of attention to her appearance and began going out on dates most nights of the week.

Too old for baby-sitters, Blake was alone in the house much of the time. He tried calling his parents at work to talk with them but found that his calls were usually unwelcome. Feeling lonely, he soon learned that his big empty house was the perfect lure to attract friends. His friends were in awe of the big house and the beautiful mother, but Blake set them straight: "Mom goes out with different guys all the time; I guess she's kind of a slut. She spends all of Dad's money on herself, to buy makeup and clothes." He had similarly harsh words to describe his father: "Dad has no life outside of his job. He's like a zombie."

Rather than being impressed with his parents' hardworking lifestyles, Blake was repulsed by them. He adopted the image of a party guy who just cared about having a good time. He was naturally intelligent but stopped doing any work, so the A's and B's that came so easily turned to D's and F's. At the house, he and his friends frequently raided his mother's liquor cabinet for parties. Blake even began sneaking alcohol into school. The end came when a girl in his grade drank too much at one of his parties and got horribly sick. Her father arrived to pick her up and discovered her crying and vomiting, surrounded by drunken kids without an adult in sight. He threatened to sue Blake's parents. This, coupled with Blake's failing end-of-year report card, clued his parents in too late to just how much their troubles had affected him. Therapy and lots of hard work over the next several months helped Blake resolve some of his hurt and anger, but in many ways the years of neglect had caused permanent damage.

PARENTAL PITFALLS TO GUARD AGAINST

Your phone rings. It could be a friend, your sister, the plumber returning your call. None of that occurs to you. Instead, you're filled with dread. Now what has he done? you ask yourself. Has he cut school again, been in a fight, been caught drinking in public? This tension is all too familiar to the embarrassed, furious, and exhausted parents of troubled youth.

Parents are also frequently on the receiving end of teen tirades, and all the arguing, worrying, and strained communication can certainly take their toll. It is nevertheless essential that you take care of yourself as well as your children, so that you will both get through these challenges. It's natural for you to sometimes be tempted to react thoughtlessly in unproductive ways out of frustration and simple fatigue at trying to solve such a range of problems. Here are the four most common parenting pitfalls to be aware of and avoid.

Don't blame yourself for your child's difficulties. Parenting a kid in trouble is both time and energy consuming. It is all too easy for you to wind up feeling guilty and asking yourselves, Where did we go wrong? Resist these unproductive feelings; they can harm your relationship with your child even more. Worse yet, they may cause you to grow detached and decide your child is just no good, a bad seed. Remember also that there are times when we all feel extremely angry at those we love. For parents, it's an understandable reaction to years of frustration, hurt, and disappointment. While anger and love can coexist, if the resentment is not addressed it will eventually erode your relationship. Your parenting practices can greatly influence your child's behavior, so your best bet is to devote your energies to fortifying your skills, not lamenting your failures.

Don't allow your teen's problems to set the stage for long-term conflict with your spouse over parenting practices. When you are struggling with a child in trouble, you may begin to see your lives as dominated by your teenager's predicament. You may argue vehemently with your spouse, one of you feeling the other is too harsh and one insisting the other is a pushover. Meanwhile, the teenager's difficulties seem to get worse.

A teenage patient's father once asked to speak alone with me. His son had been in a great deal of trouble, from frequent drinking and aggression to school truancy, and during our family meetings this father harshly placed most of the blame on his son's friends and poor judgment. There was little meaningful dialogue between them.

But this meeting with him alone was different. He slouched in his chair and partially covered his eyes as he spoke. "You know, Dr. B., my kid's not the only one with problems. I've been drinking frequently, and my wife and I argue constantly," he lamented. "We should probably get divorced. We argue about our son all the time, but I don't think he's really at fault. I'm really scared for all of us."

I told him that I admired his courage and felt that this was a beginning, not an end. When I asked if he thought his son knew about his feelings, he responded sadly that he doubted it. My heart went out to this man and I told him that his situation was difficult but could be changed with hard work on the part of himself and his family. He seemed relieved and asked if I'd help him talk to his wife about it. From that point we worked together for about six months, helping everyone in the family take responsibility for his or her part and forge a new alliance among them.

Don't even think of striking back. You do real damage when you retaliate by putting down your teenagers, violating their privacy, or taking things that belong to them. You've probably been tempted to do these things, and you're wise if you've resisted. Parents who stoop to their child's level of warfare are rarely rewarded with behavior change.

PUTTING YOUR KNOWLEDGE TO USE

Not every teenager at risk will find his way into trouble. Your child's fate is determined by many complex factors. Yes, his personality and your parenting practices do interact powerfully. Yes, sometimes good parents wind up with kids who get into trouble, and good kids result from parents with lousy parenting skills. But pointing fingers won't get us very far. The real challenge is to learn how to change your interactions with your teenagers, promote their compliance rather than their rebellion, and find palatable ways to pass on to them your knowledge about the world.

As you gain a better understanding of your teen's perspective, you will gain the insights you need to be able to pinpoint any real sources of trouble. You can also arm yourself with the knowledge of the life skills that your child needs and the risk factors that can make their life unhappy. When you know what to look for, you're in a stronger position to intervene. The teen years can be a tough time, and it's safe to say that every teenager will experience the pain, temptations, and struggles that come with the territory. As you begin to see things through teenage eyes and feel what they feel, you can become a partner in your teen's life.

WHO'S IN CHARGE HERE?
SETTING LIMITS
FOR YOUR TEEN

"Don't you have any consideration for anyone besides yourself?"

"You're forty-five minutes past your curfew—consider yourself grounded for the next two weeks!"

"You've been on that phone all night long and I was expecting an important call."

"Do you think the whole world revolves around you?"

Infants believe that they are the center of the universe. Mommy and Daddy are there to serve their needs: to keep them warm, well fed, and clean. When something is wrong, baby can let out a wail or two and someone will come running to take care of the problem.

As babies grow into children, one of the first things they learn is that the world does not revolve around them. They are told to share their toys and to stop crying when they don't get their way. They encounter myriad rules from their parents, school, and community. All children struggle with these rules, and some children have a particularly hard time getting along with others or following the rules. But learning to deal successfully with authority and limits is essential to a child's healthy development and socialization process.

When children enter their teens, the struggle to accept authority is taken to a new level: the mind-set of "I am the center of the universe" returns! Teens typically don't understand why adults expect them to conform to "stupid rules," and they act as though the world revolves around them. This isn't regression (although parents of whiny, irrational teens may feel like they're dealing with a three-year-old!); it's simply the next level in their development process. Just as a baby struggles to become an independent and responsible child, a teenager struggles to become an independent and responsible adult. Perhaps even more than children, teenagers need guidelines to identify appropriate behavior and rein in dangerous impulses. The expectations of the adult world are far higher than of the child's world, and the decisions that teens make have farther-reaching consequences. The teenage world also presents a maddening mix of freedom and restraint. Teens often feel as though they are expected to act like adults while they are treated like children. They struggle to come to terms with limits like parental expectations, school rules, laws, and ethical codes.

Teens usually dislike rules and regulations, and they scoff at their parents' generation's values. But the rules that govern the teenage world are a model of those that govern the adult world. By adapting to these external constraints on their behavior, teens learn to develop their own internal controls: the ability to delay gratification, to think before they act or react, and to use good judgment in a range of often challenging situations. Perhaps it is ironic that the more effectively teenagers adhere to the rules and expectations that matter, the better they are able to manage their own lives, and the fewer limits they need. That is the essence of maturity: exercising self-management within the boundaries of society's rules.

The limits parents set for their teens are a key part of that growth process, but limit setting can be challenging to all involved by its very nature. Because teens are valuing their independence more and more, they may see limits as intrusions on that independence. There are some naturally cooperative teenagers, but many of them act as if they're programmed to resist authority. They demand reasons for your rules and expectations—but may not accept the explanations you give them! They want to know why they can't stay out late, hang out in certain places, or drive the family car whenever they want. The most extreme kids routinely violate limits and think of their noncompliance as a personal declaration of independence. But when teens feel understood rather than controlled, respected rather than condescended to, and valued for who they are rather than for what they achieve, even the most recalcitrant will accept reasonable limits.

EXTREME APPROACHES SELDOM WORK

This may sound obvious, but as parents you must be in charge of your own home. Your duties include financial responsibilities, major decision making, and child rearing. An implicit parental bill of rights says that, in return, you're entitled to a certain amount of respect, compliance, and appreciation. Your family shouldn't be run like a dictatorship, but there shouldn't be anarchy either. As parents you occupy a different position than your children, but a family requires mutual respect and cooperation for each of its members.

If you're thinking, Gee, I don't get any of these from my teenager! your efforts at limit setting have probably failed. It's time to regain lost ground.

Let's briefly revisit a few of the extreme approaches to parenting because they often underlie the ways parents do or don't set limits. Some parents may fall exclusively into one category, while others wind up as an inconsistent mixture of two or more.

The Father-Knows-Best Approach

"I am the parent and you are the child. What I say goes. I expect you to listen to me under any circumstances. Don't question my authority, accept it. I know what's best for you and will make as many decisions about your life as I need to."

While this approach was successful with children in older days, it no longer gets the desired results (except, perhaps, among highly traditional families that resist modern society because of cultural or religious backgrounds). And really, it's not an inherently good approach in the first place. Today's society places a high value on empowering teens and letting their voices be heard; this approach goes against all that. It creates a communication barrier and feelings of resentment because it tells teens that their opinions don't deserve any attention. Parents who use this approach convey the message to their children that what they think or want is of no interest. And finally, children who are brought up this way may grow up to be demanding and narrow-minded parents themselves! Parents today have to earn the respect they demand, over time, through consistency, active involvement, and practicing what they preach. Simply insisting on deference from your teenagers, regardless of how you treat them, is unrealistic and unfair. And if you demand blind obedience, you're often rewarded with rebellion.

The Laissez-Faire Approach

This parenting style is of more recent vintage. If the father-knows-best approach represented very conservative values, then the laissez-faire approach is the very liberal view. The child is encouraged to make her own decisions, and the parents take a passive role, intervening only when necessary. Discipline for infractions is generally mild and short-lived, and some parents may simply express disappointment: "I really wish you wouldn't do that." Some of these parents are simply lazy, but many who try this approach are genuinely well meaning. They believe that by not squashing their children's personalities and wishes under parental rules and regulations, their children will ultimately be happier individuals. But because these children are given extensive responsibility whether or not they can handle it, the liberal approach carries its own set of problems. Many teenagers lack the maturity and experience they need to run their own lives, and falter without guidelines. Without anyone to emphasize the importance of long-term goals or teach them self-discipline, these teens often drift into aimless pursuits of pleasure without regard to the future or its consequences.

The Flip-Flop Approach

I've never met a parent who is purposely inconsistent with his child. Yet this pattern occurs all too often. Although these parents have good intentions, inconsistent parents find themselves fluctuating between authoritarian and liberal approaches. They attempt to set limits, but their teenager ignores or defies their guidelines. As their efforts fail, they throw up their hands and give up, allowing the child to get away with exactly what he wants. Then when they witness the effects of their teen's wild actions—being tired or hungover after a late night out, getting in

Addressing Your Blind Spots

Sometimes it's hard to be objective about your parenting practices. Try these suggestions to make sure that you're on the right track:

1. Talk with your spouse, a relative, or a close friend who is aware of how you parent. Ask them for feedback on your behavior. If they make constructive suggestions, consider them carefully, and try making the appropriate adjustment.

2. If your approach to child rearing is not working, ask yourself why. Are you too strict or too lenient? Do you run into trouble every time you try to set a limit? What is it about your approach that is causing you to run into problems?

3. The next time you and your teen are clashing over limits you have set, listen to yourself objectively. Do you like what you hear? If you were in your teenager's shoes, would you want to be spoken to like this?

4. You've probably seen that commercial: "It's ten o'clock—do you know where your children are?" Do you find you often have little idea of where your teen is or what he's doing? If you don't communicate or follow through with your teen, your rules will just be lip service.

5. Do you worry excessively about what your teenager is doing? If she has been in trouble before, you probably have good reason. If she has not been in trouble, you'll want to relax a little more and seek other, more constructive ways to spend your time.

6. Does your teenager frequently complain that you're too strict and are out of touch with the times? This may or may not be valid, but if that's the message you keep hearing, check around. Speak with other parents, the school counselor, or your pediatrician. And make certain that you are familiar with the adolescent norms that were presented in Chapter 1.

7. Finally, if you're still having trouble letting go, take a closer look at your own life. Are you satisfied with your job, important relationships, and what you've accomplished? If not, consider your options—making a change, developing new interests, or seeking professional counseling.

trouble with authorities, or even just acting smug and self-satisfied—their frustration and anger grow again, and they make another attempt to get tough. Their kid knows that his parents won't really punish him despite their threats and continues to defy them and violate their rules. Many of these parents have no clue why their efforts at discipline are doomed to fail. It's a sorry state of affairs—one that can only lead to continued problems.

STARTING TO DEVELOP A BALANCED APPROACH

The key to successful parenting is balance—just the opposite of the extreme approaches I've just described. Parents must simultaneously take charge *and* allow their children room to grow. In this you must also be models of consistency and predictability. When your children are sure about your expectations and the consequences of violating them, they're less likely to test the system.

While some parents appear to achieve this balance between control and freedom naturally, most parents have to work at it. A good way to start is with a realistic assessment of your approach to child rearing. Think hard about your answers to the following questions.

- How do you feel about setting limits?
- How much weight do you give to your child's feelings?
- How do you feel about letting go of your child?

After you have thought about and honestly answered these three important questions, read on.

How do you feel about setting limits? Do you think that limits are necessary, or that they cramp a child's style? If you can't say no without feeling guilty about depriving your child of something, you've got a problem, because giving in to a child's demands just makes them more persistent. See the sidebar for tips on how to deal with this. On the other hand, you may also be the other extreme of parent, who places excessive limits and restrictions on everything, which can also have negative repercussions for your family.

How much weight do you give to your child's feelings? Are you willing to listen to her before making a decision, or must your word be final? If your child feels you don't take her feelings seriously, she may withdraw from you and resist the limits you set. But if you send her the message that you respect her but must also consider her best interests, any anger about rules will probably be short-lived. Also, if she believes you're willing to negotiate under certain circumstances, she'll be more likely to talk things over. Of course, your child's feelings should not take on undue importance, to the extent that you are sacrificing rules and your own values just to placate your child!

How do you feel about letting go of your child? One of the hardest things parents must do is acknowledge that their teenager is growing up and may not need them as much as he used to. It's so tempting to think of your child as a *child*, not as an emerging adult. Wasn't it easier when his idea of a perfect day was to spend it with you? It's hard to accept the idea that your perfect little son is not only growing up but is growing away from you, and will probably leave the nest pretty soon. And it's okay to have fond memories—as long as you don't live in them! Your teenager is not a little kid anymore (even if he sure acts like one sometimes!) and should not be treated like one.

On the other hand, some parents are so ready for their teenage children to be out of the house that these teens feel unwanted. The parents deliver an ultimatum: their child *must* be out of the house and living in his own place by a certain age. The parents think they are helping their teens by forcing them to take this step, but for teens who are uncertain about what lies ahead of them, it is very frightening to have that safety net removed.

These three questions have a lot to do with parents' effectiveness in setting limits. Explore them honestly and address

Tips for Parents Who Have Trouble Saying No

1. Remind yourself that everyone must learn to take no for an answer sometimes. A child who fails to learn this basic lesson is likely to have conflicts with others for the rest of his life.

2. Rest assured that your child won't love you any less because you deny some of his demands. In fact, he'll respect you more in the long run.

3. Remember that you are the parent and your teen is the child. When push comes to shove, your word is final.

4. Make up your mind in advance about rules and expectations. You should be certain that they're in your child's best interests. If you have any doubts, speak with a friend who is a competent parent, check with the school counselor, or seek professional assistance.

5. State your limits clearly and specifically to avoid any possibility of confusion or misinterpretation.

6. Be assertive, not aggressive; firm, not angry. Model the behavior you want to see in your child.

7. Remember that it may take some time before your child accepts your new and firmer approach to certain issues.

8. Remind yourself that in the long run, both you and your child will be better off with a clear understanding of your authority.

them if necessary to ensure they don't get in the way of your good judgment.

A BASIS FOR LIMITS

Before we begin addressing specific limits and how to set and keep them, let me outline several guidelines you should constantly keep in mind as the basis for all limits.

First, always remember that the reason for setting limits is the good of the teenager—not because we get a kick out of it, as some teenagers would suggest. Some adults allow themselves to act upon their desire for revenge or domination, and they impulsively create unfair, mean-spirited rules that serve only to punish their teenager. This is a very bad idea. A good parent will create limits that he or she truly believes reflect everyone's best interests, and

How Normal Teens Test Us Out

All teenagers will test the limits every now and then. It's only natural for them to see how far they can push you—after all, how else can they find out? Here are some examples of what they do:

1. You made a deal with your sixteen-year-old son that he can go to a Sunday-afternoon pro football game provided that he has finished his English paper, which is due on Monday. A car full of his friends has just pulled into the driveway to pick him up, and he's still typing away furiously.

2. You're adamant about your thirteen-year-old's ten o'clock bedtime. At 9:55 she tells you she hasn't showered yet.

3. You give your teenager $40 to buy a skirt at the Gap for a school concert. She arrives home with a new sweater and tells you they didn't have her size in the skirt, so she got the sweater instead.

4. Your son just got his driver's license. You tell him you don't want him driving at night for the first month. He approaches you at 9 P.M. one evening and tells you he's miss-ing a book that he needs to study for a test the next day. Is it okay if he takes the car to pick up the book at his friend's house?

5. You insist on a zero tolerance policy for alcohol. Your daughter comes home from a football game one evening and you smell a trace of beer on her breath. She's certainly sober, but you're concerned nonetheless. You ask her about this and she tells you she just had a sip of her friend's beer.

Each of these situations poses a challenge to you. Should you overlook the relatively minor incident, or stand firm and enforce your rule? I suggest that you hold the line regarding your policy. Otherwise your teenager will be testing you at every juncture. At the very least, point out that you're making an exception for this occasion, but if it happens again, you'll certainly enforce the rule.

will feel confident standing behind them. If you've prepared yourself well and feel sure you are doing the right thing, your teen's accusations that you're setting limits to be mean or to get some sadistic pleasure will have no basis and shouldn't ruffle you.

Second, while rules must be age-appropriate, you should build in a certain amount of flexibility. Consider your child's maturity and track record, because these may not fit your stereotypical expectations of someone your child's age. When your teenager demands more freedom, take into account his recent performance (good or bad) as well as the appropriateness of his request.

For instance, a fifteen-year-old who is disrespectful and irresponsible and who constantly breaks his parents' rules doesn't deserve a late curfew, because there's simply no basis for trust. He must earn the privilege of staying out late one step at a time. Only when he shows he can behave responsibly can he have the freedom he wants. Generally speaking, a teenager who keeps his word, manages his life reasonably well, and avoids trouble should be allowed to stay out as late as his peers, assuming the evening's destination is clear and you know where he'll be. Limits should reflect the level of responsibility the young person has demonstrated.

Third, taking the time to discuss a situation with your teenager can diffuse anger over limits she thinks are unreasonable. It may broaden her perspective to understand the logic and facts behind your limits. Even if she doesn't accept your reasoning, she'll realize she's gone as far as she can. It may be hard to believe,

To Address or Not to Address

While setting limits is important, some limits need to be more flexible than others. Limits like curfews and bedtimes should be treated seriously, but they should also reflect an increased trust and responsibility you have in your teen. Certainly, if your teen repeatedly fails to demonstrate good judgment, his arguments won't have much meaning. But consider seriously the words of your teen if he has repeatedly shown good sense.

Here's a list of situations that warrant discussion, contrasted with those that ought to be nonnegotiable:

OPEN FOR DISCUSSION

Curfews (especially for special occasions)

Privileges (telephone, TV, computer)

Their room's appearance and cleanliness

Dating rules

Time spent with friends and acquaintances

Study habits

NONNEGOTIABLE

Drinking

Helping around the house

Using drugs

Attending school

Treating others with politeness and respect

Dangerous situations

School dress codes

but she'll actually get tired of arguing after a while and give up her case. That's why it's important for you to listen attentively, show you understand their concerns, and review the evidence with teens before reaching a decision.

Keep in mind that you don't have to address every protest, request, or demand. There will always be teenagers who won't be able to let go of a situation, no matter what you say; they insist on explanations for why they can't do something, and argue convincingly on their own behalf. So while I encourage parents to engage in a dialogue with their children about privileges, I also warn them to make it very clear that their word is final.

REASONABLE LIMITS FOR COMMON SITUATIONS

Reasonable limits are a ladder you build for your children to climb. With each step they get closer to the top and enjoy the freedom of choice that adulthood affords. Children start at the bottom of the ladder and gradually work their way up, proving themselves and earning your trust as they progress. The more you trust them, the fewer limits you need to set. It's all about striking a balance between taking charge of your children and letting them go.

Following are some common situations in which you'll be called upon to establish these reasonable limits, and some advice on how to handle them.

Curfew

Few teenagers are mature enough to decide what time they should come home from a party or a night out with friends. What is a reasonable time to expect them home? Many activities, such as high school dances or football games, have an approximate end time, which you can abide by. In less structured situations, you'll have to set a time based on your good judgment.

During the week, it's reasonable to expect your child home by dinnertime. On school nights, he shouldn't go out after dinner without a good reason, like an errand to run, a study session with a friend, a scheduled activity like a music lesson or play practice, or a school event. These activities all have a definite ending time, after which you should expect him to be home; if they don't come with a built-in ending time, assign one. Make sure your teen always understands exactly when you expect him home, even if it means repeating yourself.

So what about weekends, vacation, and summertime? Take into account your own personal preferences and what works best with your teen. Many parents like to assign a set curfew. A missed curfew will entail consequences like a temporary or permanent earlier curfew or even being grounded. This approach is a good one for kids who would otherwise stay out until all hours. It is also good for parents who prefer not to micromanage their teen's life; they trust that their teen will make good choices and will be home by the set time.

Other parents prefer to have different expectations for each individual situation, rather than imposing a rule that applies to all situations. Parents find out where their kids will be, how they can get in touch with them, and they agree upon an estimated return time. They may require their teen to call and check in at some point, or they may assign their child a beeper or cell phone that she is required to answer anytime they call or page. (Note: an emergency-use-only cell phone is a good thing for all teens to have, in case of a flat tire, a missed ride, or another emergency.) This is a good approach for teens who are very busy with jobs, activities, and an active social life. It also works well with parents who think that each situation should be handled individually.

You don't have to compete with the most liberal parents in setting your rules. There will always be at least one example of a friend whose parents let him stay out as late as he wants to. Don't sweat it. It's better to err on the side of caution. Your children will probably insist they're missing out on something by not being the last to leave, but that's rarely true. You also shouldn't sacrifice your own sleep and peace of mind to please your teenager. If you don't feel comfortable going to sleep until you know your teen has come home safely, let that influence the rules you make. Take into account your child's age and the level of responsibility she has demonstrated.

Rules and curfews should leave some room for exceptions. Tell your teenager that you're willing to consider a legitimate request, as long as she's willing to discuss it and provide adequate information. Special occasions that will probably qualify for exceptions include a friend's birthday party, a school prom, a concert or sporting event, and an important date, if she can explain to your satisfaction why it's so important.

School Attendance and Performance

Experts disagree about how involved parents should be in their children's schoolwork. School is the teenager's job and should be treated as such, but at the very least parents should keep themselves informed of their children's progress by checking all their report cards and progress reports. Again, parents need to take into account their child's age, his academic record, and the level of responsibility he takes for his schoolwork. It's legitimate to insist that they set aside a specific time to study (like right before or after dinner), make a genuine effort to complete assignments, and do reasonably well in their studies. Parents of students who perform poorly in school need to make even more of an effort to be in touch with their child as to what's going on in each class, when tests and exams will take place, and sometimes what homework is due each night. Chapter 9 focuses on the school issue in much more detail.

Use of the Family Car

Once your teenager has gotten her driver's license, you must decide how much freedom to allow her. Use of the family car should be treated as a privilege and a responsibility to be taken seriously. She must demonstrate that she can drive safely, abide by traffic laws, and observe the speed limit. You will be required to ride with her while she has her learner's permit, but even when she gets her license, continue to accompany her in the car until you feel confident about her abilities and good judgment. Once she is driving on her own, stay on the lookout for reckless behavior, like piling eight people in the car or speeding out of the driveway without checking for cross traffic. If she fails to see the danger in reckless driving, you should remove the privilege of using the car. The same holds true if your teenager has her own car. She's just as accountable for her actions and should be held to the same standard as with the family car. No matter who paid for the car, you remain in charge and still have the power to take away her driving privileges. You may be inconvenienced by having to drive your teen all over the place, but it's better than her getting into a car accident.

Television and Computer Time

Does your child hole up in the basement playing computer games for hours, surfacing only for meals and school? Have you given up trying to have a civilized conversation when she's riveted to the television screen? Not all teenagers manage their time very well. If they spend so much of it watching TV, playing computer games, or surfing the Net that these activities interfere with their responsibilities, you'll probably have to set limits.

The nature and extent of limits should vary with your child's situation. If you feel that he's truly addicted to the activity (he can't tear himself away from it to do his homework or participate in other activities, or he stays up well beyond his

Dealing with Dangerous Driving

Here's a scenario involving a father and his seventeen-year-old son who has had several minor car accidents.

Father: Chris, this is the third time you've dented the car.

Chris: I know, but it wasn't my fault at all. The other guy slammed on the brakes and stopped so fast that I couldn't stop in time.

Father: It's your job to stay far enough back from the car ahead of you that you can stop in time. I know you learned that in driver's ed, and I've said it before too. Were you driving too fast? Were you tailgating?

Chris: Come on, Dad, you're making such a big deal out of it.

Father: It is a big deal. People could have been hurt. You've been very lucky. And you're avoiding the question.

Chris: I wasn't really going too fast. I was just a little late for school. I'll be more careful next time.

Father: That's what you told me last time. I'm not sure you should be driving at all.

Chris: No way! How else am I supposed to get to school and to hockey practice? I'll be the only one of my friends who can't drive!

Father: I'm just not convinced anything has changed. You always seem to be in a hurry.

Chris: What do you want me to do? I already said I was sorry.

Father: Well, if you're serious about wanting to keep your driving privileges, you can call the Department of Motor Vehicles and enroll in that defensive driving course they offer.

Chris: That's really stupid. You know how busy my schedule is.

Father: That's the only way you can keep driving. Believe me, better this than the courts. At the rate you're going, it's only a matter of time before something serious happens.

Chris: This is so lame, Dad. How about if I just promise you that I'll be extra careful from now on?

Father: No, it's the class or nothing. Think about it and get back to me. But until I hear from you, no car keys.

Chris: It's not fair. You're forcing me to go to that dumb course.

Father: No, I'm just telling you what you have to do if you want to have the privilege of driving. It's up to you.

Chris: Okay, I'll call the stupid school!

This father has taken a firm and reasonable position with Chris. Considering that there have been several accidents, he would be negligent if he dismissed the matter as bad luck. The father has set a defensible limit that defines the conditions for future driving. The son, realizing that his father means business, agrees to his terms.

bedtime to engage in it), you may have to severely restrict his access or remove it completely. I suggest you begin by imposing a one- or two-hour limit on the activity, asking him to voluntarily adhere to it. Give him a few days to wean himself, because television, video games, and computer-based games and activities are all difficult habits to break. But remind him that if he can't or won't adhere to your proposed guidelines, you'll have to take more drastic measures. You may need to actively enforce the one- or two-hour limit, remove game files from your computer, change the password to your Internet service provider, or even lock up the video game system or CD-ROMs.

Telephone Hogs

Telephone battles are among the most frequent arguments in families with teenagers. Teenagers love to talk endlessly to their friends, but they shouldn't be allowed to monopolize the line at the expense of other family members. They need help to show consideration on this issue. Usually a time limit and a procedure for signaling that the phone is needed solves the problem for most families.

If your child has her own phone, naturally she'll have more leeway. But that doesn't mean you can't keep track of how much time she spends on it. Some teenagers treat the telephone as a body part, and their parents come to feel that the instrument is nearly inseparable from their children. If your teen is constantly on the telephone, you'll have to decide to what extent it's interfering with her life. If she's doing well in school and seems well adjusted in other aspects of her life, you're better off leaving her alone. However, if she can't manage her time effectively and her phone conversations are taking up time that should be used for homework, family interactions, or participation in activities, you'll have to restrict her telephone use. You might begin by limiting it to a certain time period, and only if that doesn't work should you consider taking the phone itself away.

Dating and Sexual Activity

While some teens' telephones have been ringing off the hook with admirers since the sixth grade, other teens don't start dating until much later, in high school. While some parents like to lay down a blanket rule for their kids, especially for girls, like "No dating until you're sixteen," I think that you're better off dealing with each teen's situation individually. Zero tolerance rules will distance your teen from you and put up a communication barrier. Your teen may respond with rage toward you and may see no other option but to lie to you and sneak out to meet up with their boyfriend or girlfriend.

Even though it may pain you to see your teen growing up, don't discourage them from dating. Instead, make it a condition that your teen has to introduce you to their date. This is a bigger issue with daughters because of the dangers of date rape, but it should also hold true for sons; the truth is that bad influences and emotional abusers can be of either sex. In most instances you'll feel relieved knowing who they're out with. Apply the same rules to dating that you would to any social outing with friends. Make sure you know where they're going and when they'll be back. Don't let your teen ride with a dangerous or inexperienced driver, and if they are riding with someone else, emphasize that they can always call you if they decide they need a ride.

Sexual activity is a much more complicated issue. Parents may have different approaches they wish to take with their child. Chapter 8 deals with sexual activity and dating in much more detail; it goes beyond rules and asks you to think about your values and your teen's values, presents issues you must discuss with your teen, and introduces some potential problems you may encounter.

Alcohol and Drugs

There are clear limits to alcohol and drug use that are provided by the law. It is illegal to consume alcohol under the age of twenty-one, illegal to purchase tobacco under the age of eighteen, and against the law to use illegal drugs at any age. It is in your own best interest, as well as your child's, to embrace and enforce these laws. Some parents secretly sympathize with underage drinkers, smokers, and marijuana users, often because of fond memories of their own teenage years. But it's a bad idea to explicitly encourage it, and it's an even worse idea to provide these substances to teens (yours or others) or to make your house a party haven. These parties often get out of control, and it would be a nightmare to have a substance overdose, a rape, or an alcohol- or drug-related car accident take place after you supplied or condoned the drinks or drugs. The police, the media, the legal system, and your fellow parents all look extremely unfavorably upon these types of situations.

There is nothing wrong with being honest about substance use with your children; indeed, it is important to be up-front with them in the first place since they are likely to encounter it anyway. Millions of parents enjoy a few drinks or an occasional cigarette, and some support legalization of marijuana. But again, let the law be your guide. And in addition to telling them your views, give a realistic account of the dangers involved with using these substances. Information and more discussion on drugs and alcohol are provided in Chapter 8.

PRINCIPLES OF EFFECTIVE LIMIT SETTING

Whether it's society's influence or just human psychology, teenagers don't like rules. You can safely assume that they won't ask for them, and you can count on your teenager loudly protesting many of the limits you insist on. Some of their complaints are nothing more than an act they put on, especially when their friends are involved. It's not cool to comply with their parents' rules, so they protest to save face. This type of protest usually involves clever put-downs and humor at your expense.

Unless they're really getting rude, just ignore it and quietly repeat the rules.

It's the real battles between you and your teen that take their toll on both of you. So take steps to avoid as many of these as you can. State your reasonable limits clearly, compassionately, in a nonauthoritarian way. And try to set limits ahead of time; it's much more effective than trying to set a limit in the heat of the moment (for instance, as he's walking out the door on his way to a party). Setting limits beforehand gives your child the opportunity to blow off steam, plead his case, and eventually agree to a compromise (if you feel it's justified). You'll learn more about useful negotiating techniques for instances like this in Chapter 3.

Here are my principles of effective limit-setting.

Be Firm and Considerate

Take a stand, but do it respectfully. For example: Ellie, a senior in a competitive private school, is making plans to spend the weekend with some friends. Earlier in the school year, Ellie and her parents decided on an extensive list of competitive colleges that she wanted to apply to. The deadline for college applications is next week, and Ellie has been procrastinating; there are still three applications that are barely started. Ellie's father is thinking about all of this as Ellie talks to him about her big weekend plans at a friend's house. Instead of attacking her by screaming, "You can forget about the weekend! You're not going anywhere until those college applications are filled out!" he simply comments, "I notice you haven't finished your college applications to Vassar, Smith, and Yale. I think you'll be really upset with yourself if you let them slip by. If you spend Friday night with your friends and then come home Saturday afternoon and get to work, I think you'll have enough time to get them done by Sunday night. If you'd like me to help you with them, I'd be happy to."

This isn't provocative; it's simply a neutral observation and an offer of assistance. If the daughter reacts angrily, there are probably other issues at work. The father can point this out and initiate a discussion about them.

Choose Limits Wisely

Limit setting requires good parental judgment and a touch of compassion. You won't gain much by trying to manage every aspect of your teen's life; he's likely to resent it and will never learn to be truly independent. Your goal should be to encourage him to assume increasing levels of responsibility for his own actions. Try to convey this message convincingly and often. The idea is to get teenagers to understand that you create limits based on their own past performances, not on your desire to restrict their activities. You want them to be accountable for their own actions, not to shift the blame elsewhere.

For example, let's say your teenager runs late for school every morning. He gets up at the last minute, throws his clothes on, and grabs a can of soda and a handful of cookies as he runs out the door. Although you'd prefer to see him not risk being late and have time for a proper breakfast, you have to admit that somehow he manages to get to school on time each day. I'm afraid this is one of those situations when

What to Expect When You Begin Setting Limits

Don't expect your teenager to welcome your limits with open arms. If you've been lax about limit setting or have previously failed to enforce your child's intermittent infractions, or if your child's friends have fewer restrictions, you may find the going a little tough at first. In fact, your teenagers may purposely defy you in an attempt to test your resolve, even if their defiance is just verbal sparring. They may say, "Nobody else has to be home by eleven-thirty!" "Why are you treating me like a baby?" "You're so stupid!" or, "You can't make me." And you need to be ready for these challenges to your authority.

Remind your teenagers that you're not asking anything unreasonable of them, and you intend to enforce your newly imposed limits. You can acknowledge that you've allowed them to get away with too much in the past, and were probably mistaken. But now you're setting limits because you're concerned about their actions and want the best for them. It'll probably be tough for all of you at first, but you'll get used to it. In fact, you'll find that after you've consistently set limits for a few weeks, most teenagers will accept them.

you should grin and bear it. It's probably not worth setting a limit for this situation because the ensuing hassles will generate ill will and may not accomplish their intended objective. Yes, running late is a bad habit; but your teenager will need to discover that for himself.

However, if your teenager's grades are jeopardized by his chronic tardiness, you'll need to intervene. First ask him if he's willing to get up a little earlier (with your help if necessary) and organize his preparation time better. If he agrees, give him a chance to take that responsibility. If he doesn't agree or if he fails to keep his word, inform him that you'll have to oversee his morning routine until he can get himself to school on time.

Avoid Threats and Put-Downs

Often it's not *what* you say but *how* you say it that teenagers respond to. For example, if it's eleven-thirty on a school night and your son is still watching television, you might simply say: "David, last week you told us that you'd get eight hours of sleep each night if we didn't bug you. So we want to give you a chance to prove yourself." This places the responsibility squarely on his shoulders and allows him to go peacefully. But if you sound angry and shout, "Get in your room and go to bed!" it sounds like a threat and puts him on the defensive. Guess which approach a teenager will respond to better!

Also, don't exercise your authority with empty threats. Once a teenager realizes his parents don't back up their words, he'll violate the limits more often. If he respects you for practicing what you preach, he'll be much more likely to comply.

Your tone of voice is always important in these situations: sarcasm and contempt usually provoke anger. Refrain from putting down your difficult teenager, as tempting as it may be. Young people are very sensitive and their feelings often bruise easily. Why should they accept your limits when you show them such disrespect?

And as hard as it may be, try not to say, "Because I said so," when your child questions your authority. This response makes teenagers' skin crawl; they feel as if their autonomy is threatened and their feelings are ignored. Further, they may be less likely to ask for permission in the future if they think it will be denied. These feelings can fuel defiance and further polarize teenagers and their families.

Offer an Explanation

Teenagers want reasons for the rules they're expected to follow. (Don't we all!) You don't have to apologize for limits you set, but it helps to let your children know why you set them. If they challenge you respectfully, let them plead their case before banging down the gavel. This way you keep the door open for future dialogue. I always advise parents to keep their children talking when there's a dispute, to deflect any impulsive action that both parent and child might regret afterward.

For example: It's Friday night, and your fourteen-year-old son has just informed you that he's going to hang out with his friends who live a few streets away. When you ask him where he's going, he says that they are just going to "hang around, you know, probably in the woods behind the shopping center." The woods area is poorly lit, and there have been a few rumors of older kids hanging out there at night who drink and get into violent fights. To voice your objections to this plan, you might say something like, "You know, Sean, we know that this neighborhood is pretty boring at night, and that there aren't a lot of places to go. But we don't want you wandering around in the woods. I don't know if the stories I've heard are true or not, but it sounds like you might run into some trouble. It's safe enough during the day, but it's a bad idea to hang out there at night. We can't let you go if this is the plan. Why don't you call Frank and John and come up with a better way to spend your Friday night, like going to a movie, or the sports complex on Route 6, or going out for

Holding the line

Fourteen-year-old Cindy had always acted older than her real age, and now that she was in high school, her friends included seniors and even recent high school graduates. One Saturday night in September, her new friend Steve invited her to catch a movie and spend the evening hanging out with friends afterward. He lived nearby and offered to pick her up in his car. Cindy was excited and approached her parents enthusiastically to ask their permission. To her dismay, they had serious reservations about the idea.

"Why can't you just let me go?" she said in an exasperated voice. "Steve's been driving for years already and is a totally safe driver. Besides, I don't have any other way to get there."

Cindy's parents simply restated the position they'd discussed with her previously. "Cindy, we don't like the idea of you hanging out with this group. It sounds like they're all much older than you, mostly boys, and we don't know any of them. Some of those guys are in college! And Steve may be a great guy, but we don't know that. We will not allow you to run around all night with a group of strange boys who are much older than you."

Cindy protested, "Why does it matter that they're boys or that they're older? They're my friends, especially Steve. You can't choose my friends for me!"

By then, Cindy was whining. "If you don't let me go out tonight, I won't be able to face them on Monday. Everyone will think I'm a total geek, and Steve won't ever hang out with me again. They'll think I'm just a dorky freshman who isn't allowed to do anything fun." The discussion was deteriorating.

Cindy's parents calmly stood their ground. Her mother spoke gently at this point. "Listen, honey, I know this is really important to you, but sometimes Dad and I have to do what we feel is best. If we keep arguing, things are only going to get worse. You're all going to the mall to watch that movie, so how about if Dad drops you off at the mall so you can meet your friends there? Then he can pick you up afterward if we can agree on a place to meet."

Cindy was crying now. "You don't let me do anything. It would be so embarrassing to have Dad drive me there. How could I explain to Steve that my parents don't trust him enough to let me ride with him? That just won't work."

Her father intervened. "Look, Cindy, I'm sorry, but that's your only choice. Let me know what you want to do." Cindy ran up to her room in tears and slammed the door. Ten minutes later, she was back downstairs. "Come on, Dad, hurry up or I'll be late. I'll be in the car."

Cindy's reasonably composed parents handled a potentially volatile situation well. They set their limit, offered an explanation, listened to their daughter, and held the line. If Cindy had threatened to go to the mall without permission or do something else drastic, her parents would have had to specify the consequence without threatening her. And of course, they'd have to be able to enforce the consequences, or their daughter wouldn't take them seriously in the future.

pizza? If you can come up with a better plan, then you can get together with them. And we'll be happy to drive you guys wherever you want to go."

In this situation, Sean's parents took a clear stand about a situation they didn't like, but they were graceful and logical. They acknowledged their son's feelings (of boredom), and gave him strong reasons why his plan was not a safe one. They attributed their concerns to the situation rather than their son's inability to take care of himself. This reduces the likelihood of an argument because they aren't criticizing him. And further, they offered to consider any alternatives he might propose and promised to provide transportation, thus ending the conversation on a positive note.

You want your children to know that your word is final, but that doesn't mean you can't offer a face-saving alternative every now and then. This shows them that you take their feelings seriously and can be flexible under certain circumstances. When teens are alert to this possibility, they're more likely to keep talking and work with you toward a compromise. And as we see in Cindy's story (see the sidebar), despite their initial resistance to your position, teenagers often go along with the face-saving alternative, realizing that it's better than nothing. Although they probably wouldn't admit it, they might even grasp the validity of your argument.

EXCESSIVE LIMITS

Teens and parents benefit from having clear limits

set. But these limits need to be reasonable to work. Unreasonable, excessive limits carry all sorts of risks and tend to backfire drastically, no matter how good the parents' intentions may be.

Some years ago, I worked with a sixteen-year-old girl who was consistently told to be home at nine every Saturday night. Her parents had no reason to distrust her but insisted there were many dangers out there from which she must be protected. She resented this early curfew and complained that she was being treated like a child.

Her parents dismissed her requests for a later curfew more consistent with the times her friends had to be home, and told her firmly that they were doing this for her own good. Their daughter, eager to have a social life like the ones her friends enjoyed, began to sneak out of the house late at night to meet her friends. Her parents didn't have a clue, and she felt triumphant because she was protesting their restrictive curfew and having fun in the process. But her unsupervised, late-night escapades put her at real risk. Not only were there plenty of opportunities for risky activities like drinking, drug taking, and sexual encounters, but she was at risk for real physical harm because she was sneaking around alone without anyone knowing where she was.

Late one night, her father happened to look into her room and discovered she was gone. When her parents confronted her the next day, they were extremely distressed and angry. Their initial reaction was to punish her severely by grounding her for several months. The problem was that she had never been in trouble before and, except for this behavior, had never been uncooperative or confrontational with her parents or anyone else. With great effort, I convinced her parents that their daughter's rebelliousness could be better dealt with if they gave her the opportunity to come home a little later and demonstrate that she could be responsible. They were skeptical at first, but finally agreed to accept my recommendation on a trial basis. Fortunately, when their daughter felt they understood her complaints, she readily complied with the new arrangement.

Parents should rethink unreasonable demands, such as permanent telephone restrictions, excessive study requirements, severely limiting the amount of time teens spend with trustworthy friends, and prohibitive dress codes that differ markedly from those of their child's peer group. Parents who micromanage their children force responsible or conformity-conscious teenagers to comply with expectations that embarrass them and are out of touch with the times. Excessively repressive limits get violated surprisingly often. When parents' rules make it difficult for adolescents to live the normal life their friends enjoy, they'll lie and do almost anything to circumvent these rules. These deceptions widen the communication gap between them and their parents, and these kids place themselves at risk for serious problems and for even more drastic parental measures if they get caught.

It's a different story if young people have been in trouble for some time. If they've had their chance to prove themselves and failed, rules that might be considered reasonable for adolescents who have earned their parents' trust no longer apply. Parents of teens with bad track records need to establish and enforce a set of checks and balances, and clearly spell out their expectations and consequences. These parents are in for a struggle, but they have to stick to their guns if order is ever to be restored.

HOW TO ENFORCE LIMITS

You can teach your kids to respect your limits by imposing clear and immediate consequences for unacceptable behavior. Doing so takes resolve, as well as pride in and concern for your children, and it isn't always easy. Teenagers will try all sorts of ploys, like playing one parent against the other or loudly refusing to accept your punishment. But if the limits you are enforcing are good, reasonable ones, your kids stand to learn useful life lessons if you follow through effectively. If you don't, you may actually be enabling the behavior you hoped to eliminate.

After learning that his son had cut school, Ryan's father told him that he would not be allowed to use his skateboard for the weekend. But Dad was busy with a big report the next weekend and he didn't bother to enforce the consequence he'd laid down. Not only did Ryan use his skateboard, he learned that his dad's words were meaningless. Of course, now Ryan won't hesitate to cut school again!

When you fail to follow through with a stated punishment, you have failed to teach your children that their actions have consequences. After all, that's going to be the reality they experience when they assume adult responsibilities like real jobs and paying bills. There's little incentive to change when no pressure is exerted. This enabling behavior on the part of parents explains why certain adolescents persistently violate rules and expectations.

Let's assume your teenager has violated a limit that you set. Was his action intentional, or accidental? What explanation does he have for his behavior? Does he feel sincerely bad about what happened, or is he indifferent? Is he sorry for what he did, or just sorry that he got caught? Take all these questions into consideration before determining the consequences for his behavior. If there are mitigating circumstances, you can reduce the consequences. But if he doesn't take his actions seriously, you may have to consider more restrictive alternatives. (And don't be fooled by superficial appearances. Many teens can shed copious crocodile tears when they've been busted, but two minutes later they're laughing about it with their friends. Tears and words of apology do not necessarily mean your child is actually sorry at all.)

Tom's parents had told him repeatedly that he was not allowed to go to his neighborhood swimming pool. Because he'd been in several fights there, the pool managers had revoked his privileges for two weeks. Nevertheless, his parents got a phone call telling them he'd been seen loitering on the grounds with several other kids who appeared to be his friends. When they confronted Tom with this information, he initially denied it, accusing the lifeguard of lying. His parents didn't argue with him. They realized Tom was lying and simply asked him why he'd violated their rule.

At first Tom was defensive and indignant, insisting that the pool suspension had been unfair. His father pointed out that the issue wasn't whether he'd deserved to be barred from the pool, but that he'd flagrantly disregarded the restriction. Tom quieted down a bit and finally said sadly that he just didn't have any other friends to hang out with and didn't want to be alone. His father told him that he could now understand why he'd done it, but still felt strongly that he should be held accountable.

Since they hadn't discussed any consequences for violating their rules beforehand, Tom's father asked what his son thought they should do. To his parents' surprise, Tom suggested that he go over to the pool with them and apologize to the manager. He would then ask the manager if there was anything he could do to make amends. His parents thought this was reasonable and agreed. As it turned out, the manager assigned Tom a cleanup project at the pool as a sort of payback. Tom also apologized to his parents for breaking their rule and seemed sincere. By this time, his parents felt the issue had been satisfactorily addressed and decided against any further punishment. If Tom had refused to discuss the matter or to accept responsibility for his actions, however, his parents would have had to determine the appropriate consequences themselves, taking into consideration his lack of cooperation and evasiveness in addition to the pool incident.

Five Steps to Enforcing Limits

It's essential to enforce any limits that you establish. Here's a sequence to follow that will help you accomplish this:

1. Think long and hard about a reasonable consequence for any infraction of your rules. If your teenager's actions don't directly relate to your rules (they usually will), explain why their actions were inappropriate. The consequence should be meaningful, relatively short-lived, and instructive.

2. If possible, inform your child in advance of what the consequence will be. If this is not possible, explain your rationale for the consequence at the time you impose it.

3. Try not to sound harsh and vindictive. You certainly have a right to be angry, but you're better off focusing on your concern and hurt rather than criticizing them directly.

4. Let your teenager know that you will be checking on her during the period of her restriction. And make certain that you do.

5. When your teenager nears the end of her punishment, review the rule she broke and make certain that she has learned from her experience.

DEFINING PUNISHMENT: INSTRUCTIVE VS. PUNITIVE

So how do parents determine appropriate consequences for their teenage children who violate limits? Often our instinctive reaction is to "teach them a lesson": to arrange a consequence harsh and severe enough to ensure the infraction won't happen again. This strategy makes perfect sense in theory but doesn't always work in practice, because many teenagers feel no regret for their actions and simply vow not to get caught again. Also, teenagers who frequently get into trouble develop immunity to punishment. They say to themselves, I've already lost my freedom, so things can't get any worse. I might as well keep breaking the rules and enjoy myself. This is why we need another definition of "teaching a lesson."

To teach your teenager something useful instead, make the lesson instructive rather than punitive. This raises the question of how to define punishment. Theoretically, an effective punishment should weaken the intensity of the undesirable behavior, that is, make it less likely to happen again. When parents tell me they've had their child on a punishment for several months and the misbehavior has continued, I tell them the punishment is suspect. Sure, it makes parents feel they're at least doing something, but there's absolutely no point in continuing a consequence that doesn't accomplish its intended purpose.

Effective punishment should teach, not humiliate. That's why I prefer to think in terms of constructive *consequences,* rather than punishment. After all, you should base your actions on concern for your children, not a desire for revenge. Try to keep your negative emotions in check when you prescribe a consequence.

Here's an example of a message that's useful rather than vindictive: "Judd, you know you've broken our rule about going to a party where there's no adult supervision. We really don't like to put restrictions on your life, but we need to be sure this won't happen again. So we've decided to punish you by grounding you for the next two weekends. We hope you'll learn a useful lesson from this. If you can convince us it won't happen again, we can go back to our old agreement." A consequence doesn't have to be severe and long-lasting to be effective. Just make sure you get your essential point across: "We will not tolerate any violations of the reasonable limits we've established for your own good. If you abuse the right to go out, then you may lose the right to go out."

Physical punishment is ineffective with adolescents. It's dangerous, humiliating, and harmful to the parent-child relationship. There is no justification for physically disciplining your teenager; therefore, I strongly urge you to avoid it. Parents who rely on physical punishment are usually angry, frustrated, and immature themselves. Their failure to display restraint and self-control sends the unfortunate message that aggression and violent behavior are acceptable, and their teenage child is likely to follow suit. Furthermore, there is a thin line between excessive physical punishment and abuse.

In fact, teenagers (especially boys) are large and strong enough that physical altercations can be dangerous for both parent and child. Often, when parents behave aggressively, their teen retaliates. I've heard many stories about fathers and sons getting into fistfights, and daughters who respond to a slap across the face by smacking their parent back. Both parties are usually sorry afterward, but a lot of damage has been done. Generally, parents who rely on physical punishment are in frequent conflict with their child. Worse yet, the boundaries between parent and teenager are obscured because the parent is reverting to childlike tantrum behavior. Even if your teenager initiates the aggressive behavior, it is best to avoid a physical showdown.

To avoid getting yourself involved in punishment that may be ineffective or even dangerous, think hard about what consequences would be effective with your child. Taking away a privilege usually works well. Just remember the privilege has to be something your teenager values, or the punishment won't be very productive. Teens who spend a great deal of time talking on the telephone, watching television, using the computer, driving their car, or listening to music will immediately feel the loss if any of these pleasurable activities is taken away. These activities are not risky in and of themselves, but they're important to most teenagers, although going without them would not be harmful. Other privileges that can be rescinded include having friends over to the house, late bedtimes, and relaxed curfews. Just make sure that the privilege you are taking away is appropriate to the severity of your teen's misbehavior; if it's too mild they won't take it seriously, and if it's overly severe they'll feel angry and frustrated.

One punishment that gets mixed results is sending the teenager to her room. Many young people treasure their privacy and may actually be pleased to be isolated from the family. You could try a creative twist on this idea and deprive them of the pleasures found there—remove their telephone or Internet access—or of the privacy itself. I've known several parents to go so far as to remove the door from their child's bedroom. I think this should be reserved for only the extremest cases, but it certainly makes the point.

The bottom line is that teens must learn to take their parents' rules seriously, and the parents must be consistent in enforcing limits. This often demands that you maintain your composure under fire. Few teenagers take punishment easily. They argue, provoke, threaten, and deny responsibility—anything to avoid punishment. If you want to teach them a useful lesson, you have to stand firm.

Learning to Impose Consequences Calmly

Whenever your teenager breaks a rule and you need to impose a consequence, first ask yourself how you're going to enforce it. This can be quite a challenge with teenagers because you can't possibly monitor everything they do. In the majority of households today, the parents both work full-time. If you order your child to come home directly from school, forbid him from having friends over, and require that he stay there until you get home from work, he'll have plenty of room for noncompliance. You could call home to find out if he's there, but you wouldn't be able to tell if he had company. And if you insist he do his homework during this time, you will need some way to check on it.

I'm often asked, "How tough should I be?" My answer is that you must decide how important it is to get your message across. Sometimes this can be done with minimal fanfare, while at other times it takes a lot of effort. In some instances, the natural consequences of violating social norms can take the place of parental punishment. If your child is caught shoplifting, for example, the store may decide to press charges. That in itself may be enough to keep him from doing it again, and you won't need to punish him further. If there are no natural consequences, you should consider arranging for an experience similar to what would happen to your child in the real world.

Grace Under Fire

The next time you need to enforce a limit by imposing consequences, try to follow these suggestions:

1. Take a deep breath and tell yourself you won't come out screaming. You have every right to be angry, but anger expressed calmly and directly makes your point effectively.

2. State your consequence clearly. Explain why you've decided on that punishment.

3. Don't give your teen the impression that punishing her gives you pleasure. You want her to understand why her actions were wrong and to refrain from repeating them in the future. You don't want her to strike back because she's angry about how she's being treated.

4. Define any exceptions to the punishment in advance (for example, if your child follows your guidelines willingly, you may shorten the restriction by a week).

5. Explain the provisions for enforcing the consequence (you'll be checking on him nightly, say, to make certain he's there and off the phone).

6. Let her know what you'll do if she breaks the rule again. This is not a threat, but simply a statement of the intended consequence.

7. When the punishment has ended, review the incident and make sure that your teenager has learned a lesson. Then return to business as usual.

For example, if your son breaks a neighbor's window while playing baseball in your yard, you should make sure that he apologizes to the homeowner and pays to replace it. And in situations like a violation of rules that are strictly between parents and their teen, the parents need to create logical or appropriate consequences. These can be among the most difficult to enforce; I know of several parents who have intentionally stayed home on a Saturday night to make sure their children didn't leave the house.

THE ART OF CONFRONTATION

Consider again what we discussed about teenagers in the last chapter. They don't always perceive things the way that adults do, they can be very sensitive (or highly sensitive in certain areas), and they often try on different, cooler, tougher personas. Their parents often embarrass them and can't compare to their friends, who are the center of their universe. These characteristics don't make them a very receptive audience. So you'll need to really be on your toes every time you challenge their misbehavior. The trick is to do it without fueling further conflict.

Following the principles of effective confrontation will help.

Phrase Your Grievances in a Nonjudgmental Way Your Teenager Can Tolerate

When things aren't going well, teenagers can be irritable, moody, and defensive. For this reason, approach contentious issues carefully. It's easier for teenagers to hear objective observations than judgments. Consider the difference between "Jen, it's one-thirty in the morning" (this opens the door to further dialogue) and "Jen, you're two hours late getting home from Krista's! You never do what you say you're going to do! Why can't you follow the simplest instructions?" (this slams it shut). A teenager is sure to respond defensively when she's accused of something, even if she's clearly guilty!

Some teenagers will respond angrily no matter how you phrase your observations. In these instances you'll need to remain composed and stick to the issues at hand. An irritable or overly defensive response is usually an admission of wrongdoing. So if Jen says, "So what?" her father would respond: "If you don't have a decent explanation as to why you were late, I think I'm heading off to bed. I'm going to think about this tonight, and I'll let you know what the consequences will be tomorrow. But if you'd like to explain anything to me, I'm ready to listen." This leaves the door open for further dialogue but also makes it clear that the matter will not be dropped. Jen is offered two alternatives. She can either discuss the matter further or allow her father to determine the consequence.

Hold Up a Mirror to the Young Person's Behavior

You want your teenager to see herself as others see her and to be aware of how her actions affect the family. So when she's done something wrong, first identify the infraction and then challenge it. If you're critical or threatening, she'll probably tune you out, walk away, or counterattack. She has to be held accountable for her actions, of course, but you need to get her attention first.

If your daughter was rude to your dinner guests, for example, before criticizing her, ask how she thought she sounded. Remind her of the things she said or the manner in which she said them, and then explain why you felt they were inappropriate. Simply state your observations in neutral tones; while you may feel tempted to use a harsh or sarcastic tone (either to get her attention or to vent your frustration), it's a bad idea. Ask her to state back to you the things you brought up, and ask her how she thinks she will behave the next time she's in a similar situation. If you are comfortable with role-playing, try reenacting the situation together. A little humor can make role-playing more fun, but please avoid parody or mockery, which can hurt feelings.

Give with One Hand and Take with the Other

Don't forget to acknowledge the positive things in your children when you challenge them with your concerns about them. In the following example, eighteen-year-old Jerry had a history of marijuana abuse but had successfully completed a drug treatment program. He had been clean for the past year and was living at home, going to school, and working part-time. Recently, though, his parents had grown increasingly concerned about his behavior. Here's what they could say to Jerry so that while they honestly voiced their alarm about him, they also validated his good points and emphasized that they cared about him:

"You know, Jerry, we really are glad that you're living at home. We think it's been working out well, and you've been very responsible about balancing your classes and work. But Jerry, something's been bothering us. You always seem on edge lately. When we try to talk to you, you get angry and walk away. Since you started hanging out with those older guys at work, you're never at home. Even when we see you, something just doesn't feel right to us. We can't help wondering if you've started smoking pot again. When you completed your drug treatment program last year, you told us that you would never use again. And your former counselor said that if you ever relapsed, we should seek immediate assistance. We're scared, Jerry, and we're not going to turn our backs on you. We've made an appointment to talk with a drug counselor who can help us to figure out what's going on, and to help you if you're feeling tempted or are using again. It's for Monday night when you aren't scheduled to work, and we expect you to come with us."

These parents began their confrontation positively. They told their son they were pleased he was living with them and enjoyed having him around. This avoided putting him on the defensive and set the tone for a more constructive conversation. Then they expressed their concern, shared their observations, and set a limit. They avoided threats and stayed focused on the task at hand. Their son was expected to see a counselor with them. They didn't have to threaten him with consequences beforehand, although if he refused, they'd then have to consider one.

Offer Viable Alternatives

Parents don't have to be overbearing, harsh, or combative to effectively challenge a teenager's thoughts or actions. A successful confrontation should challenge behavior without making it a win-lose proposition. Give your teen alternatives, so she'll feel she has some control over the situation. To do this, you need to be sensitive to the feelings of young people and know how to tell them things they don't want to hear in a way they can accept.

Here's an illustration of a successful confrontation. Paul was on restriction for two weeks for breaking a curfew. Even so, he demanded that his parents let him go to a Pearl Jam concert on the coming weekend; one of his friends had extra tickets. His parents reiterated their position and said they were sorry, but he had to pay his dues. Paul tried to plead his case, but his parents held their ground. His mother, to sidestep the escalating tension, offered him three face-saving alternatives: to go to a later concert, take his parents with him to this one, or drop the discussion.

Paul quieted down for a minute and stopped to think about his options. Going to the concert with his parents was simply out of the question. It would be embarrassing and take the fun out of it. So he'd have to settle for a future concert; hopefully Pearl Jam would continue to tour and would come again before too long. He wasn't thrilled with the idea, but he was able to let go of the argument at that point. Paul might have insisted he was going with or without their blessing, in which case his parents would be wise not to physically restrain him. Under those circumstances, their best bet would be to avoid enabling his actions (for example, by not giving him money or the car) and to make it clear there would be further consequences, and then to follow through on them.

Take an Honest Look at Your Situation

Sometimes we should remind ourselves that the apple doesn't fall far from the tree. That stubborn, uncooperative, uncommunicative, and defiant child of yours may take after you. This is hard to swallow, but if you can admit your own short-comings and confess that your child is not the only one who needs to make some changes, your child will feel at least partly vindicated. You'll be opening the door for discussion by saying that you too are fallible. This makes it easier for her to admit her own failings and accept your discipline a little more readily. It helps to keep in mind that all parents act as role models for their children. If you stand by your children despite their difficulties, they'll be more likely to come around sooner or later.

I worked with one father who argued relentlessly with his son, Todd. One of the topics that they constantly fought over had to do with his son's study habits. The father insisted that Todd study at his desk instead of lying down on his bed, and he object-ed to his son playing music while he was studying. Todd, of course, saw no problem with this, as his grades were satisfactory. Neither father nor son was willing to budge an inch.

The resemblance between the two of them was uncanny. When they were arguing, they both had the same facial expres-sions, right down to the drawn eyebrows and pursed lips, and their arguing styles were similar. Too similar, because neither would succumb. To break this deadlock, I thought it would help if Todd's father admitted to his son that he could be unreasonably stubborn at times. When I suggested it to him, he immediately refused. I continued to bring up the idea to him when we met one-on-one, and finally he admitted that he felt that an admission of his own faults would mean that he had lost the argument, and that his son would see him as weak. I pointed out to him that the argument was already a lose-lose situation, so that he could only benefit. He seemed surprised by this perspective, and then agreed that he would think about it.

The next week, Todd's father admitted to him that he knew he was very stubborn and that he suspected it sometimes got the best of him. He proposed a plan where in future clashes Todd would calmly tell him when he felt he was being unreasonable. He agreed to try to do the same for Todd, to talk things out rather than yelling. Further, he promised to listen to his son's complaints and try to be more flexible. Although Todd was very skeptical at first, he softened his position in response to his father's overture.

The two ultimately resolved their studying argument by agreeing that Todd would sit up in bed when studying and lower his music a decibel or two. Two months later, they both admitted that the studying arrangement was working out fine, and that even though it was tough to change their stubborn ways, they were slowly learning to admit when they were wrong and to discuss problems rather than fighting. It was a promising start.

Maintain Grace Under Fire

Only a saint would be able to set and enforce limits for their teenager without ever getting upset. I often tell parents that if they expect to get angry sometimes, they won't be disappointed or blame themselves when they do. The key is to manage this anger without letting it get the best of you. Teenagers will often take advantage of their parents' anger, seeming to know that an angry parent isn't a rational parent. Some teens enjoy egging their parents on when they lose their temper because the parent loses control of the situation. Other teens step into the role of the victim, so they can manipulate their parents' anger and subsequent regret to their own advantage. And worse yet, other teens use their parents' anger as an excuse to ignore the rules or obligations set for them.

For all of these reasons, parents need to find ways to calm themselves down before entering the arena. Here are some suggestions:

- Talk to yourself in the heat of the moment. An inner pep talk can sometimes help: remind yourself that you've been through this before and know what will happen if you keep arguing. Listen to the voice inside you that says that you're going to stay cool and in control without stooping to your teen's level. Often, just telling yourself to calm down helps! Think about something pleasant to distract yourself from the conflict and show your restraint in the child's presence. This sends a powerful message: "I can handle myself in the face of your provocations, and I'll stick with limit setting until it's finished." And don't rule out the old count-to-ten rule that you learned in kindergarten; it works for younger kids, and it can work for parents too!

- If calming yourself down doesn't work, you should remove yourself from the situation. A break will give you time to collect your thoughts and allow your child to settle down as well. Even if the issue is left temporarily unresolved, it's better to put it on hold than to do or say something that will damage your relationship with your teen.

- You might also call on your spouse or another significant person in your life for support. Let them step in and take over the heated discussion with your child. Your teenager may welcome another's presence because that person brings a fresh perspective and perhaps allows him to get his point across.

OUTSMARTING TEENAGE PLOYS

Let's face it. Teens can be extremely clever. They can come up with endless excuses and schemes to get around your limits and consequences.

Forewarned is forearmed, so I want to alert you to some of your teenager's tricks and teach you some of your own. Here's a collection of some of the ruses I've seen over the years. Learn to recognize them.

The Old Sleepover Trick

The teenager politely asks his parents if it's okay to sleep over at a friend's house. Unbeknownst to the parents, the friend does exactly the same thing with his parents. This way both are free to do as they please, as late as they want. Another variation is to sleep over at a friend's house who has fewer rules (if any!) to contend with. This maneuver can be used to get to parties, late-night concerts, and unsupervised time at another house.

The cure for this is simple: if you're at all suspicious, call the friend's house beforehand and check with his parents. If you find out after the fact, impose a meaningful consequence and take steps to make sure it won't happen again. It helps to get to know your kid's friends, and if possible, his parents as well. That way, you will find out whether the rules they have are similar to your own, and by getting to know the parents you'll form a network of support and information. This is much more difficult than it was

Strategies for Challenging Difficult Behavior

1. Approach him directly with your concerns. Don't beat around the bush. Tell him exactly what behavior disturbs you and why.

2. Make certain that your concerns are backed up with facts. Be prepared to tell her what you've learned and how you learned it.

3. Stick with the issue at hand. Don't allow yourself to get sidetracked and dwell on past grievances.

4. Allow your teenager the opportunity to offer an explanation for her actions.

5. After you've listened attentively, challenge the credibility of her explanation. If it's plausible, tell her that you'll consider it but are still suspicious. If her explanation is preposterous, don't argue the point. Tell her that based on what she has told you, you're assuming she's guilty.

6. If you're too angry to think clearly, don't impose your consequence on the spot. Express your feelings directly but let him know that you'll be giving the matter further thought.

7. Make certain that you revisit the issue after you've all had time to think about it.

8. Consider asking your teen what he thinks you should do about the situation. Sometimes your children's answers will surprise you.

when your child was in elementary school, but it is possible.

If your teenager is trustworthy, you should not feel the need to check every time he sleeps out. On the other hand, if he has a spotty track record, tell him in advance that you will be routinely calling until he has regained your trust. This alerts your teen to the fact that you're not a fool, and it may dissuade him from trying to deceive you again. It also says that you're being up front with him and not resorting to the kind of dishonest behavior he's been practicing.

The Late-Night Sneak-Out

This strategy is especially popular with teens who've been grounded, but it can be used to circumvent any parental rule. Typically, the teenager willingly accepts her punishment or curfew (maybe *too* willingly—if your teenager has been throwing a fit for days but is suddenly all smiles about her restrictions, watch out!) but makes plans to meet her friends at, say, 2 A.M. Either they meet at a prearranged destination or the friends pick her up. Of course, she's back in bed before her parents wake up. The telltale signs of a night out are a teen's exhaustion the next day or her sleeping much later than usual. Parents who are awake may also hear a car stopping in front of their house, pausing, and then taking off. If you suspect your teenager is up to this, set your alarm to wake you up in the middle of the night so you can check your child's bedroom.

If you find that she's gone, you can either wait up till she comes home, go out looking for her, or go back to sleep and deal with it in the morning. If you can tolerate a few more hours of uncertainty, I suggest you wait until morning. This way you won't be as exhausted, and you can take as long as you need to deal with it. Searching for your teen can be difficult and frustrating, and even if you know where she is (a boyfriend's house, a party she was forbidden to go to), it could be a horrible scene if you show up. Some parents who decide to wait until the next morning lock the door or window that their teen escaped from, or strip her bed, so that when she tries to sneak back in she immediately knows she's been caught.

No matter what you decide to do, you'll have to confront her about her actions. She'll probably insist that it's the first time she's ever done this, but I wouldn't argue the point. You should impose serious consequences for this behavior. Make certain that they will have an impact on her and that you can enforce them. At the end of this section, I'll tell you how to go about this. And if there are any precautions you can take to prevent this behavior in the future (like a second-story bedroom or regular bed checks), feel free to do so.

The Car That Moves by Itself

You go out to your car one morning and suspect it's been moved. Wasn't it closer to the garage door when you parked it? You mention this to your teenager and he swears he knows nothing about it. In reality, he's been sneaking the car out for occasional rides. (I've known kids who don't even have their driver's licenses to pull this one!)

Here's what you do. When you leave your car, write down the mileage on the odometer, and check it again the next morning. The numbers will speak for themselves, and your teen won't be able to talk his way out of it. He'll also have a hard time joyriding when you've locked a club on the steering wheel (and held on to the key, of course) or installed a cutoff switch.

The Fake ID

Ever wonder how and where your teenagers get their alcohol outside of the home? Usually in one of two ways: either they get someone older to buy it for them or they buy a counterfeit ID. Possessing a fake ID is a serious offense, and depending on how the ID was created, altered, or obtained, it can be a felony. If you suspect that your child has false identification, investigate. Ask him to show you his wallet (if he has a fake ID, it will most likely be in his wallet so he can present it at the liquor store or bar). If you find a fake ID, destroy it. (If you confiscate but fail to destroy the ID, your teen will go to great lengths to take it back and use it; it's better to cut it up.) And let him know that you'll be watching him more closely in the future.

CHOOSING YOUR BATTLES

Parents would be foolish to believe they can influence every aspect of their child's life. Good parenting requires instead that we make judgments about which issues to overlook and which to challenge. Not all battles are worth fighting.

Teenagers should be allowed to develop their own daily routines, within reason—to decide when to exercise, shower, snack, and take naps. They should also make their own choices about extracurricular activities such as sports and clubs, provided they use good judgment.

I suggest this rule of thumb: ask yourself whether a particular action is harmful to the child or anyone else. If she chooses to wear ugly or tacky clothing to school one day, she's probably just trying to express her individuality. Arguing in this situation would only weaken the communication between you. But if she seems to be wearing the same style every day and it's breaking the school dress code, getting her in trouble, attracting very negative attention, or is associated with a gang or deviant group, you have cause for concern.

Your teenager's room is another example. Many parents complain that their children live like pigs in rooms that wouldn't pass inspection by the board of health. Parents contend that having rooms like that in their house is embarrassing and they must be cleaned up. This has been the cause of countless family arguments over the years because teenagers insist that their rooms are their business and don't affect anyone else. From my point of view, a person's bedroom should be respected as a private area. Teenagers need their emotional and physical space and must be taught to honor that of others. Respect their telephone conversations, mail, and personal belongings. And don't expect them to keep the same little-kid decorations they've always had; their redecorations may make you cringe, but posters and knickknacks won't harm anyone. A messy room may be difficult to ignore, but you may do better to devote your energy to something else, or to set minimal standards of cleanliness for them. (Just ask them to keep their door shut when you're entertaining friends or family.)

The exception, of course, is when you feel that the room reflects a troubled emotional state or is truly filthy. It's time to intervene if the room has a bad odor, if old food and drinks are spilled on the carpet or decaying in a corner, if all his clothes are wrinkled and dirty on the floor, if he's burning candles or incense that you fear could cause a fire, or if the room is infested with bugs or mice. Other indications of trouble are drug paraphernalia, subversive or violent reading materials, and any types of weapons.

Parents should never turn their backs on these signs. Usually, your best course of action is to challenge your child on what you've found and not to accept any weak excuses. If you have any doubts, seek professional assistance. We've all heard stories in which parents overlooked telltale signs that were indicators that serious trouble was brewing. It's always better to err on the side of caution.

Here's a scene involving a mother and daughter trying to agree on a privacy issue. This sort of discussion occurs often with normal teenagers and is something you must all be prepared for. During the conversation, parent and child exchange feelings, reassure each other, and end up with a mutual understanding.

Mother: Jackie, every night you go to your room, lock your door, and spend hours on the telephone.

Jackie: So? I've got lots of friends to talk to.

Mother: Well, we'd just like you to spend some time around the family. You know, sitting and talking, or watching TV.

Jackie: That's so boring. You and Dad watch all those boring news shows. I'd rather be in my room.

Mother: But what do you do up there for the whole night?

Jackie: I don't know, just stuff. What are you so worried about, anyway?

Mother: I just wonder if it's healthy to be in your room for so long.

Jackie: Look, Mom, what are you so worried about? My room is the one place where no one can bother me. I can talk to my friends without worrying that everyone is listening to every single thing I say.

Mother: But I'd just like to see you once in a while.

Jackie: Then why don't you just come to my room and knock?

Mother: I guess that's fair enough. It's just that I worry about you and am afraid that you're shutting me out. I really do trust you, you know.

Jackie: Stop worrying so much! I just like to be by myself sometimes. You know I'll come to you if I have any real problems, like I did last year when I was having trouble in algebra. Duh!

It's not unusual for parents to feel that they're sometimes losing touch with their teenagers. Fortunately, Jackie is reasonably mature and isn't doing anything wrong, and she understands that her mother is overreacting. After some discussion, Jackie reassures her mother that she has nothing to be concerned about, and the mother agrees to back off.

The bottom line is that sometimes you must bite your tongue and let your child find her own way. Exceptions should be made, of course, if you feel she's in danger; in general, the less successful teens are at managing their own lives, the more you'll need to intervene.

THE GOODWILL BANK

I'm fond of telling families about my concept of the goodwill bank. I consider it an essential ingredient of harmonious family living. Although we don't routinely describe the process in this way, the concept governs many of our actions. Essentially, the idea is that every time a teenager is honest, responsible, and helpful, he makes a deposit in this imaginary account. Parents are the bankers, and it's up to you to decide when the account is earning interest and when withdrawals can be made. As teenagers accumulate goodwill in their accounts, you should respond with increased leeway and privileges.

But this goodwill bank is also a two-way street. When you parent in a kind, loving, and responsible fashion, you generate similar good feelings in your children. And while they probably won't mention it, they'll be much more likely to cooperate when you seek their assistance. So if you make it a point to display goodwill, you're setting the stage for a more cooperative, problem-solving environment. It certainly won't circumvent all problems, but it will give you a reserve to fall back on when the going gets tough.

In operating a goodwill bank, your job as parents is to take charge in a firm, caring, and consistent manner. This is not an easy task, but the greater the trouble your teenagers face, the more important it is for you to intervene decisively and effectively. As a parent you have every right to be suspicious when your child's behavior has been erratic or there have been problems in the past. Don't ever let your teenager tell you otherwise, because there's too much at risk. Your own observations and intuitions are important; trust them. But don't lose sight of your child's past performance and the level of responsibility she has assumed. If her goodwill account has a hefty balance, you shouldn't be trailing her every move. It's unnecessary and can lead a perfectly normal teenager to be angry and resentful. A little trust can go a long way.

As we've discussed throughout this chapter, the purpose of setting limits is to help your children learn restraint, exercise good judgment, and ultimately become responsible adults. You should challenge their misbehavior to make them accountable for their actions and to help them think twice before doing the same thing again. Many teenagers complain vehemently that their parents set unreasonable limits and watch over them too closely. At times you'll be tempted to give up and let them have their own way to keep the peace. Don't do this unless you're certain that they're not at risk of getting into trouble.

Besides, you probably have far greater influence than you think. As you learn to harness this limit-setting power, your teenager will respect you more and more, and ultimately appreciate your efforts.

CHAPTER THREE

BUILDING
BETTER
RELATIONSHIPS
THROUGH
BETTER
COMMUNICATION

"You act like I'm still a baby.
You barely even know who I am."

"You always overreact. I don't know why
I bother telling you anything."

"What do you care anyway?"

I see an average of thirty patients a week. I would say that almost half of them complain that they can't talk to their parents without arguing. Many of these teens act nonchalant, snickering at how pissed off they make their parents, or patronizingly describing how their parents freak out about everything. When I see groups of teens, they try to outdo one another with stories about whose parents yell the most, threaten the direst punishments, and leap to the most absurd conclusions. And yet teens are genuinely saddened and frustrated by the communication breakdowns between themselves and their parents. When I meet with parents, it's the same story; they may talk big to their friends about their teens' obnoxious attitude, but in reality, they want nothing more than to be able to get along with their children. These are typically parents and teens who—deep down—care about one another very much. So why can't they talk to one another?

Good communication is a fundamental human need, crucial to forming strong relationships with others and finding our role in society. We all feel the need to make ourselves understood and to understand other people. When we are unable to communicate our feelings to someone, we react with frustration, embarrassment, or anger. Depression, poor self-esteem, and feelings of isolation and alienation can result from repeated inability to communicate with and relate to other people.

As important as communication is at any time in a person's life, adolescence is arguably the time when it is critical. Because parents are their children's earliest teachers and role models, you have already set the tone for communication in the family. If your children haven't developed the essential skills by the time they reach adolescence, you need to help them catch up—both to facilitate communication within your family and to prepare your children for the rest of their lives.

Failure to communicate obviously just makes existing problems between parents and teens worse. Family members need to learn to talk to one another in ways that create an atmosphere of love, mutual respect, and understanding, without screaming, demanding, and threatening. Harmonious communication is essential in helping to keep your children out of trouble and dealing with trouble if it arises.

CREATING A NURTURING ENVIRONMENT BY SHOWING YOU CARE

Parents love their children, and children, at least deep down, know that. But with everything else going on in the troublesome teen years, it often becomes especially difficult for parents to express that love and for teens to feel it on a regular and consistent basis. The simple truth is that young people who feel their parents' love are less likely to get into trouble. Feeling loved encourages pride and self-worth in teens, and places extra value on their actions. And it makes teens more receptive to your feedback, diminishes their need to seek harmful connections outside the home, and increases their desire to participate in activities of which you approve.

But translating those intangibles of love and caring into action may not be easy; it requires you to seek opportunities to demonstrate your affection. When your teenager feels that you share in both his successes and his disappointments, he begins gradually to count on you, knowing you're there for him through thick and thin.

Following are some things you can do to send this message to make sure your teenager knows you care.

How to Tell When Your Teens Feel Unloved

■ He makes frequent self-deprecating remarks.

■ She never seems to trust your compliments and strongly rejects them.

■ He adamantly states that he doesn't care what you think or feel.

■ She is extremely sensitive to any feedback or criticism.

■ He is willing to be friends with anyone who will offer him acceptance, including selfish, negative influences.

■ She gives up easily when she is misunderstood or her requests are not immediately met, sighing, "Never mind," or, "Just forget it."

■ Other people in his life tell you that he seems desperate for approval.

Show Affection Through Your Actions

Actions often speak louder than words. Most parents have been warned by their children to avoid public displays of affection, and their private overtures seem to go unnoticed, but that doesn't mean you should give up. Teenagers need regular reassurance. With hugs or through notes and indirect gestures, let them know you love them. One mother showed her son an ad in the newspaper about a sale on some video games he wanted. She told him if he had the money saved, she'd be happy to take him to purchase them. In a similarly thoughtful gesture, a father subscribed to *Seventeen* magazine for his office and took it home to his daughter every month. You may not receive the thank-you of your dreams—a halfhearted hug, a shy smile, or an offhand "Thanks" may be the best you'll get—but these simple gestures show you care.

Another important way to show affection is giving the gift of time: make yourself available to your teen on a regular basis. One way of doing that is to establish a regular family function. Insist that you all have dinner together on certain nights each week or that several hours on Sunday be set aside for family activities. Your children will probably resist this idea, especially if it's a recent innovation. And as busy as our lives get, all family members (especially you, parents) will have to sacrifice pursuing some other activity during that time. But after a while, this family time will become a valued part of your family life. And don't let your children tell you that their friends never spend time with their families. It's probably not true, and even if it is, it's nothing to be proud of.

Remember that there's a big difference between being with your children physically and being with them emotionally. Even though you're sitting in the same room, if you're engrossed in separate activities or watching TV, there may be little engagement. Emotional connection—which is the goal—demands paying active attention to one another. It also helps to give this family time a purpose. If you keep your children away from friends and activities for family time without it being quality time, they'll feel trapped and resentful. Organize this time around a meal, a family project, an athletic activity everyone enjoys, or a favorite TV show you all love. It doesn't have to require major planning or expense to bring your family together.

Be Curious About Their Interests

Some of the activities that occupy your children may seem foreign to you, but they give you a wonderful opportunity to display curiosity and concern. Say your son is taking electric guitar lessons and spends hours practicing. You may not especially enjoy his type of music, but you know it's his passion, so ask questions about his progress and request that he play something for you. After you listen attentively, find a way to compliment him on his skill and then ask him more about the music, like who wrote it and why he likes it.

Music, in general, is an important part of most teenagers' world. Your daughter has probably set all of the buttons on your car radio to her favorite stations, so you have exposure to her music whether you like it or not. Ask about the types of music she listens to. If you don't know about the different types and how they vary from one another, ask her to explain and give some examples. You don't have to pretend to like the music if you truly don't, but you should be accepting of her preferences. She may feel just as critical of your tastes as you do about hers, but that doesn't mean you can't learn something from each other and use it as an opportunity to connect.

Computers and the Internet are also areas that modern kids know a lot about. So follow the same principle of expressing interest if your teen is a computer buff. Ask him about his favorite Web sites and have him show you new things you can do on-line. Although teens won't show you everything that they do on their computers, there are some things they will be pleased to demonstrate. If you share your teen's computer interest, you can collaborate together on projects, like school reports and research. And even if you don't know much at all about computers, your teen may enjoy playing the role of the expert and teaching you some things. It might be especially fun for you to ask him to help you set up an e-mail account or to create a Web site. Many teens have created sites for themselves, so this will give him a chance to demonstrate his skill in a way that opens the door to more interaction between the two of you.

Whatever your children's particular areas of interest, it may be difficult for you to muster enthusiasm if you hold a low opinion of that interest. If that's the case, then you've probably had thoughts that their time could be much better spent—on studying, sports, community service, or any other wholesome activity you prefer. But unless you feel that their interest is really harming them (and it probably isn't), spare them the lecture. The last thing you want is for your teen to intensify her focus on her interest as a means of protest, or to halfheartedly take on an activity simply because it will please you. Anyway, parental boycotts rarely quash teenagers' interests; they just send them out of range of your radar screen. Ideally you want to foster responsible but independent and self-sufficient thinkers, so in the long run, you'll all be better off.

Sometimes you'll find that your children resist all your efforts at sharing their interests. If they do, ask yourself why this is the case. Do they feel you'll be judgmental and critical? If so, you'll need to convince them that you'll approach their passions with an open mind. Are they afraid you'll take the fun out of their pursuit by monitoring their progress too closely and trying to control it? Then they're just exercising healthy independence, and while you should show interest, keep some distance and avoid passing judgment or criticism. Are their interests illegal or dangerous? In this case, you may need to pursue the matter with or without their blessing. Finally, they may be private about all aspects of their lives. This means you'll need to sharpen your communication skills (as explained later in this chapter)

Simple Ways to Demonstrate Unconditional Love

1. Make it a point to regularly compliment your child. Not in a fake, Eddie Haskell, "That's a nice hat, Mrs. Cleaver" kind of way, but in a genuine way. Comment on her talent at piano, his good grade on a history test, her computer expertise.

2. Try to be thoughtful and considerate of her feelings. Remember the names of her friends, her musical interests, and her other likes and dislikes.

3. Share in her successes and failures. Convey your pleasure in her achievements, and let her understand that you know how she feels in the face of disappointment.

4. Accept him as he is. Don't try to mold him into a clone of yourself. Let him know that you respect his individuality, even if some of his choices make you uncomfortable.

5. Be there. Go to his football games, even if he doesn't start; his chorus recital, even if the school concert will be over two hours long; the school play where he has a bit part in one scene. It will make a difference to him.

6. Take her thoughts and feelings seriously, and allow her to influence you every now and then. She should know she has a real impact on your life.

7. Tell him that you love him, regardless of whether he'll say it back to you.

and try to improve your relationship as a part of that process.

Whether your children are athletes, artists, social butterflies, or anything in between, I encourage you to go out of your way to learn what's important to them. I can assure you that your efforts won't go unnoticed. When you meet them on their own turf, they feel that you value who they are. And when you accept their interests, you are in effect accepting them.

Help Them Pursue Their Interests and Activities

You can both show your affection and demonstrate that you're aware of your teenagers' interests by looking for opportunities to help them pursue those interests in thoughtful ways. Cut out an article about something your son has talked about—maybe a rock group, a basketball game, or a television special. Tell him that when you saw the piece you immediately thought of him. One father, browsing through the newspaper, came across a notice for a book signing by an actress whom his daughter admired. He offered to drive her to the bookstore that weekend so she could purchase the book and meet her idol. His daughter was thrilled.

If your child has a gift or talent, help him to pursue it. If your son is a lacrosse player, take him shopping for all the equipment he needs, show up at his games, and look into summer sports camps together. If your daughter likes working with little kids, help her to find a part-time or summer job as a babysitter or working at a camp or day care center, and help her learn about careers with children. You don't want to control your child; rather, you want to encourage him, to be his biggest fan.

Take your kids to places they enjoy. After all, many of the pursuits and interests of young people are purely for the sake of fun! It could be a lake, an amusement park, a sports complex, or a concert twenty miles away. They may take off with their friends, but they won't forget that you brought them. (This gesture will be especially appreciated before your teen is old enough to drive.) My father used to pile a bunch of us into his big old car every weekend and cart us off to some local activity. To this day, I remember how he made himself available to give us rides when we were looking for something to do. My father passed away a number of years ago, but his legacy—"I can always find the time if you need me"—lives on. It's a tradition that I've happily carried on with my own children.

Trust the Magic of Special Occasions

I've known many families who manage to celebrate holidays and important events together, even despite the level of tension in the household. Teenagers often play down the significance of such occasions, but they always appreciate the family rituals and traditional ceremonies.

Justin, for example, had been at odds with his parents for some time, arguing frequently and feeling he had little in common with them. But even though his parents were frustrated and angry, they wanted to show they loved their son, and so on his sixteenth birthday they decided to throw him a surprise party. They contacted his friends, made the arrangements, and succeeded in catching him off guard when he walked into the house and everyone shouted "Happy Birthday!" Justin was tearful, speechless, and touched. The party was a success and a lot of fun, but more important, his parents had sent him the important message that they loved him. Following the party, the family tension seemed to lessen somewhat, and Justin gradually became more accessible to his parents.

You don't have to rely on holidays to enjoy this magic, either. Your family can create its own special occasions. Take everyone out to dinner at your son's favorite restaurant when he gets a good report card, or give a card or small gift to your daughter to celebrate her landing a position in the elite school singing group.

Recognize the Importance of Forgiving

Teenagers have a way of trying your patience with their demands, their noncompliance, their lack of motivation. Since they insist they know everything, you can feel pretty frustrated. You watch them make mistakes and cringe as they fail to follow your well-intentioned advice. Yet through it all, you must maintain a steady appearance of concern. If your children are to genuinely believe you're in their corner, they need to know you can forgive them for their mistakes.

This isn't always easy. You can count on feeling angry, hurt, and rebuffed at times. When your teen lashes out at you, your natural reaction may be to strike back and make him suffer as you have. And when he gets himself in trouble after ignoring good advice, "I told you so" may be on the tip of your tongue. Rise above these inclinations and find a way to show him that your caring is unconditional. In other words, you can condemn his actions but you must make it clear that you still love him. This sort of consistency is the foundation for a close relationship: knowing that your loved one will stand by you despite your mistakes and shortcomings.

Have Fun

All this talk about caring, and we haven't even mentioned the importance of learning to enjoy being with your children! Sharing a good laugh every now and then helps you feel more comfortable with each other, especially when relationships are strained. A sense of humor is contagious. If you can laugh at yourself once in a while, your teenager is likely to laugh at himself. Remember that a person with a healthy sense of humor makes others laugh—though not at anyone else's expense. This is especially important with teens, who are so sensitive and fragile that they often fear others are making fun of them.

There's humor to be found all around, if you just look for it.

Some families tell jokes and amusing stories at the dinner table, while others spontaneously make up silly songs or awful puns, or find funny situations together. Try asking your child to tell you about the funniest person he knows. Watch a hilarious movie together, share corny jokes with him, or tell a story about something funny that happened to you. Create a tradition of swapping humorous stories.

Opportunities to have fun together usually become rarer as your kids grow older, so take advantage of every chance you get. If mealtimes and car trips are the only things you do together, insist that the television, radio, and Walkman be turned off. Your teens may complain that there's nothing to talk about, but most families can come up with such nonelectronic entertainment like word games and trivia contests, as well as conversation.

HOW TO AVOID UNDERMINING A NURTURING ENVIRONMENT

Beware of Mixed Messages

Parents send mixed messages anytime they say one thing and do another. Such inconsistency is rarely intentional but it strongly affects your children, leaving them cynically wondering what you really feel. Even worse, they'll eventually stop taking you seriously (another name for a parent who sends these mixed messages is *hypocrite*). Recently, a teenage girl told me her father insisted that he was interested in all aspects of her life. Yet he could never remember her friend's names. She knew he never forgot his business appointments or colleagues' names, so she concluded from this inconsistency that he just couldn't be bothered with the details of her life. This basic incongruity is too much for children to tolerate, so they assume what their parents do is more valid than what they say.

To avoid these problems, take a look at your own behavior and ask yourself if you're giving consistent messages. If you're

Common Examples of Mixed Messages

Are you guilty of any of these inconsistent behaviors that send mixed messages to your teen?

1. You tell your teenager you're interested in how her field hockey team is doing but you never go to any of her games.

2. You assure your child that you'll be patient while helping him with his math homework, and then you start to show annoyance when he fails to understand your explanation of a problem five minutes into your work together.

3. You insist on the importance of having a family dinner each night, but you often work late and arrive long after the others have finished eating.

4. You yell at your daughter for spending too much time on the phone, but you spend hours and hours gabbing away on the phone yourself.

5. You remind your son he can always come to talk to you, but when he takes you up on the offer, you tell him you've brought a lot of work home from the office and can't talk until the next day.

not, you'll want to work on your communication skills by following the suggestions later in this chapter. You can ask your spouse or children for feedback and then show them all that you're trying to change your ways.

Avoid Subtle Rejection

Mixed messages are one form of subtle rejection. Another example is giving your child a gift that you think he should have but that he doesn't want. Sometimes this type of gift giving is the result of a misunderstanding, but it surely is a disappointment to a teenager and feels like a clear example of thoughtlessness. Young people have told me about getting birthday presents from their parents that weren't on the wish lists they had been asked to prepare—clothes they never wear and books they had no intention of reading.

Seventeen-year-old Sandra reported, "I like to wear very trendy clothes, and my conservative parents don't really understand my taste. So in the weeks before Christmas last year, I cut out pictures from catalogues for them and told them the names of my favorite stores. Come Christmas Day, I opened my presents to find long, blah skirts, cotton turtlenecks, and baggy sweaters. And they were from good stores like Lands' End, so they weren't cutting costs. I know I should just be thankful that they cared enough to buy me gifts at all, but it was obvious they didn't care about what was important to me. It was depressing." Gifts that don't take the recipient's feelings into account rarely accomplish their objective of making that person happy. It's easy for teenagers to conclude that these gifts mean you don't care enough to figure out what they really like.

Don't Rely on Guilt

Laying guilt trips on your child can do as much damage as mixed messages and subtle rejection. Don't remind them constantly of the sacrifices you're making for them or how good they've got it compared to other kids (or compared to your own childhood). While you may think you're teaching your child to be appreciative, you're doing more damage than good. Eventually your child will tire of hearing how wonderful you are and how

Ten Worst Guilt Trips

■ Finish your dinner. There are starving children around the world.

■ I'm embarrassed to go out with you when you're dressed like that.

■ What will people think when they hear you don't want to go to college?

■ Your grandmother would have a heart attack if she knew you were going out with that girl/that boy/those friends.

■ It hurts me so much to watch you throw away your life this way.

■ After all I've done for you, after I've worked so hard and given you so much, how could you do this to me?

■ Just do it for me. It's not such a big deal.

■ What makes you think you're so special? When I was a kid, my parents would never have let me get away with that.

■ I just know I won't be able to sleep tonight if I know you're out with those kids.

■ We're not angry; we're just very disappointed.

ungrateful she is. And she'll be hurt that you feel you're doing her a favor by being the good parent she deserves.

HOW TEENAGERS AVOID TALKING

Showing sincere affection, having fun together, and avoiding the pitfalls of guilt and subtle rejection all help to establish an environment in which more comfortable family interchanges can occur. So let us now turn to the actual communication process between you and your teenager.

The biggest obstacle you may face is getting their attention, because it is typical for teenagers to avoid their parents. Teens may avoid you because they value their privacy, feel uncomfortable talking about their feelings, or fall prey to their moods. In most teenagers these feelings will pass in a matter of hours or a couple of days at the most, and they'll approach you when they feel the need to talk. It is important to wait out such a period of avoidance calmly and be prepared to talk when it ends. While you can make gestures of outreach, you can't force your teen to talk to you.

If your teen has been going out of his way to avoid you for weeks, even months, and it's clearly not just a temporary phase, he probably really needs your help. Maybe he is unhappy about his life but is unable to admit it to you, or has convinced himself that you couldn't possibly understand what he's going through. He may be involved with alcohol, drugs, or other illicit activities and is denying that he has a problem. But it should be clear to you that something is going on.

Teens who go out of their way to avoid their parents at all times are making a veiled plea for help, and you must heed it. Even though they insist on being left alone, they usually want very much to connect with their families and don't know how to do so. Many of them are angry and alienated and don't know how to express their feelings directly. They can't get their

Normal Teenage Communication Habits

Keep these things in mind before you assume that you have a communication problem with your teenager:

- Teenagers are often in a hurry. They may be abrupt and cut your conversation short, but they don't always intend to be rude.

- They'll talk to you spontaneously every now and then, but regular lengthy conversations are the exception rather than the rule.

- Whether you like it or not, they'll talk to their friends more than they talk to you.

- They'll usually come to you when they need you.

- They'll be uncomfortable talking about certain personal matters, like sexually related issues, bad or humiliating experiences, and their own shortcomings.

- At times they'll be moody and will avoid conversation with you.

- Although they may avoid you often, if something is bothering them that concerns you, you'll hear about it, even if it's in a roundabout way.

needs met appropriately because they've never learned to communicate properly, so they resort to innuendo and demands. On the surface they are aloof, apathetic, or superficially cheerful, but a closer look reveals loneliness, hurt, and feelings of failure.

Following is a description of four unhealthy roles that teenagers adopt to relate to others. Each role has its own unique communication style that serves a specific purpose: to avoid dealing with real feelings and stay distanced from everyone else. There will be times when you find that your children fit several of the profiles, and they may even switch from one style to another when you least expect it. But remember this frustrating behavior is rarely intentional. Due to their lack of communication skills or experience, these teens actually think they are protecting themselves. In order to really communicate with your teen, you need to identify her defense tactics and figure out how to get past them.

The Shut-Down Teen

A shut-down teen is one who almost never communicates, so you're never quite sure what's going on inside him. This may be the most familiar teenage communication style—or noncommunication style. A teenager like this will be difficult to draw out. He has little to say to you and doesn't generally respond to your overtures. A typical conversation might sound like this:

Parent: How was school today?

Teen: Fine.

Parent: Anything interesting happen?

Teen: Nope.

Parent: So what's happening in your life these days?

Teen: Nothing.

This lack of responsiveness gives you very little to go on. You don't know if your child is being noncommunicative because he

How to Know When Withdrawal Has Become a Serious Problem

■ He has been isolated from your family for at least a month, avoiding you and rejecting your overtures to engage him in conversation. When you see him, he is usually moping around the house aimlessly.

■ Other adults involved with her (like neighbors, relatives, or school personnel) have also noticed the withdrawal.

■ His current behavior pattern is markedly different from his past behavior.

■ She won't talk about anything that's going on in her life and insists that you leave her alone.

■ He has drifted away from his friends and spends increasingly longer periods of time locked in his room.

■ Your persistent efforts to reach out to her have been unsuccessful.

feels sad or depressed, angry or rejected, or just doesn't feel like talking. What's really going on behind the apathy? The ambiguity leaves you feeling concerned and ineffectual.

In a situation like this you have to assume responsibility for building bridges. You may be tempted to leave your teen alone and wait until he comes out of his cave, but hanging back can be risky because the problems that led to his isolation can rapidly get worse. Your job is therefore to help him understand that you're interested in him, determined to establish a relationship, and not about to judge him. Be patient but persistent in seeking some common ground. Even if he has nothing to say, talk to him about something, anything, of interest. Maybe he'll pick up on the topic or come back to it later, and maybe not. What's important is that he'll know you're not giving up on him.

The Small-Talker

This young person talks a lot without saying much. Sound familiar? As parents of a teen exhibiting this communication style, you may feel you don't know her very well because she typically describes events in detail without expressing her feelings about them. Whenever she can, she shifts the focus of conversation away from herself and onto other people. This practice makes her appear interested but is actually a safe way to avoid exposing herself.

Teenagers like this are often cheerful on the surface, but we wonder what's going on inside. Generally they're neither self-confident nor happy, and they doubt that anyone really cares for them. A lot of their energy is devoted to maintaining one-sided relationships from which they stand aloof. Sometimes these teens have a reason for this self-protective behavior. Maybe their trust has been violated in the past, or maybe they have grown up in families or cultures where feelings, especially negative ones, are not discussed. But it's a real problem when their small talk interferes with getting close to others. The small-talker may joke around a lot, make light of his feelings, and change the topic of

---

Ten Suggestions to Engage the Small-Talker

1. Say, "So you've told me all about the time your friend Jane had at the dance. How about you?"

2. When he is talking about something in his life in a strictly factual, emotionally neutral way, ask, "How did it make you feel when that happened?"

3. Model open behavior, being certain to reveal your own feelings about people, events, and so forth.

4. Don't be afraid to speculate about what she's really feeling. Say, for example, "I bet it upset you when your friends went to the mall without you after you had all made plans."

5. Purposely guess wrong about his feelings, knowing he may feel compelled to correct you.

6. Small-talkers are often afraid that their real feelings will be ridiculed or put down. Encourage her to speak by giving affirmation when she ventures her own opinions, and emphasize that it is okay for people to have different views on the same issue.

7. When appropriate, ask him what his best friend or girlfriend really feels about the topic you're discussing. It may be easier for him to disclose his own feelings in the guise of a friend.

8. If you feel uncomfortable about her constant beating around the bush during conversation, don't be afraid to tell her so. She may not be aware of what she's doing, and even if she is, pointing it out might help her to address and change this behavior.

9. Offer him alternatives to small talk. For example, ask him what advice he'd give someone else in the same situation, or tell him that you really respect him when he has the confidence to voice his own opinion. And of course, remind him that what he says will not be held against him.

10. Anytime she deals with you forthrightly, make certain that you call it to her attention, and tell her how good it makes you feel.

---

conversation. You'll often be struck by his ability to avoid any personal disclosures.

Small-talkers are detached from their feelings for several reasons. First, they don't believe that another person would be interested in what they really feel. Second, they are afraid that if they did open up, people might somehow use it against them (for example, make fun of them, violate their confidence, or think less of them). And finally, they don't believe that expressing their feelings would change the situation.

To begin to connect with teens who exhibit this communication style, you have to demonstrate that you care about them, that their feelings are important, and that you want to hear about them. Think of it as your responsibility to try to get to know them better. You'll frequently have to shift the focus of your conversation back to them. For example, if your child matter-of-factly describes his friend being kicked out of class, ask how he feels about the incident. Or if a teenager talks about the new school security officer being mean, inquire if she's had any firsthand encounters with him. The trick is to prevent them from getting bogged down in details and skirting their own feelings. Redirect discussions so they have to consider what they think personally. When they finally tell you, listen carefully, paraphrasing their words so that they know you understand what they've said.

The Victim

Some kids are convinced that they have been unfairly victimized or taken advantage of, and they see themselves as helpless pawns in the struggle of life. Sometimes they're right—abuse takes place in many different forms, and it can come from the people these kids trusted the most, including parents, friends, neighbors, and teachers. This abuse could be emotional, physical, or sexual, and it may have happened years ago or just weeks ago. The result is that these teens are gun-shy and always prepared for the worst, unable to trust other people or share much about themselves.

If a child has really been the victim of abuse, he needs professional counseling. This is one of the toughest issues any parent could ever face. When parents learn that their child has suffered abuse at the hands of someone, they often share the same helpless, angry, victimized feelings as their children. And as hard as it is on a family when a child suffers abuse, it's far worse when the child's abuse comes from one or both parents. Parents all want to believe that they act in their children's best interests, but sometimes their own problems—drinking, abuse, or marital con-

Are You Behaving Abusively?

■ Do you find yourself repeatedly lashing out at your teenager for relatively minor infractions (forgetting to take out the trash, spilling something by accident, or dawdling in the bathroom)?

■ Do you rely on physical punishment as your primary form of discipline?

■ Do you constantly put down your teenager?

■ Did you ever hurt your child when he was younger?

■ Are you convinced that your teenager deserves to be treated harshly?

■ Does your family ever tell you that you get really mean?

■ Do you take out your own frustrations on your child?

■ Do you have a serious dependence on alcohol or drugs to the extent that it affects your personality and behavior?

If you answered yes to any of these questions, consult the Appendix in this book for sources to which you can turn for help. You owe it to both your family and yourself to find the courage to deal with your problems immediately.

flicts—get in the way. Keeping painful incidents a secret or brushing family problems under the rug does no one a favor. Everyone suffers in the long run, because harmful situations will always come back to haunt everyone involved. In such a situation your whole family needs professional help immediately. The healing process is a long, painful journey that requires honesty, courage, and trust. There will be many setbacks and moments of despair and rage along the way. But in the end, the feelings of self-worth and confidence your child will recover make it worth every bit of the effort.

Fortunately, most teens don't fall into the category of being serious victims. The teens I'm talking about are self-proclaimed victims. They manipulate others into feeling guilty by twisting their words or actions around into personal affronts, or else they make people feel sorry for them with their tales of woe. Then the victims play upon these emotions of guilt or pity to get what they want: attention, possessions, friends. Of course, when their act doesn't work, these victims are laughed at and viewed with contempt.

Why would a teen who isn't really a victim act like one? Victimhood is greatly a matter of perception. These victims have interpreted everyday setbacks or unhappy moments to be episodes where they were treated badly or used. Other characteristics of these victims include an insatiable appetite for indulgence and difficulty accepting no for an answer. They are truly self-centered and unrealistically expect that things should always go the way they want. They don't like being forced to do their own work, and they usually give up easily. Victimhood is a passive approach to life that often requires little effort on their part, other than some self-indulgent dramatics. And yes, sometimes it gets them what they want.

If your child is a false victim, you are struggling with feelings either of guilt or of frustration. You can begin to help her by challenging her on her self-centered views and actions. Don't just accept her "poor me" statements; ask her why she feels that way, or what she could do to change her life for the better in the future. Tell her how it makes you and others feel when she constantly complains about how miserable her life is. And finally, encourage her to take a more proactive stance toward life. Suggest ways in which she can communicate her needs more clearly, as well as ways that she can create her own happiness and success. Deliver this message at a time when you are not in conflict and do so in a clear, objective, nonthreatening way. Eventually she'll have to develop another style of relating to people, based on mutuality rather than self-righteousness.

The Approval Seeker

This final communication style may seem fairly benign to you, but it will definitely have a negative effect on your teenager. Like adult chameleons we all encounter in our professional and social lives, teens who are approval seekers are desperate for others to like them and will do almost anything to be accepted. Sometimes it's hard to find fault with these approval seekers when they are students who do excellent schoolwork to gain approval from their teachers, or children who try to act like the perfect son or daughter to win approval from their parents. But the reality is that these teens are often unable to voice their true opinions or make their own decisions.

The approval-seeking tendency gets more dangerous when teens seek approval from their peers, because they are very susceptible to negative influences. This sort of teen gets drunk because all his friends are drinking; she has sex prematurely to please a boyfriend. Low self-esteem and insecurity results, because their relationships are based on false grounds. They worry that people wouldn't like them anymore if they went against popular opinion or what is expected of them.

If your teen is an approval seeker you have to be very careful, because she may never really tell you what she feels out of fear of saying the wrong thing. Instead she'll try to second-guess you so she can mirror your opinions. Worse, she may display an alarming lack of objectivity about her friends and her own behavior. She's afraid of rejection and probably depends on someone to make decisions for her. This fear of independence is not what you want.

Approval-seeking teenagers must learn to communicate their real feelings and wishes directly. They rarely trust their feelings and can't see themselves in a positive light. Don't let them get

Helping Teenagers Communicate Their Real Feelings

Here are some actions you can take to help your teens learn how to share their real feelings:

- Emphasize to your children that what they think is important. Express curiosity and listen carefully to what they tell you.

- Stress the importance of being truthful. Let them know that you value this quality and tell them why.

- Be honest and open about what you feel. Don't be afraid to reveal your own foibles.

- Think back to your teenage years and try to share an experience of yours that seems relevant to theirs.

- Show them that you love them unconditionally.

- Make it a point to speak regularly about events in your life and theirs.

away with vague statements like "Whatever you want is fine." And avoid falling into the trap of speaking for them. Instead, try to help them learn to communicate their real feelings. "What is popular is not always right, and what is right is not always popular" is a saying that speaks directly to the approval seeker. Teach them to be strong and independent.

One last thought: if you are unconsciously pushing your child to be an approval seeker, search yourself to make sure you aren't letting high expectations cloud your perception of who your child really is and what he is really interested in.

ENCOURAGING TEENS TO TALK BY UNDERSTANDING THEM BETTER

Many teenagers find it difficult to talk to their parents about themselves, not because they're naturally quiet or lack conversation skills but because close relationships with their parents seem to undermine their own independence. Of course, this attitude isn't taken by all teenagers, but those who are at risk for getting into trouble seem to take pride in distancing themselves from their families. Whether your children are reluctant or willing to talk, you'll need to find some conversational tools to open the door to further communication. Following are some ways to gain information about your teenager that you can use both to understand her better and to have topics for conversation.

Observe Them with Their Best Friends

If you really want to learn more about your teenager, try watching how she relates to her best friends. You'll no doubt be struck by the difference between those conversations and the ones she has with you. Her closest friends seem to know her innermost secrets, and their conversations are full of jokes, nicknames, and references that you can't even pretend to understand. This may be a huge contrast to the tense, sparse verbal exchanges that take place between you and your teen. The difference is that your teenager knows her best friends really understand her, care about her, and will stand by her no matter what. Her thoughts and stories are received with sympathy, compassion, and little or no judgment. Don't we all know teens who spend hours talking on the phone each evening (often with friends they just saw that day in school!), calling each other back to share the littlest details they forgot to mention the first few times?

You don't have to be your teen's best friend, but you can learn a lot about how she's doing by observing one casual conversation. Don't eavesdrop on your child's private conversations, but if she's around you in the kitchen or family room, just pay attention. You may even learn a thing or two from her friends about being a better listener.

Show Interest in Their Friends

Always remember that young people feel it's safer to talk about someone else than about themselves. Ask how their friends are doing in school, what their interests are, and how they get along with their families. After some initial surprise, teenagers will usually answer questions like this and unwittingly reveal information about themselves in the process. The only time your teen will be reluctant to talk is when the answer is unflattering or negative. If you suspect that may be the case, voice your interest in a general way, such as, "How is Renee doing these days?" or, "What has Erik been up to lately?"

Sometimes it can also be interesting to initiate a discussion with your child's friend in his presence. Teenagers generally don't like their parents to pry into the lives of their friends, but they're often surprised to see how receptive their friends are to such conversations. Of course, this is because their friends believe, like them, that anyone is better to talk to than their own parents! If you can arrange this, your children may also see you as a neutral person they can vent to, confide in, or seek advice from. It's a win-win situation.

In such a conversation, be prepared to handle whatever that friend has to say. If you're presented with a situation that you disapprove of or that involves something risky, you'll need to bite your lip and keep your remarks neutral. When it comes to your teen's friends, think of yourself as an adviser rather than a parent. And remember that each time you successfully do this, you'll score points with your child. He'll trust you a little more, and may emulate his friend by confiding in you. So think of the opportunity as a dress rehearsal for an upcoming situation in your family.

Tune In to Teen Culture

You may be taken aback by some of your children's interests, but staying in touch with teen culture will have a big payoff for you. Although there's no need to become an expert, spend time learning about what's important to them. Some magazines that are generally pretty in touch with teen culture are *Teen People, Entertainment Weekly,* and *Rolling Stone.* The magazines your teen buys will be more specialized to his interests, so ask to borrow an issue or two. MTV doesn't exactly mirror real life, but it does show the latest trends. Join your teen for an episode of his favorite TV program—and try to keep any disparaging remarks to yourself, or you won't be a welcome companion next time! Take note of the movies your teen goes to see with his friends, and ask him for a short summary when he gets home. And notice the clothing teens wear, their hairstyles, and the slang they use, because that's also part of their culture.

What you learn will give you insight into the world as your teen sees it, as well as rich material for discussion. You'll then be

What's Wrong with This Dialogue?

Your communication style sets the tone for interactions in your family. Teenagers, perhaps more than any other age group, are quick to pick up inconsistencies in your words or actions, so you must look carefully at how you relate to your children. If there's a long history of conflict in your family, you're probably frustrated and angry, and these feelings emerge in how you talk to your teenagers every day. You may have an edge to your voice, speak more loudly to them than to other people, or resort to sarcasm and criticism. As a result, your communication with your teen will suffer.

This dialogue illustrates anger, misunderstanding, and poor communication skills:

Fiona: Mom, I'm sleeping over at Heather's house tomorrow night.

Mother: No way, Fiona. It's the middle of the week. Why don't you ever use good judgment?

Fiona: You're such a bitch! You make a big deal out of everything.

Mother: If that's the way you're going to talk to me, then this conversation is finished. You never show any respect for your father and me.

Fiona: I could never respect you. You're just so out of touch. Are you going to let me go, or not?

Mother: Considering the way you treat us? Give me a break!

Fiona: I can't stand you. You're so uptight! None of my friends' parents are like this.

Mother: Well, if that's your attitude, you can just stay home this weekend as well.

Fiona (in tears): This house sucks. I'm out of here. Whether you like it or not, I'm going to Heather's tomorrow night. I'm not going to let you ruin my life.

Neither this mother nor Fiona is able to get her message across in such a way that the other will listen. The mother often responds with sarcasm, and both indulge in name-calling and accusations. The mother is infuriated by her daughter's lack of respect, and the daughter is tired of being nagged and criticized. Rather than speaking directly about their own feelings, each blames the other, which is evident in the messages beginning with "you" rather than "I." ("You are" messages come across as accusations, while "I feel" messages are personal and thus difficult to challenge. See page 125 for more information about I-language). Finally, rather than focusing on the issue at hand, they use it to bring up old grievances and generalizations about behavior over time ("You don't use good judgment," "You *never* show respect"). Clearly, both mother and daughter need to do some work to correct their misunderstandings.

If Fiona's mother had been versed in communication skills, the conversation might have gone something like this:

Fiona: Mom, I'm sleeping over at Heather's house tomorrow night.

Mother: Well, it's the middle of the week, so I'm not crazy about the idea. I'm concerned that you'll stay up late talking and won't study for your test.

Fiona: Oh Mom, you make such a big deal out of everything! I think I'm old enough to be trusted now.

Mother: Wait a minute. I didn't say you couldn't go.

Fiona: Well, the way you said it made me feel that way.

Mother: That wasn't my intention. At this point I'm considering it. I really just wanted to hear some more about the sleepover.

Fiona: So, what do you want to know?

Mother: Well, why is it so important to you that you sleep over? Can't you just study late and then come home?

Fiona: God, you always treat me like a baby. Just forget I asked.

Mother: Fiona, please listen to me. You just told me you really wanted to go. I'm trying to give you a chance to explain. If you're willing to talk about it, we might be able to work this out.

Fiona: All right, I'll try to answer your questions.

Mother: That's all I'm asking. It's much easier for me to give my okay when I feel like I have all the facts.

This time the mother doesn't react angrily to Fiona's comments. She stays focused on the issue on the table and shares the reason for her concern. Fiona is clearly impatient and frustrated, but the conversation doesn't turn ugly this time because her mother is able to stay with the task at hand. Despite some mildly provocative remarks, the mother concentrates on expressing her own feelings without striking back. And eventually, Fiona is able to follow her mother's strong example. In the end, both are left feeling better.

Of course, not all conversations with your teen will run as smoothly as this one, but you have to try to create an atmosphere conducive to sharing both positive and negative feelings.

in a better position to meet them on their own ground. They may find your knowledge of teen culture disarming or hilarious if you haven't expressed it before, but they will usually greatly appreciate your interest and will be only too happy to correct any mistaken observations. I'll have more to say about current fads in Chapter 8 and will help you understand which are typical for teens and which should cause concern.

THE BASICS
OF COMMUNICATION

You've been communicating since the day you were born, so going back to basics may sound simplistic. But I actually find it extremely helpful with my patients, who in many cases have lost touch with what productive communication entails.

In general, good communication involves one person speaking clearly while the other listens attentively, leading to mutual understanding and a format for problem solving. It seems simple enough, doesn't it? But many families fail at it. Misunderstandings can easily thwart communication between parent and child, and all sorts of misunderstandings regularly occur. Sometimes each party jumps to the conclusion that the other can't possibly understand his position and dismisses any interchange as useless. Other times someone may bring up past grievances, which will quickly sidetrack a conversation, since the natural response to verbal assault is self-defense. Here are some ways to avoid these pitfalls and carry on more productive conversations with your teen.

How to Begin

In any conversation, first make sure you have the other person's attention. Establish eye contact, observe what that person is doing at the moment, and be attentive to whether the person is alert, bored, tired, and so forth. With teenagers, this process of establishing attention is especially important because they so often seem to be in a hurry and it's not much use trying to talk to someone who's distracted or resentful of intrusion. So, choose your moment wisely. One girl's father told me about a time when his daughter was leaving the house to meet some friends and he politely asked her to wait a minute so they could talk about something. The daughter walked right past him without saying a word. "I could actually feel the breeze as she flew by," the father laughed.

It's pointless to try to stop your children when they're on the run because their priorities are different from yours. Matters relating to their friends and the daily business of their lives are paramount, and conversations with their parents usually of distinctly secondary interest. However, if you watch them carefully, opportunities will certainly arise. You'll find them puttering around the house, glancing at the newspaper, flipping through TV channels, or looking for something to do. These are golden opportunities, so seize them.

For casual conversations, which are fairly easily initiated, simply approach your child and begin talking. If your topic is interesting or touches on something familiar to him, your teenager will jump in. Don't expect the conversation to last too long. Teens' attention spans are often shorter than those of adults, particularly in conversations about adult matters.

If you have a more important issue to discuss, you'll want to preface the conversation by asking your child if he's willing to sit down with you for a few minutes. If he tells you he's busy or in a hurry, you'll need to accept that for the moment, but get him to commit to a time when he's willing to talk. Consider times before or after dinner, at bedtime, or while he's riding with you in the car. If your teenager continues to avoid the discussion, you'll need to insist on a time. If necessary, tell her that she won't be allowed to engage in a certain activity until you've had the discussion.

What to Do When Your Teenager Keeps Brushing You Off

If your child seems genuinely troubled about something, you'll have to find a way to engage him. It's okay to be brushed aside a few times, but there comes a point when you must insist on a discussion. Here are some specific suggestions:

1. Tell your teenager what you're concerned about and why.

2. Clearly state your need to have a real discussion with him. If he tries to brush it off, be persistent.

3. If she doesn't respond when you first bring up the discussion, allow her about a day to get back to you.

4. If he continues to avoid a discussion, place a time limit on how long you're willing to wait (several days is reasonable). Give him a definite date by which the discussion needs to have happened.

5. If the definite date arrives and she is still avoiding you, remind her of this and offer her one final opportunity.

6. If she still won't talk to you, do not drop the matter. Do not give up. This is a sign that something serious may be going on.

7. Try to find someone else in his life who might be able to talk to him (for example, another family member, a good friend, a teacher, or a school counselor). This person can be someone your teen knows better than you do, but he should be someone you feel comfortable enough talking to as well.

8. If she continues to defy your requests for a discussion, inform her what the consequence of further avoidance might be.

9. Follow through with the consequence if necessary.

10. If you continue to be unsuccessful in engaging him in a discussion and believe the matter is serious, seek professional consultation.

Questioning and Listening Skills

Listening attentively is as important as speaking clearly in conversations with your teen. Always keep in mind that you can learn something from your children, and be sure to convey this message to them. This openness will make it easier for you to pay attention to them and for your teenagers to talk to you.

Be sure to stay focused on what they're saying and don't change the subject. Try to repeat their message in your own words to convey that you understand what they're saying. If your daughter complains that her brother gets away with more than she does, you might say, "What I hear you saying is that you think we are more lenient with your brother than we are with you, and that makes you angry." That will free her to say more about her feelings without making her feel judged in any way.

A lot of my young clients complain that their parents get preachy in conversations, so they give up trying to tell them things. It's important that you swallow any temptation to say, "I told you so," or, "You know what the moral of that story is?" Would you like your boss or your spouse to interrupt your heartfelt confidences with comments like that? You should also stick to specifics and not globalize the problem. For instance, if a child lost an expensive jacket at a party you should avoid saying something to the effect that she is always losing things. Comment on the one incident and focus on what can be done to avert a similar situation in the future.

And ask relevant questions to keep the discussion moving. This response on your part shows your interest and your eagerness to receive more information. But a warning: don't ask your teenagers questions they can't answer. If you ask your son why he's doing so badly in school, he'll probably answer, "I don't know," or just walk away. It's better to ask him what's wrong with the school or his teachers, a question he'll be happy to answer. It would probably also be futile to ask a moody teenager, "What's the matter?" Better to ask if he would like to be left alone—at least you can expect an answer to that question.

Checking Out Their Frame of Mind

Concerned parents should learn how to tune into their teenagers' moods so as to enhance communication and connect emotionally. A parent who senses her child is excited about something should try to mirror that feeling with enthusiasm of her own. If your son is animated about a dance he's going to, you might comment on how good he looks, or ask about the band or DJ or who else will be there. If your daughter is fired up about something unfair that happened in school that day, ask her about the incident, commiserate with her over any injustice, and express your empathy about the situation. Be especially careful not to seem indifferent to your teenager's mood; that is a surefire way to discourage him from future dialogue.

Because your teenager's frame of mind will vary frequently, you'll need to be a careful observer to pick up on changes. Don't be alarmed if he sometimes resists your overtures. Simply continue to comment on his moods and make certain that you invite a response. Your unwavering interest will usually pay off. However, there will be times when you'll want to step back, because an overly intrusive approach can drive your teenager away. You'll know you're overdoing it when he starts getting annoyed and complains about your bugging him all the time. Remember that sometimes it's not what you say, but how and when you say it. So try to learn from experience.

It will take you some time to develop the habits of clear communication and active listening. Allow at least a month before expecting a difference in the pattern at home. At first you may have to plan carefully before you initiate a conversation. Consider exactly what message you're trying to get across and ask yourself how you plan to convey it. Many parents impulsively blurt out their anger or criticism, only to be sorry when their teenagers get defensive and strike back. It's always important to question your own behavior as well as your teenager's.

STRATEGIES TO PROMOTE DIALOGUE

There is no substitute for taking an active interest in your child's life, but sometimes communicating with teens can feel like a verbal version of hide-and-seek. They come home, race to their rooms, and lock their doors. Certainly, your children should have their private time. And their room is a sanctuary where it's perfectly appropriate for them to spend hours on end listening to music, talking on the telephone, working on the computer, and doing their homework. But they should come up for air every now and then.

You should expect them to spend some quality time with you, but don't be unrealistic. If you're actively talking to them for ten or fifteen minutes a day, you're doing well. When they believe you are genuinely concerned about them and not judging them, they're more likely to share what's going on in their lives. Following are some suggestions to encourage teenagers to talk more about themselves on a regular basis.

Tell Stories About Yourself

Your children may not speak freely about themselves, but that doesn't mean you can't. Think about experiences you've had that may be relevant to your teenager's life. If you tell them about some dilemma you faced when you were young, it lets them know that you too are fallible. They'll express their feelings more freely when they see you are willing to do so. And don't ask if they want to hear or wait for an invitation; just pick the right moment and start talking. A formal "Back when I was your age" story will sound like a lecture, but a casually told, interesting story gives your teen room to digest the story on his own and doesn't force any messages.

One father told his son about an embarrassing moment in his teenage years. He'd never learned how to dance to fast music and went to great lengths to cover it up; the only dancing he would ever attempt in public was the "slow song sway." During a crowded school function, he asked a girl he really liked to slow-dance to "Stairway to Heaven." Unfortunately, after several minutes the tempo picked up and it turned into a fast-paced rock song. There he was, stuck on the dance floor surrounded by couples dancing crazily, not knowing what to do. His son, who also hates dancing, got a big kick out of this story.

Sharing such amusingly embarrassing experiences helps you to build a foundation of openness. When your children see your human side and hear about the same feelings they experience, they are more likely to talk to you about their own feelings when something worrisome comes along. Not only does this foundation promote dialogue; it increases the closeness between parent and child.

Make Inferences About Their Thoughts and Moods

Even if your teenager doesn't readily tell you what's going on with him, you can speculate. He may give you cues, both spoken and unspoken. Despite what he says, he usually wants to be noticed. When he looks worried, tired, annoyed, or otherwise distracted, comment on what you're observing, describing rather than judging. If he seems depressed, you might say, "It seems like you've been staying around the house a lot lately, and you seem like you don't have much energy." This gives him a chance to pick up on your observation, and is far less intrusive than asking directly if he's depressed. Most teenagers would rebuff a question like that anyway, even if they were.

Don't Interrogate or Lecture

Many teenagers tell me they feel their parents talk to them as if they're on the witness stand. Needless to say, feeling interrogated doesn't make for good conversation. Teenagers are very sensitive to intensive questioning and tend to withdraw when pressed. The more questions you ask, the less likely they are to answer. Keep this in mind and police yourself for excessive intrusion into your child's thoughts. If you have serious questions that must be answered, pick only the most important ones to ask.

Also, remember that class is *not* in session, and you're *not* the learned professor. In other words, skip the lecture! Try to balance how much you talk with how much your child talks. This will ensure that he's involved in the conversation. Unless teenagers get a chance to contribute, they'll tune out and fail to receive their parents' intended messages. After a big lecture, Mom may think she's really taught her daughter all about abstaining from sex, when the reality is that her sexually active daughter tuned out her well-intended but out-of-touch ramblings awhile ago, and daydreamed about her new boyfriend instead.

Seize the Moment

Every so often, you have your teenager's undivided attention—when this opportunity arises, talk to him. The fewer the distractions, the better; you just can't compete with

Ten Ideas for Judgment-Free Conversation

1. Make certain that your tone of voice is neutral.

2. Try to precede your comment with a positive statement.

3. If you're sharing an observation on her behavior, allow for other possible explanations. Don't jump to conclusions until you have all the facts.

4. Ask him what he feels about a specific issue before telling him how you feel.

5. Remind her that you're trying to be objective.

6. Try to make your comments descriptive rather than critical.

7. Be brief and stick to the issue at hand.

8. Avoid making sweeping generalizations, especially about other teens.

9. Try to be receptive to his comments about you.

10. Use gentle humor when you can.

his friends, the television, or a sporting event. Rides in the car, times when your teenager is desperately bored, and joint household projects are potential times for discussion, as are family rituals like mealtimes, bedtime, and holidays. For several years, my teenage son and I have met in the kitchen at around ten-thirty on weeknights for a snack. This is a sort of sacred time, because for about ten minutes we have each other's undivided attention. We've shared a great deal this way over the years, even if I've gained a few pounds in the process.

Ask for Their Opinions

Like most parents, you may find it easier to give advice than to receive it. But you should seek your children's opinions every now and then. This lets them feel that they're being helpful, and that you respect them and are open to their thoughts. Since teenagers are convinced they know everything, they'll be only too happy to give you the benefit of their vast experience!

Depending on their interests, you can ask your children's opinions on which outfit you should wear, which new movie you should see, or what birthday present you should buy for another family member. Discussion is easily initiated if you comment that they know more about certain things than you do and you'd appreciate their help. Look for areas where they excel, like their best school subjects, music, computers, fashion, or sports. Try asking their opinion about such mundane subjects as what tonight's dinner menu should be, or what kind of car you should purchase next. And once you're in the habit of sharing thoughts, there's no reason you can't have conversations about more serious topics as well. How does she feel about her grandfather living with you, or her older sister getting married?

Teenagers are pleased to learn that their opinions matter to you. When they are convinced that you're genuinely interested in what they think, they are more likely to share their thoughts and ask for your own opinions. Sometimes their forthrightness will pleasantly surprise you; other times you'll be shocked. You might even get a fresh perspective and some good advice along the way. In effect, you're setting the tone for an interchange that bridges the gap between parent and child in an exchange based on mutual respect and trust.

Ask Which Friend's House Is Their Favorite Place to Hang Out

I always find it useful to ask teenagers to describe the house of a friend where they enjoy spending time. This should be done in a spirit of curiosity and goodwill. After all, you shouldn't have to apologize for wanting to know more about their lives. But be careful that you don't come across as prying. You don't want them to feel that you're doing detective work.

When I posed this question to my client Aaron in a family meeting, he told us enthusiastically about life at his friend Dan's house. It seemed like Dan's entire family got along really well, joking with one another, helping one another out, and doing things together. The house felt pleasant and relaxed. I asked Aaron if he thought Dan's parents trusted their son. He smiled broadly and said, "They sure do. I wish my parents could be like that." At this point, I turned to his parents, inquiring if they would like the atmosphere in their home to resemble that of Dan's. Both strongly concurred and expressed their willingness to work on their family life. With that, we had the basis for change.

This approach, based on curiosity about others, can promote communication and understanding in several ways. It gives you an idea of the kind of atmosphere the teenager finds comfortable, it allows you to exchange ideas about how family life ought to be, and it encourages goodwill, with you and your child agreeing that you can all take positive steps to improve your home life.

Avoid Intrusion

A few words of caution about curiosity. While you want to foster familiarity and communication with your teenager, be careful not to violate his personal space. When you feel shut out of your teenager's life and you wonder what's really going on with him, you're tempted to gather information covertly: eavesdropping on his telephone conversations, going through his room, or reading his e-mail, notes, and journal. Such detective work may be justified under extreme circumstances, when you are really faced with a problem that must be confronted. (These serious circumstances are addressed in detail later in the book.) But when you're playing Sherlock Holmes just out of curiosity, watch out! Your intentions may be good, but you are invading their privacy, and what you find out may mislead you.

Be careful not to violate your teen's personal space.

Several years ago I was working with a depressed sixteen-year-old client, and seeing her family as well. One day I received a frantic call from her mother, who insisted on seeing me immediately. It seems that her mother had gone through her room, a highly private sanctuary that few were allowed to enter. She had read one of her daughter's diaries, which contained accounts of wild, detailed, graphic sexual encounters between her daughter and several different boys whom her mother didn't know. This was completely out of character and a total shock to her mother; she had suspected that there were things she didn't know about her daughter, but promiscuity was the last thing she expected. Her mother was sobbing, torn between fear and fury.

I had been seeing her daughter for several months and had gotten to the stage where she had really opened up and begun to talk about her deepest issues. She was an intelligent, kind girl who unfortunately felt isolated, uncomfortable, and awkward around other people her age. She had retreated into a world of books, and also spent hours writing stories about romantic encounters laced with adventure that mostly starred an idealized version of herself. I thought that sexual promiscuity sounded just as out of character as her mother did, and I suspected that what her mother thought to be a diary or journal was really a notebook in which she recorded her fantasies.

"Mrs. Jones, have you considered the possibility that these diary entries might be fictitious?" I asked.

She looked at me incredulously. "You think she made this whole thing up?"

"Well, it wouldn't be the first time something like this has happened," I responded. "She's got a vivid imagination, she's probably read books and seen movies that contain sexual scenes, and it's likely that she's experienced deep crushes and sexual attractions." While her mother considered this, I went on. "If it was someone else, I might think you had a real problem, but we both know that it doesn't sound like her at all. I don't think you should say anything to her about reading her diary. If you did, you'd have to admit that you went through her room against her specific wishes, and it would only make things worse. She would feel angry and violated, and would never trust you in the future."

The mother reluctantly agreed to drop the matter and to act as if nothing had happened. As it turned out, her daughter eventually told her that she used her writing to express her fantasies, and the mother was able to respond with interest and compassion.

If parents come across something incriminating that they feel they must act upon, like a pack of cigarettes in a coat pocket or drug paraphernalia in a sock drawer, well, that is something else altogether. My point is not that parents should ignore or justify clear signs that trouble is brewing. I am merely saying that when parents go snooping around in their teenage children's lives, they generally find mildly unsavory things that they didn't really need to know about.

NEGOTIATION: LIFE AT THE BARGAINING TABLE

Young children need direction and normally follow adult instructions without too much protest, but teenagers, though they still need guidance, often resist rules no matter how many logical, sensible, adult conversations you have with them. This puts you in a dilemma: you have to be in charge of your teenagers' lives, but you also have to give them room to grow. You will be with them less and less as they grow older, so part of your being in charge means helping them internalize rules for good behavior to ensure they will make appropriate decisions on their own.

During their adolescence, your children typically assert their independence by refusing to accept your rules and limits on blind faith. Instead, they question your authority and try to bargain. It's tempting for you to say no and refuse to discuss the matter when they resist. But cutting them off won't solve anything in the long run. It's more fruitful instead to let them discuss the differences of opinion. Listen to what they have to say, and weigh their beliefs against your own. There will be plenty of times when you'll acknowledge their feelings but will make it clear that the rules will remain in place. But surely, every so often, they'll make some excellent points, and rules that they may have outgrown can be adjusted in their favor. When teenagers are encouraged to express their feelings and when they feel their words do matter to you, they'll be more likely to accept your final decision in these showdowns, and to develop their own decision-making abilities in the process.

It is better, then, to think of these interactions as processes of negotiation. People of all ages use the skills of negotiation and compromise to get what they want when someone stands in their way. Negotiation is especially well suited to resolving disputes between parents and adolescents because it allows teenagers to express their viewpoints, teaches them good problem-solving skills, and eases the tension that arises when your teen feels completely misunderstood and treated unfairly. Further, your willingness to negotiate conveys respect for your teenagers, thus increasing their willingness to talk to you. Good negotiation can defuse anger and redirect a stalled relationship, helping you to direct your teen toward healthy decision making and away from violent, angry approaches.

A good way to start is to choose a subject that has been a minor issue between you and your teenager. I suggest you begin with something relatively common and specific that is not contentious. Some examples are difficulty waking up in the morning, regularly showing up late for dinner, or a chore that is frequently left undone—all behaviors we observe in typical teenagers. You can introduce the negotiation by announcing that you think she's old enough to be in on the decision-making process and that you have an issue you'd like to address. Even if she's been in trouble, you're now offering an opportunity for a new beginning. When she sees that you're willing to let go like this, she will likely loosen up and respond to your offer.

Principles of Negotiation

Before any conversations take place, spend some time thinking through these principles of negotiation.

1. Enter the negotiation with realistic expectations. Maybe you think your teen should be in bed by ten every night in order to be well rested. (Probably that's true!) But is ten an appropriate bedtime for his or her age group? The truth is that most teenagers stay up at least another hour, if not more. A ten o'clock bedtime will probably be difficult to enforce and will provoke innumerable fights between you and your teen. Stay in touch with the appropriate expectations for your teen's age group. What are the school's rules and policies for his grade? How much homework is he assigned each night? What curfews and rules do his friends have?

And consider your teen in realistic terms. How is she doing in school? How responsible is she? How much patience does she have? What sorts of friends does she spend her time with? This is not to remind your teen of her past shortcomings and failures during your negotiations; that would be highly counterproductive. Instead, use this basic information to keep the negotiations based in reality.

2. Set a positive tone by proposing negotiation as a new alternative to explore. Many teenagers bargain because they like the idea of gaining concessions from their parents. At first they don't think about making any concessions themselves, although the negotiation process calls for it. Not all teenagers will readily negotiate their differences with parents, so I suggest you initiate the process by reminding your child that you often reach stalemates when discussing certain issues. Acknowledge that it's frustrating for you, and ask if she feels the same way. Assuming the feeling is shared, emphasize that stalemates are often the result of angry, inflexible fighting, and that through negotiation, the two of you may be able to reach a different, more successful resolution to your problem. Propose that you both try negotiating instead of fighting the next time the two of you experience a difference of opinion. She has nothing to lose and everything to gain.

Recommended Guidelines for Speaking to Each Other During a Negotiation

To increase the likelihood of a successful negotiation, each participant should agree to the following guidelines:

- All of the participants in the negotiation process are on equal footing, regardless of age, gender, or role in the family.
- When one person is speaking, the other(s) must listen. If this is hard to stick to, you can either take turns after an agreed-upon signal or simply raise hands.
- If a participant feels that they must interrupt, they must ask or signal for the speaker's permission first.
- Each participant must address the other participants with respect, even if there is a disagreement of ideas.
- No yelling, screaming, name-calling, or sarcastic comments. No criticism, lectures, moralizing, or blaming. And absolutely no physical lashing out (hitting, shoving, and the like). These are all highly counterproductive.

- If one participant is saying something that is truly upsetting for another participant to to listen to, tell them, and they will stop.
- No bringing up past grievances. The only exception is if a participant has a bad track record in a certain area and another participant feels it must be addressed to ensure that things will be different this time.

3. Establish a calm and patient climate for negotiation. Structure your negotiation session beforehand to reduce the outside factors that would cause the conflict to escalate, like limited time or an uncomfortable public setting. Choose a mutually agreed upon time and place. Specify who will attend the negotiation (will it simply be you and your teen, or should other family members or friends be present?) and be sure no competing activities will distract any of you. Then decide how long the initial discussion will last. I strongly recommend that both you and your teen use the "I-language" guidelines for negotiating, even if it seems awkward at first. (See the sidebar.) I also highly recommend that all the participants in the negotiation become familiar with using I-language and that I-language be required.

I-Language

One of the goals of negotiation is to avoid attacking or blaming the other party. Using I-language can help you to accomplish this goal. I-language is a way of expressing yourself without making inflammatory statements. When someone has done something to make you upset or angry and you want to let that person know how you feel, instead of making an accusatory "you" statement, express yourself with an "I" statement. Let the person know how you were affected by their actions by speaking with the pronoun "I," as in, "I felt really hurt by your angry words this morning, Rob."

Imagine that Mom is really angry at her daughter, Stephanie.

She wants Stephanie to know how she feels about her behavior. Notice the difference between the following ways to express her anger.

Mom Statement #1: "Stephanie, you are driving me crazy! You still haven't cleaned your room, even though you know you're supposed to if you want to go out this weekend! It's a disgusting pigsty! And you forgot to feed Fluffy last night too! You are so irresponsible and self-centered!"

Mom Statement #2: "Stephanie, I am really feeling frustrated. I know you want to go out this weekend, but I see that your room hasn't been cleaned yet, and you know that it has to get done before you can go out. I'm also upset because you forgot to feed Fluffy last night, and she went hungry. Let's come up with a plan to deal with these two problems."

In both statements, Mom is expressing her frustration to Stephanie. The difference is that in the first statement, she is attacking Stephanie with angry put-downs. This may be how Mom really feels, but this approach is likely to make Stephanie feel angry and defensive, even if she recognizes that she messed up. In the second statement, Mom's "I" statements make her message a personal one, and therefore difficult to object to. Mom also offers Stephanie a new plan, whereas in her first statement she has already condemned Stephanie to failure.

I-language takes some practice to get used to. It requires you to cool down from an initial negative reaction and speak in a reasonable tone, which is tough when you're in the heat of anger. But once you make an effort to use it, I-language becomes more and more natural. It is not useful just during the process of negotiation, but in all areas of life.

Your teen may feel impatient with all this "production," and his natural inclination at first will probably be to get this discussion over with quickly. Convince him that patience is to his advantage, because it will give you both the time to explore all possible options. And warn him that if he tries to rush you into a decision, the answer will probably be no.

4. Plan to include points on which you are willing to compromise,

Paving the Way for Negotiation

Preliminary steps may be necessary to move out of a standoff and into a negotiation process with your teenager. Fifteen-year-old Sean, for instance, simply informed his parents that he was planning to go to the beach with his friends over the weekend. He offered no explanation about whom he was going with, how he would get there, or where he was going to stay. His parents insisted on more information before they would consider his request. Sean refused, saying they should trust him. The situation had all the makings for a major conflict.

His parents had several options at this point:

■ They could back off and let him go. This would be acquiescing to his demands and trusting his dubious integrity and responsibility. They would be taking a real chance in this situation, not knowing what Sean was doing or who he was doing it with. They would also be weakening their position as authority figures.

■ They could persist in their request for further discussion, trying to convince Sean that sitting down and talking was the best way to solve the problem. If Sean agreed to talk, they could consider his request and then make a more informed decision about his proposed trip.

■ If Sean refused to discuss anything, they could take matters into their own hands and call his friends' parents for more information. This would make Sean angry at his parents for intruding, although they'd have every right to do so under the circumstances.

■ If Sean's refusal to talk continued, and his parents couldn't get accurate information, they could set a firm limit. This would mean telling him that he could not go to the beach under any circumstances, unless he chose to share the necessary information with them. And if he violated their limit, there would be specific consequences.

As it turned out, Sean remained adamant in his refusal to discuss the issue and insisted that he was going with or without his parents' permission, no matter what they were able to find out on their own. They were backed up against the wall.

Wisely, his parents chose to set a very serious but firm limit. Since Sean had not behaved responsibly in the past, they told him if he left for the beach without permission, they would treat him as a runaway and notify the police; the choice was his. At first Sean was quite angry about this, but it didn't take him long to decide to sit down with his parents and provide further details.

His parent's strong—but not hysterical or emotional—stance formed a background against which Sean and his parents could enter into a negotiation process to determine under what conditions he could go to the beach.

and remember that it's better to negotiate up than down. Say you're going to negotiate with your daughter over her weekend curfew. How late are you willing to go? Perhaps you would prefer it if your child was home by eleven-thirty but you are willing to go as late as twelve-thirty as long as she firmly adheres to it. When your daughter tells you she should be able to stay out as late as she wants, tell her that you'd rather she be home by eleven, but that you're willing to compromise with her. Then you can hold out for eleven-thirty or twelve and listen to your daughter's rationales and reasoning. If, at this point, you give in to a twelve-thirty curfew, your daughter will really believe that the negotiation process worked in her favor and gained her an hour and a half (she probably didn't really think you'd go for that no-curfew-at-all stuff).

It also helps to tell your teenager when agreements are only temporary. For example, in the curfew negotiation above, you might tell your daughter that for now, her curfew will be twelve on weekend nights, but that it may be moved to twelve-thirty if she can successfully prove herself capable of making it home on time. Teenagers often rise to a chance to prove themselves and will often respond more favorably to a rule they're not fond of if you offer them the possibility of review after a successful trial period. (Of course, defining the trial period can be another negotiating point!)

5. Decide ahead of time what is not negotiable. There will be times when you'll have to put your foot firmly down, because sometimes your teenager's requests will be unrealistic, risky, or too demanding of others. Make sure your children know you're willing to discuss their requests but sometimes they'll have to take no for an answer. When you encounter one of these non-negotiable points, explain clearly and logically why it is not a possibility, and try to suggest alternative solutions. It's important to make it clear to your child that while the negotiation process requires you to treat each other as equals, you ultimately have the final word.

6. Do not allow yourself to be intimidated. Negotiation is achieved through calm discussion, not through threats or loud shouting. If the negotiation is not going in the direction your teenager wants, he may react angrily and call you names, scream at you, insist you don't know what you're talking about, or threaten to do whatever he wants even if you say he can't. If this occurs, you'll need to step back and tell him that you're not going to negotiate under those circumstances. Make it clear that you're trying to treat him with respect and you expect the same courtesy from him. If his defiance persists, leave the room and tell him that you'll talk again when he's prepared to be more reasonable.

Steps to Follow During the Negotiation Process

So you've chosen your issue, prepared well beforehand, and are now about to sit down with your teen for the actual negotiation. What else can you do to increase the likelihood of a successful outcome? I recommend that you follow these steps at least in your first negotiations so that both you and your children will stay focused on the issue at hand.

1. Identify the problem. Defining the terms of the issue might sound easy enough, but what if each family member perceives it differently? Make sure everyone has their say, each taking a turn to define the problem as they see it. Then try to work together to come up with a definition of the problem that incorporates everyone's perspective. If you can't reach an agreement, simply propose that you agree to disagree. What you've agreed on is that there is more than one problem to be addressed.

Sabrina, for example, was a sixteen-year-old whose parents felt she was unwilling to help around the house. Both her mother and father had full-time jobs, but they pitched in with the household chores. Sabrina, on the other hand, contributed little and was stubborn about complying with their requests. She complained that she had a heavy load of schoolwork and was tired of her mother's nagging her to do chores on top of that.

For this problem to be successfully negotiated, both Sabrina and her parents needed to verbalize that each understood the other's feelings. At the outset of the negotiation, Sabrina's parents acknowledged to Sabrina that they understand that she feels burdened by her schoolwork and is upset by her mother's nagging. And Sabrina eventually let her parents know that she is aware of how hard they both work, and realizes that they need more assistance from her. After this step, some of the anger and tension was diffused, and all three family members were able to agree that the real issue was to define a reasonable workload for Sabrina.

2. Come up with possibilities. Each member of the family should be given the opportunity to offer ideas without fear of criticism. This is not the time for anyone to be judgmental. Share your thoughts as your teenager listens; then reverse the process. It goes without saying that all parties must remain attentive and respectful. Squelch any urge to make angry or sarcastic remarks—concentrate on being open. Write down each proposed alternative. When everyone agrees all the possibilities have been covered, review the list together.

After Sabrina and her parents agreed on the need for a list of appropriate chores for Sabrina, they begin to generate solutions. Sabrina spoke first, suggesting that cleaning her room, emptying the trash, and putting dirty dishes in the dishwasher are quite enough for her. Her mother blurted out, "That's not even half of what I do." Before Sabrina can counterpunch, her father stepped in. Addressing his wife, he said, "Wait a minute. We agreed we were just going to share ideas. How about telling us what you think?" Her mother, back on track, suggested that Sabrina vacuum the house as well. The father then said he'd like to see Sabrina do the chores she has proposed and also pick up after herself around the house. Now the family has several possibilities on the table to work with.

3. Evaluate the proposed solutions. After all participants have expressed their ideas, evaluate the alternatives. You can begin by discussing the pros and cons of each. If the conversation gets heated, suggest taking a break. When everyone has cooled off, resume the discussion. Continue until all the participants are satisfied that all points of view have been adequately considered. Then you can move toward a final decision.

When Sabrina's family evaluated the alternatives, neither parent felt that their daughter's proposal would be a sufficient contribution to the household. Sabrina was unhappy with this but let her parents speak. When it was her turn, she reiterated her position that cleaning her room, taking out the trash, and loading the dishwasher are plenty. She rejected her mother's idea about vacuuming, but not her father's suggestion that she pick up after herself.

4. Commit to a course of action. Once you've evaluated the alternatives, it's time to make a choice. Each participant will probably have to give a little. Teenagers not used to the compromise process may interpret this as defeat, but you can assuage this feeling by pointing out to him any gains he made or points that you gave in on, and ask him to give the proposed solution a try. After you reach an agreement, talk briefly about how to enforce it. I recommend that

Ways to Improve Your Technique in Conversation and Negotiation

1. Pretend that you're strangers. If there's too much tension during your talks, agree to pretend you've never met before, and treat each other like strangers. This lends a touch of humor to the situation and enables each of you to get some distance from the problem.

2. Hang up a bulletin board, chalkboard, or dry-erase board. Each family member can post suggestions about any topics of discussion that will be addressed at the next family meeting. This allows everyone time to think about them in advance.

3. Ask each family member to write down their list of grievances, and exchange them before the meeting. This enables parents and children to express their complaints in a less threatening fashion. The lists should be read prior to the meeting and discussed only if all parties agree.

4. Use scorecards during family meetings like those judges hold up after performances in the Olympics. This technique lightens the atmosphere and provides a way to tell the other person how you feel about their efforts to communicate. For example, you can agree to rate such categories as talking without criticism, listening carefully, and trying to compromise. The scoring ranges from one (very poor) to ten (excellent).

both you and your teenager suggest and write down consequences for violation of the agreement, to underline its seriousness and avoid future arguments.

Everyone in Sabrina's family was eventually able to agree to
the father's suggestion. The mother, however, expressed reservations about her daughter's ability to carry out her part of the bargain. Sabrina, for her part, doubted her mother could stop
nagging her. To cement the deal, the mother volunteered to
relieve Sabrina of her responsibilities for one week if she nagged
her. This pleased Sabrina, who offered to cook dinner for the family if she failed to abide by the agreement.

5. Meet later to review results. Once you've chosen an alternative and everyone has had time to give it a chance, meet again
in a week or two to review how things turned out. Say how you
felt about what seemed to work and what didn't, and let everyone else have a chance to speak. If everyone is satisfied with the
outcome, agree to use your new skill when future problems arise.

I should say that despite your best intentions, your teenager
will sometimes refuse to negotiate or even to talk to you. This
often happens when there's a history of trouble, poor communication, and little indication that things might change. Time is of
the essence—you must convince her that it's to her advantage to
address your differences of opinion. Remind her that the family
situation is already miserable and that there's nothing to lose by
trying.

Reverse psychology sometimes works too. Try challenging
your child by telling her that you think she's afraid to talk to
you. She might be inspired to prove you wrong. If need be, give
her some time to think about an issue if she refuses to discuss
it. This lets her save face by approaching you on her own terms.

If push comes to shove, remind your teenager that you're not
going to drop the matter. Let him know you're prepared to do
whatever is necessary to get the family back on track. One of the
goals of negotiation is to develop a positive mind-set that will
help all of you address issues that come up during the course of
adolescence.

Moving Toward More Productive Conversations

One of the most hotly contested issues you will negotiate with your teen is parties. Some high school parties are harmless, friendly get-togethers where parents are present and subversive elements are not. But many parties are not so innocent. Your teen will be quite reluctant to discuss these with you because alcohol or drugs will probably be involved, and these parties are often thrown when the parents are out of town. Your teenager will probably be very defensive discussing them.

Let's look at a successful negotiation to resolve an issue all parents will probably face sooner or later. This teenager is desperate to go to a party, and his parents, with good reason, are reluctant to let him.

Kyle: You know, Mom, there's a really big party coming up after the basketball game next weekend. I really want to go.

Mother: Do you know any of the details, Kyle? Like who's throwing the party and where they live?

Kyle: All I know is that it starts about ten-thirty, after the game.

Mother: That's pretty late. Will the parents be around to supervise?

Kyle: I don't know. What's the big deal, anyway?

Mother: Well, for one thing, you were in trouble a few weeks ago for drinking and getting home late.

Kyle: Yeah, but I've already been punished for that.

Mother: I just don't know about this, Kyle. I'm going to have to talk to your dad and see what he thinks.

Kyle: Come on, Mom, just be cool about it. Most of my friends are going.

Mother: All I can say now is that we'll get back to you. If you keep pushing me, though, the answer will be no.

Kyle: Mom, you're so lame!

(A few hours later, Kyle's parents speak and agree to talk further with him the next evening. The dialogue resumes at that point and continues as a negotiation.)

Father: Kyle, your mother has told me about the party next weekend. We've talked it over and agree it sounds pretty risky.

Kyle: Come on, Dad! Just once, can't you cut me some slack?

Mother: Kyle, you know we've got a problem here. Can you just tell me what you think the problem is, so we'll know you understand?

Kyle: All right. You're uptight because you don't know anything about the party and you're worried I'll get drunk or come home late, or whatever.

Mother: That's pretty close.

Kyle: So, what do you want me to do?

Father: Well, to convince us there isn't anything to worry about.

Kyle: You treat me like such a baby! None of the other kids go through this interrogation.

Mother: Look, you said you really wanted to go. Discussing this with us is your only option.

Kyle: Well, then let's get it over with.

Father: All right. First, we're worried that the parents won't be home. What can you tell us about that?

Kyle: I don't know, Dad. No one told me whether they'd be home or not.

Father: Well, we could call them and find out.

Kyle: That would be embarrassing.

Father: I'm sorry, but that's the only way we'd consider it.

Kyle: Well, do it if you have to, but don't tell them you're my parents.

Mother: Okay, we'll try to be discreet. But remember, if the party giver's parents won't be home that night, you're not going. Is that understood?

Kyle: Yeah.

Mother: And we have other worries too. Like you getting drunk again. We've told you this many times, but we don't ever want you or any of your friends driving while under the influence of alcohol.

Kyle: We're not stupid, Mom. There's always someone sober around who can do the driving.

Mother: I'm glad to hear that, but whether or not you drive, we would insist that there's no drinking for you.

Kyle: You're both so out of touch. Almost everyone drinks at these parties!

Mother: Maybe, but you're the one we're concerned about. Do you have any ideas about that?

Kyle: No, maybe we should just forget it.

Father: Kyle, wait a minute. What if you agree to come into our room when you get home so we can check to see if you're sober. That would help us a lot.

Kyle: I'll do whatever you want. Just let me go.

Mother: Well, we're getting closer to an agreement, but I'm still worried about you getting home on time.

Kyle: Okay, what if I call home and check in? Or Dad could just meet me outside at a certain time if I don't take the car.

Mother: I think we could live with that.

Kyle: Thank God. Does that mean that this discussion is over?

Father: Almost, but there is one more thing.

Kyle: Now what?

Father: Well, we want you to tell us what should happen if you break your agreement.

Kyle: Oh. Well, what if I agree to stay home the next two weekends? Would that make you happy?

Mother: That's fair enough. Let's give it a try.

This dialogue illustrates how Kyle's parents successfully handled the negotiation process. First they insisted that he define the problem: they had no information about the party and were worried about him getting drunk again. Then they explored the alternatives with him: he could let them call his friend's parents, and check in with his own parents when he returned from the party to show them he was sober. Finally, Kyle proposed the consequence for any violation of their agreement.

Kyle's parents initially directed the discussion. This is often necessary when a teenager is reluctant to explore the issue. When Kyle was ready to give up, his parents encouraged him to keep talking. So Kyle stayed with the discussion and eventually reached an agreement that would enable him to attend the party. The family would certainly need to review the outcome the day after the event. If it was successful, there would be a basis for future negotiations. If Kyle failed to abide by his agreement, he would have to face the predetermined consequences. And of course, his negotiating position would be weakened for the next party.

CHAPTER FOUR

HELPING YOUR TEEN DEVELOP GOOD SELF-ESTEEM

*"No, I don't have plans for this weekend.
Who'd want to hang out with a loser like me?"*

*"Look at my thighs.
I'm totally disgusting.
Nobody is ever going to want
to go out with me."*

*"Another D. I'm such an idiot.
I'll never get into a decent college."*

*"I knew I wouldn't make the varsity team.
I can't do anything right."*

THE VALUE OF GOOD SELF-ESTEEM

Teenagers with positive self-esteem genuinely believe they're decent, competent, and lovable. At the same time, they readily acknowledge their shortcomings and seem to get by nicely despite them. When faced with difficulties, they're not afraid to trust their own judgment. A sense of pride underlies their actions. They think before they act, and know how to exercise discretion. These teens aren't always sure of themselves, but they're not afraid to ask for help.

Positive self-esteem doesn't require popularity or high achievement, just self-acceptance. Several years ago I met a young woman at a school leadership conference where I was a consultant. At sixteen, Rita felt good about herself. She wasn't an academic superstar or a future Olympian, but she had her own circle of friends, many interests, and family connections that meant a lot to her. Rita had the usual adolescent concerns about appearance and popularity, but they never got her down for long. From time to time Rita faced minor setbacks, like failing to make the cheerleading squad and not having a date for her sophomore year homecoming dance. But when she was upset, she talked about her feelings with her friends and her parents. Then she usually started to feel better and could get on with her life.

Once, she told me, she'd been approached by some acquaintances at a party and encouraged to try the drug ecstasy. She'd simply said, "No, thank you," and walked away, feeling confident that her decision wouldn't win or lose her friends and knowing she could do without a chemically induced high. This was a teenager with pride and a sense of her own identity. She had convictions and was willing to stand by them.

Rita had been raised to feel loved and valued for who she was. Her parents set appropriate limits for her but took her requests seriously. They recognized her strengths and encouraged her to work on her weaknesses. Her confidence that they were behind her in all she did served Rita well in her teenage years. She was self-assured and accepting of the foibles of others, well on the way to becoming a mature and productive adult.

Teenagers like Rita are certainly not perfect. But in their hearts they believe they are "good enough." This feeling is essential to positive self-esteem. It is one of the many rewards of good parenting: seeing your children accept themselves as they are. Rita's story illustrates a reasonable amount of self-satisfaction combined with efforts to improve herself. Her parents' expectations for her were realistic, and they provided unwavering support. This helped Rita feel that she was doing the best she could. And that's exactly what you should ask of your teenagers: that they try their best.

SELF-ESTEEM PROBLEMS HIDE BEHIND VARIOUS FAÇADES

Low self-esteem can be at the root of many behavior problems. Drew, for example, was a fifteen-year-old whose parents brought him to see me because he was sad, angry, and uncooperative. Since primary school he had been socially awkward and the brunt of jokes. In response, he struck out at others and got into trouble afterward. To make matters worse, he was nearly failing in school, was isolated from his classmates, had no friends his age, and insisted that he no longer cared about what others thought or what happened to him.

When I met Drew he was withdrawn and defensive, with excuses for everything. He protested that he didn't need my help or anyone else's, and complained vehemently about being blamed for things that weren't his fault. Why wouldn't people just stop picking on him and leave him alone? None of his multiple school detentions, home restrictions, or other punishments had had any effect on his misbehavior. During our first meeting I commented that he didn't seem very happy for someone who was doing his own thing. This surprised him and he grew quiet.

When I suggested that other kids in his situation would feel pretty lonely, he nodded and looked down at the floor dejectedly.

It took several months of our working together until he felt comfortable enough to reveal his true feelings. As he did, a tragic, lonely picture of Drew emerged. Drew desperately wanted to be liked, but his attempts to befriend other teens had been rebuffed, probably because of his strong will and overreaction to people's comments. In addition, his parents criticized him, his older brother teased him, and no one seemed to have time for him. Consequently, he went to great lengths to get attention. Unfortunately, the attention he got was generally negative, since he didn't know how to behave in a way that got positive attention. When he got in trouble, he was quick to shift the blame onto someone else and protest his innocence, but inside Drew saw himself as a total failure. Drew's cumulative experiences added up to a lack of pride in himself. He had abandoned his efforts in school and at home and viewed the world as unfriendly. Once I asked Drew if he had any good qualities he could tell me about. His response has stuck with me over the years. "Doc," he said, "the only thing I can think of is that I sleep a lot. At least then I'm not in anybody's way." What a sad example of the damage criticism and rejection can do—and the lengths to which teens may go to disguise poor self-esteem.

Some teenagers, on the other hand, project an image of self-confidence, but beneath the cheerful, upbeat surface envied by their peers lies a pool of discouragement. These popular, sociable, well-dressed, and apparently successful young people have also gone to great lengths to hide their poor self-esteem, but in just the opposite way than Drew did. Where Drew's bad self-esteem made him lash out at the world, these teens project a happy façade and turn their unhappiness inward, upon themselves. In truth, these teens are neither genuinely self-confident nor at peace with themselves. The inconsistency between their public and private selves is a signal that all is not well.

My experience, though, is that many of these teenagers will acknowledge their discomfort when they're in a safe environment. Several years ago I asked a group of teens I was working with to create a picture on a blank T-shirt. I often use this exercise to help kids get to know one another. This group's specific task was for each to show his or her public image on the front of the shirt and something more private on the back. Most of them drew a cool-looking teenager on the front and something personal, but relatively unrevealing, on the back. But one young man who seemed full of confidence—despite the considerable trouble he had gotten in recently, he projected the aura of a cool, James Dean–like rebel—drew a picture of an apathetic, smug teenager with a cigarette hanging out of his mouth on the front, and on the back, to everyone's surprise, pictured a little boy sitting in a corner with tears running down his face. He told us grimly that he often felt that way when he was alone. Here was a powerful illustration of the disharmony between a young person's image and his real feelings. Fortunately, this teenager was able to admit that he didn't like himself much and got the support he needed from his peers to work to improve his self-esteem.

Frequent criticism, rejection, and failure can erode any child's self-confidence as surely as can physical abuse, alcoholic parents, and a dysfunctional family. Poor self-esteem can lead to depression, behavior problems, and substance abuse. Many teenagers won't readily admit that they're unhappy with their lives; this reluctance is understandable since admitting unhappiness takes great courage and leaves them feeling vulnerable. They've been expending a lot of energy to pretend everything is fine when it isn't, but it can nevertheless be hard to let go.

ASSESSING YOUR TEENAGER'S SELF-ESTEEM

If you're the parent of a teenager who has self-esteem problems, it is important that you start your child on the process of building confidence in herself. Because poor self-esteem hides behind many masks, you should be on the lookout for the following attitudes and behavior patterns. Teenagers may use some or all of these for protection when they lack confidence in themselves.

"Who Cares?"

Young people who make it a point to proclaim that they don't care about anything are usually fragile and unsure of themselves. Because they've been disappointed and hurt often, they've gradually cut themselves off from their real feelings and can no longer let themselves be optimistic about anything. Their indifference has become a screen for their poor self-esteem and a shield against further letdowns.

One boy, for example, who was frequently punished by his parents, continued to violate their rules and told them that he didn't care what they did to him. Unfortunately, he probably meant it when he said he didn't care; he had given up any hope of avoiding punishment and was convinced there was no way out of his situation. Clearly, his indifference was actually a reflection of his unhappiness. Likewise, a fourteen-year-old girl with ongoing academic problems began to express her opinion that school doesn't really matter and abandoned her efforts to succeed. Her teachers described her as unmotivated and unreceptive to their overtures; she responded to them by saying that she saw no point in trying since she was going to fail her classes anyway. True to her word, that was exactly what she did. Again, we clearly see that she adopted an apathetic façade to protect herself from situations that might disappoint her if she did try and then did not succeed. Whether this hardened, indifferent attitude stemmed from conscious or unconscious effort, the result was the same.

Prolonged indifference can sometimes go hand in hand with depression. Sometimes depression comes as a result of being hurt and rejected repeatedly, or stems from a terrible experience, like the death of a loved one. These teens' lives are permeated with feelings of profound sadness and loneliness, and they view the future without hope, resigned to their misery. Because they feel so hopeless and because it hurts to acknowledge their feelings of sadness and loneliness, some depressed teens take the position that nothing really matters to them. That way they insulate themselves from further disappointment. Unfortunately, this cover-up soon becomes second nature to them, and as they seal themselves off, their underlying depression escalates.

Finally, abject apathy may be a tip-off to drug use. Serious drug users usually insist that family members (along with any friends who would voice objections) leave them alone, and they fail to maintain meaningful connections with their school and family. The highs that drugs bring also yield devastating lows, and drug users become indifferent as things that once mattered to them fail to bring any pleasure or happiness. Drug addicts pay a great price for their indifference, as their lives are generally very unhappy.

"Don't Mess with Me!"

Angry and defiant teenagers aren't exactly bursting with self-confidence either. These teens typically manage to keep others at a distance by walking around with a bold, aggressive attitude, determined to hide their vulnerability and pain by fighting off anyone who might expose weakness. It's difficult to be around these teens because of their abrasive, rude natures and, for many, their tendency to have trouble controlling their aggressive behavior.

One young woman, for instance, constantly questioned the authority of one of her teachers. Anytime this teacher commented on her behavior, she grew angry and accused him of picking on her. She began to respond defensively to his most matter-of-fact comments to her. Her reactions became so extreme that the teacher began to avoid her and taught his class as though she were no longer a member. She couldn't let on that her feelings were hurt by his rejection of her; instead, she became even more abrasive.

Another teenager provoked fights wherever he went. He assumed that his peers were out to get him and often reacted aggressively to their neutral comments. Because of his poor self-esteem, he usually failed to correctly assess their intentions and jumped to a negative conclusion. One time, one of his baseball teammates made a joking comment about his new haircut. His teammate was just kidding, but he thought he was being attacked, and responded by screaming angrily. Under these circumstances he could be almost certain that no one would ever get to know him—or ever want to.

Rebel Without a Cause

Most teenagers protest convention every now and then. Some teens seem to enjoy shocking their parents and other teens. Others rebel now and then because they don't want to be seen as carbon copies of their parents or generic, one-of-the-crowd teenagers. Still other teens buck conventional norms when they find themselves questioning those norms or when they just think it's cool to behave unconventionally. Usually those essentially healthy actions will be intense but short-lived, or ultimately harmless. However, sometimes the nonconformist's behavior becomes intense; she lashes out at those around her and adopts an angry, rebellious, or contemptuous attitude that does not simply fade away. These teens attack everything that dissatisfies them in their lives, but this sort of nonconformity can also reflect teenagers' dissatisfaction with *themselves*. When they go out of their way to consistently present an objectionable appearance, espouse controversial views, or vehemently reject their family's values, they may be covering up deep hurt.

I've worked with many nonconformist teenagers who are contemptuous of their mainstream peers or families. Sometimes they've been the brunt of taunts and ridicule at school. Other times they are members of families where they feel like a misfit, or a screwup, or unwanted. When exploring these feelings together, we've been able to uncover the anger and pain of rejection that they've felt over the years. Rather than acknowledge their own sadness, which is too much for them to handle alone, they rebel against the conventions they feel shut out of, conveniently posing as proud individualists.

Ten Telltale Signs of Poor Self-Esteem

Observe your teenager carefully to see if any of these thoughts and behaviors regularly occur. If they do, there's a strong chance he or she suffers from inadequate self-esteem.

1. She blames herself whenever something goes wrong. If her academic bowl team loses a match, she is certain it's all her fault.

2. He gives up easily when faced with a challenge. He tries out for a sports team but then quits after one day, insisting that practice is too rigorous.

3. She always assumes the worst possible outcome in a situation. If she takes a test, she's certain that she failed.

4. He often expresses the feeling that he's worthless, dumb, unattractive, or boring. You'll hear him talking about why other people don't like him.

5. She thinks in all-or-nothing terms: everything is either all good or all bad. One of her teachers, she may say, is absolutely the greatest, while another is terrible. There is no happy medium.

6. He avoids new situations. When invited to a party where he knows hardly anyone, he finds an excuse to stay home.

7. She allows others to take advantage of her. She may lend her classmates money, knowing that they won't pay her back.

8. He routinely blows events out of proportion. If his soccer team loses its first game, he assumes that the entire season is down the drain.

9. She never gives herself credit when things go well. If she gets a good test grade, she says it was just luck, and wasn't she stupid to miss the few questions she did?

10. He believes that his current situation will never change. He says he will always be unpopular, or won't ever go on a date, or will never do well in school.

QUESTIONS TO HELP YOU IDENTIFY LOW SELF-ESTEEM

The behavior patterns of young people lacking self-esteem described in the previous section are relatively easy to spot. Discovering other clues might take some detective work.

Begin by trying to answer the questions below. You may be able to reshape some of the questions so that you can pose them directly to your teenager, and if you've established good communication with him, he may surprise you with forthright answers. However, if he volunteers little information, you'll have to rely more on what you observe and hear from other sources.

To discuss these issues with your teen, you should approach the questions in a friendly, relaxed spirit. Find a time when your teenager is in a reasonably good mood and seems available to talk with you. Make sure that distractions are minimal, so you have an attentive audience.

What Would Their Friends Say About Them?

Try asking your teenagers how their friends might describe them. If they answer honestly, you may find what they say surprising, because teens' close friends are usually privy to thoughts and feelings they don't share directly with parents. When I tried this with one boy in the presence of his parents, he said that his best friend would probably say he was afraid to ask girls out. This surprised his parents since he was always talking to girls on the telephone. The close friend, of course, knew that the boy experienced extreme anxiety before making those calls, desperately afraid of being rejected.

If your teen resists telling you what his close friends might say or gives a clichéd response of few words, you have two options. The first is to ask him how he'd feel if you really did ask a few of his friends what they thought about him the next time those friends were over. This may surprise him, but hopefully he will begrudgingly give you an okay. In that case, you should consider trying it the next time you have the occasion. (Of course, you'll ask them in a way that seems interested, not prying. Ask his friends to describe him in his presence, so he won't worry about what they might have said and they won't feel they're going behind his back.) But if he says strongly that you should mind your own business, then back off. Your second option is to pick up on more subtle cues. Try to be a good listener when you're around your teen, either alone with him or around others.

Finally, think of your child's friendships as a reflection of her interests and personality. Teens especially tend to choose like-minded peers to spend their time with. A boy who has trouble with school will seek out friends who scoff at academics. The same is true for teens who drink or violate their parents' rules. Despite what your child says about his friends, they probably all have the same priorities he does. When your teenager's self-perceptions change, so does his choice of friends.

How Do They Interpret Events and Situations in Their Lives?

Teenagers' outlook on life colors their perceptions; their optimism or pessimism is directly related to their assessment of their worth. A discouraged boy who fails his first two science tests and concludes the course is a lost cause is not likely to bother studying for future tests. Teenagers who approach life pessimistically and always expect the worst have poor self-esteem. They lack the confidence to believe that they have control over their own destiny. By contrast, a teenage girl might react to her team's losing an important basketball game by resolving to practice more and play harder the next time. This young woman has a positive outlook on her life. Rather than look upon the defeat as a prophecy, she uses it to motivate herself to try harder—certainly a reflection of more positive self-esteem.

Most of us have a set of internal standards to measure ourselves by. Our definitions of what is acceptable are based on the messages we've received over the years. These yardsticks determine our satisfaction with our performance and our relationships. Ask your teenager what he considers a reasonable expectation for a given situation. What does he think would happen, for example, if he decided to run for a class officer position, like class president? If he says that's a stupid idea because no one would ever want to vote for him anyway, you have a clue to his self-confidence. This young man sees himself as unpopular with his peers and just doesn't believe he has anything to offer. He's unlikely to be disappointed because he won't take a risk. This approach to life provides insulation from failure, but also discourages effort.

The more negative a teenager's interpretation of situations, the worse her self-esteem. To identify this type of thinking, observe how your child reacts in an ordinary situation that is not emotionally charged in the way an exam or sporting event is. For example, your daughter buys a shirt she really likes, and when a friend comes over, she asks her opinion. The friend, unaware of your daughter's need for reassurance, says simply that it's okay. Your daughter is upset afterward, assuming that her friend was just placating her and didn't really like the shirt, so she returns it to the store the next day. She's programmed to turn a relatively benign remark into a criticism.

How Easily Influenced Are They?

There's a strong connection between poor self-esteem and susceptibility to peer influence. Often, the more desperately a young person seeks approval, the worse he feels about himself. It's one thing to go along with the crowd when it's socially acceptable, but quite another to do risky things that can cause harm. The latter suggests unrest accompanied by poor judgment. Take a careful look at your child's need for acceptance, his ability to say no to his peers, and his comfort level when he's alone. If he falls short in each of these crucial areas, it's safe to assume that he lacks confidence in himself.

Again, if you look closely you'll find subtle signs of this willingness to be influenced. You may notice, for instance, that your teenager flip-flops when it comes to plans, depending entirely on what his friends are doing. He'll say, "I'm staying home tonight because I've got a lot of homework," but as soon as someone calls, he's out the door. Or he may act dramatically different when his friends are around—often being sarcastic, dishonest, and disrespectful, which he hopes his friends will see as being cool. Of course, this behavior is for the sole purpose of gaining his friends' approval.

YOUR CONTRIBUTION TO BUILDING SELF-ESTEEM

A teenager's self-esteem is determined by many factors. Parents can't do everything, and many things that affect your teenagers are beyond your control. Nonetheless, you can lay the groundwork for a more positive outlook on life and point them in the right direction.

Use Praise Liberally

Have you and your children forgotten how to compliment one another? Do you interact with your teens more through criticism than anything else? As negative feelings mount, parents and teenagers find it increasingly difficult to talk to one another and forget the pleasant relationship they may have enjoyed years ago. This destructive cycle can easily become self-perpetuating when anger dominates daily life. To break this pattern and begin to improve your teenager's self-worth, the best place to start is with honest praise. Never underestimate the power of the compliment. Almost all young people are pleased to be acknowledged by their parents, and sincere praise is one of the building blocks of self-esteem.

Your assignment is to catch your children being good. If you are the kind of person who instinctively finds fault, work at finding something worthy of praise in your teen's behavior, personality, or achievements. If your son comes home from a football game with his uniform bloody and torn, don't complain about the state of his clothes; instead, share his elation over his team's win. If she gets a B+ on a test she studied hard for, praise her success instead of asking why it wasn't an A. Try to make positive comments on as many aspects of his life as you can. This way he won't feel that you value him for only one particular trait or attribute. When you do this consistently, you create a comfortable atmosphere and invite more productive dialogue. It may feel awkward and forced at first, but keep reminding yourself that this constructive step will lead to a more productive relationship.

If praising your child is new for you, start with something basic, credible, and nonthreatening. If she says something funny at dinner, for instance, use the opportunity to tell her you appreciate her sense of humor. If she's concerned about a friend who's going through a rough time, praise her for being such a supportive friend. While you should focus your criticisms of your child on the specifics of things she does wrong, you should make your praise broad and general. If you don't approve of a skirt she's wearing, comment only on the choice of skirt, but if you like a particular blouse she's wearing, compliment not just the blouse but her taste in clothing in general.

Pay careful attention during the course of a week and you'll find many chances to compliment your child. If you practice this regularly, you'll be on your way to shifting the negative climate in your home. But remember that it's a gradual process. You'll need to be patient and stay focused on the task. Even the most basic skills can take time before you can use them effortlessly. If complimenting people, even those you love, is difficult for you, it will take time and constant attention to become second nature.

But avoid overdoing it. If you've never been the type to lavish praise, it will sound peculiar if you're praising every little thing your teen does. If you can't find something genuine to praise right away, keep looking, and avoid false praise. And remember, you're still allowed to speak out about things you are upset or angry about.

If you keep it up, eventually your teenager will start to think of you as an ally rather than an adversary. Your expression of goodwill gives him subtle encouragement to compliment you about something; the emerging warm feelings are contagious. Best of all, your teenager's self-esteem begins to improve as he reaps the benefits of your praise.

Challenge Their Negative Thinking

If regular praise can strengthen self-esteem, negative thinking can have the opposite effect, so you should encourage your teenagers to share their self-doubts, pessimism, or sad thoughts as a step to overcoming them. This is easier said than done, of course, because teens tend to hide their private thoughts. Your job is to help them feel safe enough to share their feelings. When they do open the door a crack, be careful not to downplay their concerns by being dismissive. If your son mentions his nervousness about an upcoming exam, don't automatically blow it off with a comment like, "What are you so worked up about? It doesn't really matter that much!" If your teenager doesn't think you're taking him seriously, he's likely to retreat to his private thoughts again.

Once you know about your teen's specific concerns, you can challenge negative thoughts that interfere with his self-esteem. I've discussed how you can open channels of communication. Now, assuming you've gotten your teenager to share his pessimistic interpretations of events, proceed to question him. Essentially, what you're trying to do is get him to look at his thoughts more objectively and present positive alternative ways of thinking. This is best accomplished if you work together.

In the following example, an eleventh-grade student named Lucy has told her mother that none of the boys in her class want to ask her out. She feels hopeless, and her mother is trying to challenge this negativity.

Lucy: I hate guys! They're such jerks. Guys never pay any attention to me, except maybe to ask about a homework assignment or something geeky like that. I'm really starting to hate going to school.

Mother: So why do you think that boys aren't paying attention to you?

Lucy: I'm just not one of the popular girls. You know, my friends are nice, but we don't get asked to any big parties or asked out on dates or anything. We sort of keep to ourselves.

Mother: Do you feel that boys totally ignore you?

Lucy: Well, it's not like I don't exist completely. But they always seem too busy to stop and talk.

Mother: You mean you just assume they don't want to talk to you.

Lucy: Well, yeah. I can tell they're not interested.

Mother: Wait a minute here. No one has ever teased you, have they?

Lucy: No, but . . .

Mother: Have you ever noticed any of the boys looking at you?

Lucy: Well, once in a while, but they're probably thinking I wear nerdy clothes or something.

Mother: Hold on. Since when can you read minds?

Lucy: Well, I never get asked out, do I?

Mother: That's true, but couldn't there be another reason why the boys don't talk to you?

Lucy: I can't think of any.

Mother: Well, I can. What if they don't think you're friendly? Isn't it possible they don't say much to you because they figure you're not that interested?

Lucy: I guess so, but I doubt it.

Mother: Well, have you ever bothered to check it out?

Lucy: What does that mean?

Mother: That means you could be friendlier to one of the boys who talks to you a little and see what happens.

Lucy: I could never do that! I'd be terrified.

Mother: Well, you could do it while one of your girlfriends is there. That would make it a little easier, wouldn't it?

Lucy: I guess so, but it would never work.

Mother: Maybe it's worth a try. You know, I can think of another reason they don't talk to you that much. I bet you could too if you tried.

Lucy: I don't know, Mom. Maybe they think I'm too fat and ugly. Or maybe they think I'm stuck-up or my friends are geeks. I guess anything is possible. What reason can you think of?

Mother: Because they like you! You know, they might want to ask you out but they're nervous about trying.

Lucy: No way!

Mother: Remember I told you I knew your father almost a year before he asked me out. When he finally got around to it, he said he was afraid I'd say no.

Lucy: All right, all right. So what am I supposed to do?

Mother: Just try talking to one of the boys who you know a little and would like to get to know better.

Lucy: I know who I want to get to know better. I just don't think I can do it.

Mother: It's not as hard as you think it is. Try talking to him like you would to a friend instead of thinking of him as someone you've got to impress.

Lucy: But Mom, I don't know what to say to him.

Mother: I'll make you a deal. You start a conversation a few times and see what happens. If it doesn't work, I'll get you that blue Abercrombie shirt you've been begging me for. Either way, something good will come out of it.

Lucy: Are you serious?

Mother: Very.

Lucy: I can't believe I'm going to try this. Mom, I'll kill you if he ignores me.

Mother: It's worth a chance. Like you tell me, sometimes you've got to go for it!

In this conversation, Lucy's mother challenged her daughter's negative thinking in a relatively nonthreatening way. She encouraged Lucy to express her thoughts and then helped her come up with alternative explanations for the boys' behavior. Lucy will have to check out the other possibilities on her own, but her mother has planted a seed of doubt. As Lucy learns to scrutinize other situations more objectively, she'll be better able to dismiss the negative thoughts that hold her back, and this will strengthen her self-esteem.

Sometimes teenagers have physical conditions that encourage poor self-esteem—bad skin, crooked teeth, a weight problem, a speech impediment. If your children face challenges like these, be careful not to patronize them or let them use the challenge as an excuse for a lack of confidence. Instead, try to help them appreciate their other strengths.

Over the years I've devised a game that I play with my teenage patients to help boost their self-image. I've collected a large number of high school pictures of famous people. As you might imagine, some of these stars did not look very attractive in their teenage years. So I show my patients these pictures of short, homely, overweight, bespectacled, and awkward adolescents. Some examples include David Letterman, Gloria Estefan, Marilyn Manson, Sean Combs, Dennis Rodman, and Julia Roberts. Then I ask the teenagers to guess who they are today. Many are shocked to learn that today's celebrities once looked very ordinary or unattractive.

The point is that their unbecoming or unremarkable features did not hold them back. They went on to develop their talents, work hard in their chosen fields, and ultimately succeed. And this is precisely what I'm trying to get my patients to do: develop the belief that they too can alter their current situation. It's an interesting and entertaining exercise you can do with your children. By the way, my source for these pictures is *People* magazine. Every year or two they publish an issue that features high school photos of sports, movie, and rock stars. I suggest you have your scissors ready!

> Self-discipline, determination, and a positive vision for the future change destinies.

I've also found it helpful to share stories about famous people who have succeeded against the odds. Magic Johnson, Cher, and athlete Dan O'Brien all had learning disabilities. Walt Disney was fired by a newspaper editor for lack of ideas, and the one and only Michael Jordan was not initially selected for the basketball team when he entered high school. I ask teens to think: what if these people had given up? Again, the message is that self-discipline, determination, and a positive vision of the future have changed many people's destinies. Teens need to be reminded that their future won't necessarily reflect the way they feel now.

When negative thinking dominates a young person's existence, he may become depressed. Sometimes this is obvious, sometimes not. As you observe your child carefully and note any change in his behavior and mood, remember that teenagers are notorious for trying to disguise poor self-esteem. Trying to help can put you in an awkward position: if you buy into their excuses, you inadvertently perpetuate their problem, but if you lean on them to face their feelings, they may grow angry and protest. If your child is depressed, I urge you to get professional help. Depression is a treatable illness, and intervention can make a big difference in his life.

Value Your Teenager's Uniqueness

In adolescence, more than at any other age, individuals feel better when their parents recognize and appreciate what is special about them, especially if they are unappreciated by the rest of the world. Is your teen athletic, academic, artistic? Intense, laid-back, funny, or serious? Intellectual, intuitive, or street smart? All teens have positive traits, but sometimes they don't know what their own strengths really are. That's where you come in. Whether it's a bright smile or a pleasant disposition, a well-refined talent or a dormant interest, find something that distinguishes your teenager and let him know you value him for it. When they genuinely believe you appreciate them, they won't get angry so often. Your children's special traits are an integral part of their identities. Their feeling of uniqueness promotes their self-worth because it's something that can't be taken away from them.

Patrick's father put this principle to good use. He was an avid Monday night football fan, but despite his overtures, his son showed no interest in watching the games with him. So the father took a different tack. He acknowledged that football was his thing; he followed the stats and took pride in knowing a lot about his pastime. But he also realized that his son had different interests and that he probably felt just as strongly about them as the father did about his. In fact, Patrick was a real history buff. He devoured historical novels and texts and was intrigued by anything of historical significance. Patrick had a wealth of knowledge that his father grew to admire.

So at every opportunity, his father asked Patrick about his take on events where history had a bearing. Whether it was a presidential election, a conflict in the Middle East, or a recent archaeological find, his father sought his counsel. During family dinners, he'd frequently say: "Let's ask Patrick what he thinks. After all, he's our resident historian."

This father's approach generated goodwill between Patrick and the rest of the family and it provided an opportunity for ongoing discussions. His family's pride in Patrick's knowledge of history helped him carve out his own niche of expertise and built up his self-esteem.

Promote Competence and Initiative

Teenagers must feel they can exercise some degree of control over their environment in order to feel more secure with themselves and comfortable with the world around them. But not all teenagers move at the same pace. Some need continued limits and supervision because they fail to exercise good judgment and don't know how to be self-reliant. You may need to address this before you can promote their competence and initiative. Other teenagers are well on their way to taking responsibility for themselves and should be recognized for their efforts. You'll need to observe your child carefully to determine where she falls on this continuum. If she's doing poorly in school and you suspect she's cutting class regularly to sneak off and smoke pot with her friends, she's probably taking little initiative to change things. You'll need to keep a close eye on her and begin with very small steps to increase her competence.

This feeling of competence and mastery over challenges is a major contribution to the development of self-esteem. Often the feeling evolves slowly and requires active parental involvement in the early stages. You should not hesitate to help your teenager in every way you can with his journey, whether it's quizzing him on his Spanish vocabulary for a test, driving him back and forth to hockey practice, picking up art supplies that he requested, or anything else you can do to be supportive. But it also helps teens to believe that their accomplishments are the results of their own efforts, not yours. Assure your teen that you'll be there to catch him when he slips up. But remember: you want your teen to feel that he made it on his own. Trusting one's own abilities while accepting limitations is a key part of self-esteem.

It's also important for you to help your children learn to trust their own abilities and develop their independence as part of this process. When your teenager approaches you with problems, you may be tempted to simply solve them. Your daughter wails, "Dad, I have to do a report on the Middle Ages and I don't know where to start!" "Here's what you should do," you say, ready with a solution, not wanting to see your child struggle. Don't do this. It may be a quick fix, but it doesn't help your teenager learn to solve her own problems. It may even make her more dependent on you. Next time your child asks for your advice or help, ask her instead, "What do you think you ought to do?" This shifts the burden back to her by challenging her to come up with ideas of her own.

It would be nice if at least one area of competence could be identified for every teenager. Encourage your youngsters to try new and different activities; they'll usually find something they can hang their hats on. It may not be a sport or a particular talent, but there are many other possibilities, like a school-related club or organization, a job or volunteer assignment, or a hobby. When teens develop expertise on any topic, it accords them a certain status with their family and peers.

Taking the initiative to do something and finding it rewarding confirm one's competence. Think about the times you've created or assembled something, or fixed something broken. Didn't you feel satisfied afterward? Of course! You made it happen. This is the feeling you want to engender in your children. Initiative, competence, and self-esteem will serve them well their whole lives.

Help Set Goals

Feelings of competence and self-esteem aren't achieved overnight by anyone. They come from learning to be realistic, taking small steps, and keeping one's goals in mind. Does your teenager have specific goals, both short-term and long-term, or is he just drifting along without any purpose? Has he worked hard to achieve a goal, or is he used to quitting when things get tough? Your teen's vision of the future will shape his actions today; without future goals, the present becomes devoid of purpose, empty hours to while away. Here's how to teach your teens to set goals:

- Help them to set goals realistically and think through their plans. Because they are often unrealistic, teenagers tend to take on too much, wait till the last minute to do things, and fail to assess situations objectively. Try to slow them down a bit. Ask them to think out loud about their plans. Have they considered all the facts? What is the most likely outcome of their actions? Have they learned anything from past experiences? This is where you come in as the voice of reason. Teens need to learn that goals can't just be pulled from a hat like a rabbit; they must be carefully thought out and then systematically implemented.
- Teach your teenagers to break tasks into smaller parts. They should feel that each step is something they can accomplish without getting stressed out. Taking small steps enables them to chip away at problems gradually and experience modest successes rather than failure. Have them write down the sequence of steps first. Then they can tackle each one as a separate challenge. The broader goal, of course, is reached by completing each of the steps in the series. And they should set their own timetables.
- Encourage them to ask for help when they need it. They should learn that there is no need to feel ashamed by requesting help; in fact, those asked will usually be flattered. Setting goals and working toward them does not have to be a lonely affair. Teens can appeal to friends, family, and teachers for support.
- Have them practice goal setting whenever they are faced with a situation that seems formidable (for example, school projects, sports, and other forms of self-improvement). Remind your teenagers that realistic goal setting and step-by-step building are applicable to a variety of situations.

Model Self-Confidence

You don't need to wear a happy face all the time to be a good role model for your children. Let your kids see you as you really are.

Appropriate sadness, disappointment, and worry are natural parts of life. You need to demonstrate consistency between your words and your actions. If you tell your child that you have serious financial concerns, you shouldn't be spending money frivolously. If you do, he won't take you seriously; or worse, he'll think you're irresponsible. Remember that your nonverbal messages, such as facial expressions and body posture, are as powerful as your words.

When you deal with what life has handed you with equanimity and maturity, your children are likely to do the same. Genuinely self-confident parents feel no need to prove themselves. Their attitude to life is realistic and allows them to tolerate good and bad times. They face challenges with enthusiasm, savor successes, and accept disappointments as well as they can. Not only do they accept themselves, they accept others as well.

Clearly, your child's self-esteem is influenced by yours, and your outlook on life will certainly be transmitted to them. If you're bitter and critical, they'll come to feel they can't please you, or that they're unworthy, or that life as an adult is miserable, so why bother? If you're content with what you have, they'll sense this and develop a similar attitude. If you acknowledge your mistakes and try to do the right thing, they'll eventually follow suit.

Impart Your Cultural Heritage

You have to accept yourself—your appearance, intelligence, personality, and ethnic or religious identity—to respect yourself. Your heritage, in particular, lies at the core of who you are. Your own sense of pride has been developed through your upbringing over the years. It's the product of the messages you've received, your experiences with others, and ultimately your self-acceptance. Somehow you must convey this cumulative wisdom to your children.

Here are just a few of the many ways you can make your children more connected to their roots.

- Attend a family reunion. If one isn't scheduled, consider organizing a get-together. Remember that weddings, funerals, and religious confirmations also serve this purpose.

- Keep a family photo album. Every now and then, sit down with your children and look at the photographs. You'll be surprised by their curiosity.

- Make a family tree, frame it, and mount it in a conspicuous place. (There are lots of on-line services that can help you when your own family records and recollections fail.) Sooner or later your children will look at it and probably have questions for you.

- Tell your children about your family history whether or not they ask. You can mention that their grandparents did the same with you and you weren't thrilled. Even though your teens may seem inattentive, they'll remember most of what you tell them. And they'll probably return at some point to request further information.

- If possible, visit the family grave site every few years. Teenagers often balk at this seemingly morbid activity, but remind them that death is a natural part of the cycle of life and should be acknowledged. Make this journey a celebration of your family heritage by sharing stories and feelings about family members who have passed away.

- Display a few personal items that have been handed down through the generations. These promote a sense of family pride and offer an opportunity for discussion when others inquire about them.

- The next time someone in your family celebrates a milestone birthday or anniversary, hire your child to put together a collage from the family photographs. If you have old movies, all the better.

Although teenagers often make faces when parents talk about their family backgrounds, they're likely to recall these discussions for years to come. The messages you convey about your heritage can be powerful, so approach the subject with pride. Make sure your child appreciates that she needs to know where she's been to know where she's going.

One Family's Tradition

The mother of one of my clients made it a point to tell her son about her Italian heritage. Her grandparents had immigrated to the United States in the early part of this century. When they arrived in New York, they had few possessions and no family to turn to. Despite this, her grandfather was able to get a job as a shoemaker and worked long hours to support his family. Although he was exhausted on the weekends, he reserved Sundays as a sacred time with his family. That was when they explored all that New York had to offer. The mother remembered well her parents sharing their fond memories of family trips to Coney Island.

Although their early years in this country were a struggle, the family stuck together and managed to make the most of what they had. After years of hard work, the grandfather was able to open his own shop and eventually prospered. To this day, a portrait of him standing proudly in front of his store hangs in the family room. The mother saw her family legacy as aspiring to something, working hard at it, and never forgetting loved ones. Although her son often winced when she told this story, he too became proud of who he was and where he came from.

Help Young People Comfort Themselves

Just as our cultural heritage contributes to our identity, emotional security supports us. As your children grow older, you won't always be there to help them in times of distress. I find it quite useful to explain to children that when someone cares for you deeply, they're with you in spirit during difficult times. You can initiate this conversation on an occasion when your child feels sad or disappointed about something.

First, express your empathy with their feelings; then share a similar experience of your own. Explain how you drew strength from thinking about someone who comforted you in the past—a special teacher, a coach, a family member, a minister, or a best friend. Then ask your child to think about a person in her life who was solidly in her corner when she needed support. (Don't expect to be that person. Although you are solidly in her corner, she needs someone a step removed from her everyday life.) Whether or not that person is still there for her, with practice she can learn to recall these memories when she feels fearful, sad, or alone.

Encourage your teens to imagine that the special person is present, saying the things that used to make them feel safe and secure. Have them close their eyes and describe the person as they remember him—appearance, voice, touch, and mannerisms are important. Finally, tell them to hold on to those images; they will be their allies throughout life.

I discussed this idea with a young man several years ago. His grandmother had died when he was twelve years old, but he vividly remembered her always being on his side. "Even when I used to get in trouble, she would hug me and tell me everything would be all right," he said. "I remember when I came home from school with a note from my teacher. I'd been in a fight and she wanted my mother to come in for a meeting. Well, Grandma was over at the house and she saw the note before my mother. She told me she wanted to hear my side of the story first. After I told her I was at least partly at fault, she just looked at me and said, 'Don't worry, I'll love you no matter what you do.' God, I miss her."

Many children are lucky enough to have memories like this. We would all like our children to feel they can count on us even when we can't physically be with them. Talk with your teens about your own fond memories and encourage them to express theirs. Remind them that they have a resource to comfort themselves at stressful times. As they learn to harness these powerful images, their self-esteem will be enhanced.

ACKNOWLEDGING ACHILLES

There's more to a balanced view of oneself, and that is being able to accept one's vulnerability.

Achilles, the warrior from Greek mythology, had been

dipped by his mother into the river Styx at birth to protect him from harm. However, the water hadn't touched the heel by which she'd held him. Not knowing this, and assuming he was invincible, Achilles was killed during the Trojan War when an arrow struck this one vulnerable spot.

We all have such places of vulnerability. The fear of rejection, for example, looms large for most of us. Like their parents, teenagers avoid facing their weakness for several reasons: They fear being ridiculed, They're not sure how another person will react to their disclosure, They feel it's easier to avoid thinking about something that's bothering them than to face their discomfort. But vulnerability isn't something to run from. Coming to grips with it is an important part of emotional health and self-esteem.

Building self-esteem is a delicate balancing act in which we have to take pleasure in our strengths while acknowledging our weaknesses. Help your teenagers recognize and accept their limitations. Adolescence is a time of life when children can feel invulnerable. Not only do teens deny their mortality, but many of them seem unaware of the risks they take. You can see this sense of invulnerability in many aspects of their lives: many drive too fast, drink too much, have unprotected sex, and experiment with dangerous drugs. Yet despite the facts, they're convinced they're in no danger, and until tragedy strikes, they give little thought to changing their ways. This is precisely why you must alert your child to her own vulnerability. Not only will it enhance her self-esteem, but it may also be a matter of life and death.

You send a message to your children about your own vulnerability every time you deal with adversity. If you talk about it openly and show you're willing to face it, your children learn that they can too. Many young people have told me how shocked they were to see their parents break down and cry at their grandparents' funerals. When I ask them how this made them feel, they usually say they were relieved and sympathetic. They always seem pleased to have learned that their parents were vulnerable.

But you don't need a sad occasion or a crisis to share your

feelings. There are plenty of chances in everyday life. Tell your teenager about painful memories of your own adolescence, your embarrassing moments and your disappointments. These disclosures are appropriate ways to encourage him to feel less threatened by his own feelings of humiliation or defeat. But bear in mind that there are certain boundaries that shouldn't be violated. Details about your marriage, your sexual activities, and the private matters of other adults are simply not your teenager's business.

And when you share a personal experience with your children, be sure to tell them how you got through it. Don't hesitate to express your fears and self-doubts, stressing that they were perfectly natural under the circumstances. And let them know where you found the support and inner strength to stick with it. Then look back at the experience and talk about what you'd do differently if it occurred again. During your discussion, encourage your child to ask questions and react to the story you've told. Even if your teen just listens, she'll gain something from your experience. If she doesn't listen when you're talking, try to find another way to get your point across.

As you encourage your children to grow in self-esteem by acknowledging vulnerability, be aware of the role gender may play in the way you address your teen. When children are young, we're conscious of their vulnerability. We comfort both boys and girls when they cry and sympathize with their fears. By the time they begin elementary school, however, we start to treat them differently. We continue to give girls some leeway but hold boys to a different standard. We hug our daughters when they fall and tell our sons not to be crybabies. "Why are you making such a big deal over losing your stuffed animal?" parents ask their little boy. "We'll buy you another one." The cultural imperative of discouraging boys from showing their weakness but forgiving it in girls is at work here. When these messages persist throughout childhood, boys learn to mask their real feelings.

The tides have shifted some over the last few decades, but longtime cultural norms are hard to shake. Our culture doesn't encourage the open expression of feelings, especially for men. Feeling threatened by sadness, fear, and uncertainty, many men bite their lips and pretend they can't be hurt. When you teach boys to hide their feelings and encourage girls to show theirs, you inadvertently perpetuate gender differences. No wonder men get such a bad rap for being insensitive. They've been in training since their early years.

It's more culturally acceptable for girls to express their feelings, but girls are also sometimes the victims of outdated cultural perceptions. Many people think it's fine for girls to express their sadness, frustration, or disappointment because they are "the weaker sex." According to stereotypes, girls (and women) are victims of their own moods and emotions, and are less in control and capable than men. This is a more subtle form of stereotyping than the masculine edict that "boys don't cry," but girls suffer when they are told they can vent their feelings but are not taken seriously when they do.

Give your children the clear message that it's okay to vent their feelings, and help them learn healthy ways to do so. This is not just true with small children; it's true for teenagers, adults, everyone.

HELPING YOUR TEENAGERS FACE THEIR VULNERABILITY

You can safely assume that all teenagers have fears, insecurities, and worries, and you'd be foolish to think you can make them go away. But you can lessen their impact by listening nonjudgmentally and making your children feel understood. Ideally, you should serve as a sounding board for their anxieties, a safe haven where they can speak their minds. They'll be inclined to isolate themselves at first, but they can be brought out with some of the communication techniques I suggested in Chapter 3, like telling stories about yourself, making inferences about their moods, asking for their opinions, and listening actively. When you've used those for several weeks, you can proceed to intro-

Getting Boys to Open Up

It's no secret that boys have more difficulty expressing their feelings than girls. But you can help get past the macho roles that make it even harder for boys to show their emotional side. Here are some suggestions:

■ Send your sons a clear message: "You don't have to be the rock of Gibraltar. It's not necessary to be macho and stoic all the time. In fact, no one expects you to be devoid of emotions. Grown men do cry, and there's nothing to be ashamed of."

■ Look behind angry and macho behavior. Your son may be hurting and asking for help indirectly.

■ Routinely remind boys that their feelings are important. If they seem upset or withdrawn, express your concern and curiosity. If they don't respond, try to talk about what you think they're feeling. For example, if you think your son is upset about his acne condition, you might say, "I remember when I was fifteen and had pimples all over my face. I was afraid they'd never go away. I was miserable." This provides your teenager with the opportunity to say, "Yeah, me too." And perhaps he'll even tell you more about what he's going through.

■ Expose your children to people who don't fit the conventional gender roles. Some examples include female legislators, male nurses, female police officers, and male flight attendants. Fathers and mothers can also shake the stereotypes at home. Dad can prepare dinner and do the dishes; Mom can rake leaves and mow the lawn. And your children can do both!

duce more sensitive issues. But remember, you'll need to continue practicing these communication strategies because old habits change slowly.

The following conversation illustrates how a parent might encourage a teenager to express his vulnerability.

Mother: Tom, I've noticed you've been pretty sad the last few days. Is everything all right?

Tom: Yeah, I guess so.

Mother: Well, you don't seem like yourself. Is it because Pammy hasn't called in over a week? That's pretty rare, considering how much you usually talk on the phone with her.

Tom: Things have just changed a little, that's all.

Mother: Does that mean you're not going out with her anymore?

Tom: Well, not exactly. She just said she needed some space.

Mother: I know how much you care about her. Were you upset when she told you that?

Tom: I'd rather not talk about it.

Mother: I remember when my high school boyfriend told me it was over. I was devastated for months. I thought I'd never find anyone else like him.

Tom: I don't understand. It doesn't make any sense. And my friends are all telling me she's not worth it. You know, saying I should just get on with my life.

Mother: I can imagine how sad you must be. It's really lonely when a relationship ends. Besides, you and Pammy were together for almost a year.

Tom: I guess I feel like it was my fault. She said I spend more time with my friends than I do with her. Maybe if I hadn't gone out with the guys last Friday night . . .

Mother: Have you tried talking to her about it?

Tom: Yeah, but she's got her mind made up.

Mother: I'm really sorry. I know how much it must hurt. I liked her too.

Tom: It totally sucks.

Mother: Well, let me know if I can do anything to help.

Like Thomas's mother, you want to convey the message that there's no reason to be ashamed of vulnerability. We all feel better after we've been able to express our feelings, and shouldn't need to pretend otherwise. You can help by sharing your own experiences and listening attentively to your child's. Your subtle permission to be honest about feeling sad strengthens your children's self-regard by narrowing the discrepancy between their private and public selves. We're all eager to acknowledge our strong points and hesitant to admit our limitations, but we also have strengths and weakness that coexist and influence each other. If you're determined to hide your vulnerability, you'll waste a lot of valuable energy trying to convince others that everything is fine.

It's been said that the good parent speaks to the teenager's heart, not his head. That's what I'm getting at when I say you need to help your child share his vulnerability. Help him find the words to express what he really feels, not what he thinks you or others want to hear. If he thinks you're interested only in his successes, he'll be reluctant to share his frustrations and disappointments. I strongly encourage you to reward your child's efforts as enthusiastically as you do his accomplishments. Even if he has mediocre grades, if he believes you're proud of him because he does his best, he'll have the heart to keep trying. If he's convinced that only winning, getting straight A's, or being the life of the party will please you, he'll be resentful when he can't do everything, and probably give up.

When teenagers can share their frailties with a friend or parent, they usually wind up feeling closer to that person. Once they feel accepted rather than criticized, they can be a little more forgiving of themselves. This will help free them from the power of their negative thoughts and strengthen their self-esteem.

PORTRAIT OF A RESILIENT YOUTH

A young patient of mine named Ricky showed great self-esteem and had the kind of emotional resilience I hope you'll be able to foster in your children. His childhood was less than idyllic; his parents' marriage was an unhappy one, and there were few family outings, vacations, or even meals all together, since his mother and father avoided spending time with each other. As much as this hurt Ricky, he was able to roll with the disappointments and take pleasure in his accomplishments. A cheerful kid

Paving the Way to Emotional Resilience

1. Make certain your child knows that you love him.

2. Try to be available when he needs you.

3. Supervise his activities and stay involved with his life.

4. Provide reasonable limits based on the degree of trust he has earned.

5. Keep the communication channels open. Talk to your child regularly and encourage him to talk to you.

6. Spend quality family time together.

7. Invest the time to build your teenager's self-esteem.

8. Promote meaningful connections with other adults who can serve as mentors and role models for your teenager.

9. Make certain that you display the behaviors you encourage in your child.

10. Hold him accountable for any wrongdoing or hurtful behavior toward others. And be certain you are consistent and follow through on any consequences you impose.

who got along well with others, Ricky played on several sports teams and was enthusiastic about his participation. Despite a reasonable effort at school, his grades were unexceptional, but his parents were able to accept this and reminded him that they just wanted him to do his best.

When he was twelve, Ricky's parents divorced. He'd been aware of their conflict but hoped they would stay together. When he learned of their decision, he was upset and told them so. To his parents' credit, they managed to keep him out of the middle. They reminded him that the separation wasn't his fault and reassured him that they would always be there for him. It helped that both parents cared deeply for him and were able to work out a viable joint custody arrangement. During the year following the divorce, Ricky immersed himself in his studies. He joked about having two homes, a double allowance, and twice as much fun with his parents separately. Clearly, he was distressed under the surface, but he was encouraged by his parents to tell them openly about his feelings, as they did about theirs. He was able to vent his general frustrations in a healthy way—through his sense of humor—and could air his feelings of sadness or anger in discussions with his mother or father.

Ricky understood that his parents split up because of their fundamental incompatibility. Although their separation meant a major life change for him, he was fortunate in that his basketball coach and his guidance counselor both took an interest in him and encouraged him to continue his efforts and take on more challenges. Ricky kept himself busy during that difficult year of transition. Gradually he came to believe he was competent enough to accomplish some of the goals that he set for himself. As time passed, he became more independent and self-directed. His parents took pride in his efforts and often told him so. By his senior year Ricky was doing well in school and working toward going to the college of his choice. His emotional resilience had served him well.

Ricky's story illustrates several of the traits we observe in resilient teenagers. His parents' unwavering caring and reassurance prevented any damage to his self-esteem, one essential ingredient of resilience. Ricky also established meaningful connections with others, which provided additional support for him. As a result, Ricky felt that he was competent and able to achieve some of his goals on his own. Finally, his sense of humor served him well, enabling him to see the positive aspects of a difficult situation.

STRATEGIC PARENTING:
PROMOTING INDEPENDENCE, GOOD JUDGMENT, AND IMPULSE CONTROL

*"I can't trust you to remember
one simple thing, can I?"*

*"Why don't you ever show good judgment?
Get your head out of the clouds!"*

Y ou probably know how determined your
teenager is to fend for himself. You also know that
he still needs your guidelines and limits. No matter
how responsible a sixteen-year-old may be about doing his

chores and telling you where he's going, he should not be allowed to stay out as late as he wants every night or blow off his homework as much as he sees fit. Balancing a young person's desire for freedom with his need for age-appropriate limits is a classic parenting dilemma. When you look at teenagers' behavior to gauge how independent they are, you'll find that the ones who are most adamant about not needing their parents are often the ones who need them the most.

It's perfectly natural for your teenager to distance herself from you. She doesn't bound into your room anymore to share the day's stories or tell you how much you mean to her. This distancing is part of a gradual move toward independence that is one of the crucial tasks of adolescence. A young adult must learn to stand on his or her own two feet. Doing so requires self-esteem and the willingness to ask for help—characteristics described in the previous chapter—along with good judgment and the ability to delay gratification, subjects to be explored here.

Because teenagers beginning to think for themselves and function independently are caught with their parents in a push-pull routine, their behavior toward you can be hard for you to accept, even painful at times. To your distress, they become increasingly critical of you as they try to differentiate themselves from their family. "Mom, why do you always wear that horrible color?" "Do you have to talk like that in front of my friends?" Although your kids, since the age of ten, have probably been rolling their eyes whenever you offered an opinion or set a rule of the house, now skepticism and resistance seem to be the rule rather than the exception. At this stage, nothing you do seems to please them, and they genuinely believe they know everything.

To get through these challenges you should provide a safe base for children to return to as they venture further and further from home. Teens will take pride in their new-found freedom but maintain the prerogative to revert to their old ways every now and then. Think of your teenagers as kites: you want them to fly but you don't want them to get tangled in power lines or float off and disappear. So you give them as much line as they need to catch the wind and soar, sensitively guiding them and alternately reeling them in and letting them float as seems appropriate. Knowing how and when to pull back on the string is the essence of what I call strategic parenting.

HEALTHY INDEPENDENCE

In the delicate balancing act of parenting a teenager, you first need to understand the difference between healthy and unhealthy independence in order to determine what limits to set and how much monitoring to do. Bear in mind that maturing is a process. Each teenager must be allowed to progress at his or her own rate; the self-direction achieved by one child at thirteen may not appear in another until seventeen. Many experts even suggest that adolescence now extends through the college years because many young adults don't enter the working world until they're at least twenty-one. They continue to face new challenges until that time comes, but are expected to become increasingly responsible and independent.

Here are some of the most common ways in which healthy adolescent independence is expressed.

Self-Reliance

Self-reliant teenagers approach both work and play with an independent spirit. They believe they can do most things on their own, rarely needing you to oversee them, but asking your help with occasional formidable challenges. They enjoy people's company but are equally comfortable by themselves. This is the spirit you want to promote in your child.

Independence comes more naturally to some teenagers than to others. From early on, self-reliant children are more inquisitive, exploratory, and self-directed than their peers. They're able to play alone for extended periods of time, and they're also receptive to learning new skills. The majority of teenagers are able to achieve such independence at some point as they master each of the essential life skills. At the end of this process, they feel self-confident, goal-directed, and prepared to face challenges.

Independence from Family Values

Sometimes the teenager expresses his emerging independence by choosing a path quite different from the one you had in mind for him. This can be a hard pill to swallow. Consider the young man from a family of professionals who decides to become an auto mechanic. His parents have exposed him to other career choices and he's not interested, so there's little they can do to change his mind. Forcing him to comply with their expectations would only make him resentful and possibly rebellious.

It can be distressing to watch your children make decisions different from those you would like. But if the choices won't hurt them and will give them satisfaction, you need to accept their decisions. After all, they have a right to be happy, and it's not your place to tell them how to go about it.

This is not to suggest that you abdicate your authority, however. You want to do everything you can to steer your children toward the values you believe in, whether they be a work ethic, lifestyle choice, or religious identity. But if, after all this, they're still determined to march to the beat of a different drum, so be it. Encourage them to do the best they can on their chosen path.

Self-Protective Independence

Sometimes independence of thought and action can insulate teenagers from stressful or dangerous situations. When alcoholism or marital problems cause conflict at home, for example, some youth manage to distance themselves from their parents and get involved in their own activities. They may find jobs, spend much of their time at friends' houses, or get passionately involved in sports.

If your teenager is avoiding you more than usual, ask yourself why. Maybe she fantasizes about a more pleasant home life or loses herself in some interest while shut away in her room. Such behavior isn't always related to a teen's home life or her relationship with a parent. It could also be indicative of more serious problems, such as depression (see Chapter 4) or substance abuse (Chapter 8). Spending mental or physical time and energy away from a stressful home is a healthy adaptation to a difficult situation, but it's also a sign that parents need to face the problem the child is escaping.

UNHEALTHY INDEPENDENCE

Some young people assert their independence through misguided actions like defying authority, behaving aggressively, and adopting a negative, cynical attitude. Such teens are usually unsure of themselves, though they'd like to view their actions as expressions of their independence. More often than not, they are afraid, confused, or lonely, while pretending to be the opposite. This type of motivation is obvious in teenagers who attach themselves to negative peer groups like gangs. They present themselves as free agents but are just as dependent on their peers as they once were on their parents.

A Reasonably Independent Teenager

Ben, a former neighbor of mine, was a high school junior with several good friends and a fairly good school record. He spent much of his free time in his room listening to music, talking on the telephone, and reading magazines. His parents worried about him being too isolated, but Ben seemed content with his life. Occasionally, if he was tired, he chose to stay home when his friends went out on a weekend. To his credit, he didn't feel he had to go along with the crowd.

Ben's teachers described him as a cheerful student who participated actively in class. He occasionally disagreed with his classmates' ideas without worrying about the group's disapproval. He finished most of his assignments without complaining, but sometimes admitted he needed his parents' help with difficult projects. Ben had begun to think about colleges and had sent off inquiries on his own. He had some thoughts about his future and was considering a career in computers.

At home, too, Ben was reasonably self-sufficient. He'd learned to cook for himself and could do his laundry when necessary. His parents felt he was responsible enough to handle considerable leeway with his weekend curfews. Although he rarely abused this privilege, he once came home drunk. The following morning he apologized to his parents and agreed to forfeit his driving privileges for two weeks. It didn't happen again.

Ben is a good example of a teenager who is independent and responsible enough to deserve the trust of his family and teachers.

Some teens, in another expression of unhealthy behavior, run away from home because they feel angry and rejected. They feign indifference and demand emancipation. If only their parents would let them live away from home, they complain, everything would be fine. Underneath this exterior, however, lurks poor self-esteem and the need to have someone to depend on. Rarely do teenagers like this achieve healthy independence without resolving these issues.

Yet other teenagers flagrantly violate conventional standards and show contempt for mainstream conformity. There are certainly rugged individualists among the kids who reject conformity and superficiality, but here I'm referring to those outcasts—alienated teens—who are profoundly unhappy about not fitting in with their peer group and maybe their family as well. Rather than coming to terms with these norms or trying to address their inadequacies, they choose a more dramatic course of action, such as outrageous dress, body piercing, or affiliation with marginal groups. Driven by anger over earlier rejection and a fierce desire to justify their differences, these youngsters are rarely comfortable with themselves despite their protests to the contrary. Their rage can make them dangerous to both themselves and others.

Sometimes expressions of unhealthy independence are a more extreme outcome of a teen's misguided but understandable attempt to cope with a difficult family situation. Fifteen-year-old Tammy, for example, refused any direction from her parents and was quick to remind them that they couldn't tell her what to do—not even call her for dinner. Tammy sneered at both affection and punishment from her parents. She tried to show that she didn't need anyone, wandering off by herself and managing to get by without any money in her pocket.

Tammy's parents told me that she'd been fiercely independent since her childhood and, they assumed, just didn't need other people. That couldn't have been more wrong. In reality, their daughter was isolated, lonely, and sad, having abandoned her efforts to connect with her relatives and peers. Her superficial independence was a smoke screen for what was missing in her life.

As I learned with further probing, Tammy's parents themselves were aloof and undemonstrative, so their daughter had learned to entertain herself at an early age in response to her parent's lack of involvement. That need to rely on herself had grown over time into a rejection of any suggestion of relying on anyone else. If you have a child who is behaving toward you like Tammy, don't dismiss it by simply saying she's difficult. Rather, pay attention to the real message she's sending; most often it's a call for help. And you should heed it by looking at your own behavior as well as your child's.

PROMOTING HEALTHY INDEPENDENCE

What you want for your child is genuine self-determination—independence that stems from positive self-esteem and a history of success. You want him to take responsibility for his behavior so you don't have to do it for him. This kind of independence of thought and action will help keep teenagers out of trouble.

How Independent Is Your Teenager?

Ask yourself these questions to gauge your child's independence and judgment:

1. Does he always check with friends before making a decision? If so, he probably does not trust his own judgment and is too dependent on others. You'll learn what to do about this later in the chapter.

2. Do you feel like you always have to watch over her? If you do, she's probably not trustworthy and has exhibited poor judgment in the past. On the other hand, if she's a responsible child and you're still worrying yourself sick, the problem may be yours. You'll want to find other pursuits to devote your energies to. (If you still can't let go, consider seeking professional assistance.)

3. Does he usually think about things before he acts? If he doesn't, you have an impulsive child on your hands. He probably fails to consider the consequences of his actions and exercises poor judgment in many situations. You'll learn what to do about this in the section on developing impulse control.

4. Would she walk away from a risky situation? If the answer to this question is no, your child lacks good judgment. Further, if

Preparing for Your Teenager's Independence

Some parents let go of their teenagers naturally, while others find it's a struggle. Here are some suggestions to help you with the separation process:

■ Try to recall when you were a teenager. Think about the pride you felt when you began to do things on your own—and the resentment you felt when your parents held you back.

■ Remind yourself that your teenager's emerging independence is an essential step toward becoming an adult, and be proud that you're making a contribution.

■ If you find yourself cringing every time your son announces he's going out for the evening, take heart: you're not alone. These are perfectly natural feelings, which will pass. You'll need to bite your lip at first, but you'll get used to it and even begin to enjoy your increased free time.

■ Remember that your teenagers' independence is not a rejection of you; it's an affirmation of them-

selves. So try to take pride in their accomplishments.

■ Prepare yourself for your child's independence in advance. If you've allowed your life to revolve around her, it's time to shift gears.

■ Resurrect old interests and develop new ones. Find projects around the house, travel to a place you've always wanted to see, or join an athletic club. Edna St. Vincent Millay captures this spirit of reinventing yourself: "If to be left, or left alone, then lock the door and find oneself again."

■ Devote your time and energy to building significant relationships. Get to know your spouse again, look up an old friend, or have the neighbors over for dinner.

■ Remember that your teen's emerging independence is the beginning of a new era. Although you may feel like you're losing him, you're actually redefining your relationship. You'll probably find that he talks to you more when he sees you less!

she frequently succumbs to negative peer pressure, she is too dependent on others for approval. I'll help you to deal with negative peer pressure in Chapter 7.

5. Is he willing to talk to you about his actions? Usually, teenagers who refuse to talk with their parents are avoiding taking responsibility for their actions. Their judgment is often hampered and their proclaimed independence may be a disguise for their unrest. You'll need to look carefully at your child's behavior to determine why he's unwilling to discuss his actions with you. If it's a communication problem, you'll want to refer back to Chapter 3. If you suspect substance abuse or other illicit activities, refer to Chapters 8 and 10.

No parent can single-handedly ensure that a child becomes independent. So many factors, both in and out of the home (family conflicts, sibling rivalry, peer pressure, media violence), affect a young person's development that you can only try to influence circumstances within your reach. Although you can't control the time your teenagers spend with peers away from home or what they read or hear about on the news, there is still much you can do to foster their healthy independence.

Assess Your Attitude

Ask yourself how you feel about your teenager's emerging independence, about letting her go. Do you genuinely believe that you can get along without her and she can get along without you? Or does part of you wish she'd stay around a few more years? Can you allow her to find her own way, knowing that she may stumble? If these things are difficult for you, you may have to do some soul-searching or look for support from people who've dealt with similar experiences.

Years ago I worked with a mother who had a lot of trouble pulling away from her teenage son. She'd been divorced for years and had counted on him to help her run their home. The boy did chores, baby-sat for his younger sister, and served as his mother's sounding board. As he approached his sixteenth birthday, though, he began to spend more and more time at parties, Friday night football games, and outings with a girl he liked. Now when his mother asked for his help with something, he often told her how busy he was and asked if he could do it another time.

The mother found herself feeling lonely and dejected. While

she knew her son needed to make his own way, she began to discourage his steps toward independence, trying to make him feel guilty about all the responsibility on her solitary shoulders. Fortunately, she had the presence of mind to eventually realize what she was doing and sought my help. We determined that she needed to cultivate a life of her own and invest herself less in her son's. With support, she was able to redirect her energies and allow her son the space he needed to separate and assert his autonomy.

Many parents grapple with mixed feelings about their children's emerging independence. If you can face this ambivalence honestly and acknowledge the healthy need to let go, your children should do fine. But if you try to hold on to them for dear life, using them to fill your own unmet emotional or social needs, you may introduce new problems that take on a life of their own.

Teach Responsibility Routinely and Gradually

For most teenagers, independence is learned, not born. You give your sons and daughters the tools to work with, but they have to use them. If they need your help, you'll give it, but the competent parent lets a child know which expectations he is responsible for meeting on his own. By fulfilling their responsibilities, teens prepare for an adult role in society.

There are plenty of opportunities in daily family life for teaching responsibility. Let's look at two of them: sleeping schedules and chores.

Waking up on time and going to bed at a reasonable hour should be, in most cases, your teenagers' responsibility, not yours. You should initially monitor this behavior, but turn it over to them as soon as they're ready. Many teenagers complain that they can't get up on their own and need us to help them—interesting, considering how often they tell us to leave them alone! Yet they'll stay up all night if they get the chance. I doubt any teenager has asked for help getting to bed on time. They simply don't think of sleep as a priority.

You can fall into a trap if you agree to get your teenager up in the morning. He'll assume that it's your job and won't learn a useful lesson. If you want him to behave responsibly, insist that he take charge of himself. You can't force him to fall asleep on demand, but you can get him to agree to be in bed by a certain time. If he's exhausted every morning, his routine needs adjusting, and you may need to intervene.

Having said this, I must add that most teenagers struggle with getting up on time in the morning. Recent evidence suggests that adolescents have later sleeping and waking patterns than people of other ages, making early school days a problem and late-night activities attractive. Some high schools have even changed their schedules to accommodate these patterns. Nonetheless, getting out of bed and getting ready for school are opportunities for your teens to demonstrate responsibility. If you act as their personal wake-up service, you're just prolonging their dependence on you.

Chores provide similar opportunities for teaching responsibility. Although it's natural to expect that teens will be resistant to doing chores, at least from time to time, domestic responsibilities do serve an important purpose. Not only do they contribute to maintaining the family unit; they also foster accountability and team play. When you ask your child to do the dishes, walk the dog, clean his room, or take out the trash, you're hardly imposing. Such duties prepare teens for self-sufficiency and will serve them well when they have to perform these tasks for themselves in adult life.

There's nothing like firsthand experience to drive home this point. Let your daughter oversleep a few times and miss an activity that's important to her. Let her laundry pile up until she has nothing to wear. Leave unwashed dishes in the sink until there are no more clean glasses, or "forget" to cook dinner or stock the refrigerator. Believe me, she'll get the point soon enough that the household doesn't run by itself. If your teenager fails to get the message, you may be tempted to give in, but I strongly suggest that you hold the line. It may be hard to tolerate the mess or the empty refrigerator while your child tunes it out, but I assure you that your strike won't go unnoticed.

When teaching your children responsibility, first make sure they appreciate the benefits of learning to care for themselves. Next, create situations that let them exercise these skills, and tell them you're available to teach them whenever they're ready to learn. Finally, try to make some of these activities more appealing. When you send your son to the grocery store to do the week's shopping, encourage him to pick out some of the foods he wants for dinner. Prepare a meal together every now and then, reminding him that cooking skills will serve him well when you've left him alone for a day or two (something most older teenagers would relish) or when he goes to college and wants to avoid the dining hall. Of course, you'll want to make the connection between his demonstrated self-sufficiency and your increased trust of him.

Teach Self-Management

Young people develop a certain mind-set as they learn to care for themselves. With each success, they find it easier to face new challenges with enthusiasm rather than trepidation. You can help with this development by assisting your children in defining the issues they want to address and supporting them when they try. You'll find plenty of opportunities to discuss your children's priorities with them. They'll often comment on teams they'd like to make, cars they'd love to own, and colleges they want to attend. You'll often have to be the voice of reason. If your sixteen-year-old wants to go to a good college, for example, he may have to choose between going out on weekends and devoting additional time to his studies.

The money issue frequently comes up with teenagers. They want parents to pay for everything; parents tell them money doesn't grow on trees. Most teenagers have lists of things they want and want immediately, usually heavily influenced by peer pressure and advertising. Some beg, others demand; only a few give up. Try to redirect pleas for money into learning situations. If your teenager desperately "needs" a new Discman, for instance, and asks you to buy it for her, tell her you understand that it's important to her but you won't give it to her now. If she can't wait until Christmas or her birthday, ask her if she has any ideas about how to get the money to buy it. Her first response may be to borrow it from you! Keep asking her for other suggestions. Take advantage of this opportunity to teach the value of saving. Rather than summarily dismissing her request, suggest jobs around the house or other ways to raise cash. While she may balk at your proposals, she'll ultimately learn to defer gratification.

Giving teenagers an allowance can be especially helpful in teaching them to manage money, as every week they're faced with the decision of whether to spend or save. This decision-making process helps them prioritize and gives them time to think about how badly they want certain items. Some teenagers will save for something over several months, while others will give up on

Ten Questions to Guide Your Teenagers Toward Good Decisions

1. What have you done in the past when faced with a similar situation?

2. What did you learn from your experience?

3. Is there anyone you can talk to who has been through a similar situation?

4. Can you imagine how you'll feel after you make your decision?

5. What's the most likely outcome of your decision?

6. What would you advise your best friend if that person was faced with a similar dilemma?

7. Can you delay the decision a little longer in order to give the matter further thought?

8. Is your decision based on what everyone else is doing?

9. If you had ten seconds to make your decision, what would it be?

10. Have you weighed all the pros and cons of each possibility?

Each of these questions helps your teenager to think further before taking action. Your goal is to help them to be more independent and exercise good judgment, so try to be a consultant, not a traffic cop.

their original idea when they see the length of time involved. Eventually, a valuable lesson is learned: satisfaction comes from patience, persistence, and a certain amount of sacrifice.

Guide, Don't Control

We're all tempted to micromanage our teenagers' lives for their own good—telling them when to study, which activities to participate in, and how to dress for occasions. However, anytime you help a child with something he could complete on his own, you slow his progress toward autonomy.

It's a real challenge to know how much to intervene in issues like homework, room decorations, or moral dilemmas. Young people often invite you to assume their burdens, wondering why they should struggle with something you can do so easily. The answer is that if they learn to do things for themselves, they won't be dependent on others. For some teenagers, this is a very scary proposition.

Rather than telling your children what to do, ask questions to direct them toward reasonable courses of action. If your son, for example, has the option next semester of taking either an advanced math course or an easy basic skills class, ask him to evaluate the pros and cons rather than telling him which you think he should take. Naturally, you're inclined to push him into the college prep class. But if you impose your will, he won't have a chance to think the issue through. So instead, keep quiet, even if you have to suffer through listening to the supposed advantages of the basic class, which you know he could coast through easily. After you've listened to what he has to say, you could ask how the course will affect the strength of his college application. If that doesn't change his decision, ask him why he feels so attracted to a class that won't challenge him.

As difficult as it may be for you, your child should be the one to make the final decision. If he doesn't, don't be surprised if he blames you when things don't work out. Sometimes you have to allow your children to make mistakes so they can learn from them.

However, you're the parent, and you retain the right of refusal. If your child's decision is based exclusively on laziness or on what his friends are doing, you have every right to intervene. This parental prerogative is especially important when your teenager routinely shows poor judgment and doesn't think for himself.

You may have already noticed that decision making can be a double-edged sword. On the one hand, your teen will tell you to let her make her own decisions; on the other, she blames you for not making a decision for her. "Why didn't you remind me my paper was due tomorrow and tell me to work on it?" they lament. If this leaves you feeling damned if you do and damned if you don't, you're not alone. Young people are determined to be independent—but only when it's convenient for them.

To be self-sufficient, your children will need initial help with decision making. If they can't make sensible small decisions, they won't be able to make big ones. A teenager who has trouble picking out her own clothes, budgeting her study time for a final exam, or getting around town by herself will hardly be able to make an informed decision about college.

Use your instincts when deciding whether to help your children function more independently or to persuade them to delay important decisions that have repercussions for the future. It can be a relief to many teenagers when their parents set reasonable limits on things they propose to do. The road to independence can be a long one. I suggest you discuss your feelings with other parents you respect and keep abreast of effective parenting practices to make sure you are on track.

Encourage Productive Time Spent Alone

The more solo activities young people feel comfortable with, the greater their self-direction. Teenagers who can't deal with unstructured time alone are at risk for trouble because boredom can make them discontented and restless, leading in turn to poor judgment.

How to Know When You're Being Too Hard on Your Kids

■ You feel that anytime your child is relaxing, he's wasting time.

■ You expect your teens to be accountable for everything they do during the day.

■ You've decided which activities she should participate in, because they'll strengthen her college application.

■ You forbid him from going to any unchaperoned teenage activities (concerts, a night at the mall) because there is always danger present.

■ Your child is upset because she feels she's being treated differently than her peers, and she hasn't given you any cause for concern!

If any of these signs apply to your situation, I suggest you seriously weigh the pros and cons of your position. Ask yourself what would happen if you relented. If you're convinced that your child would flounder but there's no documented evidence, you're probably worrying excessively. In this case, confer with someone who is knowledgeable about teenagers (school counselor, pediatrician, minister). There are risks that accompany overparenting: your teenager may come to resent you, and worse yet, she may rebel against your excessively tight control.

Owen was a teenager I worked with who couldn't tolerate being alone. He told me that he sat around for hours waiting for his phone to ring in the hope that one of his friends would call to invite him out. Owen felt lonely and jumpy when he was by himself and didn't enjoy doing things alone. He thought reading was boring, talking to his parents was out of the question, and television was satisfying only for a little while. Owen lacked the confidence and self-direction to come up with activities of his own, so he depended on other people for stimulation.

Teenagers like Owen are not unusual. But sometimes there's more than what we see on the surface. Some young people are genuinely afraid to be alone. They've never overcome their childhood fears of strange noises, burglars, and in some cases even thunder and lightning. Others perceive solitude as a stigma, believing that if they are alone, people don't care about them. And that thought triggers sadness and feelings of worthlessness. In both cases, young people are in need of assistance. They must learn to face and conquer their fears and will need your support and understanding to do so. If their fears persist, you should seek professional help.

Even with typical teenagers, you may have listened to them complain for years that they have nothing to do. If you've responded by taking it upon yourself to entertain them, you've probably increased their dependency on you. But if you've encouraged them to develop interests, find something to do in their rooms, or just relax without anyone around, you've planted the seeds of self-sufficiency.

Teach Your Children to Keep Busy

Expose your children to new activities and hobbies to encourage them to develop a range of interests. They can listen to different types of music, collect something, keep a diary, learn to play an instrument, paint or draw, or simply read for pleasure. Offer suggestions, but let them make the final choice. Never, ever, let them blame you for having nothing to do. They are responsible for entertaining themselves.

Most children seek out their friends when they have free time, which is healthy and normal, but it's also good for them to stay at home without their friends every so often. Not only does this encourage self-direction, it relieves some of the pressure they may feel to go along with the crowd. Some teens will fight the idea of solitude, desperately clinging to their friends to entertain them. But it is imperative they learn to enjoy their own company as much as that of others.

The computer, and more notably the Internet, has created innumerable opportunities for young people to entertain themselves. Some teens make good use of computer time, but others seem to find trouble when they surf the Net—either ending up on sites that are tasteless or obscene or just wasting enormous amounts of time idly surfing. Consequently, you may need to supervise how they spend their time. Excessive dependence on the computer, television, or telephone is a bad sign. It suggests that the teen may be avoiding something else she needs to be doing or that her range of interests is too narrow. Worse yet, she could actually be addicted to the activity. An addiction is something a person can no longer function without. If that sounds like the case, you'll need to help her break her dependence. Limit the amount of time she's allowed to spend on the activity, and if that doesn't work, remove the device for a while. What you want is, as always, balance. For a teenager who develops diverse interests and can comfortably spend time alone as well as with peers, there's nothing wrong with some TV or computer time.

Support Activities Outside the Home

While it's important for young people to learn to spend time by themselves, it's also important to push them out the door sometimes. You may say, "Well, that's no problem! My teenager can't get far enough away from home!" But is she doing something constructive when she's gone? Simply hanging around a friend's house watching television, playing video games, or making telephone calls isn't independence, although it's certainly better than drinking or smoking pot.

There are a number of ways you can encourage your teen to participate in activities that develop self-reliance. Ensuring that at least some of their time is spent in an outside activity that fosters self-reliance is a good place to start. A job can achieve this goal. If your child does want a job or you want your child to have one, make sure you limit the hours he works.

Volunteer work or community service can serve a similar purpose. Young people can feel they're making a positive contribution to society by volunteering at a hospital, retirement home, or homeless shelter. The rewards for this type of work are self-esteem, a broadened perspective, and a sense of autonomy, which are more valuable than money.

Another way teenagers can develop self-reliance is by traveling on their own. Expensive fares to faraway destinations are not realistic for most of us, but even local travel is valuable, exposing young people to new experiences, encouraging them to function on their own, and forcing them to deal with people outside their usual circle of acquaintances. A cheap and easy way to encourage solo travel is to suggest your child use public transportation to get to lessons, the library, or get-togethers with friends. Traveling even locally helps teens learn to ask directions, follow time schedules, handle money, and rely on themselves if things go awry.

If you're worried about your child getting lost or something terrible happening to him, make sure that he has a way to contact you if he needs you. Give him change for a pay phone, for instance, or loan him your cell phone or calling card. Most teens are ready for this by age fourteen or fifteen. If your child feels uneasy, you might introduce this by going with him the first time. Whether it's at camp, on a school tour, or on a summer adventure, if your child is able to be relatively self-sufficient, he'll come back with a stronger sense of independence and be ready to tackle other challenges.

Reward Independent Behavior

As your children gradually assume responsibility and become more independent, be sure that you recognize and celebrate their efforts. Their emancipation can feel threatening to them and also to you because it makes you feel less needed. But take heart: your teenagers' move toward self-reliance is a positive reflection on your parenting. As they learn to do more things for themselves, their horizons broaden and they naturally move away from their parents. You wouldn't want it any other way. They won't forget that you're there for them when they need a shoulder to lean on. That feeling of security is essential to true independence. Now that they're growing up, encourage them to spread their wings and find their own way. How else will they fly?

Elise's experience reflects a teenager's independent behavior and parental support for her efforts. At sixteen, early in her junior year, she wrote to several colleges and requested information packets. She chose small colleges that were distant from her home, even though she was close to her parents. When her parents saw the brochures arriving, they complimented Elise on her initiative and expressed interest in the schools. The prospect of their daughter attending college far away saddened them, but they wanted it to be her decision.

Mike's actions provide another example of independent behavior coupled with parental support. The previous year, he and his best friend Eric were constantly getting each other in trouble when they played on the same countywide soccer team. When faced with the decision about whether to rejoin the team, Mike elected to play on another team instead because he felt he'd be less distracted and could devote his full energies to the game. His parents applauded his decision, knowing it took courage to choose the less familiar situation. They told Mike that they'd be happy to drive the greater distance to his games and would attend as many as they could.

Allow for Some Nonconformity

Nonconformity has existed through the ages. At times it has been a harmless statement of protest against convention, but it has also been a catalyst for social change. You may not especially like nonconformists, but you should respect their right to self-expression. Indeed, the First Amendment is a cornerstone of democracy.

Naturally, there will be times when your children do things you don't approve of. I'm not talking about illicit or dangerous behavior, but about wearing outlandish clothing or listening to obnoxious music or identifying with an extreme political position or social cause. In the sixties, parents wrung their hands over their children's bell-bottoms, long hair, and peace marches. These seem quaint today, and their proponents have gone on to become successful in mainstream careers.

The occasional statements teenagers make to assert their individuality and independence are usually age-appropriate and

How to Tell When Your Teens Are Ready for Increased Levels of Responsibility

1. They give you their word and keep it.

2. They manage their study time and do reasonably well in school.

3. They usually do their chores around the house.

4. You can relax (somewhat) when they're out.

5. They're willing to talk to you about most of their activities.

6. They've abided by the rules and curfews that you've imposed to date.

7. They can admit when they've made a mistake—and learn from the experience.

8. They demonstrate good judgment in most situations.

9. They enjoy peer approval but they're not controlled by it.

10. They have clearly defined activities and interests.

Remember that occasional lapses of responsibility (usually minor) will occur in typical teenagers. They'll forget to do a chore or show up fifteen minutes after their curfew. But in such cases they acknowledge their mistakes and learn from them. If they've demonstrated a consistent pattern of responsible behavior, you should continue to increase their leeway as they mature.

even useful. Not long ago I heard a story about a teenage boy who went to school dressed in girl's clothing. The principal found this inappropriate and sent him home for the day. When his parents were informed, they didn't fly off the handle but were curious as to what prompted their son's actions. It turned out that he was protesting what he felt to be the school's double standard in its dress code. Girls were allowed to wear flannel shirts, combat boots, and T-shirts to school, as long as they were accompanied by a skirt, whereas boys were required to wear a coat and tie at all times.

The young man's parents supported their son, understanding that his action didn't hurt anyone and was simply his way of championing free self-expression. Cross-dressing may not have been the route they would have chosen, but they saw his nonconformity as a sign of his strength of character and independence of thought. Consequently, they met with the principal and persuaded him to rescind the reprimand. This story eventually appeared in the school newspaper, and everyone looked back on it as a benign high school prank. The perpetrator had pride, a sense of humor, a healthy rebelliousness, and confidence in his freedom to think and act independently.

Perhaps your teenager marches to the beat of a different drum on a more continual basis. Genuine nonconformists are not in search of attention. They strongly believe in what they're doing, whether it's their dress, interests, or political or social involvement. They're comfortable with themselves and are guided by the courage of their convictions. It may be hard for you to watch your children steer away from the mainstream, and you may be tempted to suppress their individuality. If you try, it probably won't work. If they're determined to change something they feel is unjust, your best bet is to offer some guidance about how to protest appropriately. It's one thing to circulate a petition or write a scathing editorial, but that's a far cry from taking over a building or endangering others.

Create Opportunities for Your Teenager to Assume Responsibility

Although teenagers can assert their independence through healthy nonconformity, the strongest indicator of self-reliance is trustworthy and responsible behavior. As assuming responsibility is the proving ground for independence, your children will need chances to demonstrate it.

By the age of twelve, children are asking to be dropped off at the movies or at the mall to meet their friends. Provided their destinations are safe and familiar to them, these are reasonable requests. If they consistently show up when and where they promise to, you have a basis for trusting them.

As teenagers get older, they can demonstrate their responsibility by managing their studies, baby-sitting for younger children, and shopping for family groceries, all of which are springboards to further independence. You can also allow them to do their own clothes shopping and have their own house key. If your teens avoid these responsibilities or are discouraged from attempting them, they may not develop the prerequisites for mature behavior.

Before leaving the subject of healthy independence, I'd like to share one final thought. There's a big difference between being self-sufficient and never needing anyone. The independent teenager will keep some ties to people she depends on, but simultaneously take responsibility for herself. This is no overnight process. You must continually monitor your children's behavior while allowing them opportunities to function autonomously.

DEVELOPING GOOD JUDGMENT

No teenager can be healthily independent unless he can exercise good judgment. Most teenagers would describe themselves as discerning despite their propensity for impulsive behavior. The self-assured teen assures you, and believes himself, that he would know the right thing to do in a difficult situation. Unfortunately, he doesn't necessarily do it.

Before teenagers can learn to trust their own judgment, they must have self-confidence, along with a body of experience to refer to, the ability to tell the difference between dangerous and benign situations, the ability to anticipate the consequences of their actions, and the conviction that they should do what is in their best interests. It's no easy task to teach your children to reflect on their actions, defer gratification, and make thoughtful decisions. Since you can't be with them everywhere they go, all you can do is make sure they know what is right. In this section, I'll list some ways you can help your children think and act more maturely to solve problems.

Help Them Anticipate the Consequences of Their Actions

At the heart of good judgment is forethought, the most basic reasoning skill. Most teenagers are in a hurry. They don't like to be bogged down in details, and they tend to make abrupt decisions that can get them into trouble. Many are sorry about their rash behavior afterward and learn things the hard way. There's usually little or no harm done, but for some teenagers the consequences of poor decision making can be disastrous. Almost daily we hear about young people overdosing on drugs, getting into car accidents, facing an unwanted pregnancy, or taking violent revenge on others. Their impulsiveness and poor judgment will forever alter the course of their lives.

If only making your children consider the consequences of their actions were as simple as telling them what's best for them! To open their minds, you must talk without lecturing, listen without judging, and lead them to their own conclusions. Of course, you want your teenagers to stop a moment, think about what they're doing, and anticipate the most likely outcome. This may seem simple enough, but you can get sidetracked if you don't stick to some basic guidelines.

I suggest you teach your teenager to allow at least a few minutes before making any decision with consequences. Remind them that this delay will be difficult at first, but it won't hurt them. Then have them practice resisting the pressure that others place on them to take immediate action. For example, ask your child to imagine a situation in which her friends are planning to drive to a neighborhood to hang out and it's a place where drugs are rumored to be sold. She's not sure she wants to go, but her friends say: "Are you coming or not? We don't have all night." Encourage your teenager to buy some time when she's unsure. She can say: "Don't rush me, I need to think about this." Or, "If you're in such a hurry, why don't you leave without me?" It'll seem silly at first, but it's an important first step because when she has a few minutes, she can think about what's likely to happen when they get there. Are her friends just looking to meet boys and flirt a little? Or are they planning to use drugs, hook up with strange boys, or seek other forms of dangerous excitement? Is this really what she wants to be doing? Finally, she can ask herself about the most likely outcome if she uses drugs or winds up in a car with boys she doesn't know. She'd be placing herself in danger and could get hurt or arrested. Is this a risk she's willing to take? By thinking ahead, teens can usually anticipate the consequences of their actions. If those consequences are undesirable, they can bow out of the situation.

Remind Your Teens That Their Feelings Are Important

Why give someone power over you whose judgment may be no better than yours (or maybe worse)? Tell your children that you trust their judgment and feel that they should trust it as well. If something doesn't feel right to them, they should listen to their gut feeling. And of course, there will be times when they lack sufficient information to make an informed decision—in which case they should defer action. That's where good judgment comes in.

Teach Your Children to Recognize Risky Situations

Encourage teenagers to think ahead and imagine what might happen in a range of possible situations—an unsupervised party with alcohol, for example, or a date with someone who has a reputation for being a drug user, or a test where they see someone cheating. Don't lecture when you discuss these situations with them. Plan how to use familiar examples to illustrate results of good and bad judgment.

Finally, make sure to build their self-confidence (using the guidelines in Chapter 4). Teenagers with pride in themselves trust their judgment because they don't have to check with others for approval. They have a well-developed set of beliefs that govern their actions. And when faced with a difficult situation, they instinctively think about what's prudent under the circumstances.

Talk About Examples of Poor Judgment

The mass media are full of stories about people who've made poor decisions and suffered the consequences; these include athletes, rock stars, even presidents. Discuss these lapses of judgment with your teenager and ask for his take on them. For example, should the media come down hard on an NBA star who gets thrown out of a play-off game for yelling at the referee? What happens to the rest of his team because of his behavior? You can find hundreds of other examples in books and movies. Most people disapprove of those whose rash decisions jeopardize the well-being of others. The message you want to convey is clear: if you don't think before you act, you may regret it. If you ask your teenager what that person might have done differently, he will usually be able to tell you a more prudent course of action.

In your home, try to nurture a climate for discussing significant events that illustrate good or bad judgment. If your teenagers feel free to express their opinions and debate them with you, they will refine their judgment in the process. As they think more about a situation, they get better at assessing it accurately. Anytime you subject your ideas to the scrutiny of others, you test the waters of good judgment. To become healthily self-reliant, children have to learn to be receptive to other people's feedback.

Explore Examples of Good Judgment

Teens can also learn from examples of people who've shown good judgment in a crisis: the passerby who jumps into a river to save a drowning child, the teenager who prevents a friend from driving home drunk, the student who defends a friend against school bullies.

I recently heard about a teenage boy who saved a life through quick thinking and decisive action. On his way home from school one day, he stopped by a sick friend's house to say hello. When no one answered the door, he got worried. He went around to the back of the house and entered through the porch, and when he went into his friend's room, he found her motionless on the floor next to an empty bottle of pills. Knowing that his friend had been depressed, he realized she'd taken an overdose. He called 911, and while he waited for the ambulance to arrive he brought pillows to make her comfortable, and he carefully monitored her breathing and pulse rate, saying encouraging things the whole time. Fortunately, the rescue squad arrived quickly and took his friend to the hospital, where they pumped her stomach and saved her life.

Teenagers who hear this story agree this teenage boy "did a cool thing." This may be an extreme illustration of composure under stress, but good judgment will also come in handy in daily situations involving peer groups, school, and family. Because the well-prepared, rational young person is at a decided

Testing the Waters of Good Judgment

Here are ten examples of daily situations that call for good judgment. Be certain to discuss each of them with your teenager, particularly if he's making poor decisions in any of these areas.

1. How much sleep to get each night

2. How much time to allow to get to school

3. How long to talk on the telephone

4. Whether to borrow something from a sibling without asking

5. How much money to carry with you

6. How to dress in inclement weather

7. How low to let your car's fuel tank go

8. Whether to eat breakfast

9. What to spend your allowance on

10. When to let your parents know your whereabouts

These are conversations you should have with all teenagers at least once. If you find yourself bringing them up over and over again, you'll need to work further on their ability to exercise good judgment.

Looking at Serious Issues from a Responsible Perspective

Teenagers don't routinely discuss serious issues (smoking pot, drinking, responsible sexual behavior) with their parents. So you'll need to find ways to bring these issues up in a nonthreatening fashion. Here are some tips that should help:

■ Tell your children you'd like them to convince you they know about current issues of concern. Of course, they'll insist that they already do. At this point, just say you're pleased to hear this, and ask them to educate you further. You can use this forum to raise legitimate concerns and find out where they stand on the issues.

■ If your teenager takes an irresponsible perspective on an issue (like saying it's okay to get drunk every weekend), you'll need to challenge his thinking. Ask him where he got his information, and be certain to alert him to the risks. And read Chapters 8 and 10 to learn how to deal with these specific behaviors of serious concern.

■ Discuss as well situations in which young people experienced serious consequences for their lapse in judgment. For example, a young man had his license revoked because he was driving under the influence of alcohol. Ask your child about her reaction to that situation. And what should the young person have done if he thought about the consequences in advance?

■ Find out how your children feel about the legal drinking age, minors smoking cigarettes, or teenage pregnancies.

Fortunately, teenagers have opinions on most of these issues, and are only too happy to share them—which opens the door to further discussion about mature and responsible behavior.

advantage in all sorts of life situations, the more you can encourage this type of thinking in your child, the better. Teach him how to handle emergency situations; encourage him to become certified in CPR; give him all the skills you can to boost his confidence.

It goes without saying that you also need to model good judgment for your children. A parent who treats injuries calmly and reacts to crises with practical skills sets an excellent example. Share what you've learned from your own experiences, both successes and failures. Someday your child will remember them when he needs them.

Sixteen-year-old Chris recalls a story about his father. When Chris was a child, his family was attending a special party at a neighbor's house on a warm summer evening. Chris's father was upstairs on the second-floor balcony when he spotted a woman who had fallen into the pool and was clearly unable to swim. He shouted down to the partygoers, "There's a woman drowning in that pool!" Everyone made a lot of commotion, saying, "Someone's got to rescue her," but no one did anything. Chris's father ran down the stairs, through the back door, pushed his way through the crowd, and dove into the pool in his best suit to rescue the woman. Chris later asked his father why he dove into the pool and ruined his suit, and his father replied, "Son, if not me, then who?" To this day, Chris models himself after his father, who kept his head in an emergency and knew when he needed to get involved.

As you find many daily situations that call for good judgment, you should discuss them with your child as often as you can. For example, your teen needs to decide when to study and when to play, when to speak up and when to keep his mouth shut, and when to leave a party if trouble's brewing. Teenagers are usually reluctant to discuss these events because they consider them no-brainers. But don't let them brush you aside. Tell them it'll make you feel better to know that they've listened to some of your examples and provided some of their own. Then you won't have to hassle them about it anymore.

Have a Dress Rehearsal

Like most other skills, developing good judgment takes practice. Because teenagers are convinced they know everything and don't need your help, you're going to have to find a way to persuade them to talk about matters of judgment. This is made easier by the fact that you have something they desperately want: the keys to their freedom.

Next time your child asks to do something that requires you to trust her, seize the opportunity to test her judgment with a hypothetical situation. For example, if your sixteen-year-old wants to go to a party with older friends, discuss what she'd do if they offered her marijuana. Most teenagers will assure you they'd turn it down and dismiss your concern, but don't let the discussion end there. Ask why she'd turn it down and how she'd do it. If she can't come up with at least one reasonable answer, she shouldn't be allowed to go.

Parent-child dialogues like this are essential to your child's developing good judgment. When you question your teenager about how he might handle a tricky situation, try to be as sincere and patient as you can. Invite him to think out loud and share his perspective. This allows you to gauge his judgment. Such discussions can't guarantee compliance, but they can satisfy you that your child has given some thought to potentially compromising situations. And the more he examines his actions beforehand, the less likely he is to use poor judgment.

In another example of this process, a fifteen-year-old named Todd has been invited to spend a weekend at the beach with a friend's family. Todd's parents are worried that the boys will wander off by themselves and get into trouble on the boardwalk.

Mother: Todd, your beach weekend sounds like fun, but there's always the possibility of trouble when a lot of kids hang out together. We'd like to talk over some of our concerns with you and be sure you can handle a problem situation.

Todd: Oh, Mom, don't worry so much. We're not going to do anything wrong. We'll just chill out, hang around the shops, play some basketball.

Mother: Maybe so, but we'll feel better if we know you're prepared. You've probably heard some of the same stories that we have.

Todd: You mean about the fights and kids getting busted for drinking beer.

Mother: Yes.

Todd: Well, we wouldn't do that. You think we're that stupid?

Mother: No, I don't think you're stupid, but I'll rest easier knowing you can handle an uncomfortable situation if it arises. You seem to know about the things that can happen. Let's talk about what you would do.

Todd: What do you want me to tell you?

Mother: Okay, what would happen if your friend wanted to go to the beach at night and there were teenagers drinking there?

Todd: I'd probably go, but I just wouldn't have anything to drink.

Mother: I'm glad you're being honest, but can't you see any risk in that?

Todd: Well, I guess there's always the possibility of something bad happening when kids get drunk. But I'd stay away from any troublemakers.

Mother: I'm glad to hear that, but I still think you'd be better off staying away from the general vicinity.

Todd: All right, we'll try to. But don't expect us to sit around and be bored the whole weekend. We'll still be hanging out around the boardwalk.

Mother: Well, you've addressed my concerns about drinking, but what if some rowdy kids approach you and try to start a fight?

Todd: Don't worry, I can take care of myself.

Mother: That wasn't exactly what I had in mind.

Todd: What do you mean, then?

Mother: I mean, could you get out of that situation?

Todd: Mom, I'm not going to let anyone push me around.

Mother: I wouldn't expect you to, but there are alternatives to fighting.

Todd: Like what?

Mother: Like just walking away without responding to their provocations. Fighting in self-defense is one thing, but letting someone egg you on to fight is different.

Todd: Well, I guess I could get out of a fight if it wasn't necessary.

Mother: That's really all I'm asking. Just that you and your friend try to avoid trouble.

Todd: Okay, Mom, we'll do what we can.

Todd's mother feels uncomfortable with him hanging out at the beach but wants to give him a chance. She appropriately expresses her concerns and encourages him to discuss them with her. Todd reluctantly agrees and they explore the potential risks together. His mother points out that he can avoid trouble by exercising good judgment and staying away from teenagers who drink and try to provoke fights. After some discussion, Todd agrees that he will go along with her request. His mother feels more comfortable knowing that her son can evaluate a situation and make the right decision. Of course, this dialogue is for illustrative purposes, and doesn't necessarily represent every twist and turn a conversation might take. But the more prepared you are, the more likely your conversations will flow smoothly.

Teach Social Problem Solving

To some extent, poor judgment comes from not being able to solve problems. Fortunately, you can help your teenagers learn skills to face social dilemmas. Social problem solving resembles negotiation. The difference is that kids must learn to do it on their own. To introduce the exercise, I suggest that you remind your children that if they can handle frustrating situations, you will trust them more and their lives will be easier. When they tell you, as most teenagers naturally will, that they can already deal with things and don't need to learn anything new from you, use their freedom from your supervision as your bargaining chip.

These are the five steps of social problem solving you should help them follow:

1. *Identify the problem.* Look carefully at the situation and determine what it is you're up against. Make sure that there's only one issue to be addressed. If there are more, you'll need to specify them before you proceed. In the event that you can't identify the problem, seek the advice of someone you trust and respect.

2. *Ask yourself what you want to happen.* After you've defined the problem, think about it and decide what you would consider a favorable outcome. You should be able to specify your goal for the situation—and make certain that it's realistic.

3. *Consider the options.* Think about all your possible choices in the situation. Don't try to figure out the best one at this point. Simply go over the possibilities in your mind (write them down if it helps) and make sure you're prepared to implement them.

4. *Evaluate the possible consequences of each option.* Now it's time to review the most likely outcome of each choice. It's important to be honest with yourself here. Try to think about your past experiences, the advice of others, and your gut feeling. Then try to predict the consequence of each of your possible actions.

5. *Choose the best alternative to get what you want.* After proceeding through the first four steps, you'll need to make a decision. Don't expect to have 100 percent certainty, but you should have the satisfaction of knowing you've weighed available alternatives. Now it's time to go forward with your chosen plan.

Many of us do follow these steps automatically, and they are not hard to learn. With some coaxing, teenagers can apply this simple approach to trouble at school, family issues, and social situations. It will strengthen both their judgment and their feeling of competence; and of course, you'll trust them more.

Here's how a teenager could apply these steps to a challenging situation. Kurt has just learned he's failing math for the third quarter because of his poor attendance and missed assignments. His parents are upset, but rather than jumping to conclusions and punishing him immediately, they first ask him what he intends to do about the problem. Kurt doesn't really know, but asks his parents if there's any way he can avoid being severely grounded. They agree to consider holding off punishment if he'll follow the problem-solving exercise. Here's how Kurt applied the steps in the sequence:

1. *Identify the problem.* Kurt has just learned that he's failing math and has to do something fast. He's facing punishment from his parents as well as a bad report card that could hurt his college plans.

2. *Ask yourself what you want to happen.* Kurt knows the desired outcome in this situation: he wants to raise his grade for the next quarter.

3. *Consider the options.* His first option is to ask his teacher whether he can get an extension on the work owed, as well as some extra help after school. His second option is to make up the missed work on his own and hand it in, hoping it will raise his grade. After further thought, Kurt discovers a third option: dropping the course, taking an incomplete, and finishing it in summer school. This would solve his attendance problem and maybe get his parents off his back. And of course, he has the option to do nothing and fail.

4. *Evaluate the possible consequences of each option.* Kurt thinks carefully about each of his available options. Evaluating the possible consequences of each, he tries to imagine the most likely outcome. He can certainly ask his teacher for help, but he's not sure what her response will be. Will she give him a chance, or will she reject or even insult him? He can work on his missed assignments, but there's no guarantee the teacher will change his grade. If he drops the course, he'll be off the hook but

Tips for Dealing with Irresponsible or Risky Behavior

- If it's a first offense, discuss their breach of trust and make sure they understand why it was wrong. Ask for their assurance that it won't happen again. Then, based on your conversation, decide whether or not a consequence is necessary. If there was a natural consequence (like school suspension or a hangover), and you're satisfied that they're appropriately remorseful, further action may be unnecessary. On the other hand, if the offense was more serious (like physical harm to others or violating the law), you may need to impose an equally serious consequence as an ongoing reminder.

- If your teenager has been in trouble before, you'll need to stress your serious concern and impose a meaningful consequence. As the saying goes, the punishment should fit the crime. Thus a teenager who gets a ticket for reckless driving should lose his driving privileges for a few weeks; one who violates her curfew should be grounded the following weekend. Be sure that your child learns something from the experience; if she continues to misbehave, she probably hasn't.

- Always make certain that you hold your teenagers accountable for their actions. Before you impose specific consequences, make sure that they're enforceable. And finally, use time-limited punishments. Indefinite grounding leads to anger and resentment, and you don't want your children to feel trapped. So inform them that when they've paid their dues, they can get on with their lives.

he'll have to sacrifice six weeks of his summer vacation. And if he fails, he'll have to repeat the class next year, possibly jeopardizing his future.

5. *Choose the best alternative to get what you want.* Finally Kurt decides that his best bet is to ask his teacher if he can arrange some kind of contract to raise his grade. He knows that he's taking a chance and that he'll have to work hard and is prepared to make the effort. Kurt feels relieved with his decision, even though he's uncertain what his teacher will say.

When he approaches his parents with his proposed solution, they're impressed and receptive. They agree to withhold punishment since he seems to be taking responsibility for his poor grade. Through the problem-solving process, Kurt has used good judgment and found a viable approach to his dilemma. As it turns out, his teacher is happy to help him, and he eventually raises his grade.

Give Them a Chance

So far, I've talked about teenagers developing good judgment by practicing their reactions to anticipated problems. But they'll often have to make decisions in situations they haven't faced before and aren't prepared for. Sometimes you simply have to let your children prove themselves. If you've helped your child learn to assume responsibility and exercise good judgment, the odds of a successful outcome are good. When your teen knows you have confidence in him, he's often motivated to maintain your good faith. Trust him, keep your own counsel, and cross your fingers. Be sure to follow up on how things work out.

Make Sure They Learn from Their Mistakes

If you give your child a chance and he messes up, you'll have to discuss what went wrong and why, and whether consequences are necessary. Let's return to my earlier example of Todd going on a weekend beach trip. He's assured his mother that he'll stay away from the drinking crowd, but he slips up and has a few beers. Worse yet, the police pick him up on the boardwalk and escort him and his friend back to the beach house. Assuming Todd admits that he was wrong, his parents should impose a consequence (such as a weekend restriction) and ask what he'd do differently if faced with the same situation again. This is the only way they can find out if he's learned anything useful from the experience. It doesn't guarantee he won't get into trouble in the future, but at least it makes him more aware of his alternatives.

The truth is that sometimes things do go wrong. Most teenagers will drink, break their curfews, and cut a few classes now and then. Many will make bad choices. But as long as you deal directly with such issues when they arise, you'll be doing your best. If your teenager still shows poor judgment despite your efforts, you'll need to consider more stringent measures.

Encourage Them to Use Their Common Sense

Let's assume you've given your children ample opportunity to develop good judgment and you've helped them learn from their mistakes. They have still another element on their side, and that's good old common sense. Surprisingly, intelligence, good judgment, and common sense don't always go hand in hand. I've known many bright, responsible, and well-brought-up teenagers who lack this most practical of traits.

Parents often ask me, "Why do my kids go out without a coat when it's thirty-five degrees outside?" "Why does my daughter spend six hours in the sun without putting on suntan lotion?" "Why won't my son wear his retainer when the orthodontist has told him it's the only way to keep his teeth straight?" These mysteries drive parents crazy, and your children can't understand why.

What's going on with them, anyway? Well, for one thing, teenagers hate being told what to do. For another, they see their friends making reckless decisions and copy them. Also, teenagers just don't consider the consequences of their actions. It's not because they don't know any better; it's just that your adult concerns don't seem very significant to them. Unfortunately, sometimes kids are aware of the consequences but do something foolish anyway, just because it's cool.

Where does this leave you as parents? You have two choices when your children don't act sensibly. The first is to let them make their little mistakes and hope that they'll learn from the natural consequences. So they get cold without their coats on or suffer from painful sunburns—who does that really hurt anyway?

Gauging Your Teenager's Common Sense

Here are ten situations you can pose to your teenagers to see how much common sense they have. Ask them what they'd do in each situation:

1. You're driving in an unfamiliar neighborhood and get lost. *An acceptable solution:* Look for a service station or a store and ask directions.

2. You have a big exam the next day, and one of your friends calls you to go out that evening. *An acceptable solution:* Tell her that you'd love to, but you have to study.

3. You're playing in an unsupervised soccer game and hurt your leg in a collision with someone. *An acceptable solution:* Stop playing and ask a friend to escort you home.

4. You're out with your friends and realize you're due home in ten minutes. *An acceptable solution:* Head for the nearest phone booth and call home to let your parents know where you are.

5. A classmate keeps bugging you while the teacher is talking. *An acceptable solution:* Ignore the per-

son or ask her to stop. If that fails, raise your hand and ask the teacher to let you move.

6. You're at a party and notice that several people are taking drugs. *An acceptable solution:* Leave the party.

7. Someone on the street approaches you for money. *An acceptable solution:* Say, "Sorry, I don't have any change."

8. You're in a department store and realize you've lost your purse. *An acceptable solution:* Go to the nearest cashier or security guard and ask where the lost and found is.

9. You're home alone and hear someone trying to break into your house. *An acceptable solution:* Call 911.

10. There's a power failure in your neighborhood and the lights go off. *An acceptable solution:* Find a flashlight or a candle.

Your other option is to challenge them every time they're about to do something foolish. If you do, beware; your blood pressure will shoot up and your kids will still annoy you.

I don't mean to downplay the importance of common sense, for you should help your children use the practical knowledge they have. When solutions to problems aren't obvious to them, encourage them to think harder. Maybe they can tap their experience for clues in the current situation. Since teenagers often overlook the obvious, help them slow down and think logically. For example, use the timeworn lost-and-found strategy if your teenager's favorite CD is missing: ask him to think about when and where he last played it and retrace his steps from there.

Your teenager may insist that she already knows what she'd do, but remind her that it will make you feel better to hear her go over it with you. The more children can rehearse hypothetical situations, the faster they'll think when they're faced with a real dilemma. I've always been amused by the sheepish smiles on teenagers' faces in discussions like these when they realize they might not have chosen the right course of action.

THE IMPORTANCE OF IMPULSE CONTROL

Unfortunately, common sense doesn't always inhibit the impulsiveness of teenagers, and being impulsive can get in the way of their judgment. Poor impulse control can cause people of all ages to offend others, get angry too easily, and make decisions without thinking. Because teens are especially impulsive, they're at greater risk for trouble.

Teenagers are impulsive for several reasons. First, they lack experience and maturity. This absence leads them to rash actions without forethought. Second, they're impatient and self-absorbed, and they live in the moment—seeking immediate gratification with little regard to the consequences of their actions. And finally, a small number of teenagers (about 5 percent of the population) have attention deficit disorder, a condition that fuels impulsive behavior. See pages 376–378 for specific information about ADD/ADHD.

You can help your teens improve their impulse control by alerting them to the dangers of unchecked impulses and teaching them to delay their actions by thinking first. Examples of impulsiveness might include a pedestrian who rushes into an intersection, ignoring the Don't Walk sign, and is hit by a car; or a teenager who throws his chair after his teacher reprimands him and gets suspended from school. Both people act impulsively and pay a price. And both situations could have been avoided if these individuals had stopped and thought for a moment.

Explain to your teenagers that there are advantages to being cautious rather than reckless. For one thing, our judgment improves when we allow ourselves time to deliberate. This discourages us from making decisions that aren't in our best interests. For another, whereas many teens are drawn to wild, unpredictable types, most will admit that their best friends possess some measure of reliability and steadiness. They'll also usually acknowledge that their impulses can get them into trouble. Approach this in a spirit of comradeship, not attack, and you should be able to slow them down a bit. Following are some suggestions to help you to accomplish this.

Try to Improve Their Frustration Tolerance

Patience is the flip side of impulsiveness. Teenagers have to learn to delay gratification and tolerate frustration. You can help them by devising situations that require planning ahead, taking small steps, and learning to wait. If your teenager wants a new bicycle, for example, tell her that she'll have to save a certain amount of money for it. After she reaches this goal, you can contribute the rest.

If your child gets frustrated by school assignments and abruptly gives up, work with him to establish a plan to address it further. Tell him that each night you'll work with him for the first fifteen minutes. Then he'll work alone for the next fifteen minutes. When he feels ready, he'll call you back to check his work. After that, he'll take a ten-minute break and then resume his studies. He'll have your support, but he'll still be responsible for his work, and he'll have breaks to look forward to. Once the plan is in action, monitor him inconspicuously to make sure he doesn't reach a point where his frustration becomes intolerable. At first this exercise will seem awkward, but you'll find he'll get used to it in a few days. Hopefully, over time this will reduce his impatience. If the plan doesn't work, consider shorter time intervals, oversee him more carefully, or consider a tutor. You'll find more information on dealing with school issues in Chapter 9.

Another way to reduce impulsive behavior is to steer your teen toward an extended task like assembling a model airplane, doing a jigsaw puzzle, or playing a game that demands forethought. Find the right project to match her interests and temperament; if she's wrapped up in an enjoyable project, she'll learn for herself the values of patience and planning ahead. While she's working, be sure to stop by every so often and compliment her on her efforts.

Another interesting exercise is to ask a teenager to build a house of cards while you try to distract him. I like to present this one as a challenge, explaining that he might find it funny or annoying, but it's great way to build his determination. Tell him to try to concentrate while you blast music, tell jokes, or warn that the cards are going to fall. Teenagers get a kick out of this one and try their darnedest to stay focused and in control. If your son asks you to try it, by all means do so!

Get Them to Think About Their Actions

Impulsive teenagers usually react without thinking. Some say they can actually feel a brief period of tension just before they respond. The idea is to get them to slow down and reason before they act. Start a discussion about a hypothetical situation and ask for their automatic reaction. You want them to respond without thinking, so you'll have a sense of how impulsive they're likely to be.

For example, you might ask, "What would you do if you were at a party and someone bumped into you and spilled a drink on you?" If the first response is, "I'd throw my drink on

Five Steps Toward Making Your Teenager Less Impulsive

Try these skill builders to help your child develop better impulse control:

1. Make them aware of what they're doing. When teens behave impulsively, ask them to describe their action afterward. They should pay particular attention to how quickly they reacted, what they thought to themselves (like, I'd better grab the ice cream or I won't get any), and what the other person's reaction was to their behavior. With their consent, you can even video-tape them in a situation that fuels their impulsive behavior. You'll have to be on the lookout for the propitious moment, but the time will come. Afterward, they can watch themselves in action and get immediate feedback.

2. Model behavior that displays forethought and restraint; then get your child to do it. For example, you can perform a task by talking out loud. As you work on a project, say: "I'm thinking about what I'm doing, I need to go slowly and carefully, and I need to check my work." Then get your child to do the same thing. After they've learned to talk out loud, they can think about it to themselves as they work. You can do the same thing with a hypothetical situation that's provocative. Pretend that someone's bugging you and say out loud: "I'm not going to react till I've decided on the best course of action," or, "I'm not going to let him get to me, because that's what he wants to do."

3. Use practice drills. You'll want to work on all the exercises I've described in this section. Another worth trying is to shout "Freeze" when your teen is about to react impulsively. For example, if they look like they are about to rush out of the house, you yell "Freeze" and they stop in their tracks. You'll need their cooperation on this one, but if you plan it beforehand, they'll view it as a chance to avoid an argument that could lead to further conflict.

4. Support their efforts. Whether or not you're around, your teenager should work on all the suggestions in this chapter. Encourage them to report their successes and failures, and praise them for their perseverance in addressing such a difficult issue. Anytime you notice them thinking before they react, call it to their attention and express your approval.

5. Be patient. Both parent and teen must realize that change doesn't occur overnight. Your child has probably been impulsive for some time and assumes that's just the way it is. If you all work at it, you'll begin to notice some small changes after a few weeks. They'll start thinking a little before they react, and they'll learn to identify the situations that trigger their impulsive behavior. It may take several months before some of these long-standing patterns are broken, but the effort is well worth it.

them!" or, "I'd yell at the person," you have some work to do. Another question to get at this issue: "What would you do if you were driving and the light turned yellow as you approached the intersection?" The impulse-prone teenager will say, "Step on the accelerator and try to beat the light," which is clearly risky behavior without discretion. Or you can ask, "Imagine that you're standing in the cashier's line at a department store and the person in front of you drops a twenty-dollar bill but doesn't notice. What would you do?" Many impulsive youngsters would pick it up and pocket it without a second thought.

What you want your teenager to do in discussions like these is to ponder what he might do differently if he took the time to think first. Usually he'll admit he can be hasty and agree to give the matter further thought. That's really all you're asking—that he try to think before he reacts. If he can also consider the consequences of an impulsive action, so much the better. The more practiced he is at thinking out loud in your presence, the more likely he is to do it on his own.

Impulsive people often fail to consider the feelings of others. The teenager who jumps in his parents' car and immediately turns the radio on at full volume is thinking only of himself, as is the kid who bursts into the bathroom without knocking, grabs food without waiting his turn, and takes personal belongings without asking. Talk with your children about how they feel when they're the ones on the receiving end of this behavior.

Have Them Practice Delayed Reactions

I always find it helps to role-play potentially difficult situations in advance. Help your teenager practice this strategy. If she expects, for instance, to be provoked by someone in her class, you can pretend to be the offensive classmate while she works on skillfully handling the situation. Help your teenagers anticipate as many problem areas as you can. Their job is to focus on thinking before they react; yours is to support them in delaying their responses.

There's a drill I recommend for parents and teens called "code red." First, explain to your child that there are often arguments where everyone gets angry, says things they don't mean, and usually feels worse afterward. Then tell your teenager you'd like to create a situation where each of you has the power to stall an argument. The family agrees to use a signal—a clenched fist, a code word, a loud whistle—to let others in a heated discussion know that one member is close to losing control. After signaling, the angry party is given some space until he can regain his composure. This emergency maneuver allows him a few moments to think about what he's doing. This may not always avert a crisis, but it gives you a viable alternative to overreacting. After some practice with these *reaction delays,* your teenager's fuse (and yours) should grow longer.

Model Patience and Self-Restraint

Raising an impulsive teenager can be nerve wracking. You'll often find yourself on the verge of losing your temper, but as an adult you have to go out of your way to exercise self-restraint. Nothing productive comes of a parent and teenager locking horns. Resolve to prevent yourself and your child from making hasty decisions and acting impulsively. If your teen demands an immediate answer, insist on time to think about it. To slow her down, tell her you'll get back to her in a few hours. If you allow her to rush you into a decision, you'll reinforce your child's impulsiveness.

Here's how one parent resisted her impulse to overreact to her daughter's immediate demand. Tory announced without notice that she had to go to her best friend's house in the next hour because there was a surprise party she had forgotten about. She was prepared to blow off her soccer play-off game and the team party afterward. Her mother was against the idea because Tory had already missed one game and the team was counting on her. She stayed controlled and resolute, despite her daughter's pressuring her for an immediate answer.

Tory: Mom, I can't go to the soccer game tonight. There's an important party at Julie's house and I have to be there in an hour. You've got to take me.

Mom: Wait a minute. You have a commitment to your soccer team. I don't think it's such a good idea to miss this game.

Tory: I know that, but this is my best friend's party. What am I supposed to do, miss it?

Mom: Under the circumstances, maybe you'll have to change your plans a little bit. I'm sure we can work something out.

Tory: Mom, you don't understand. It's, like, a matter of life and death. Come on, let's just get going.

Mom: Didn't you think about this in advance?

Tory: Well, I knew about it, but I forgot. Please, can't we just leave?

Mom: There's still a little time. Why don't we try and think about our options here? Can you sit down for a few minutes?

Tory: Okay, but let's hurry. I've got to be there soon.

Mom: I understand Julie's party is important to you, but you have to consider the feelings of the girls on your team. Slow down and think about this. Isn't there a way you can work it out?

Tory: I don't know—maybe go to the game and then go late to the party?

Mom: It seems to me that's a reasonable solution.

Tory: But I want to be there when the party starts.

Mom: I understand that, but sometimes we have to compromise a little to honor our commitments. You're in such a hurry sometimes that you don't stop and think about your alternatives.

Tory: Well, I really want to go to the party. But I guess my teammates are counting on me.

Mom: I'll tell you what. Why don't you call one of your friends, explain the situation, and tell her you'll be a couple of hours late for the party? We'll go to the soccer game, and as soon as it ends, I'll rush you to Julie's house. I'm sure she'll understand.

Tory: Do I have to?

Mom: I really don't want to force you, but I think it's the right thing to do under the circumstances. Don't you?

Tory: I guess so. Where's the cordless phone?

When your teenagers attempt to act impulsively, resist their pressure and keep them from bringing you down to their level with demands. You'll need to slow them down and get them to think about some reasonable options. Teenagers are usually impatient for solutions. This sense of urgency isn't a problem in itself, but impulsive thinking can impair their judgment—so you must intervene.

In this chapter I've explored the interrelationship of age-appropriate independence, good judgment, and impulse control. Strategic parenting will help you zero in on your teenagers' shortcomings in these areas and build on their strengths. You want your teenagers to do the right thing because they've thought the situation through, not because they fear your reaction. As you reduce their propensity to act without thinking, you'll pave the way to their ability to use better judgment.

If you can raise independent children who can think for themselves, make sensible decisions, and delay gratification, you can rest easy knowing that they'll avoid trouble and seek adaptive pursuits in their lives.

DON'T LET THEM LEAVE HOME WITHOUT EMPATHY AND MORALITY

"How could you have cheated on this test? Didn't we teach you right from wrong?"

"How can you be so rude to your grandma? Her feelings must be really hurt."

"You act like you don't care about anyone but yourself. You must expect the whole world to revolve around you."

Empathy, morality, and values define a person. Their presence or absence determines whether one is cruel or kind, sensitive or callous, thoughtful or thoughtless. They are signs of a person's maturity, regardless of his or her actual age. Teenagers who are empathetic and have strong values are less likely to get into trouble; they possess more insight and self-awareness.

Empathy, the ability to identify with another person's feelings, is at the root of good social behavior. Empathy is not reserved exclusively for friends and loved ones; it should include strangers as well. Once we're able to put ourselves in others' shoes and recognize how our actions affect them, we begin to care about how we treat them. Closely related to empathy is morality—a sense of right and wrong and the foundation of good character. Some suggest morality is the fabric of which an enduring society is woven, for internal moral standards lead us to experience both pangs of conscience and, when we've done what is right, feelings of satisfaction. In the absence of a moral code, people act according to impulse and disregard the rights of others. Finally, values are the underlying set of beliefs that govern our actions. These beliefs are passed down to children from their families from early childhood through the teenage years.

Although teenagers aren't always noted for exuding empathy, you will notice that they respond compassionately to many situations. Here are some examples that show you they're on the right track:

1. They complain about a classmate being treated unfairly by the teacher.

2. If a friend is injured, they go out of their way to help them get the medical attention and support they need.

3. They volunteer for school projects to help the less fortunate.

4. They are affected by tragic news stories and feel compassion for those who were hurt.

5. When someone in the family is sick, they ask how that person is feeling and make an effort to help out around the house.

6. They pass a car accident and express concern about whether anyone was hurt.

7. They drop some change in the cup of a homeless person.

8. They notice younger children picking on someone and stop to intervene.

9. They make an effort to express kindness to less socially acceptable teens without caring if they are cool.

10. They display noticeable responsibility for their pets or those of others.

Naturally, most teenagers won't exhibit all of these concerns, but they will make related comments every now and then. When they do, express your awareness of their compassion and try to be responsive to their concerns. Your appreciation for their feelings will only reinforce your teenager's positive actions.

In this chapter I'll further explore the importance of these three traits and tell you how you can detect them in your teenager. I'll alert you to the role you play in building your child's character, and I'll help you encourage moral reasoning in your teens, model appropriate behavior for them, and hold them accountable for their actions. By the end of the chapter you'll be able to challenge your teenagers' self-centered thinking and redirect their energy to activities that will elicit empathy.

ASSESSING YOUR TEENAGER'S EMPATHY AND MORAL PERSPECTIVE

Some young people show signs of compassion from a very early age, responding naturally to the needs and feelings of others. Preschool teachers are often touched by the kind and sensitive gestures of small children. A little boy, for example, sees a playmate crying because her toy is broken; he goes over to the girl and gives her his own toy to comfort her. Another little boy in the same situation, however, might tease the girl for being a crybaby. Most children tease one another every so often, but do so without malice and have an innate sense of decency that keeps them from going too far. But if teasing becomes a chronic pattern, it suggests an early absence of empathy and is cause for concern. Certain children are clearly unreceptive to the feelings of others and, even more alarming, are untouched by a concern for others.

One useful way to gauge the extent of your teenager's identification with others' feelings and the soundness of his moral code is to ask how he felt about a movie, book, or television episode that explored serious or moral issues. You might also just tell him how you were affected and see how he reacts. Opportunities such as these are commonplace—especially if you're in the habit of talking with your children on a regular basis. Teenagers are usually willing to voice their opinions about movies they've seen, and you can guide the conversation to an exploration of their feelings about the characters. In one movie, for example, a teenager traveling by himself is accosted by hoodlums and forced to turn over his money. What do your children think the experience was like for that young man? Did they feel sorry for him, or just say that it was his tough luck? (Make sure you don't confuse an issues-oriented movie or book with a simple tearjerker. For example, *Dying Young* is a tearjerker whereas *Erin Brokovich* offers an opportunity to discuss empathy.)

Here's another example. In a television episode, a girl learns that one of her good friends is selling hard drugs to elementary school kids. She struggles with what to do but eventually turns him in to the police. How does your teenager think the character feels? And what would he do in her shoes? The answers you get will reflect your child's ability to feel empathy for the girl. The more he can relate to predicaments like these, the more sensitive he is to others' feelings.

Morality in the Media

There are many books and movies that can spark interesting and instructive conversations on values and morals. Try reading or watching some of the following with your teen and then discussing the choices characters made and what kind of values they showed. There are too many good books and films to list; these are just a few of my favorites.

Books

Animal Farm

The Chocolate War

A Clockwork Orange

The Contender

The Diary of Anne Frank

The Giver

Go Ask Alice

Holes

Huckleberry Finn

Lord of the Flies

Of Mice and Men

The Outsiders

The Red Badge of Courage

A Separate Peace

The Scarlet Letter

Siddhartha

Summer of My German Soldier

That Was Then, This Is Now

To Kill a Mockingbird

Movies

The Accused

Boyz N the Hood

A Bronx Tale

Clueless

The Color Purple

Do the Right Thing

Donnie Brasco

A Few Good Men

Forrest Gump

Goodfellas

Heathers

High Noon

Malcolm X

Philadelphia

Rain Man

Saving Private Ryan

Schindler's List

The Shawshank Redemption

Stand by Me

Welcome to the Dollhouse

Observe your teens' reactions to real situations as well. If they don't seem to be affected by the misfortune of others, something is probably lacking. Many teenagers in trouble are strikingly indifferent to how they affect other people. This deficiency is so prevalent and so damaging that we must examine how to help our children develop compassion and reasonable moral standards.

There are certain signs that signal a child who lacks a conscience. They include:

- Playing down the significance of harm or distress they inflict on others.
- Apologies that seem superficial and insincere.
- Seeming unaffected by others' misfortune.
- Appearing to enjoy getting away with things.
- Punishment seems to have no effect on them.
- Thinking only about themselves.
- Feel like you don't really know them.
- Remarks like, "She had it coming," "Who cares about a loser like him?" or, "It serves him right."

If your teenager is displaying several of these signs, he is at serious risk for trouble. His dismissive reactions toward the feelings of others are a reflection of his self-centered attitude. In the absence of compassion and guilt, he is free to act according to his whims and hurt people without regard to the consequences.

HOW TO AROUSE YOUR TEENAGER'S EMPATHY

The messages you give your children when they're young are powerful. Take the example of a little girl who notices a homeless person. She mentions it to her parents, who comment on how lonely and difficult it must be for the person to go through life like that. They ask her how she thinks the person might feel and remind her of how fortunate she is. These parents are planting the seeds of empathy.

But what if the parents dismiss or even ridicule the unfortunate person's condition? The effect on the child will be quite different, for they have given her little basis for a compassionate response and missed an opportunity to teach her something useful. Worse yet, she is likely to respond in a similar way the next time she encounters someone less fortunate than herself because she's gotten the message that such suffering is no big deal or is even amusing.

By the time your children reach adolescence, they should possess the ability to empathize with others. If they come up short, they'll need to be challenged, educated, and stimulated. Fortunately, most teenagers can learn to be more sensitive to the feelings of others; in this section, I'll give you some suggestions for working on this. It will take some effort, but the payoff is enormous. Everyone who comes into contact with your teenager will be pleased with the change, and in time your teenager will realize that he's better off for it.

Make a Case for Empathy

The first challenge is to convince your children how important compassion is. Teens might not see the point. "Why bother?" they may ask. Or they may complain that people will think they're weak if they're sensitive. They'll be able to come up with plenty of excuses to avoid facing their own vulnerability. I have found that they often need specific examples—either ordinary people or media heroes—to understand that people who are kind are well regarded.

You can help by making it clear to your teenagers that you value empathy. Tell them about compassionate people who have touched your life, and perhaps theirs. Seek out examples in everyday life of people displaying compassion for others: helping an elderly woman with her groceries, stopping to help a stranded motorist change a flat tire, or paying attention to someone who is ignored or a social outcast. You'll need to convince your children that they'll feel better about themselves after helping someone out. I've never forgotten the words of Cousin Brucie, a well-known WABC radio disc jockey in the fifties and sixties. He often ended his programs saying,

"Remember, kids. It's nice to be important, but it's more important to be nice."

Without empathy, a teenager will find life lonely—a message that will usually impress teens because, despite what they say, most of them would like to have closer relationships. All they have to do is look around them to see that people who have good interpersonal skills seem to have an easier time. Not all of them ooze compassion; in fact, the coolest and most popular kids can be rather insincere. But in the long run, the popularity of people who are high on image but low on substance is short-lived. They can't sustain the interest of their peers. Unfortunately, high school offers too many examples of mean-spirited people seeming to get ahead. Remind your children of people like Bill Gates who were nerds in high school but ended up better off than the cool people in the long run.

Most teens know that when they're down, seeking out people will help them feel better. Reinforce this with examples from their own lives. Here's a case in point. Joann, a junior in a suburban high school, was friendly, upbeat, and well liked by her peers. Many students thought of her as a good friend and often went to her for advice. This was no coincidence: Joann's concern for others was obvious. When someone had a problem, she listened carefully, tried to relate to it, and then helped the person come up with a solution. In this way and others, she made other teenagers feel more comfortable.

Needless to say, Joann was always included in outings, parties, and other group activities, for she was the kind of person her classmates wanted to be around. No one seemed to consider her a Goody Two-shoes or a nerd just because she was sincere, straightforward, and willing to express her feelings openly. While she was a typical teenager in some ways, her ability to empathize with others distinguished her from the others. Joann gained respect and acceptance just by being herself. Your child will readily identify people at his own school who are genuinely nice in the way Joann is.

Talk About Empathy-Inducing Situations

There are situations that call for compassion all around you. Unfortunately, many teenagers are so concerned with their own immediate problems that they fail to see the big picture. It is your responsibility to expose your children to real-life compassion. You can watch the news or point something out in a newspaper or newsmagazine. Some parents cut out articles or forward online stories to their teen's e-mail address when the topics are of interest. If you call your teen's attention to something, follow it up with a discussion. The dinner table is the classic place for these conversations, but really they can happen anywhere. Ask your child what she thinks about a particular issue. If she seems reluctant or unable to come up with an opinion, ask her to put herself in the shoes of someone involved. Offer your own opinions, but don't turn it into a debate if your child has a different opinion from yours, and don't lecture. You'll both benefit more from a calm two-way discussion.

You should also consider exploring with your teenager the human impact of disasters like Hurricane Mitch: high winds and flooding destroyed countless homes, killed thousands of people, and devastated the landscape of Central America. Hundreds of thousands of people were left homeless, starving, and desperate, with years of recovery ahead of them. These tragic events received wide media coverage across the nation, and the news images of a grieving population, starving children, and utter chaos would have been hard to ignore. But although most teenagers were aware of these events, they probably gave the matter little thought. It seemed so far removed from most of their lives that they could easily turn their backs on it. Many sensitive parents and teachers tried to make certain that young people understood the consequences of the disaster by exploring with them the effects of the hurricane and the feelings of the victims. Some went further and involved their children in collecting donations of food and clothing for disaster victims.

Here are ten suggestions to help you open your teenagers' eyes to others' misfortune and get them more involved with worthy causes:

1. Make certain that they're informed about what's going on in the world around them. Encourage them to read the newspaper and listen to the news.

2. Don't allow them to dismiss the significance of events that seem removed from their lives.

3. Emphasize the importance of sharing what you have with those less fortunate than yourself.

4. Ask your child to make a small contribution to the charity organization of his choice.

5. Encourage your child to spend his summer volunteering. The pay may be minimal or nonexistent but it will be a great experience (and as a bonus, it looks good on college applications).

6. Stress your admiration for famous humanitarians like Mother Teresa and Martin Luther King, Jr.

7. Show them that helping others brings a sense of personal satisfaction. If your words are insufficient, they need to experience these feelings firsthand.

8. Contact their school to learn about opportunities to participate in community service projects, philanthropic student organizations, or fund-raisers.

9. Arrange for them to take part in worthwhile projects where other teenagers are working (Habitat for Humanity, telethons, and disaster relief drives).

10. Allow them to volunteer for a worthy cause as an alternative to punishment.

You may also want to point out issues of local concern, not just ones that receive national media attention. Every community has its own issues; some examples might be the quality of the schools, the local political scene, local construction or development, and housing and homeless issues. Teenagers who regard international affairs as too far away to affect them might care more about issues that will directly affect them.

Ask Your Teens How They Would Feel If It Happened to Them

"You never really understand a person until you consider things from his point of view—until you climb into his skin and walk around in it."

—Harper Lee, *To Kill a Mockingbird*

As you discuss serious events with your teenager, ask him to put himself in the other person's shoes. You don't have to wait for a catastrophe to ask your teen to imagine how another person is feeling. Even small misfortunes and disappointments can lead to lessons.

Sometimes your children will provide you with the material for such a discussion. They may approach the matter casually, but be assured that they are seeking your input. Teenagers need to talk about what's on their minds, especially when they feel bad about something. One girl told her parents about a boy being beaten up on the school bus. She described it matter-of-factly and said she knew the boys who did it. Her parents were shocked by her indifference and pressed her to tell them how the boy reacted. When she admitted that he was upset and embarrassed, her parents asked her how she might feel in his place. She grudgingly admitted that she would have felt much the same. At this point, her parents reminded her that she too had been picked on when she was younger, and they asked her what

A Lesson in Compassion

Even though it is difficult to discuss illness, divorce, substance abuse, and other serious things that may threaten a family member, make the effort. Your child will benefit from an honest, open discussion and it will help him sort out his feelings. Then he will be able to feel empathy for those in unhappy situations. In this conversation, a father and his teenage son talk about a close relative who is dying of cancer.

Father: Philip, I guess you know by now that Uncle Mickey's cancer has been spreading fast. I'm afraid he doesn't have much time left.

Philip: Yeah, I heard Mom talking about it last week. He's always been such a good guy. He used to take all of us places when we were younger.

Father: It's been really tough on your cousin.

Philip: Well, Mark never talks about it when I see him.

Father: What do you think is really on his mind?

Philip: I don't have a clue!

Father: Come on, now. What do you imagine he's feeling?

Philip: Well, I guess he must be pretty upset. He and Uncle Mickey have always been pretty close.

Father: I can think of a few other reasons he's probably scared now.

Philip: How do you know?

Father: Well, I went through it when your grandfather died. I was nineteen.

Philip: Were you afraid of being alone?

Father: Yeah, I was. I couldn't imagine what my life would be like without my dad around. It took a long time to get used to.

Philip: I bet that's what Mark is thinking about. He must be so scared, but he doesn't talk to anyone about stuff. Can we do anything, Dad?

Father: What do you think?

Philip: Well, we can invite him over to our house a lot more. Maybe even let him know we'll be there for him. You know, do stuff together, try and keep his mind off things. And I guess I could talk to him a little bit about it.

Father: What would you say?

Philip: I'd tell him I'm sad too. And that I think Uncle Mickey's pretty cool and I'm going to miss him when he . . . you know.

Father: I know, Philip. I think that would really help.

Philip's father wisely helped his son become aware of what his cousin was feeling. He didn't lecture, but offered Philip some direction and shared some of his own experience. As often happens, the son picked up on this and was able to empathize more with the situation. Our lives are full of occasions like this to gently elicit our children's compassion.

she would do if a situation like this occurred again. "I guess I would tell the bus driver or get some other kids to help out," she responded in a serious tone of voice. Finally, she was able to understand her true feelings and to figure out on her own what she should have done.

Whether it's disappointment over failing to make a sports team, sadness about a college rejection, or devastation by a divorce, you can explore misfortunes that affect people your teen knows to help her recognize how she feels and experience compassion for them. Learning to feel empathy will sharpen her judgments about appropriate behavior and help her think twice before hurting someone.

Little Things That Count

Teach your teens that compassion should be a part of their daily lives. Here are some situations that provide the opportunity for teens to act compassionately:

- A little boy falls off a playground swing and starts crying. You go over to comfort him.
- Someone approaches you collecting for the Muscular Dystrophy Association. You give him a few dollars.
- You find a lost kitten in your neighborhood. You take her home with you and put up a sign providing information about how to contact you.
- You notice a handicapped person struggling to get a door open. You stop to help him with it.
- Your teacher asks for volunteers to help with an after-school project at a Head Start program. You sign up for the project.
- Your little sister is upset because she doesn't understand her math assignment. You offer to help her out.

There are opportunities all around us to display compassion. Encourage your teens to respond accordingly. Acknowledge their efforts when they do.

Encourage Them to Express Their Feelings

Not only do you want your teenager to empathize with others' feelings, you also want him to express his own. In our earlier discussion of vulnerability, I pointed out how important it is for young people to be able to acknowledge their weaknesses, disappointments, and hurts. Besides making them more comfortable with themselves, being sensitive to their own feelings also tunes them in to the feelings of others. Encourage your children to express their emotional pain over both minor and significant events. The better they can identify their own feelings, the more they'll be able to relate to those of others.

I often ask young people to recall a time in their lives when they were embarrassed, hurt, or taken advantage of by another person. Admitting to such incidents is not always easy, but with support they will usually describe an episode from their past. If they have difficulty, I will offer examples that other teenagers have told me, or I might share my own recollections of childhood run-ins with the neighborhood bully. I can still remember being terrified and screaming "Keep your hands off me" as he pinned me to the ground. Often, teens tell me stories about an excessively critical teacher, a parent who belittled them, or a time when their friends left them behind. As they describe the feelings that accompanied the incident, I encourage them to relate those feelings to someone else who has experienced emotional or physical distress. This usually helps them make that crucial empathic connection.

Several years ago, while I was working with a mildly depressed boy named Peter, he recalled his anguish over playing on a seventh-grade recreational basketball team years earlier. He readily admitted that he wasn't very good at the sport and had signed up at his parents' insistence. Unfortunately, his teammates were harsh and critical of him. They teased him about being a poor shooter and complained to the coach when he entered the game. To make matters worse, they didn't pass the ball to him, even when he was open for a shot. Needless to say, he was angry and humiliated, thinking of that year. He couldn't have been happier when both the season and his short-lived basketball career ended.

However, to his credit, Peter turned things around. He took up tennis that summer, practiced hard, and devoted himself to the game. Eventually he became a fairly good player and made his high school tennis team three years later. Now here he was sitting in my office telling me about a kid who was holding back the team. When Peter ridiculed the young man's poor strokes and slow reaction time, I reminded him that he was once that kid. Peter grew quiet and seemed to digest the impact of my words. He knew very well how the boy felt, but those were feelings he'd conveniently forgotten. Our discussion generated empathy that would hopefully lead him to be more merciful in the future.

Show Compassion Yourself

If you want your children to be sensitive to the feelings of others, you have to be sensitive too. As you go about your daily business, your teenagers are watching you carefully. It would be foolish to think they'll listen to what you tell them and ignore what you do. You must set the standard for respecting and caring for others. When people suffer or endure hardship, take care to show the compassion you are naturally feeling for them.

Opportunities for modeling compassion are everywhere. You can make donations to charity, go out of your way to help a distressed neighbor, or display sensitivity to your own parents. Make it a point to be courteous to those around you, and your children will learn to be courteous and respectful as well. Most important, treat your children with the respect you'd like them to accord you. If they say an event is important to them, try to respond with compassion and understanding. This is not quite as easy as it sounds because sometimes your teenager's reactions seem disproportionate. We're all inclined to show compassion for tragic disappointments, but sometimes we can't relate to our children's distress over more mundane issues.

Here's how one mother displayed empathy in such a situation. One day when her son came home from school, he mentioned that a teacher had ignored his efforts to participate more in class. Although he was doing well in the subject, he interpreted the teacher's response as displeasure and felt hurt. Instead of challenging her son for overreacting, the mother shared in his distress. She commented on how upset he must have felt and related a similar experience that she had in college. In no way did she belittle his feelings. This seemed to comfort the young man, and he was able to move on to something else. His mother's sensitivity assuaged his disappointment and gave him a model to follow for times when he wants to extend similar compassion to someone else.

Here are ten tips that will help you become more sensitive to your children's feelings:

1. Remember that both normal and troubled teenagers' feelings are easily bruised. Whether or not they admit it, your comments have an impact on them. So try to think before you speak. Ask yourself how your child might react to your comments. If you feel she might interpret them negatively, try to find a better way to phrase them.

2. Put yourself in your child's shoes. Try to recall how you felt when faced with a similar situation in your youth and what you did about it. Share those feelings with your child.

3. Observe your child carefully. If she seems upset, forlorn, or detached, make a nonjudgmental comment ("I've noticed that you're quiet today").

4. Don't ask them questions that they can't answer ("Why didn't you score higher on the SATs?" or "Why didn't you make that foul shot?"). Also, try to avoid questions where the answer seems obvious ("Does your ankle hurt?" when she just sprained it a few hours ago and is still writhing in pain, or "Is something upsetting you?" when she is crying uncontrollably).

5. Help your teen to put his feelings into words. For example, you could say: "If I were in your shoes, I'd probably feel . . . ," or, "I guess you're pretty upset about that poor grade."

6. Tell them you're sorry to see them unhappy (if they've admitted it), and offer to do anything you can to help. Do bring home little things to show you care, like their favorite dessert or a rental movie.

7. Don't be too emotional or dramatic. If they're already upset, the last thing they'll want is to contend with your reactions. No doubt they'll welcome a cool head in the situation.

8. Try to follow their emotional lead. If they seem like they need to be left alone for a while, respect their wishes. On the other hand, if they seek your counsel, try to put aside what you're doing and make yourself available.

9. Provide opportunities for them to talk to you when they're ready. Pop your head in their room, stop by when they're having a snack, or approach them when they seem bored.

10. When they seem upset, put your arm around them and tell them how important they are to you. They may not respond directly, but they'll appreciate the gesture.

Hold Teenagers Accountable When They Hurt People's Feelings

Not only must you display empathy toward others; you must insist that your children do the same. Many teenagers have told me that if they'd known how their words or actions would cause pain, they would not have said or done what they did. This is why it's so important that you hold your children accountable for cruel behavior.

The following story poignantly illustrates a girl's flagrant disregard for a classmate's feelings. Let's take a look at how her parents handled her thoughtless behavior and helped her learn a useful lesson.

Sara had recently moved to Washington, D.C., from rural

North Carolina and started ninth grade in a new school. Like so many other teenagers, she wanted desperately to be accepted by the cool girls. Well aware of this, Jessica and her friends teased Sara unmercifully about her clothes, her southern accent, and her taste in music. Sara had trouble fighting back and was devastated by their criticism. One day she came home from school frantic, crying to her mother that she couldn't take it anymore.

Many teens are short on empathy because they're so preoccupied with themselves.

Word of this incident traveled quickly, and Jessica's parents found out about it a few days later. They were furious with her. They sat her down and insisted that she account for what she'd done. Her mother tried to make her see how she had hurt Sara, but Jessica stubbornly insisted that it had all been in fun.

"How can humiliating another person be fun?" her mother asked. "You may have enjoyed it, but can you imagine how she must have felt?"

"I guess I hadn't thought about that," Jessica answered quietly.

"Well, I'm sure Sara must feel horrible," replied her mother. "We expect you either to get this straightened out or to accept the consequences."

Jessica objected to having to apologize to Sara, but faced with a choice of that or being grounded for two weeks, she agreed.

The following day, Jessica reluctantly visited Sara's house. Sara listened quietly as Jessica told her she was sorry about what she and her friends had done. Tears began streaming down Sara's face. Jessica was stunned by this reaction because she really hadn't thought Sara had felt so bad. Soon both girls were sobbing and hugging each other. Jessica felt ashamed of what she had done and told Sara about something similar that had happened to her when she was younger. Afterward the girls felt a sense of camaraderie. Jessica had learned something that would stay with her for a long time: failing to take another person's feelings into account is selfish, shortsighted, and hurtful.

On occasion, your teenager may refuse to apologize, saying, "I don't care what you do to me." In this case you'll need to impose a stringent consequence and make certain that it's enforced. If the callous behavior shows no signs of abating after you've repeatedly imposed consequences, you'll want to consider more serious measures.

In most cases, change does come, but sometimes it takes longer than it did with Jessica, so you need to persist in your efforts. Many teenagers are short on empathy, not because they don't care about other people but because they're so preoccupied with themselves. They may need prodding to open their eyes and hearts. Here are some other ways you can do this.

Speak for the victim. To ensure that your children's emotional repertoire includes empathy, take on the persona of a victim. Call attention to a hurt party's feelings and talk about the incident as if you experienced it firsthand; in effect, you're the voice of the victim. The less sensitive teenagers are to the misfortune of others, the more you'll need to challenge them.

Have them face their victim. This is another way to elicit your child's empathy. As we heard in Jessica's story, facing the person harmed by thoughtlessness can have a cleansing effect. Young people who are forced to listen to a description of the pain they've caused another person often feel embarrassed and even humiliated. This reaction often occurs in trials, hearings, and meetings arranged between perpetrators of crimes and their victims. Teenagers who are guilty of inflicting physical or emotional pain on others should be held accountable for their actions and need to hear about the distressed feelings they have caused.

Have them write a letter. If circumstances prevent a face-to-face encounter, you can insist that your teenager write and send a letter of apology to someone he's hurt. Challenge him by saying that his actions were intolerable and he should feel ashamed of himself. The purpose of this letter is to show he understands the distress he's caused and assumes responsibility for it. To take this further, ask him to reverse roles, writing a letter as if he were the victim and not the offender, describing the harm done to him and the pain he felt as a result. Then discuss this letter with your teenager to be sure he understands the impact of his actions on the other person.

Personalize the incident. Of course, some antisocial youth are devoid of compassion and won't be moved by these exercises. You have to go to great lengths to penetrate their shells. Sometimes you can do this by personalizing the incident. Imagine that one teenager beats up another but refuses to take the matter seriously. You might ask, "What if that had been your little brother getting hurt by someone older than him? Then would you feel any different?" Some kids will acknowledge that they would be affected and angry.

Personalizing an incident can generate an empathic response, but in some hardened teenagers it might elicit a desire for vengeance instead. Unfortunately, this is as close as these kids can get to compassion: it's an eye-for-an-eye, tooth-for-a-tooth mentality. Such young people are at the greatest risk for a continued pattern of antisocial behavior. Their self-centered thinking lets them tune out the feelings of their victims and act on impulse. Later I'll be talking about ways to challenge these difficult youth by placing them in situations that evoke compassion. This is not easy because they've grown accustomed to their ways.

Be on the lookout for these signs of antisocial behavior that suggest your child is heading for serious trouble:

1. He shows little or no remorse for his actions. Even after he gets in trouble, he says, "So what?" "I don't care," or, "It serves them right."

2. She is unwilling and sometimes unable to identify how her victim feels. She can't seem to grasp the pain, distress, and anguish that she has caused another person.

3. He continually places blame outside himself. Regardless of the circumstances, he insists that the incident was the other party's fault. If he is in a fight, for instance, he insists that the other person started it.

4. She seems unaffected by punishment. Despite the imposition of consequences for her behavior, the pattern of misbehavior continues unabated.

5. His thinking is extremely rigid. He simply can't see why his actions are wrong.

6. She insists that her peers can do no wrong and defends them to the hilt.

7. He displays little or no incentive to change his ways. As far as he's concerned, everything is just fine.

8. She seems to derive pleasure from hurting other people. You'll often note her smiling as she describes the harm she inflicted on someone.

9. His thinking is self-centered; that is, he is concerned only about his own wants and needs. This pronounced sense of entitlement permeates his existence.

10. She places excessive emphasis on the importance of vengeance rather than conflict resolution. The way she sees it, if someone wrongs you, you get them back for it; talking about disagreements is simply not an acceptable solution.

Youth who display the above characteristics are seriously deficient in empathy, an essential deterrent to antisocial behavior. They're in need of powerful interventions to alter their destructive behavior patterns. You'll learn how to work with them in Chapters 10 and 11.

Challenge Your Teen's Self-Centered Thinking

You should expect some self-centered thinking in normal teens. Typical teens are often excessively concerned about their appearance and their immediate circle of friends, but they do not behave in a hurtful fashion to others and they do display some compassion. Unfortunately, some young people act as if the world revolved around them. They're oblivious of others' feelings and justify their own hurtful behavior by placing blame outside themselves. A teenager who is suspended from school for attacking a teacher insists that the teacher provoked him for no reason. The fact that he cursed out the teacher first was irrelevant to him; he simply can't see the role he'd played in the incident.

These self-centered kids pose a serious problem to those around them. They twist reality to suit their own needs and can't take anyone else's feelings into account. One striking characteristic of their thinking is the way they minimize their problems. They really don't think their antisocial attitude is a big deal. They blame everything on other people and invent elaborate rationalizations for their behavior.

I've heard a lot of excuses from teenagers in trouble over the past twenty years, but one in particular stands out. A young man I was counseling was caught stealing cigarettes from a convenience store. During a group meeting, we discussed the episode with his peers. One girl asked him why he'd done it, and he answered something to the effect that he'd felt like it. He couldn't understand why everyone was making such an issue out of it. The cigarettes, he said, were grossly overpriced, and he was teaching the store owners a lesson. Besides, he continued, laws prohibiting the sale of cigarettes to minors were dumb, and there was no reason to abide by them. This answer shows the characteristic egocentricity, minimization, and shifting of blame of a self-centered teen.

Self-centered thinking is especially dangerous because it gets in the way of compassion and empathy. When teenagers tune out the feelings of others, they feel free to act according to whim. This stokes their antisocial behavior and lets them evade responsibility for their actions. Challenge these masters of the excuse, as one mother did after she learned her son had taken another boy's bike and damaged it.

Mother: I got a call from David's parents yesterday. They told me you took his bike, rode off with it into the woods, and then just abandoned it after it got all scratched up.

Tim: Yeah, but it serves him right.

Mother: How can you say that?

Tim: Well, I heard he was talking about me behind my back, so I had to show him what happens when he does that. It's no big deal.

Mother: I don't consider stealing and damaging someone's property to be "no big deal." It's a serious matter.

Tim: But someone had to teach him a lesson.

Mother: What gives you the right to treat someone like that?

Tim: Well, I just felt like it. I guess I was pretty angry about the rumors he was spreading.

Mother: Can you imagine how upset—and confused—he must have felt when you took his bike away from him? How would you feel if someone did that to you?

Tim: I wouldn't like it either, but he should have thought about that before he talked about me.

Mother: Well, this type of behavior is intolerable. Your father and I expect you to call David and apologize and to be responsible for repairs. And there will be other consequences as well. You'll be grounded for the next two weeks and your allowance will go toward paying for the damages.

Tim: Do you have to make such a big deal of this?

Mother: Yes, I do. It worries me that you're not taking this incident seriously. The proper way of handling your feelings toward David would have been to call him and have a conversation about it. We'll be watching you more closely from now on. And if anything like this happens again, there will be more serious consequences.

This is one way to challenge your child on self-centered thinking. If he tries to minimize the seriousness of his actions and shift the blame, stand firm, raise the issue of empathy for the victim, and impose consequences if necessary. One conversation like this won't immediately make your child more compassionate, but it's a step in the right direction. If your teenager is harming other people, he should be carefully monitored and held accountable for future transgressions.

Make it a routine to challenge your child's self-centered thinking. Below you'll find suggestions for working on each of the excuses they offer.

- Teenagers often minimize the significance of their actions with statements like, "The kid wasn't hurt that bad when we beat him up." You can respond with, "You say it's no big deal, but I think it is. He was physically abused—teenagers are charged with assault for offenses like these. You wouldn't feel this way if you or one of your friends got beat up."
- When teenagers blame others for what they do, challenge their cop-outs. If your child says, "I ran out of class because the teacher was going to suspend me," come back with something like, "So you mean it's her fault you left class? Was there anything you might have done that provoked this? I'm sure she had strong feelings about your behavior."
- A teenager with a sense of entitlement puts undue emphasis on his own point of view, showing self-centered thinking. If he complains, "How dare my coach yell at me? I don't have to take that," you could answer, "I'd be mad too if someone disrupted my practice. You don't seem to be considering his point of view. Can you imagine how he felt?"

You'll need to be persistent about challenging your child's excuses. Try to seize every opportunity, stick to your guns, and don't let them off the hook. It may take several months before you see noticeable changes. But your efforts will usually pay off.

A Meaningful Experience

A teenager recently told me about a moving experience he'd had. He'd appeared in court for a vandalism offense and was offered the option of thirty days of community service in a nursing home or six months' probation. He reluctantly chose the nursing home assignment, having little idea what to expect. His duties were to walk around the floor and make himself available to residents who needed his help. This involved recreational activities, assistance with daily routines, and just sitting down to talk.

It wasn't long before an elderly woman attached herself to him. She was frail and lonely, and she told him about departed loved ones, played cards with him, and literally leaned on him for assistance. Every day she eagerly awaited his arrival and told him how happy she was to see him. When it came time for him to leave, she'd hug him tightly and say, "Do you have to leave now? Please promise me you're coming back tomorrow. You're all I have." The young man didn't admit it at first, but he was quite moved by this.

The month passed quickly, and his new friend grew increasingly feeble.

When his stint was over, he realized he'd grown to care deeply for her and, after some deliberation, chose to continue as a volunteer in the nursing home. The woman told him that his mother should be proud to have him as a son and that she wished he were a part of her own family. As the young man shared this with me, I was struck by his pride, compassion, and tears. His heart had been touched.

This is just the kind of experience I recommend, one that gives meaning to a young person's life, generates empathy, and builds self-esteem. This is far more effective than punishment because it builds a bridge between antisocial behavior and compassion. Teenagers don't have to be in trouble to serve others, of course. Anyone will learn from volunteer work and become richer for the experience. In fact, you can have your whole family volunteer to work on a project together. This creates the opportunity to build further bonds with one another while building self-esteem and fostering compassion.

Involve Your Teenager in Helping People in Need

We've looked at ways to develop the sensitivity and compassion of self-centered teenagers who are prone to trouble. Volunteer work with community projects, religious institutions, and service organizations can also have a powerful effect on your child's thoughtlessness, by exposing him firsthand to people less fortunate than himself.

Not surprisingly, the youth we've been talking about are not the most likely candidates for volunteer projects. Thus, if you are to guide them toward morality and compassion, you may have to initially persuade them by offering the alternative of a more stringent punishment for violating the rights of others. Or you can simply insist that they make restitution for harm they've done by doing some type of community service. Judges do this all the time. Helping out at a homeless shelter, a nursing home, a Head Start program, or a hospice lets young people do something meaningful for people in need, opens their eyes to deprivation and suffering, and gives them a boost of self-esteem. Many teenagers in serious trouble have never felt appreciated and are touched by the recognition they receive in return for this kind of service.

Empathy is not only a prerequisite for making friends; it is a deterrent to trouble. Many teenagers can be reached through the alternatives presented in the previous pages: by discussing tragic events with them, by helping them imagine how the victims feel, and most important, by living the type of life you advocate for your children. They may not be receptive at first, but if you persevere, you can plant the seeds for compassion. Caring is contagious. As young people learn to feel more for others, they'll find that they get something back.

DEVELOPING A SENSE OF MORALITY

Morality is a system of beliefs about right and wrong that governs the actions of compassionate people. It is the emotional yardstick by which all of us are measured, and grows out of our upbringing, experience, and orientation toward others. No society would survive without a moral code, so it is imperative that children internalize these beliefs when they're young, with the help of family, school, and community.

Parents are the most important architects of a child's morality. The child absorbs the beliefs her parents convey about right and wrong, good and evil, and eventually develops a conscience. Some don't learn these lessons and stray from the paths laid down for them. The foundation for morality is already laid by the teenage years, but if your child is deficient in this area, there are a number of things you can do to strengthen it.

Plead the Case for Decency

This may sound obvious, but parents should impress upon their children the value of being a decent, moral person. Ideally, we would like our teens to understand the benefits of living in a moral society and how everyone ultimately benefits from living a morally good life. Of course, this will be too abstract for the more self-centered teen; he doesn't care about the greater good because it does not directly benefit him. In these cases, parents need to point out ways in which their teens will directly benefit from leading a moral life. Reasons include (1) we feel better about ourselves when we do the right thing or help someone out, (2) we have better self-esteem and a more positive outlook on life when we know our actions are morally sound, and (3) people will think good things about us if we display sound morals, and ultimately we will reap the benefits of good actions.

Since few teenagers routinely dwell on issues of morality, you need to look for familiar examples to illustrate sound moral judgment, just as you did with empathy. These examples can come from news stories, recent movies, or lessons from history. If you ask American teenagers to name a truly good and moral person, they're likely to think of Martin Luther King, Abraham Lincoln, or Mahatma Gandhi. They would describe each of these figures as being concerned about the human condition and devoted to change. Does your teen admire these figures, or does he simply dismiss them as people from long ago? These people all struggled hard for what they believed in; does your child believe that it's worth fighting hard for what you believe in? Or does he regard their struggles as foolish and not worthwhile?

If you ask American teenagers to name someone who was immoral or evil, they're likely to think of Adolf Hitler. Most seem acutely aware of the Holocaust and agree it must never be allowed to happen again. But if you ask them how a person can grow to be evil, they're often hard-pressed to answer. It is easier to think of society's villains as inhuman monsters, but challenge your children to think more deeply about how and why people can do such terrible things.

Today's young people can, on the surface, distinguish moral behavior from immoral, and good from evil, but they may not hold themselves to high moral standards or even understand why they should. This is partly because of the moral contradictions they see around them. Unscrupulous businesspeople are praised for donating thousands of dollars to charity. Politicians make false promises to the people while serving their own interests; no one reacts very strongly anymore when a politician is caught lying. Lawyers are encouraged to use immoral tactics, so long as they win their cases. Actors, athletes, and other role models indulge in the very evils that they verbally condemn.

The message that society sends our teens is Machiavellian: the ends justify the means, and nice guys finish last. This is something that not only celebrities and leaders embody, but also everyday people, including parents. While everyone is willing to pay lip service to the importance of morals, actions speak far louder than words. It is tough enough when a teenager observes this attitude in society; it is far worse when he sees his parents embody this hypocrisy. Parents need to teach their children that morals are not for losers, nor are they something to be exercised at one's own convenience.

Be a Positive Role Model

A teenager once told me that her father had reprimanded her for cheating on an exam. The young woman asked her father how he could be such a hypocrite when he'd cheated on his income tax. Embarrassed, the father explained that was different because the money was going to support the family. After some thought, his daughter responded that her cheating on exams was probably justified as well since it would get her higher grades, admission to a good college, a good job, and the approval of her parents. Need I say more?

Practice what you preach. If you're paying for your purchases at a cash register and notice you've been given too much change, would you call it to the clerk's attention? If you dent someone's car in a parking lot, would you stop to leave a note? Either you do the right thing or you don't. All the rationalizations in the world won't change your being caught in a moral lapse. Sometimes you give in to the temptation to drive much faster than the speed limit, walk into a show or event without paying admission because there's no one at the door, or tell a lie to cover your own shortcomings. But if you complain when your teenager does something even slightly unethical, you'd better be prepared to be called a hypocrite.

Of course, nobody's perfect. To be fair, you should allow your teenagers to make mistakes along the way, as you certainly have. Try to be honest with your children, as you want them to be with you. By all means, encourage them to be decent people, but take the precaution of acknowledging your own inconsistency and make a point of modeling admirable actions like volunteering, making charitable contributions, or helping a neighbor or a friend. Finally, if you notice your children acting in a morally responsible way, let them know how proud you are of them. With luck, you might hear the same thing from them someday.

Develop Moral Reasoning

Even if you're determined to help your teenagers behave morally and decently, things can get in the way. These things include impulsiveness and age-appropriate selfishness, as well as pressure from peers. A teenager's life is filled with moral dilemmas whose solutions require an informed conscience: knowledge of someone dealing drugs, a friend with a false ID, a parent with a drinking problem, and so forth. To face these challenges, your child needs to know how to do the right thing, but that's not enough. He also needs to believe he's genuinely better off for having done it.

There is considerable research suggesting that young people who think in moral terms are more likely to act in a moral fashion. Since you're rarely around when your children confront a moral choice, discuss some hypothetical situations with them. This will at least give you an idea of how they think and a chance to challenge their moral reasoning in the abstract and raise it to a higher level. To illustrate, I'll share a moral dilemma I pose to young people I work with. I ask them to put themselves in the protagonist's shoes and come up with the right thing to do.

Here's the situation: a teenage girl is at home one night when her parents get into a huge argument. Her father, who has been drinking, is angry and aggressive. Her mother is furious too, shouting at her husband for being a poor provider. Before the girl knows it, her father strikes her mother and knocks her to the ground. The mother screams that she won't take this abuse from her husband and calls the police. Witnessing this battle, the young woman has a difficult decision to make. She knows the police will question her about what happened, and she needs to decide how much to tell them. After all, she has a good relationship with both her parents and doesn't want to hurt either of them. But she also knows abuse is wrong and something has to be done.

When I ask teenagers what they would do in her place, I get some interesting answers. Some say she should leave the house before the police arrive so she can avoid the decision altogether. I challenge this response because it's a cop-out. Others think the mother got what she deserved for provoking her husband! The ones who say this are clearly functioning at an early stage of moral development: anything goes as far as they're concerned, and there's no need to abide by the norms of society. They too must be challenged on their shallow interpretation and asked if

Some Topics for Raising the Issue of Moral Dilemmas with Your Teenager

1. Cheating on exams: should they turn a fellow student in if they notice that person violating the school's honor code?

2. Election campaigns: should a candidate fight dirty, that is, seek out and publicize sordid information (which is sometimes unsubstantiated) from an opponent's past?

3. Paying income tax: is it justified to report less income than you've made in order to save money, and then rationalize that the government can spare it?

4. Harassing someone who's different from or weaker than yourself (for example, in culture, ethnicity, age, or physical condition): is it fair to take advantage of people who are in the minority or who may be unable to defend themselves?

5. Turning in a friend who's dealing drugs: when someone's placing others in danger, should you blow the whistle, or turn your back?

6. Finding someone's credit card: it may be tempting to hold on to it or even use it, but it's not yours, so what do you do?

7. Starting a terrible rumor to get back at someone: they'll never find out you started it, and if they do, you'll just deny it.

8. In a tennis game, calling a ball out (that was in) to win a point: it seems like it's no big deal, but is there a moral principle at stake— the importance of honesty?

they would say that if their own mother were being hurt.

Teens whose moral reasoning is a little further developed sometimes ask who has treated the daughter better, her father or mother? They're trying to determine whom she owes more to or, worse, who might give her a better deal if she takes that parent's side. This is clearly a self-serving interpretation and also needs to be challenged. Teens should be made to understand that a girl whose mother has been hurt and whose father has been drinking shouldn't use the situation to gain advantage.

Finally, some teenagers see this story from an appropriate moral perspective. They comment that abuse is wrong under any circumstances and that the father may be an alcoholic. They see only one defensible action: the girl must tell the truth when the police come and let the chips fall where they may. Some go so far as to add that if the father really cares about his daughter, he'll understand that she's doing it for his own good. This may be the only way he will get the help he needs.

You may find it fascinating to have such discussions with your own teenager. You can initiate these conversations by inquiring about their take on any event that reflects moral issues. If you've convinced them that their opinions are important, they'll probably respond to your overtures and the conversation can be a springboard into exploring their own moral dilemmas. I encourage you to share with them your own struggles over difficult decisions and what you've learned from your mistakes. Don't condemn them if their initial answers are shallow and lacking in thought; instead, challenge their responses with further questions. You want your children to feel safe enough to talk about confusing situations in their own lives. Ideally, they'll use you as a resource when they need to decide on the right course of action.

Promote Guilt in the Service of Decency

When your children commit an immoral offense that hurts other people, you want them to feel bad afterward. As I've said, empathy induces guilt. This doesn't mean you should routinely subject your children to guilt trips. At its worst, this is ineffective and causes resentment. But there's a lot to be gained by arousing pangs of conscience in your child. When you induce your teenagers to think about the impact of their behavior on other people, they can feel remorse, apologize, and resolve not to do it again.

One of the best ways to gauge young people's sincerity is to observe whether they express remorse. Juvenile court judges have learned this lesson well. They listen carefully to testimony and try to determine whether or not offenders take their actions seriously. Then they ask themselves whether the teenager genuinely feels bad about hurting someone or denies the significance of what he's done. Finally they think, Are this kid's words sincere, or are they measured and shallow? As parents, you must also learn to read these cues. The guiltier your children feel when they do wrong, the less likely they are to repeat their actions.

When your teen has hurt someone, or been caught in a lie or a breach of trust, follow these suggestions to plant the seeds for appropriate guilt. Stick to your guns and don't let them off the hook until you're satisfied that they get it.

- Insist that they consider their impact on their victim. As we have discussed, make certain that your teenager is aware of the distress he caused and can repeat it back to you. This includes both the physical and emotional repercussions of their actions. When you have these dialogues, don't allow your child to rush through them saying, "I know, I know." It's not lip service that you're after; it's genuine empathy.

- In explicit terms, tell them why they should feel ashamed of themselves. Challenge them on their exploitation of others to make themselves feel better, and tell them that they've let you down. If they don't feel ashamed of what they've done, you'll need to monitor their actions. If their actions become extreme and they still show no remorse, seek additional resources to help you address the problem.

- Refer back to the moral codes you've taught them over the years. Stress the importance of respecting the rights of others. Reiterate your beliefs, and make sure they understand why you try to live by them. Stress the importance of moral codes and challenge their violation of societal norms.

- Remind your children of how fortunate they are. This seems trite, but you'll need to get the point across. Tell your teens how fortunate they are to live in a democracy with a strong economy, to have a home, and to be with people who love them. Point out the opportunities available to them if they are willing to make a reasonable effort. And if their immoral behavior is seriously hurting them, try to expose them to what's in store if they continue on that path.

- Frame their insensitive actions as immature and selfish, emphasizing their disregard for the feelings of others. Don't allow them to confuse bravado with courage. Insist that they are self-centered and acting like a younger child. And challenge them if they say they want to be treated like an adult when they're not acting like one.

It's going to take time to get your teenager to experience guilt after they've done something wrong. The lengthier their pattern of misbehavior, the longer you'll need to work on these issues. You can have an impact on a first offender in a few weeks, but if there's a persistent pattern of antisocial behavior, you'll need to spend at least several months working on it, and there's no guarantee of success. See Chapter 11 for a discussion of more seriously troubled youth.

Hold Them Accountable for Immoral Behavior

When your teenager does something wrong, there should be a consequence, preferably one that serves a useful purpose. That is, the consequence should ensure that she feels so bad about what she's done that she won't want to do it again. I've talked about the value of having the offender face the victim. Accountability sometimes requires going further and making sure she understands why her actions were wrong.

In this example, a mother questions her daughter's explanation for taking an item from a church bazaar.

Mother: Melissa, where did you get that belt you're wearing?

Melissa: Someone left it on the table where I was working yesterday.

Mother: Wasn't it for sale?

Melissa: Yeah, but no one bought it. It was just lying there.

Mother: So you just decided to bring it home with you.

Melissa: Oh, Mom, I'm sure they won't miss it. Besides, I was helping out at the bazaar.

Mother: Maybe no one noticed, but I don't like the idea.

Melissa: It's really no big deal. It's not like I stole it or anything.

Mother: You did steal it! And it's the principle of the thing that bothers me.

Melissa: What principle?

Mother: Why don't you tell me? That's what I want you to come up with.

Melissa: You mean why I shouldn't have done it?

Mother: Exactly.

Melissa: This is really stupid.

Mother: No it's not. I think what you did was wrong. Can't you see why?

Melissa: Well, I guess I could have asked someone's permission.

Mother: That's part of it. What else?

Melissa: I don't know. You mean because it didn't belong to me?

Mother: That's the point I'm trying to make. Maybe no one would have minded if you'd asked if you could have it.

Melissa: But I didn't.

Mother: Melissa, do you understand why I'm saying this?

Melissa: I guess so. It wasn't right to just assume I could take it.

Mother: Now I think you understand. There's something I'd like you to do.

Melissa: What?

Mother: Straighten this thing out on your own.

Melissa: How?

Mother: You tell me.

Melissa: Well, I guess I could call Mrs. Jones. She was in charge of the table. I can tell her I took the belt home and ask her if it's okay.

Mother: That's a good idea.

Melissa's thoughtless act offered the mother an opportunity to teach her daughter a moral lesson. It's the kind of thing that can happen with any teenager. Hold your children accountable for even minor infractions in order to prevent major ones. Through moral accountability you can create an enduring understanding of moral behavior.

THE IMPORTANCE OF VALUES

Values are closely intertwined with empathy and morality; in fact, "morals" and "values" are often used interchangeably. But the two are not the same. Morality distinguishes right from wrong, good from evil. Morals are generally viewed in terms of black and white; even though different people hold different moral codes, each moral code is clear as to what is right and what is wrong. Values are the specific principles or qualities that are considered valuable and important. Values are more subjective than morals because certain people put greater emphasis on qualities that, for whatever reason, are more important to them. If values can be visualized as black and white (with or without shades of gray), morals can be visualized as the North Pole or the North Star; something fixed by which we can orient ourselves.

As they mature, your children need to develop their own set of values because you won't always be there to guide them. These values will define who they are and what they believe in. These values influence our actions as powerfully as do our morals. A teenager who lacks a basic belief system is like a raft without a paddle, floating whichever way the stream flows. If you succeed in passing on a value system that will serve as an internal guide for your children in your absence, they'll be well on the way to becoming decent, caring people who are mindful of the rights of others.

It's not hard to spot teenagers with a weak value system. Their behavior seems random and unfocused, and their amorality makes them self-centered, immature, and impulsive. They are easily led into antisocial and illegal activities because they are susceptible to peer pressure. Teens without values are usually followers, seeking the approval of anyone who will accept them. Teens with a well-developed value system, on the other hand, are less likely to get into trouble. Five basic human values that every healthy teen should possess are honesty, respect, generosity, courage, and forgiveness.

Honesty

This is perhaps the most important determinant of one's behavior toward other people. Teenagers who value honesty are typically sincere, trustworthy, and likable. They take responsibility for what they do and treat others with respect—although all teenagers have occasional lapses. This is complicated by the fact that many people stretch the truth a little, even though they agree that it's dishonest to tell an outright lie. For example, your daughter might not consider it dishonest to buy a formal dress from a store, wear it one evening, and return it the next day. Your children have probably seen you pretend to a salesperson that you're interested in buying a computer when you're actually just comparing different models for a future purchase. These situations can be interpreted in several ways. Some would call any misleading behavior dishonest, while others would think of it as pragmatic in certain situations. In fact, such behavior is probably not hurting anyone, but it is taking advantage of a situation. You'll need to stress that it's the moral principle behind the action that counts: honesty should govern all your daily actions.

The best way to raise an honest teenager is to be an honest parent. Your behavior and beliefs strongly influence your children in this area, so be sure to create an environment in which honesty is valued. Set a good example by keeping your promises and answering your children's questions forthrightly. They're watching you carefully and drawing conclusions from your behavior about what is right. As I've suggested, if you're inconsistent, your "justifiable" exceptions can confuse the issue.

Encourage your children to be truthful and help them see that they'll be better off for it both spiritually and practically. People will trust and respect them more and they'll have the pleasure of a clear conscience. If you also prepare yourself for your teenager's slips on the way to maturity, you can use them as teaching opportunities. When a young person confesses spontaneously to wrongdoing, acknowledge his courage before dealing with the problem.

Young people need to know that honesty is appreciated but won't always mitigate the consequence of poor decisions. Sometimes you may wonder if your child is being honest with you when you ask her for information. She may give you a vague answer when you ask, for example, where she was the previous night. Some parents would say, "Look, we just want you to be honest with us. We won't punish you if you tell us the truth." This is a useful approach, but some young people take advantage of it, interpreting it to mean that as long as they confess to wrongdoing, their parents will let them slide.

Respect

Honesty is one form of respect for others. Respect also involves politeness, awareness, and an open mind; it means to accept people as they are, including their ethnic background, socioeconomic status, and intellectual ability. Reinforce this acceptance by arranging your teen's participation in recreational activities and field trips where they'll meet different kinds of people. You can also tap the media for inspiration.

Parents should create an atmosphere of respect between themselves and their teens. Parents have the right to demand respect from their children, as long as they exhibit behavior that deserves their children's respect and as long as they will treat their child in kind. Respect goes a long way; it will enable your teen to understand and accept your wishes when they run counter to his immediate wishes.

Rudeness is far more prevalent and accepted today than in previous generations. Television and movies model and glorify rude behavior and irreverent humor. Do not allow the media to determine your teen's behavior. The wisecracking repartee on *South Park* or any number of sitcoms may be funny to your child, but he must understand that it would not be suitable in real life.

"Respect" has become something of a buzzword lately, so your child will probably ask for it even if he's done nothing to deserve it. It's up to you to teach your child the meaning of the word as well as how to behave respectfully and to earn respect for themselves.

Respect is an indispensable character trait. Promote the Golden Rule of treating others with the same respect you want for yourself. If you can instill this value in your children, they'll respect themselves as well.

Generosity

You want your teens to look outside themselves and their own little world, so you should look for ways to teach them to be generous toward others. Generosity means being selfless rather than selfish. It also means that teens appreciate the good things they have (money, possessions, friends, love) and, through compassion for others, wish to share these things.

Generosity involves giving freely of yourself to others. Whether it's your time, money, or a specific skill, there are many opportunities around us to show generosity. Encourage your teenagers to share what they have: her gift for working with little children, his mastery of outdoor skills, or her collection of postcards from around the world. Even a limited amount of time spent in sharing helps to develop a generous spirit.

I've already discussed the value of volunteer work (such as working in an animal shelter, tutoring, or coaching) and want to emphasize the spirit in which it's done. I know families that practice a tradition of giving during the holiday season. They collect old books, games, and CDs and head as a family to the local children's hospital to make their donation in person. Such acts of kindness are always well received.

Young people should learn to offer their assistance because it's the decent thing to do, not because it's required of them. Certainly, you'll need to set the stage early on, but the goal is to teach your children to act generously because they'll do good for others and will feel like a better person for it. Anything that helps teenagers see the value of selflessly giving something of themselves to someone or some cause is a worthwhile activity. In many cases, a teenager's time is the most precious gift they have to offer—so encourage them to be generous with it.

Courage

When I think of courage, I think of the lion in *The Wizard of Oz*. His courage was in him all along, and he simply had to find it. This is how I like to address the issue of courage with teenagers. I tell them courage is an interesting mixture of pride, guts, and independence of thought. Courageous people aren't afraid to speak their minds. Their convictions are important to them, and they're ready to defend someone else if necessary. I present this as a healthy expression of risk taking in the service of decency, which always appeals to them.

Some teenagers might consider dangerous behavior a form of bravery, but I don't buy that. On the contrary, it's cowardice. People who look for shortcuts or illicit ways to get what they want are afraid to do things the hard way, afraid to fail, and unsure of themselves. I never hesitate to remind young people of this, and I urge you to do the same.

Make sure that your children don't confuse courage with bravado either. Acting tough, intimidating others, and denying one's true feelings are often a smoke screen for inner unrest. Truly courageous people, on the other hand, don't need to impress others with their actions. In the movie *Good Will Hunting*, the main character, Will Hunting, is a janitor with a brilliant mind. Initially he displays bravado, indifference, and a jaundiced attitude toward academics and the world around him. Will is fearful of closeness with others and revealing his real self. But through his work with a caring psychologist, he is challenged to utilize his abilities and find out who he really is. Will ultimately develops a trusting relationship with his therapist—facing his fears and finding the courage to move on, make a fresh start, and pursue a meaningful relationship with a young woman who loves him. It's a touching portrayal of the journey from bravado to courage and maturity.

It's your job to help your children see that courage comes from within and grows with experience. Encourage it early in your child's life so he'll develop the conviction that he can act on his own behalf. As he grows older, opportunities to exercise his resolve will increase. He'll often face situations in which doing the right thing will mean going against his peer group. If you've taught him to value his integrity, he'll be able to stick to his guns.

Your own acts of courage are perhaps the greatest inspiration to your teenagers. I recall one young man proudly telling me about his mother's struggle with cancer. She'd been ill for several years and was determined to survive against the odds. There were many times when she felt miserable, but she continued her daily responsibilities despite her discomfort. Somehow she was able to keep a cheerful disposition throughout her ordeal.

The boy visited his mother in the hospital following surgery and was amazed that the first thing she did was to ask how the family was getting along. How odd, he thought, that she should be concerned about them when she was going through such suffering. Sitting in my office, he said he now understood that this was truly an act of courage and unselfishness. Sadly, his mother passed away the next year, but she left him the legacy of her courage and inspiration.

There are more everyday examples of young people's courage all around you. Standing up for someone in trouble, holding a friend's hand while she gets stitches (especially if you're a queasy sort), and admitting to being wrong are all brave in their own way. Recognize these actions as courageous and call them to your children's attention. Encourage even small risks in their lives.

Teenagers are often faced with situations that frighten them, such as presenting papers in class or asking someone out on a date. When you help them face their fears, you promote a very useful type of courage.

Forgiveness

This final value is especially important because many teenagers take even the smallest slights to heart. When they're hurt, they can carry around a grudge for a long time. It's not unusual for them to mobilize their friends to blacklist a person who's insulted or humiliated them. The more troubled the teens are, the more intense their hard feelings. They store their pain, stay angry, and want to get revenge. As you know by now, excessive anger can lead to violence. Consequently, these teenagers must not only deal with their anger but also learn to forgive those who have wronged them.

Forgiveness is a value stressed by every moral and religious tradition, but despite the high priority placed upon it, people continue to hang on to their resentments. Forgiveness is especially difficult to teach because it has to come from within. You can talk about it easily enough with your teenagers, but that doesn't always help them let go of their anger.

If you want your young person to be more forgiving, model forgiveness yourself, and watch out for mixed messages. If you tell your child to forgive someone who's offended him and you haven't spoken to your brother for years because of a family feud, you're clouding the issue of forgiveness. Your child should know that it's a last resort to sever a relationship with someone who has hurt you, even though you do have a right to protect yourself if your trust is continually violated. And if you constantly remind her about a mistake she made for which she apologized, what are you telling her about forgiveness? You don't have to overlook all her mistakes, but you should give her additional chances.

Another way to model forgiveness is to teach your child to say he's sorry. Apologizing requires understanding the other person's motives and the circumstances that led them to do what they did. Everyone makes mistakes and must take responsibility for them. When one person apologizes, it puts the other in a position to forgive. The words "I'm sorry" and "I forgive you" allow relationships to flourish and endure. This is not something to be taken lightly. When your teenagers make mistakes, demand sincere apologies and don't accept mere lip service to satisfy your demands.

The hardest part of forgiveness is learning to forgive people who have hurt us who do not apologize or feel sorry. Self-esteem is the key to this type of forgiveness. This may be a difficult process for your teen because if she has been hurt by someone, her ego is likely to be bruised. Help her rediscover pride and confidence in herself; only then will she be able to rise above the hurtful actions of others.

In this chapter I've looked at how empathy, morality, and values determine good character. Empathy lets us step into someone else's shoes, moral development governs our perceptions of right and wrong, and a strong value system determines who we are and how we choose to lead our lives.

Parents provide the building blocks for these essential traits. Through your role modeling, your teens come to see that virtue is more than mere words. Ongoing discussions of events stimulate thought and challenge preconceived notions. You must hold your children accountable for their actions and make sure they learn from their mistakes. Finally, you should guide them toward experiences that soften their hearts and strengthen their resistance to adverse influences. Doing so will encourage them to stay focused on productive activities and keep them away from trouble.

CHAPTER SEVEN

RESISTING NEGATIVE PEER PRESSURE

"I get depressed when I'm not around my friends. I feel like I'm missing out on something."

"You know, you just gotta do what the boys are doing. I mean, show them that you're in."

"It's not what's right that matters; it's what's cool!"

"I never buy a CD without checking with my friends first. I don't want my friends making fun of my music."

"I almost always go along with the crowd. I wouldn't want to be the one to spoil the fun for everyone else."

No **influence in your teenager's life** is as powerful as peer pressure. At its best, it can mobilize his energy, motivate him to strive for success, and encourage him to conform to a healthy group norm. At its worst, peer pressure can impair good judgment and fuel risk-taking behavior, drawing a child away from the family and positive influences and luring him into dangerous activities.

No matter what kind of peer pressure your children face, they must learn how to balance the value of going along with the crowd against the importance of making their own decisions. And you must ensure that your teen is comfortable with himself so that he will be able to achieve that balance. I have found in my practice that the more comfortable a teen is with his identity, the less susceptible he will be to negative peer pressure—a force that almost always leads kids to some form of trouble. Don't let anyone, including your teen, tell you that negative peer pressure is not your business. It most definitely is, and you must find a way to teach your teenager how to deal with it maturely and responsibly.

Peer pressure comes in many different forms. I find that when most parents think of peer pressure they imagine variations on the type of situation where a bunch of teens are drinking or smoking something while one abstainer is being taunted that "everyone's doing it." This is only one way in which peer pressure can exert itself.

Peer pressure usually depends on the kind of peer group your child hangs out with—or the one she aspires to. Some teens run with the popular crowd. They may worry that not going along with their friends will make them outcasts or at least less popular. Then there are kids who are not in the popular group but would like to be. These teens are likely to go along with things in the hopes that it will buy them the acceptance and elevated social status they crave. There are other groups where one strong personality dominates and that person uses his or her influence over the others to lead the group into trouble. And there are kids who are not popular per se but have their own cliques. They are usually known by stereotypical labels: punks, geeks, deadheads, burnouts, and so on. Kids who are a part of these groups do not worry about what the mainstream kids think, but they worry intensely what members of their own group do. While they may think (or look like) they are bucking trends, they may be succumbing to a different set of pressures.

WHY PEER PRESSURE IS SO POWERFUL

As I've mentioned before, the very nature of adolescence compels teens to keep a close eye on their peers. They are struggling to define their own identities, and because they're not yet sure who they are, they're self-conscious and curious about how other people behave. It's natural for them to try to understand themselves by looking at their friends to see how others are resolving the same issues.

Even little kids worry about making friends and being liked. But during adolescence, these fears intensify. Adolescence brings with it so much awkwardness and uncertainty, as teens find their bodies, interests, and priorities all changing at once. Belonging to a group of friends affirms their self-worth and supports them as they negotiate the rocky path toward adulthood. As they distance themselves from their parents, they increasingly use their friends as their primary confidants and rely upon their advice and support. Naturally, close friends are well suited to this role because those are the people most likely to rubber-stamp the individual's feelings and patiently listen to his or her ruminations on life. In a normal situation, a close group of friends offers a sounding board as well as camaraderie and solace. But in a bad situation, teens adhere to their friends' bad or ignorant advice and opinions instead of thinking for themselves or seeking a more informed opinion. Some teenagers fail to realize when they have become excessively dependent on their friends in a way that robs them of their independence and individuality. In these cases their friends have become a crutch—a way for teens to avoid making their own decisions and developing their own personality and tastes.

THE EFFECTS OF PEER PRESSURE

It's not surprising that peer pressure has such an impact on your teenager's clothes, language, attitudes, and behavior. Even reasonably independent teens are not immune to the culture of conformity. Whether you like it or not, the opinions of your teenager's peers often carry more weight than yours. After all, who does she spend most of her time with? Trust me: she's not concerned about whether you think she's cool. But if one of her friends should look askance at something she does or says, that could make her crumple in a heap of insecurity.

All teenagers will be exposed to peer pressure at one time or another. Parents may worry about their children's susceptibility to adverse influences, but most teenagers seem to have a sense of when things have gone too far and when they should make their own decision rather than just going along with the crowd. And usually the influence of the peer group gradually subsides as young people mature.

Most teens I talk to don't necessarily see peer pressure as a bad thing; it's just a part of their lives. You've probably been struck by the change in your child's behavior when his friends are around. It's as if he has a special personality reserved for his

Types of Peer Pressure

1. Positive peer pressure. Any situation in which peers support and encourage constructive actions for one another is positive peer pressure. This is the type of age-appropriate peer pressure that we want to encourage. For example: team members push one another to get psyched up for a big game, or a friend encourages your teen to stay home and study hard for an upcoming exam.

2. Neutral peer pressure. This is the naturally occurring peer pressure to go along with the crowd in a way that's not harmful to others. This type of pressure occurs frequently in the teenage years and should not be considered a problem. For example: your son's friends encourage him to go with them to the movie they're all dying to see, or a friend tells your daughter that everyone's going to the football game Friday night and asks if she's coming too.

3. Negative peer pressure. This undesirable peer pressure to do something that places a teen in danger or is hurtful to others is definitely cause for concern. For example: your daughter's boyfriend encourages her to try using ecstasy and insists it will be fun, or your son's friends ask him to bring his baseball bat when they gather to drive around town so that they can knock down people's mailboxes.

All teenagers will succumb to peer pressure every now and then; it's perfectly normal. But make certain that your child can resist negative influences because consistently taking excessive risks and engaging in hurtful behavior suggests a more serious problem.

peer group. Since being cool earns them status, teens devote a lot of their energy to this pursuit.

What's considered cool and what's uncool varies widely from year to year and from school to school. Cool behavior can range from dressing in trendy styles to being good at a certain sport to being sarcastic to parents; uncool behavior often includes displaying excessive affection and obedience toward parents, reaching out to an unpopular classmate, and expressing interest in schoolwork.

While not all teenagers follow the cool/uncool code of their social set, they're certainly aware of it. Many feel they have to act a certain way because it's expected of them. That explains why they put on a show for their friends, going out of their way to do things that would never be tolerated in their own homes. It's all to gain acceptance from their peer group.

It usually takes some convincing to get your teenager to understand that peer pressure can be dangerous. If you talk to him openly, observe his behavior carefully, and listen to him non-judgmentally, you'll begin to understand the pressure he's under. He may be coaxed to drink, smoke cigarettes, and use drugs, encouraged to cut school, dared to join his friends in other risky activities, or expected to be cruel to unpopular kids. Teens are able to weather this onslaught if their resolve is strong, but it helps them to know that you understand the enormous pressures they face.

Parents Talk About Peer Pressure

"I can't stand the kids my son hangs out with. They all look suspicious to me. I'm never sure what they're up to, and I'm afraid he'll just go along with anything they say. I don't know what to do about it."

"Our daughter spends most of her time worrying about what her friends will think. The clothes she wears, the food she eats, the movies she sees . . . everything she does seems to be for an audience. We try to talk her out of it sometimes, but she won't listen."

"Peer pressure is probably our greatest fear. We like to think our kid is informed about all the dangers out there, but you never know. It just takes one convincing teenager and a moment of weakness, and boom, he's in trouble."

Do these voices sound familiar? Most of you know very well how susceptible your teenager is to outside influences. You worry a lot about it, and with good reason. There are so many ways for today's youth to get into trouble. Alcohol and drugs are readily available, the pressure to be sexually active is strong, pornography and hate group propaganda are available on the Internet, firearms can be bought by almost anyone, and having fun sometimes lurches consciously or unconsciously into hurting other people. This gives parents a lot to worry about.

You desperately want your children to use restraint and good judgment when they're tempted to do inappropriate or illegal things, but this can be very difficult for a teenager craving acceptance. Therefore you have to take an active role in helping your teen develop a tough skin toward peer pressure. You can't supervise them every hour of the day, so you have to prepare them for making decisions on their own. If you've discussed the risks with them, instilled in them a sense of pride, and raised them with a solid set of values, they'll be more likely to withstand the pressures they'll face and more likely to choose friends who are positive influences. They might even be better off for the experience of resisting challenges.

WHAT MAKES TEENS SUSCEPTIBLE?

Certainly, all teenagers are susceptible to some degree of peer pressure. They want to be accepted by their friends and will make certain accommodations to ensure they are. But most have the sense to know when a situation endangers them or is cruel toward others and will draw the line when they have to. Troubled teens, however, seem unable and/or unwilling to do this. They repeatedly fail to exercise good judgment and ignore their parents' admonitions.

Without question, the more vulnerable a teenager is to negative peer influence, the more liable he is to get into trouble. Peer approval becomes an addiction for the teen at risk: he simply can't get along without it. His feelings of anger, insecurity, and alienation leave him desperate for companionship at any cost. It's no surprise that troubled teens often seek out the company of other estranged, angry, and destructive kids. Their superficial bonding takes on the aura of a cult, a tight group united against the outside world whose members rely heavily on one another for support, acceptance, and security. Unfortunately, when teens in a group stop thinking for themselves and discard the values they've been taught, they're usually headed for trouble.

Children who are prone to negative peer pressure are usually affected by the following factors.

Poor Self-Esteem

Young people with poor self-esteem are typically more susceptible to outside influence than others. They look to their friends to provide them the support and acceptance that they cannot find within themselves. Many have experienced rejection in the past, so they are eager to please. Often they'll do anything to gain acceptance or keep their place in a group. They rely on their friends to make decisions for them, don't take responsibility for their actions, and often find themselves in compromising situations. All of this results from their inability (or unwillingness) to assert themselves and say no when they should.

One teenage girl, Karen, was desperate to be one of the popular girls, so she invited everyone over for a big party on a Saturday night when her parents were out of town. Her classmates showed up en masse, with tons of beer and liquor. They broke windows, carelessly stained carpets with spilled beer and cigarette ashes, and ruined furniture, all of which cost her furious parents hundreds and hundreds of dollars. Karen pretended she was having fun, but she was really miserable at how her "friends" were destroying her house. But she never asked anyone to stop or stood up for herself. She achieved some notoriety for her wild party, but no more popularity than she'd had before the party, and probably lost some peoples' respect.

Feeling Unwanted

Many teens feel rejection by their peers or from their family members. Some have felt this way since they were small children. Their parents may have been emotionally undemonstrative,

How to Tell When Peer Pressure Is Too Great

- She worries about losing her friends if she doesn't go along with the crowd.

- He does something that is very uncharacteristic of him (for example, he and his friends bully a younger child, although he has always been gentle with kids).

- He abandons his school efforts, stating that studying hard is for geeks and losers, and he and his friends would rather have fun.

- She drastically changes her mannerisms and language or adopts an artificial personality to imitate someone cool.

- She drastically changes her appearance, which she had previously been satisfied with.

- You suspect he's hanging around with members of a gang, cult, or other unhealthy organization.

overextended and exhausted, or wrapped up in their own problems. And alienated teens have often felt shunned by their peers since they started school. They failed to make friends at an early age because of their anger, insensitivity, tactlessness, or self-centeredness, and got used to being the outsider. By now these teens have probably given up trying to be liked and understood by their peers or family members. But they still long for friendship and acceptance, and they'll usually join any group that will tolerate them. Their years of anger and alienation make them eager to cause trouble, and that's what these groups of lost souls usually enjoy. The news in recent years is full of stories of children like this whose feelings of anger and rejection drive them to appalling violence. In most of these cases, such dramatic outcomes could have been avoided.

Teens involved in gangs are a particularly extreme example of excessive peer pressure. Often such teens forgo their own identities to adopt the characteristics of the gang members. Many report family histories of rejection, neglect, and even abuse. The gang offers them a powerful sense of belonging and security, so they readily embrace the strict rules, closed-mindedness, and norms of bravado, violence, and antisocial behavior. You'll learn to identify signs that your child is gang-involved in Chapter 10, and what to do about it. Cult-involved teens (those in groups of Satanists, skinheads, and extreme religions, for example) pose a similar problem. They are highly susceptible to peer influence and often lose their ability to think for themselves. In these cases it's unlikely that you'll be able to wean them away from the negative influence on your own. If your child is involved with a gang or a cult, you'll need outside assistance to break him away from his unhealthy dependence. See the Appendix for specific resources to help you to face these challenges.

WHO'S A BAD INFLUENCE?

The conventional wisdom is that undesirable peers are the ones who get your children into trouble. If only things were that simple! It's a real challenge to determine which of your children's friends really put them at risk. Obviously the ones who drink too much, behave aggressively, play truant from school, and violate social norms qualify as personae non gratae. But what about teenagers with long hair, body piercing, and unconventional ideas? Is your child risking anything hanging around them?

You have to make these judgments based on more than appearance. I've known many polite, well-dressed, and seemingly responsible teenagers who are sneaky and contemptuous of adult authority under the surface. I think of them as Eddie Haskells—Wally Cleaver's friend on *Leave It to Beaver*, whose smooth façade seemed to belie a more troubled interior. These kids are every bit as dangerous as their more conspicuous counterparts. Try to judge your children's peers by their track records, not their clothes or hairstyles.

Be careful not to leap to false conclusions based on surface details. Unless you have reasonably concrete evidence of another teenager's wrongdoing, you may be better off letting your child make her own decisions. Your suspicions could drive her toward an even more negative peer group, and if you keep criticizing her choice of friends, she'll soon stop listening to you. One young man told me, "My parents are so paranoid about my friends that they check on everything I do." He became so angry about their intrusion that he stopped following their rules. "If they're so convinced I'm going to get in trouble," he said, "I might as well just do it."

My advice is to bite your tongue if your teenager's friends don't look like poster children for the Boy Scouts until you learn more about them. If they stay out of trouble, get their school-work done, and support one another, leave well enough alone. By the same token, if your child's friends are constantly in trouble, no matter how clean-cut they look, you have every right to intervene.

INSULATING TEENAGERS FROM NEGATIVE PEER PRESSURE

Everything I've said in this book should help you keep your children out of trouble. Open communication will allow them to talk to you when they need to; appropriate limits will help them develop better self-control and gradually take on responsibility; and grooming them for independence will help them make their own decisions instead of just going along with the crowd.

But the most powerful resistance to peer pressure comes from within. Young people who have positive self-esteem and well-developed values are far less likely to feel pressure. They trust their own judgment and stick to their beliefs. They can take their peers' opinions into consideration without feeling compelled to follow them.

These pressure-resistant teenagers seem to flourish in other ways as well. They're more self-directed and they have interests that occupy their spare time. As a result, they don't rely solely on their peers for approval and entertainment. Their identities are well established and they do things that are in their own best interests.

The rest of this chapter will focus on what you can do to keep your child safe from negative influences. While there is no guarantee that your child will be immune from peer pressure, these measures will ensure you've done your best. And if your best is not enough to protect your especially difficult teen, you'll read about more restrictive alternatives later in this book.

Be Informed

Make sure that you know what's going on out there. Learn the facts about alcohol, drugs, and sexually transmitted diseases and make sure your information stays current (you'll find information resources in the Appendix of this book). Try to be an astute observer of the teen culture that surrounds your child. It's your job to find out about your teenagers' friends and keep informed about your child's whereabouts. Don't hesitate to ask them where they're going, who they're going with, and when they'll be home. Stay in contact with other parents, and use your neighborhood resources (schools, health clinics, public information agencies, and religious institutions).

It is of paramount importance that your children know the facts about critical health issues (these are addressed in detail in Chapter 8). Misinformation can easily fuel a teenager's susceptibility to negative peer influence. I've had many teens tell me all sorts of misinformation they learned from their friends (coffee will sober you up to drive home if you've drunk too much; ecstasy is a completely safe drug; you can't get pregnant if you use the withdrawal method; smoking pot is not addictive). They simply assumed that their friends knew what they were talking about—but that's not always the case.

In summary, you should be well aware of the importance of good judgment by this point. Accurate information insulates young people from poor decisions. When they can readily identify their friends' misguided actions, they are far less likely to succumb to their influence. While teenagers receive some health education from the schools, don't count on the educational system to impart values, support, and appropriate limits; that's your job. I've never had parents express regret over taking an active interest in their child's life.

Invite Their Friends to Your Home

Teenagers place a great value on their friendships, whether their peers are good or bad influences from your perspective. Naturally, you'd like your child to avoid undesirable peers and spend time only with ones of whom you approve, but this won't always be the case. So if your child is subject to negative peer influence, you may want to consider inviting the suspicious friends to your house.

This suggestion may sound like asking for trouble, but let me explain. You can be sure that your teenager will find a way to hang out with his friends one way or another. The more defiant and troubled teen will even sneak out in the middle of the night if he has to. Furthermore, when he feels like you're rejecting his peer group, he may consider this a rejection of himself as well. So give him the benefit of the doubt and say that you'd like to meet his friends and get to know them better. If he's reluctant to bring them home, ask why. He may hem and haw, but should agree if you reassure him that they'd be free to just hang out without you hovering over them.

Of course, if he refuses to invite them over, you have cause for suspicion, but don't expect him to tell you why. Teenagers are very protective of their friends. Thus, you'll need to seek other sources to learn what's going on. Talk to other parents or the school, for instance, to learn more about their friends. If you learn that these friends are usually in serious trouble, you have every right to ban them from your home indefinitely; but if you get a vague or mixed message, you're better off inviting them and trying to draw your own conclusions.

But assuming they're not bad kids, you may have to look further for an explanation of your child's reluctance. Perhaps he's embarrassed by your behavior or afraid you'll ask too many questions. If so, discuss this with him. Teenagers are usually happy to get their complaints out in the open. Whether or not their gripes are legitimate, take them seriously. Needless to say, if your child is right and your behavior really is inappropriate, you should consider making some changes.

There are several advantages to inviting your child's suspicious friends to your home. First, it allows you to either confirm your suspicions or see the kids in a different light. Second, you have the added benefit of getting to know your child's friends better and your new relationship with them can become a deterrent to trouble. When the friends feel you appreciate them and welcome them into your home, they have the chance to become your allies and might tell you something you wouldn't hear otherwise. Third, you're better off having your child's questionable peers under *your* roof than someone else's. There, at least, you can provide some supervision, keep them off the streets and out of empty houses, and you'll have a better idea of what you're dealing with.

I find it useful to ask teenagers if they think their friends have their best interests at heart. Naturally, they insist they do. But, I ask, would a real friend pressure you to do something that might put you in danger? Or would he take no for an answer and drop it? Discuss such issues with your teen. If their friends seem indifferent about their safety and well-being, you're justified in challenging the friendship. Remind your child that real friends don't jeopardize one another's future.

Avoid Controlling Their Choice of Friends by Force

If you could choose your child's friends, they'd probably all be outgoing, considerate, gifted, and successful. But you rarely can. Many parents have told me that they cringe at the sight of some of the teenagers walking into their houses, sure that these guests are there to corrupt the morals of their children.

So why not tell your children they're forbidden to see those undesirables again? Because it probably won't work. Unless your children are unusually compliant, you may instead strengthen the bond between them and their friends, as well as creating a rift between the two of you. They'll probably spend even more time with those you want them to avoid, either lying to you and sneaking around or brazenly rebelling against your orders.

The more you attack their friends, the more staunchly your teenagers will defend them. If you start yelling about how terrible their friends are, your children will take it as a personal attack and will insist that everything you've heard is untrue and that you obviously don't know the first thing about their friends. You're better off trying to have a calm, rational discussion focusing on your concern about the risks your teen might be getting into with these companions. Focus on that rather than the individuals in question.

Set Rules and Limits

Your energy is better spent figuring out what's going on with your own children rather than what their friends are doing. Blaming someone else for your teenager's problems is an easy escape for both of you, but it doesn't address the mistakes he has made. Make sure you hold him responsible for his own

What's a True Friend?

Ask your child to measure his friends against these criteria for a true friend:

- Someone you can always trust

- Someone who's always there when you need him

- Someone who will talk with you about your problems or come to you with theirs

- Someone who will tell you the truth even if it hurts

- Someone who encourages you to do better

- Someone who won't encourage you to do something dangerous

- Someone with whom you can be yourself

If your child insists that his friends meet these criteria, you'll have to either accept it or point out any discrepancies you've noticed. For example, you can comment that his friends violated his trust when they snitched on him to get themselves out of trouble. He'll have difficulty accepting your feedback at first, but let the facts speak for themselves. Conversely, if your child admits that his friends don't meet the criteria for a true friend, you can help him to explore other options.

actions, even if his friends play a strong role in the decisions he makes. If he and his friends get into trouble together, you can restrict his contact with them for a specified time period as a punishment. Just don't fool yourself into casting your son or daughter in the role of helpless victim when he or she isn't.

But if your teen's friends really do get into trouble all the time, you should also ask yourself why your teen is spending time with them. Does she think it's the best she can do? Is she going through a rebellious phase that will probably be short-lived? Is she trying to spite you? This is usually the most important issue to address, and it explains why restrictions on those she spends time with should serve a useful purpose. Not only do you want to keep her out of trouble; you want to give her gratifying alternatives to destructive friendships.

Sometimes your teens will spend time with friends who are unquestionably a bad influence. This is difficult to address because your children will likely deny or refuse to discuss that their friends get in trouble, regardless of any incriminating evidence. In this instance, tell your teens what you know (for example, their friends sell drugs or have recently been suspended from school) and how you know it. Then explain why you feel they're a bad influence and can't be trusted. Don't argue about the validity of the facts; just take action. Under these circumstances, you must limit their exposure to undesirable peers as much as possible. This isn't always easy. You have to convince them that you mean business and will do anything necessary to keep them away from the undesirable peers. This could range from enforced supervision of their time to a change of schools. Most important, you'll have to offer them an alternative to spending time with their friends. (More about that later.)

Contact the Parents of Undesirable Peers

If your teenager persists in spending time with a negative peer group and your other efforts have failed, you may need to contact their friends' parents and inform them about what's going on (for instance, drinking, getting into trouble, taking other risks). Don't assume that those parents already know. This can be a touchy situation because you can never be certain what response you'll get (or what trouble you may be stirring up), but if they're willing to cooperate, you'll have some newfound allies in keeping everyone out of trouble. If you find the other parents uninterested in getting involved, for whatever reasons, you'll still be no worse off than you were before. And you'll have a better understanding of why your child's friends may be getting into trouble—their parents are unconcerned or do not provide adequate supervision. As I said earlier, it's difficult to control your teens' friendships, but that doesn't mean you can't exert pressure on where and how they spend their time.

You should not ask your teenagers' permission before contacting their friends' parents—they'll be certain to say no. But I do recommend that you let them know you've spoken with these parents, because you don't want to be open to accusations that you're behaving in a sneaky fashion. Teenagers hate it when their parents check up on them, but when teens know they're being monitored, they're less likely to test the limits, because they are more likely to get caught. This process weakens the influence of negative peers.

Help Your Child Be a Closer Part of Your Family

Kids who spend excessive time with friends, good or bad, are usually estranged from their families. They feel criticized, rejected, and hungry for acceptance from anyone who'll have them. If you want to weaken negative peer associations, you'll have to make your teenager feel more involved in your family and build his self-esteem. You'll need to improve the communication and send a powerful message that you care about him, despite any difficulties he has caused. Let me stress again the importance of meaningful family connections. Many teenagers make poor choices of friends because they are estranged from their parents. With this in mind, make a major effort to bring your child back into the fold. Set aside past grievances and tell him you want to try to make a fresh start.

Your child may be suspicious when you suddenly start treating him differently. He'll assume you have an ulterior motive and may be cautious or indifferent at first. But teenagers generally respond sooner or later to kind, genuine overtures, even if it takes some time. No, you probably won't completely lure him away from his friends—at least, not right away. Even if you despise his friends, it's important to acknowledge that your teenager needs his own friends. Yes, you should make an effort to improve your relationship, but you can't—and shouldn't—try to act like his new best friend. Just being a good parent can have enough of a positive impact.

As your child gets close to the family again, the negative peer group will seem less attractive for two reasons. First, he'll feel relieved and comforted when he realizes he can depend on his parents again. He may not admit it, but it's a comfort to know he can count on them. Second, as the family becomes part of his social sphere once again, he won't be tempted to spend most of his time away from home. The more cohesive the family unit, the more the teenager feels part of it. Once you've reopened communication with your children, you'll have more of an influence on their choice of friends.

TEACHING YOUR CHILD PEER-REFUSAL SKILLS

Assuming you have worked on your communication with your teenager, the next step is to teach her how to say no in a compromising situation. She has to learn how to exercise good judgment in every situation, whether she's invited to go out the evening before an exam, encouraged to tease someone, or asked to drive when she's been drinking. This is especially important if your child is easily influenced. Her inclination will be to simply go along with the crowd because it's the line of least resistance. Here are some suggestions for helping your teens improve their abilities to follow their own senses of right and wrong, even when it requires going against the advice and pressure of friends.

Hold Discussions About Peer Pressure

Encourage your child to talk about the peer pressures she faces. Remind her that you know how it feels and it's nothing to be embarrassed about. Share some of your own experiences, emphasizing how you felt torn between going along with the crowd and listening to what your better judgment told you. One father told his daughter about a time when his friends dared him to throw an egg at a passing car. He wanted to make his friends laugh and show them he was a fun person, but also thought it was a dumb thing to do. He did it anyway. And sure enough, after his egg hit the car, the driver jumped out, chased him, and caught him! "That was the last time I did something dumb just to please my friends," he lamented. His daughter giggled and said: "Oh Dad, that was such a lame thing to do." But she got the point, and learned that her father understood what peer pressure felt like.

Don't Let Your Children Make Their Friends' Feelings More Important Than Their Own

When you talk to your teenager about peer pressure, emphasize the importance of trusting one's own feelings. Ask her if what her friends think is more important than what she thinks. If she says yes, you're facing a problem with her self-esteem and her value system. Remind her that she has a right to express her feelings and shouldn't compromise herself just for the sake of acceptance.

On the other hand, if your daughter says that her feelings are every bit as important as her friends', make sure that she acts accordingly. If she doesn't, you'll want to challenge her on the difference between her words and actions. If she really prefers jeans and Birkenstocks but wears the same cute coordinated outfits and high-heeled strappy sandals that her friends all wear, question her decision. Ask her what she thinks would happen if she wore Birkenstocks to a party. Would her friends make comments? And if they did, could she survive them? Maybe she could start a new trend, or at least be admired for her courageous fashion choice.

Role-Play Their Response to Peer Pressure

Role-playing is another way to discuss hypothetical situations and appropriate responses to pressure. It will simultaneously prepare her for the real thing and give you a chance to see how she might handle herself. If she can convince you she knows how to deal with negative peer pressure, then you can allow her more leeway.

Sometimes it can be difficult to get teenagers to role-play situations involving peer pressure. They may think it's a waste of time or feel embarrassed. But fortunately, issues often come up spontaneously, without your forcing them. These include parties, trips, unsupervised visits to friends' houses, and other activities at which problems might arise. In these cases your teenager will probably scoff at your concern over negative influences. You have to find a palatable way to express your misgivings, and your child has to convince you that there's no need to worry. If you're both successful, there is at least some basis for trust. And through productive dialogues, you can teach your children peer refusal skills and practice them by role-playing.

This discussion concerns a sixteen-year-old girl going on a date with a college sophomore.

Angela: You'll never guess who asked me out for this weekend, Mom.

Mother: Who?

Angela: Do you remember Ricky, the guy on the football team I used to have a crush on?

Mother: Didn't he graduate a couple of years ago?

Angela: Yeah, and he's really cool.

Mother: To tell you the truth, honey, I'm not sure I like the idea of you going out with someone four years older than you.

Angela: Oh, Mom, really. I can handle it.

Mother: I don't know. A lot of college boys put pressure on younger girls they date.

Angela: What are you so afraid of?

Mother: Well, does he have a car and his own apartment?

Angela: What does that mean?

Mother: It means he's in a position to take advantage of you.

Angela: That's ridiculous! I already know him.

Mother: I wish I could feel sure there was nothing to worry about.

Angela: What am I supposed to tell you, Mom?

Mother: It would help if I thought you could handle any situation that might come up.

Angela: Like what?

Mother: Well, like if he asked you to go back to his apartment after the date.

Angela: Do we have to talk about this?

Mother: Only if you want me to consider letting you go out with him.

Angela: All right. I guess if he asked me to go back to his apartment, I'd say no, because I really don't know him very well.

Mother: And what if a group of other kids were going and they all encouraged you to come along?

Angela: I guess I'd say okay.

Mother: I still feel uncomfortable about this, Angela.

Angela: Mom, what are you freaking out about? Are you afraid he'll force me into having sex with him?

Mother: To be honest, yes.

Angela: Mom, you're really out of touch. The guys I know would never force a girl to have sex.

Mother: I wish I could believe that. Angela, I just don't know if you could handle the pressure. It's not always that easy. I really want to be able to trust you.

Angela: What can I do to convince you?

Mother: Okay, what would you do if another couple went into a bedroom?

Angela: That's them, Mom, not me.

Mother: But it would leave you just sitting there and it might be awkward. I'm just not sure you could handle that situation.

Angela: Look, Mom, if Ricky really started to push me, I'd just tell him to stop. And if he didn't listen, I'd ask him to take me home.

Mother: What if he wouldn't?

Angela: This is ridiculous.

Mother: I'm serious, Angela.

Angela: All right. If he wouldn't take me home, I'd call a cab. Or I'd knock on the bedroom door and ask one of the other kids to give me a ride. And if they wouldn't help me, I'd call Dad.

Mother: That makes me feel better.

Angela: Mom, I'm not going to let anyone pressure me to do something I don't want to. You know I left that party last month when the other kids were trying acid.

Mother: That's true. And we were proud of you.

Angela: So how about giving me a chance?

Mother: Well, I feel a little more comfortable about it. I still want to know what your specific plans are for the evening, so we can discuss what time you need to be home by.

Angela: He said he'd call today or tomorrow, so I'll let you know then.

Angela's mother shows appropriate concern about the fact that her daughter may find herself in a compromising situation, and Angela agrees to address the kind of peer pressure that worries her mother. In discussing possible scenarios, Angela sends her mother the message that she takes pride in herself and can be self-reliant. Although the mother still has some doubts, she agrees to give Angela a chance to demonstrate she's responsible.

Teens resist this type of role-playing with their parents, so don't expect these efforts to be met with much enthusiasm. It helps to make these dialogues a prerequisite for your teen, as the parents above did, when faced with uneasy situations. The unfortunate truth is that nothing can guarantee your child will be able to stand up to pressure when the time comes. However, role-playing not only allows you to gauge how your child would react in a bad situation, it also arms them with the responses they need to stand up for themselves. It helps them to identify potential trouble in advance. Your children probably won't take these discussions seriously at first. But when they realize you mean business, they'll start thinking about the dilemmas you pose, and after a while these peer-refusal skills will begin to sink in. As they learn to assert their real feelings, they'll be one step closer to staying out of trouble.

Skill Builder: Suggestions for Resisting Peer Pressure

1. Use a calm and assertive voice. Tell your friends directly that you don't want to participate in their plan to drink, cut school, beat up someone, or whatever.

2. Propose an alternative activity to your friends. Suggest that the group do something that does not involve a risk (for example, play basketball, go to a movie, or find another party, where there won't be drugs).

3. Use humor to lighten the situation. If you're really getting pressured by your friends to do something you don't want to, you might say: "What's the big deal?" or, "You're right, I am, in fact, really lame," or, "I'm not prepared to get arrested over this."

4. Directly state the risks you want to avoid. Say: "I don't want to take the chance of getting drunk again," or, "I'm not about to get picked up for shoplifting."

5. Keep saying no if your friends try to convince you. You'd be surprised how many ways there are to do this. Just a few of these ways are "No thanks," "Sorry," "Count me out," "Maybe next year," and "I think I'll pass this time."

6. Tell your friends that your parents have made it clear that there will be dire consequences if you get in trouble again and you're not prepared to take the chance.

7. Remind your friends that you've decided to stay out of trouble and you need their help to do so. Ask them to keep you from drinking or doing something foolish that you'd be sorry for afterward. A true friend would certainly respect your wishes.

8. Remove yourself from the situation. Sometimes you'll find that your friends are unresponsive to your requests. In this case, the best solution is to announce that you're leaving and will see them later.

FINDING POSITIVE PEER GROUPS

Sometimes you'll need to go further than role-playing. When negative peer influence is too great, you may need to push your children in another direction. It's a real challenge to find sufficient leverage to accomplish this.

You must carefully consider all possible incentives and consequences. Sometimes you can offer your teenager more privileges, a bonus in his allowance, or an especially desirable activity if he'll agree to get involved with a new peer group. For example, one father told his son that he'd get several tickets to a baseball game if he'd invite someone outside his usual circle of friends. While teenagers initially balk at this idea, your persistence will pay off. The trick is to promote the new friendships without attacking the old ones. Of course, you don't want your teenager to feel that you're buying him off. Although I don't routinely recommend it, there are times when bribery in the service of a good cause is worth it. Sometimes the ends *do* justify the means. Think of these suggestions as simply ways to jump-start a process that can then take on a life of its own. That is, as your child is exposed to new and different friends, he comes to see that he doesn't have to rely on his negative peer group for approval.

Many teen groups are engaged in constructive activities. Religious youth groups, school clubs, and volunteer organizations all give their members a sense of belonging. The same is true for sports teams and other activities that your child enjoys, like drama, music, or art. You should certainly encourage your child to pursue her interests. Help her to find an organization that's a good fit for both of you in terms of its focus, the degree of commitment required, and its members. It's a constructive way to wean her from an undesirable peer group, and there's the added benefit of building self-esteem.

Youth at risk of getting into trouble are reluctant to join such groups and may sneer at them, often because they don't feel they could fit in. If you think there's a group that could distance your teen from his friends' negative influence, use your ingenuity. Rather than forcing him to participate in an activity, tell him it's your condition for allowing him to associate with his current friends. In other words, he must honor your request in exchange for your respecting his. Obviously, you must be prepared to enforce this. If your teenager refuses to consider a new activity or a group of different peers, even when faced with a negative consequence, you'll have to consider more serious alternatives. For the moment, let's explore the positive influence that the right activity or organization can have on your child if you succeed in getting him to give it a try.

Kelly was hanging out with a group of kids who got drunk and high every night of every weekend—and some weeknights too. When her parents tried to stop her from spending time with them, Kelly lied and told them she was meeting someone else. It wasn't long before her parents got wise to her tricks and drew the line. For the next two months, they said, she was expected to join the teen group at their church, a strong group with many members, a roster of fun activities, and a young, in-touch leader. If they found out she'd missed even one meeting, they'd send her to a boarding school. Kelly complained vehemently that they were oppressing her and threatened to run away from home, but her parents stood firm and told her the choice was hers.

Kelly did attend the group meetings regularly and made several new friends. She thought the youth group's activities were a little hokey at times, but were mostly a lot of fun. Even better, she started spending time with her new friends beyond the context of youth group meetings. Her new friends weren't into getting high and didn't drink much, so while they did go to some parties, they were just as likely to make plans to go to a movie or out to dinner. While Kelly continued to spend some time with her old friends, she saw that there was an alternative to the constant drinking and drug use that used to take up all her time. As she realized she didn't have to get into trouble to belong to a group, she drifted away from the old friends. Her parents supported her new friendships and told her they were proud of her. Eventually, they reconsidered the driving privileges they'd rescinded when she was drinking on the weekends.

Kelly's example reflects a drastic measure by her parents—forcing her to join an activity and threatening to send her away. But in this case, Kelly had been heading toward a serious substance abuse problem, and her parents' previous efforts had failed. You'll need to gauge the seriousness of the issue to determine the consequences of failing to comply with your guidelines. Begin with meaningful short-term consequences and increase them if they are not effective.

HOOKING UP YOUR TEENAGER WITH A POWERFUL ROLE MODEL

There are other ways to bring about change. Wouldn't it be wonderful if every teenager had an adult she could look up to? I'm not talking about parents, but mentors, role models, and other inspirational adults who can offer guidance and hope.

Ideally, you would pair your teenager with people who could take her under their wing and share with her their unique experiences, wisdom, and perspectives on life, which differ in some way from your own. Find a coach, a teacher, an adult friend, or a member of the clergy who is willing to spend time with her and develop a friendly relationship. Perhaps this mentor is someone who shares a strong interest in common with your child, or who experienced similar problems growing up. Once your child has developed this relationship with someone, the mentor can use his or her influence to help your teen make positive choices and focus her energy in constructive pursuits.

Mark, for example, had been spending a great deal of time with a rough group of friends. Although they didn't get into any serious trouble, they seemed shiftless and unhappy, so Mark's parents worried about their influence. Mark seemed to live solely for his weekend time with these friends. He relied on them for entertainment and eagerly went along with their wishes in a way that suggested he was more a follower than a valued friend. His only other interest was working on the family computer, at which he spent hours on end exploring the Internet and developing his own Web sites.

Mark's parents seized on this interest as a possible distraction from the negative peer group. His father contacted the computer store where he did business and learned they had some part-time jobs for young people. Then, instead of arguing about Mark's weekend cronies, he told him he'd heard about a great job opening that involved working with computers. Considering his interest, Mark listened carefully and agreed when his father offered to take him to the store to talk to the manager. This would give him a chance, he thought, to earn money doing something he enjoyed.

When Mark visited the store, he and the manager took a liking to each other. The business needed someone who could demonstrate some of their new products on weekends. This would mean learning the new systems and becoming familiar with the software. To Mark, this job was a dream come true.

Mark got the job and spent more and more time at the store. During their hours together, he and the manager grew close. He had a lot to teach Mark about computers, but soon they were talking together about many aspects of Mark's life. The manager took an interest in Mark's plans for the future, and made a point of discussing various college and career possibilities with him. Gradually, his new mentor increased his responsibilities, and this made Mark feel competent and appreciated at the store. He developed good relationships with several other people at work and met lots of other friends his age through his position. As he began spending time around responsible people who shared his interest, he was soon too busy to hang out with his old friends, who he seemed to have less and less in common with as time went by.

This is a relatively painless way one family found to wean their teenager from an undesirable peer influence. Mark's parents built on an established interest to help him develop a meaningful connection with a powerful role model and a change of environment. As Mark grew increasingly absorbed with his new, more productive pursuits, the influence of his undesirable friends waned. In the process, he shifted his allegiance to a more positive group with defined interests. His mentor, of course, was instrumental in bringing about this change. Mark identified with his positive traits and followed in his footsteps.

How to Wean Your Child Away from a Negative Peer Group

■ Support any interests he has that don't pertain to his current group. If he doesn't have any, expose him to some possibilities. For example: encourage him to adopt a puppy or kitten from the animal shelter, or to subscribe to the Internet; urge him to go out for a seasonal sport; ask him about school clubs and organizations that might be interesting; or research community-based activities or lessons in his areas of interest.

■ Encourage him to get a part-time job to earn more money and gain good experience.

■ Contact your school counselor and ask her about any opportunities for volunteer work.

■ Give him later curfews when he goes out with other, more trust-worthy friends.

■ Try to make your home life more fun. Set aside time where you can enjoy one another without getting into serious discussions or conflicts.

■ Praise him anytime he elects to stay home rather than go out with his peers. You can further support his actions by offering to pick up a movie at Blockbuster, ordering a pizza, or helping him with a task he's working on (like sorting out his CDs or decorating his room).

■ A final thought: if he has been in trouble with the law, try to get his probation officer to enforce a separation from his negative peers by making it one of the terms of his probation.

Don't be reluctant to pursue any avenues that are in your child's best interests. And even if you receive dozens of complaints as you proceed, remember that your actions are intended to help her better manage her own life.

RECRUITING OUTSIDE SUPPORT

Sometimes you can't see any solution to the negative peer pressure exerted on your child. Despite your best efforts, she rejects all your attempts to get her to make different friends, try a new activity, join an organization, or get to know someone older who could serve as a mentor. In this case, you have a difficult decision to make. How far are you prepared to go to break the destructive cycle?

You still have several options. Parent support groups are

found in many communities. Typically made up of other parents who are struggling with their children's risky behavior, they meet regularly and offer an opportunity for you to vent your feelings. They'll also give you a chance to hear the stories of others who have been through similar ordeals. Members of these groups will encourage you to confront your children on their poor choice of friends and will help you to do so in the most effective way possible. And thanks to the support of the other parents, you'll no longer feel isolated and may find the courage to take more drastic action if needed.

An option in extreme cases might involve contacting your child's school and alerting authorities to the activities of the troublemakers your child has been involved with. Of course, this may get your child into trouble along with her friends. Consequently, you should consider the seriousness of the behavior and ask yourself if you have exhausted the less drastic options (like setting firm limits and enforcing appropriate consequences for any misbehavior). If you have and you choose to notify the school authorities, you can expect them to be on the lookout for any rule violations. (It makes the job of school authorities easier when they know they have the approval and understanding of parents whose children are causing behavioral or disciplinary problems.) And they'll take appropriate action against the offenders, exerting more powerful leverage than you can. They may even notify the police department or the juvenile court system.

Several years ago, a father told me about a scheme he'd devised to weaken the influence of his son's friends. He'd learned that their group was hanging out at the mall on weekends and shoplifting. Instead of restricting his son from going to the mall, he called the security office there and reported that his son's group was roaming around and getting into trouble. He asked for the cooperation of those officers in keeping an eye on the boys so they could catch them in the act.

Sure enough, the young man and his friends were picked up in a department store on suspicion of shoplifting. While no charges were pressed, they were banned from the mall for six months. One of the security officers added a creative touch: he told the group that one of their members had tipped him off. The distrust this produced, combined with the boys' ban from the mall, weakened their incentive to spend time together. Eventually their lack of common interests dissolved their connection, and this man's son was able to get involved in more productive pursuits.

How far are you prepared to go to break the cycle of negative peer pressure?

Be on the lookout for the following ten signs, which suggest that negative peer influence is lessening:

1. Your child begins to spend more time around the house.

2. She stops wearing deliberately offensive or tasteless clothing.

3. He shows up at home with new and different friends.

4. He's making more effort in school.

5. She seems less obsessed with what her friends are doing.

6. He begins to talk more about future plans that do not involve the old friends.

7. She has joined several new groups that do not involve her old friends.

8. He no longer insists that his life is boring when he's not off with his friends.

9. Other people (teachers, neighbors, family) tell you that they're noticing positive changes in her.

10. Your child has grown more comfortable spending time alone.

Remember that breaking away from negative peers is a slow process. It usually takes several months for a teenager to grow involved with new activities, form new friendships, and become more independent. You'll need to be supportive and patient.

WHEN ALL ELSE FAILS

You won't always be able to find creative solutions to negative peer pressure. There will be times when you're at your wits' end and nothing seems to work. Your child seems to be joined at the hip to a person or a peer group that is constantly landing him in trouble. You know you've lost control of the situation because he's flagrantly defying your rules and moving further away from the family. What's left for you at this point?

If everything else has failed, try to learn why your teen is so vulnerable to this negative influence. Is it because of insecurity or low self-esteem, or a lack of positive options, or because substances like drugs or alcohol lie at the heart of their bad behavior? Who is exerting the negative influence—a boyfriend or girlfriend? their best friend? their only friend? a group of friends? The suggestions of this chapter are appropriate for pretty much any situation, but if it's an extreme case and you need to take serious action, understanding the enemy will help you form the best plan of attack.

In some instances teens find themselves overwhelmed by their current situation, unhappy but unable to make a positive change. These teens could lack the strength to break away from their bad situation, or maybe they just can't see any positive alternatives (despite your efforts). Sometimes teens don't even realize how unhappy they were until they're in a more positive, healthy situation. It may take real intervention on your part; while this is a hard step to take, it's one that might save him. Perhaps your child would fare better at a different school; take a look at the public, private, and parochial school options in your school district. This is not a financial option for everyone, but thanks to the school choice and charter school movements, you may have publicly funded school options that you had not previously considered.

I've even known families who moved to a different neighborhood or another city for the purpose of placing their child in a new and better environment. It's a drastic measure that affects the whole family. Sometimes this approach is successful and this fresh start is exactly what your teen needed to reconnect with you and the rest of the family. A major change can also give your teen greater perspective on the situation he left, which may lead to the insight and maturity needed to seek out more positive relationships and situations. Of course, the risk in pulling up your roots and starting over is that your teenager will seek out the lowest common denominator in his new neighborhood, again finding his way into trouble. He may be so angry and resentful that he further distances himself from his family, so that he still lacks the meaningful family connections that can keep him from feeling alienated. And finally, moving will not change your child's personality; you'll have to bank on positive peer influence to alter his behavior.

Other serious responses may be appropriate. Depending upon just how defiant, out of control, antisocial, and harmful he or she has become, you can apply the appropriate severe consequence. Before you go to extremes, ask yourself (and your spouse) how far you're willing to go to interrupt this downward

Big-Screen Peer Pressure

A teen's search for acceptance is a perennial theme at the movies. Here are just a handful of films that depict peer pressure and teens' struggles to resist it and forge their own identities. Each offers an opportunity for you to discuss with your teen how the movie characters cope with pressure.

American Pie

Angus

The Breakfast Club

Can't Hardly Wait

Clueless

Heathers

The In Crowd

Never Been Kissed

Pretty in Pink

Risky Business

She's All That

Sixteen Candles

Some Kind of Wonderful

spiral. Idle threats won't work, because things are already at a serious point. So don't threaten your child with military school or juvenile court if you don't mean it. False threats will further erode your authority.

You may need to set up an intervention, hosted by an impartial third party, in which you, your family, and anyone else involved let your teen know the degree to which her bad behavior and defiance has hurt them, give her an opportunity to respond, and allow her to create a plan for the future. If your teen's situation has really gotten out of control, it may be time to remove her from your home. Options include contacting the juvenile court system, enrolling her in a wilderness school or therapeutic boarding school, or seeking a placement in a residential treatment facility. In Chapter 11 you'll learn about each of these options, and I'll help you determine which might be appropriate for your child.

The most important thing to remember is that you should never abandon hope when your children are bombarded with negative peer influences. You have a variety of options, ranging from forthright discussion to major changes in their environment. In each case, your goal is to weaken the power of the peer group. You can do this by fortifying your teenagers' resources and making it difficult for them to associate with the undesirable groups. You must take an active role in monitoring their activities and setting the necessary limits. Eventually, most teenagers will find more productive pursuits and become self-directed. Then you'll be able to have the type of relationship we all want with our children—based on trust, mutual respect, and genuine concern.

CHAPTER EIGHT

SEX, DRUGS, AND REBELLIOUS TRENDS

"Sex isn't such a big deal. Practically the whole school is doing it."

"Our parents probably all partied when they were our age. It's ridiculous for them to tell us not to drink."

"Maybe drugs are a little dangerous, but there's nothing else to do around here, and they just feel so great."

"My mom told me not to get my belly button pierced, but I'm doing it anyway. It's my body."

"So I smoke a little pot; what's the big deal? Everybody's doing it."

The world is full of temptations, and your children are exposed to them every day. Our culture is saturated with images, found in ads, movies, and TV shows, that promote drinking, glamorize smoking, and glorify sex. Today's music is filled with sexually explicit lyrics. And almost any teenager in search of pornographic material need look no further than the Internet or cable TV. This is reality.

So, parents, please be on the alert. You must know what's going on and be prepared to deal with it. This chapter is designed to help you by exploring three important aspects of the adolescent experience—emerging sexuality, the temptation of illicit substances, and the influence of dangerous trends. We'll examine what temptations are out there and what may draw your children toward them. Then I'll guide you through ways to help your teenagers exercise good judgment, self-restraint, and respect for the rights of others when facing these challenges. No matter what your teenagers' level of experience or where you are in your relationship with them, it's never too early or too late to begin helping your children deal responsibly with these aspects of life.

SEX AND YOUR TEENAGER

Roughly 50 percent of teens are sexually active by the time they graduate from high school. This means several million teenagers consider themselves adults, whether or not they accept the responsibility that goes along with adult freedom.

At its best, sex is one of the ultimate expressions of love and intimacy. The problem is that sex can also be downright danger-ous, leading to unwanted pregnancies and diseases that can for-ever alter the course of one's life. For some teens sex is a well-thought-out decision based on trust and commitment; for oth-ers it's a self-centered act rooted in immaturity. You must decide for yourself which path you want your teenagers to take and how you can help direct them along the path toward maturity.

Simply forbidding your children to have sex or date, or avoiding any discussion of the subject, is unrealistic and may even inadvertently fuel your children's rush into sexual experi-mentation, as teens are intrigued by topics adults declare off-limits. Give a movie an R rating (or even better, NC-17) and teens will line up around the theater eagerly waiting to get in. Slap a "Parental Advisory" sticker on a CD and suddenly it's a hotter commodity, particularly if there's been some controversy over offensive lyrics. Many young men have read through copies of adult magazines like *Playboy* and *Penthouse* (or worse!) despite the "For Adults Only" signs in magazine racks. And would alco-hol and tobacco be quite as appealing if they were legal for teens to use? These symbols of adult passage are like forbidden fruit for teenagers: the more they see, the greater the temptation.

TALKING ABOUT SEX

Nearly all teenagers think about sex regularly. How could they not? With all those hormones racing through their bodies, teenagers are experiencing some *very* powerful feelings that they've never felt before. Even if actual sex isn't involved, most teens experience almost painful crushes and longings. Some teens admit that they devote hours of time to thinking about sex. Yet talking about sex can be a completely different story. I once had a teenage boy tell me it was easier for him to have sex than to talk about it.

So why do some kids have so much trouble talking about sex, especially with their parents? After all, isn't sex splashed across

Some Sobering Facts

■ The average age for first sexual intercourse is sixteen.

■ Each year about 1 million teenage girls get pregnant.

■ Half of all eighth-grade and 80 percent of all twelfth-grade students have tried alcohol.

■ Two million teenagers consume five drinks or more at least five times a month.

■ Almost 50 percent of all automobile-related teenage deaths involve drunk drivers.

■ About 20 percent of high school seniors smoked pot in the last month.

(Source: American Medical Association)

our TV sets, magazines, and billboards? Well, most kids would be quick to point out that there is often a major difference between the world of Hollywood and the world their parents inhabit. Sex in the media aside, several real-life factors come into play between parents and their children when sex is the subject.

One factor is the type of communication you've had about all issues, including sex. How do you discuss important issues? Parents need to be able to carry on frank discussions with their children about important topics like sex, even when the subject matter makes everyone involved uncomfortable or uneasy. And it's important for parents to talk with their children about sex from early on, because this sets a tone for open communication in the teenage years. Further, you should make it a point to talk about healthy relationships and the role that sex plays in them. After all, schools may teach the facts, but it's up to you to impart values.

Another factor in your child's willingness to discuss sex is his self-esteem. If he respects himself and isn't afraid to show his vulnerable side, he'll be more likely to ask you questions and share his thoughts with you. On the other hand, many young people are embarrassed about their sexual feelings, convinced no one else feels as they do. Perhaps your teen lacks the confidence to ask you a question or tell you something about sex because she's afraid you'll laugh at her or get angry. Worse yet, some teens consider lack of experience to be a scarlet letter *V* and dread the ridicule of their peers. They imagine their friends are way ahead of them in these matters and worry that they'll be doomed to a life of celibacy.

How to Deal with Your Feelings About Teenage Sex

Whether or not you express them, your feelings about sex will influence your teenager's feelings. You need to feel comfortable with your own sexual past, the standards your parents, peers, and society held regarding sex, your own sexual history, and how you feel about it now. This doesn't mean that you should confess all your sexual experiences to your teen. But you need to be in touch with your own feelings to successfully achieve a level of comfort in your discussions. If you help your child to feel comfortable talking about sex, she'll be more likely to share stories, fears, and seek advice. Here are some suggestions to help you deal with your own thoughts and conflicts about sex:

1. Consider the discussions you had (or didn't) with your own parents. Did your parents talk with you openly about sex? If so, are you trying to follow in their footsteps? If not, have you considered how you can approach your own children about this important topic?

2. Think about the sexual experiences you had as a teenager. Were they healthy and age-appropriate? What did you learn from them? Would you do things differently if you had them to do over again?

3. How has the risk of contracting AIDS colored your thinking about sex? Would you behave the same way today that you did twenty years ago?

4. Ask yourself what you feel is best for your teenager (abstinence, responsible sex) and why. Then think about how you can convey your values in such a way that your child will listen. You will need to be forthright, compassionate, and nonjudgmental in your discussions.

5. Make sure that you are well informed about the issues and choices facing today's teenager (abstinence, birth control, sexually transmitted diseases). There are many books, tapes, and other materials available. Refer to the Appendix to acquire further information.

6. Are you comfortable with your teenager having healthy sexual outlets (masturbation, fantasy, and age-appropriate sexual material)? If so, let your child know that you are. If not, try to speak with someone like a member of the clergy, a family physician, or professional counselor about your feelings.

7. Can you talk openly with your spouse or significant other about sex? If so, great. If not, it's probably a good place to begin dealing with your feelings.

8. Are you realistic? Do you expect your child to adhere to the same sexual standards you hold, or behave exactly the way you did as a teen (or better!) when they actually view things differently than you do? Don't fool yourself about what your teen's real-life situation is when it comes to sex.

Here's what one sixteen-year-old told me about his sexual experience. Rob seemed like a confident teenager on the surface—dark, good looks, comfortable with himself, and reasonably conversant. As we got to know each other better, our conversations became increasingly personal. During one of our meetings, Rob's sexual feelings emerged, and this private side revealed a rather different young man.

I was surprised to learn that when it came to sex, Rob was anything but comfortable with himself. In fact, he worried that sex was on his mind far too often. He thought constantly about two particular girls in his grade, but because he was too shy to approach them, he just stared at them and wished for some opportunity to talk to them. Fantasizing about them, Rob masturbated frequently and was unable to resist these impulses. He felt ashamed and was sure something was wrong with him. He couldn't imagine any of his friends doing this.

Rob was struggling with an issue that is familiar to many teenagers but usually remains unspoken. Impressed that he'd verbalized his feelings, I wanted to help him in some way, so I shared something I'd heard from an old supervisor.

"You know, Rob, someone once told me that ninety-nine percent of teenage boys masturbate and one percent lie about it," I told him.

He was incredulous. "Dr. B., you can't be serious!"

I assured him there was some truth to the statement. After all, I'd spoken with many teenage boys over the years who expressed similar feelings, and my own adolescent experiences had confirmed the stereotype. Rob was relieved. "I've always thought I was a little weird," he said, "but maybe I'm not so different after all."

Many young people keep their sexual feelings unspoken, afraid to reveal too much about themselves. Other teens talk with their friends about sex, but this could mean that they're learning teenage myths instead of accurate information. When they finally get an opportunity to talk about sex with an adult and get reliable facts or find out that others share their feelings, they feel a great burden has been lifted from their shoulders. This is why you must make it safe for your teenagers to share their personal feelings with you. Here are some suggestions to help you create this climate of security.

Don't Pressure or Interrogate Them

The more you try to force your child to talk about sex, the less she'll want to. The best way to get her to open up is to take a relaxed and curious approach. Of course, if you're worried about the sexual decisions your teen is making, your first reaction may be to start frantically asking questions. But instead of asking pointed questions, introduce the topic in a general, nonthreatening way. If

A Productive Discussion About Sex

Mother: Lydia, did you see that front-page article in *Time* magazine? I'm so tired of hearing about all these teenagers getting pregnant. I just read that there were over one million unwed mothers last year. Doesn't anyone use birth control?

Lydia: Oh Mom, come on. You take everything you read so seriously. You know none of my friends would ever get pregnant.

Mother: How can you be so sure about that?

Lydia: I just know.

Mother: No really, Lydia, what makes you and your friends so different from the girls in this article?

Lydia: Well, I know my friends wouldn't be that stupid. We've had all those dumb sex ed classes and assemblies in school. And besides, we're seniors in high school. Believe me, plenty of people are having sex.

Mother: I don't know if that makes me feel better or worse.

Lydia: Mom, you're totally freaking out over nothing.

Mother: Am I not allowed to be concerned?

Lydia: Yeah, I guess so, but things are different now. You know, virginity isn't like a major accomplishment. Girls can make up their own minds about having sex.

Mother: I can understand that. But it doesn't mean that girls should have sex before they're ready.

Lydia: Don't you think I know that, Mom?

Mother: Maybe we should have had this discussion awhile ago. We've never really talked about sex like this before.

Lydia: Well, I'm not going to just volunteer information to you, especially when you get so uptight about everything. You've never asked me what I thought about sex before. Besides, I'm almost eighteen now.

Mother: Lydia, I know I can't control what you do, but I want to be sure you make good choices for yourself. And that you're being careful to protect yourself, you know, from pregnancy and disease.

Lydia: Well, I haven't messed up so far, have I?

Mother: No, I don't suppose you have. I just hope it's because you've been making smart choices, and not just because you've been lucky so far.

Lydia: Mom, don't go laying guilt trips on me now.

Mother: All right, I'm sorry.

Lydia: Would it really make you feel better if you knew what I was doing with guys?

Mother: I guess so.

Lydia: You won't get all bent out of shape?

Mother: I'll try not to, but I think I already know what you're going to say.

Lydia: Well, I've done it a few times, but not with just anybody.

Mother: You mean with Dale?

Lydia: Yeah.

Mother: I guess I should have known. Why haven't you ever talked to me about this before?

Lydia: I didn't think you'd understand. And I was afraid that you'd go into a panic or ground me or something.

Mother: Well, I can't say I wouldn't have, but I'm glad that you told me.

Lydia: I guess it's about time I did.

Mother: What did you use for birth control?

Lydia: Condoms.

Mother: Good. I guess I ought to make you an appointment at the gynecologist, now that you're sexually active.

Lydia: Are you putting me on the pill?

Mother: Not if you don't want to be, but you can ask your doctor about it. You shouldn't stop using condoms, because you never know what kind of STDs someone has, but it's a good idea to have backup. Can you just make me one promise now?

Lydia: What?

Mother: That you'll talk to me if you ever get into a bad situation, or if you just feel like talking.

Lydia: Okay, Mom, I'll really try.

Mother: That's fair enough. And I'll try not to be too judgmental. But I may have to bite my tongue. You know, you're doing things a little differently than I did. I don't really approve of your philosophy, but I'll love you no matter what you do.

Lydia: I really am pretty happy with my life, Mom, even though it's not exactly your way.

Mother: Well, I'm proud of a lot of the things you do. And you'll be going away to college next year.

Lydia: I'll be fine, Mom, really.

This conversation may sound familiar. Lydia has made a value decision about sex that differs from her mother's values. Fortunately, her mother is wise enough to accept her decision instead of reacting angrily. Her mother voices her concerns and is willing to listen to Lydia even when the truth is hard to accept, so their discussion is productive rather than inflammatory. Of course, it would have been better if they'd been able to talk about this when Lydia was younger, since she is already sexually active at this point, but this could be a promising beginning to a closer relationship in the future.

you're worried that your teen is having unprotected sex, you can bring up the topic of different STDs, how they are spread, their symptoms, whether they can be cured, and how they can be prevented. Arm yourself with the latest info and statistics but don't be too judgmental.

If you just want a general discussion about sex, you might start by making observations about current events or pop culture, or something you read or saw recently. You could even bring up a general topic for discussion, like the way sex is used in advertising to sell products like cigarettes or shoes, or the history of censoring movies, songs, and books based on sexual content and how much these standards have changed. Impersonal conversations like these allow young people to respond without fear of reproach, and it's usually easier for them to talk about other people than about themselves.

What you want to do is give your child permission to speak the unspoken. The topic of sex should be treated in the same way as other aspects of her life—matter-of-factly, nonjudgmentally, and sympathetically. Parents who treat sexual discussions like police interrogations usually get little information from their children. Worse yet, continually telling a teenager what she ought to do is a surefire way to make her do the opposite.

Be a Good Role Model

If you're committed to helping your children develop a healthy attitude about sex, practice what you preach. This bears repeating. Whether you've always been married to the same person, you're remarried, or you're a single parent, you're responsible for being a role model when it comes to both romantic relationships and the way you deal with the opposite sex. Treat your significant other with love, faith, and trust, and encourage a healthy relationship in which you are both independent and strong, yet loyal and committed. Treat members of the opposite sex with kindness and respect, and refrain from objectifying, insulting, or bashing any particular members of the opposite sex.

If, on the other hand, you treat others (or yourself) as sexual objects, believe in negative stereotypes or generalizations about the opposite sex, are promiscuous in your relations, or are unfaithful to your spouse or significant other, you're paving the way for your teenager's jaundiced attitude to sex and relationships. Don't believe for a minute that you can fool your child; young people are incredibly insightful when it comes to their parents' hypocrisy. This means that you're sometimes faced with the difficult decision of continuing your old ways or making the changes that are in the best interests of your child. I know of several instances when concern about the example parents were setting motivated them to work on their own issues.

Discuss Sexual Issues Regarding Others with Your Teenager

Finally, I recommend that you seize every opportunity to talk openly about anything related to sexual conduct and moral behavior. A few years ago, President Clinton's actions with a young White House intern set an unfortunate example of poor judgment and immature, selfish sexual behavior. But because of the wide publicity given to this affair and the public censure of his actions, almost all teenagers had a chance to discuss the subject. This gave parents a golden opportunity, not only to let their children know where they stood but also to ask their opinions on the matter.

You can usually rely on America's gossip-obsessed media for a current sex scandal either in Hollywood, Washington, D.C., or Anytown, U.S.A., but you don't have to wait for newsworthy events to raise these issues with your teenager. If it's a slow news day, ask your child's opinion of a movie popular among teens, like *American Pie,* that deals with the pressures and insecurities teens feel about sex. And there's probably someone in your child's life whose behavior arouses curiosity or disapproval. Even if there isn't, and you don't have a particular incident in mind, you can engineer a situation that will promote useful dialogue simply by watching a relevant episode of a popular TV show together. As I've said before, it's always easier for your child to discuss someone else's behavior than her own.

I believe you should also share your thoughts on sex and related matters with your teens. Children learn by example and take your comments seriously, despite what they might say. That's why expressing respect for the opposite sex encourages a healthy attitude in your teenager. Likewise, when you allow your children to ask questions freely and respond openly to their concerns, you promote their honesty.

I leave it up to parents to decide whether or not to share some of their own teenage experiences with their children. Feelings of awkwardness, embarrassment, misinformation, and unbridled enthusiasm are endemic to adolescence and have not changed much over the years. If you feel comfortable talking about it, you can try relating your own travails.

I know one father who told his son about how excited he was the first time he kissed a girl. He was seventeen at the time. His son listened carefully and smiled, but didn't say anything. It was several months before he confessed to his father that he had just kissed someone for the first time, and he was only fifteen! This type of parental disclosure is important for young people. It gives them subtle permission to express their own feelings and relieves some of their self-consciousness about their lack of experience.

THE IMPORTANCE OF CHARACTER TO SEXUALITY

Self-esteem plays a crucial role in shaping your teen's attitudes and decisions, and this is especially true when it applies to developing a healthy sexual identity. Teens who are generally satisfied with themselves (flaws and all) are less likely to make risky choices that have negative repercussions. A healthy self-esteem includes feeling comfortable about appearance, taking pride in strengths and self-worth, and being aware of shortcomings while working to improve them.

Help Teenagers Like Themselves

In Chapter 4 you learned how to help your child build self-esteem. Now let's see how this applies to developing a healthy sexual identity. For starters, to respect themselves, young people need to feel comfortable with their appearance. They need to know how to accentuate their strengths and accept their weaknesses. It's always helpful to learn to compensate for one's shortcomings and improve on them when possible.

Teenagers who are accepted by their families and have close friendships don't have to look elsewhere for approval. As they learn to appreciate themselves, they depend less on others. This emerging self-acceptance will bolster their confidence and help them see sex as a choice rather than an obligation or an inevitability. Even if their friends are all having sex, they shouldn't feel compelled to follow suit. Self-confident teenagers can make their own decisions based on their values, best interests, and accurate information. Independence, good judgment, morality, and a strong value system all contribute to a young person's pride—a major deterrent to risky sexual behavior.

Encourage Teens to Think About What's Best for Them

You'd be surprised how many teenagers don't think twice about the decisions they make; adolescence is a time of impulsive behavior. If only children would stop for a moment and ask themselves if their actions are in their best interests, much pain and anguish could be avoided. Here are five suggestions to help your teen to stop and think about having sex instead of simply acting on impulse:

1. Ask your teen to think about his or her values regarding sex. Does he or she view sex as a casual act, or something very special? Is premarital sex okay?

2. Encourage them to practice directly stating their feelings without being apologetic. They can practice this by themselves, with a close friend, or with you if they're so inclined.

3. Suggest to your teen that if someone is putting pressure on her to have sex, she should ask that person why sex is so important to him. If that person's reasoning is questionable, tell your teen to challenge it.

4. Urge your teen to ask him- or herself how they're likely to feel afterward if they have sex. Then ask them how they would feel if they chose to abstain. How will they feel in each scenario—will they respect, or regret, the decision they made?

5. Remind your teenager that if someone really cares for you, they will not push you to have sex before you're ready. And if someone tries to, encourage your teen to say no and reiterate their beliefs.

We've already talked about helping teens develop good judgment. Now let's apply the above principles to a girl trying to come to terms with sexual activity. Sixteen-year-old Stacy had been dating Dan for several months. She felt he'd respected her wishes and never pushed her to do anything she didn't want to do. But recently, he was trying to persuade her to go further every time they were together. Stacy pointed this out to him and told him she was comfortable with the way things were and had no desire to take things further.

Dan, it turned out, had other ideas. He thought they'd been going together a long time and were pretty close. Therefore, he concluded, they were ready to have sex. The matter was complicated by the pressure he felt from his friends, who'd convinced him it was normal to be doing more than he did with a girlfriend. They told all sorts of stories about what they were (supposedly) doing with their girlfriends, and called Stacy frigid when Dan said she didn't want to have sex. Although he cared for Stacy, he became convinced that his friends were right; he felt sexual desire for Stacy, and now he was sure that she should be fulfilling that desire. Their relationship had been strong, but he unfortunately chose sex as the emotional proving ground. This is a common scenario for today's teenagers.

Stacy had a difficult decision to make. Should she hold the line, or give in to Dan's wishes? She'd spoken with her mother about this and had told her the position she'd taken. Her mother said it was important to respect herself and warned her never to do anything she might be sorry for afterward. Stacy thought long and hard. She certainly wanted her boyfriend's approval, but at the same time she feared it was too soon for her to get involved in sexual activity.

Eventually, she came up with two options. She could go along with Dan's wishes, hoping it would improve the relationship and leave her with no regrets, which seemed like the path of least resistance. Alternatively, she could trust her instincts and tell him she wasn't ready to go any further, even if it meant him losing interest in her. She felt it was worth it to take the chance on the latter. After all, if sex was that urgent, maybe she wasn't the right person for him. So Stacy told Dan that she cared a great deal for him but wasn't ready for a sexual relationship. He was disappointed and perhaps even a bit angry for a little while, but realized Stacy meant what she said. Dan realized that he still cared for Stacy even though sex wasn't involved, and he also realized how stupid some of his friends' comments had been. He got over it, and the relationship was better as they learned they could talk openly to each other about difficult issues.

Several months later, Stacy told her mother what happened. It pleased her to hear her mother say she was proud of her. Her mother fully understood Stacy's dilemma and confided that she'd once had to make a similar difficult decision. Both mother and daughter felt relieved and were able to discuss when Stacy might be ready for a sexual relationship. Stacy now felt that her mother would respect her choices, and this made it possible for her to do what she wanted when she was ready. That's as much as any parent could hope for.

Talk About Mature Relationships

Stacy's mother had the right idea. She shared her views and helped her daughter exercise good judgment. Such dialogues about mature relationships are an essential part of family life, and parents should bring the role of sex out into the open as naturally as possible. The message you want to convey is that sex is precious. It's an act of love between two consenting adults. If you've made your children feel important and proud of themselves, they'll have good judgment and self-esteem, which are deterrents to immature sexual behavior.

Teenagers often confuse love with sex and think in short time frames. Contrary to their view of the world, getting close to another person doesn't happen overnight. This confusion can lead to trouble for young people who are hungry for acceptance and immediate gratification. It's important that you tell your child about the ingredients of good, mature relationships. Here are some essential points to make:

- Good relationships involve hard work, trust, and commitment.
- Establishing closeness takes time. There are no shortcuts to genuine intimacy.
- Honesty and open communication help to create the trust essential to any mature relationship.
- Mutual respect is necessary to sustain a healthy relationship.
- Excessive criticism, coercion, and bickering can erode a good relationship.
- There are times in a relationship when compromise is necessary.
- Sometimes it is necessary to accept another person's shortcomings and have them accept yours.

Convince your teenagers that really getting to know someone takes time. If they insist they're close to their boyfriend or girlfriend after only a few days, ask how they can be so sure. Tell them that a few days together or a telephone marathon are not remotely like an intimate relationship; there should be a strong connection between intimacy and a longer-term commitment. You want your teen to think twice before considering a relationship permanent, especially since her definition of "permanent" is quite different from yours because she lacks a realistic view of the future. It takes maturity to judge another person's character and considerable time to get to know him. That's why it's so important to discuss these matters with your children in a way that helps them realize the context in which sex should be considered.

Teach Teenagers How to Say No

Teens are often pressured to be sexual when they're not really ready. This pressure can come from the media, which often presents a glorified, earth-shattering vision of sex; lots of movies, TV shows, and novels portray teenage sex. Sometimes this pressure comes from friends who brag about their own sexual encounters and consider sexual experience, even promiscuity, to be a status symbol. (True, they're not really good friends if they don't respect someone's desire to wait—but that doesn't make it any less hard to deal with.) And sometimes pressure to have sex comes from the person your son or daughter is dating. (The stereotype is that it's the boys who pressure their girlfriends into having sex with them, and this may be more common—or, sadly, more accepted—but I have met boys who have been pressured by girls too. It works both ways.)

If your teenager has a well-developed set of values and feels secure in his choices, he will be able to rise above all the pressure and the hype about sex. On the other hand, if he lacks self-confidence or is easily swayed by the opinions of others, then he is at risk for caving in to the pressure, and possibly making a choice he will regret.

Encourage your teens to say no if they are feeling pressured to have sex. This may be something they will have to say to their boyfriend or girlfriend, but it may also mean saying no to what their friends think they should do. And it may even mean your teen needs to learn how to say no to himself if he is in a situation where he feels himself getting swept away by feelings of love or lust and is tempted to make an impulsive decision to have sex. (This goes for young women too, of course.) Getting swept away and making a spur-of-the-moment, lust-filled decision to engage in sexual intercourse can be a terrible idea; this is when condoms are forgotten, promises broken, and acts of cheating and betrayal committed.

The bottom line is that your teenager needs to know that her feelings matter, and needs to feel comfortable expressing herself. If your teenager finds herself in a sexually charged situation where she feels increasingly uncomfortable, she needs to learn how to say no firmly and clearly. Teach your teenagers that no means no. Remind them that if they're with the right person, someone who loves and respects them, he or she will respect their decision and their relationship will still be strong.

Finally, tell your children that they also need to accept no as an answer, even if they feel ready to have sex. Being told no doesn't mean that your boyfriend or girlfriend doesn't like you or that you're physically repulsive; it means that they just plain aren't ready. Young people with well-developed values guide themselves accordingly. Pride and willpower can keep them from making poor decisions about sex. But you need to go a step further to make sure your daughters can say no when faced with dating pressures. You want her to believe that her feelings matter. If a young woman is in doubt about how to conduct herself in an intimate relationship, she's better off waiting. It's worth reminding her that if a boy respects and cares for her, he'll take no for an answer.

DEALING WITH DAUGHTERS

In my years of counseling families, I have learned that parents tend to be much more worried about their daughters than their sons when it comes to sex and dating.

Daughters are precious—but it does no one any good to treat them like fragile flowers. Subjecting your daughter to unfair rules and restrictions is bound to make her angry, and she might respond by lying and sneaking around, or defying the rules outright. If you encourage weakness and passivity, then your daughter won't know how to be strong in a difficult situation. And banning boys altogether doesn't work. Neither does encouraging her to find the right boy so she'll "have someone to take care of her."

Instead, teach your daughters to be strong, independent women. Talk seriously with them about steps they can take to avoid dangerous situations. Ask your daughter to stick to the following steps when she's going out with someone (*especially* with someone she doesn't know very well):

- Make sure that you've told your parents (and maybe friends) exactly where you're going to be and when you'll be home.
- Avoid situations where it's just the two of you all alone and no one's near. Examples: parking the car in a deserted area like an empty parking lot or area way back in the woods, or being together in a house where no one else is home.
- Avoid excessive drinking or drug use. When you're drunk or on drugs, your decision-making ability is impaired and you're in a weakened, vulnerable position that someone could take advantage of.
- Always carry enough change with you to make a couple of phone calls, or to take a taxi if it's a possibility where you live. Carrying a cell phone is even better.
- If the boy you're out with does start pressuring you into doing something you don't want to do, whether it's sexual activity, drinking or using another substance, going somewhere you don't want to go, or breaking your curfew, say "no" clearly and firmly. Don't cave in—stand strongly behind your words and your beliefs.

- Look for warning signals—and listen to your instincts. If you're out with someone who loses his temper often, or gets violent when he's angry, or acts possessive and controlling toward you, or even if you just get a really bad gut feeling, bail out as fast as possible. It's far better to be safe than sorry.

Finally, tell your daughter that if she's ever in a bad situation that she needs to get out of, she can call you and you'll always come get her, no matter what time it is or where she is. And remind her that she can always come to you if she has a problem or if something bad has happened, and she'll always have your love and support.

DEALING WITH SONS

Now let's take a look at the other side of the gender coin. One of the most important things you can teach your sons is to respect women. Adolescent boys are up against some powerful cultural stereotypes of their own. Men are traditionally expected to behave aggressively, and passivity is frowned on as wimpy. A boy's friends may encourage him to get what he can and brag about it afterward. It's up to you to combat these selfish attitudes and instill an attitude of respect toward women.

Things like opening doors for women, pulling out chairs, and giving them flowers are all ways a man can demonstrate that he is considerate and thoughtful toward women. These kind gestures should be encouraged, of course, but I think it's even more important to cultivate an attitude of respect that runs deeper. Teach your sons to treat girls kindly and with respect, to take what they have to say seriously, and to place more value on substance than appearance.

And above all, emphasize to your sons that it is never, under any circumstances, appropriate to take advantage of a woman for the purpose of having sex. Using deceit, alcohol, or even coercion to have sex with a girl is cruel, dangerous, and illegal. Rape doesn't happen only between women and unknown, crazy attackers they've never seen before. It also happens when men they know and trust take advantage of them.

GUIDELINES FOR DATING

Young people usually begin coed activities in groups, which makes both them and you feel a little safer. They hang out at shopping malls, meet at movie theaters, and go to chaperoned parties. But before long they want to branch out into more private activities, and most of them can't wait to start dating.

Dating is an important rite of passage, and so it should be. But although young people need an opportunity to spend time with the opposite sex in social situations, the process should be gradual. As we've discussed, you should give your teenagers freedom in proportion to the trust they've earned from you. There are risks in this newfound freedom, for unsupervised activities can lead to trouble for irresponsible teenagers. Because dating is a privilege that goes along with growing up, you will need to establish guidelines for dating early on so you can revise them as your child demonstrates more responsibility. Here's how to take charge from the start and make sure that dating runs smoothly for both your teenager and you.

Establish Reasonable Curfews

You should already have a set curfew for your child, or else he should know when you expect him home, depending on the situation. These same expectations apply when your child goes out on his first date. The time you set should reflect your adolescent's age, the destination and activity of the evening, and his level of trustworthiness and maturity. If you're uncertain about what time to set, go with the earlier, more conservative time. You can always extend it to later when your teen has proved himself to be reliable, and as he gets older.

If your teenagers complain that all of their friends stay out later than they do, stick to your guns. It's rare to hear parents express regret over imposing an early curfew when their child started dating. On the other hand, I've heard many parents lament that they gave their teenager too much leeway too early.

Insist on Accountability

You have every right to know where your children are going, with whom they'll be spending time, and when they'll be home. If your son or daughter's date drives and plans to stop by the house to pick them up, don't let your teen dash out the door; insist on meeting the person they're going out with. They may fight you on this one, but insist on it; their embarrassment probably has more to do with nervousness than anything else. If they refuse, it may be necessary to forbid them from going out. After all, if she feels she has to hide the people she's spending time with, you have reason to be suspicious.

One father told me that his daughter's date pulled up to the house in a car that sounded like a Sherman tank. When he looked out the window and saw what he considered to be an unsafe vehicle, he called the date off. His daughter was angry but accepted his decision. In the event that the date doesn't want to meet you, you should also consider his refusal grounds for not allowing the event.

When your teen returns home from her date, talk to her about how things went. Don't be overly intrusive, but express curiosity. If this is done in a spirit of goodwill, it should encourage your children to discuss things with you in the future. After all, you were a teenager once and went through the same dating agonies and ecstasies. Naturally, they think you couldn't possibly understand what they're going through, but you can convince them otherwise. Just listen carefully, try to relate to their feelings, and don't be judgmental. In time, they'll feel comfortable sharing their dating stories with you.

Deal Directly with the Sore Spots

Certain areas are likely to lead to conflicts early on. Let's take a look at them.

Going out in cars. Should you allow your fourteen- or fifteen-year-old to go out on a date in a car? This can be a tough question, because cars mean extra freedom and extra potential for trouble, and that requires extra responsibility on both the driver's and the passenger's part. Take your teen's maturity level and previous behavior into account, along with what you know about her date, before you decide. If your child is trustworthy and you feel good about the person she's going out with, you can allow her the opportunity to behave responsibly. But make sure that you have specified the ground rules beforehand (like where she's allowed to go, when she's expected home, and that she must call you if she gets into a situation that feels dangerous or uncomfortable). Conversely, if you have any reservations about the situation, I suggest you err on the side of caution. There will be plenty of time for cars when your child is older. All things considered, you're better off playing it safe.

Parental supervision. Unsupervised activities raise another difficult question: how far should you trust your child in the absence of adult supervision? As a general rule, the younger your teenager, the greater the need for supervision. Again, err on the side of caution. If your child can't give you enough information about his proposed activity to satisfy you, don't let him go. You can always tell him that you trust him but are suspicious of the other kids, which may tone down any anger he's feeling. The bottom line is that teenagers who aimlessly cruise around with no particular destination other than a place with no parents are at greater risk for trouble. You have every reason to be concerned, so don't put your child in a situation he may not be prepared to handle.

Of course, certain unsupervised activities are more acceptable than others. Hanging out in a crowded shopping mall, restaurant, or movie theater puts young people under the watchful eye of others. You can use these situations as a proving ground for further trust. Most younger teenagers welcome the opportunity for some limited freedom and don't abuse the privilege. If they do, you'll need to restrict their activities until they can prove themselves trustworthy again.

Dating older kids. This is a very sticky issue. I don't want to suggest that all such situations are dangerous. Sometimes older teens are actually better dates because they've learned from the mistakes they've made and know to treat the opposite sex in a respectful and caring manner. On the other hand, there is a risk in your child's being exposed to someone older who doesn't have their best interests in mind and uses superior age and experience to manipulate your teen to have sex or make other bad decisions. So again, rely on your intuition. Consider your child's maturity and the circumstances of the proposed outing. It's probably appropriate for younger teens to date someone one or two years older, and older teens to date someone three, maybe even four years older. But when the age difference is greater—for example, a college student who pursuing a high school freshman, or a senior who's asking out an eighth-grader—I'd question the older person's motives. (Yes, there are exceptions, but this should be the general rule.)

Your teenager may accuse you of trying to control her and being out of touch, instead of admitting you're concerned about her safety. Don't let yourself be challenged that way or be tempted to give in. If you can't sleep at night because you're worried about what your child is up to, put your foot down. She'll have plenty of time to date older men when she grows up. Then it will be her choice, not yours.

If you do allow your child to date someone older, make sure that you meet him or her first. This gives you the opportunity to reinforce the early curfew you've imposed, screen the newcomer, and make sure that you feel comfortable with the situation. If you don't, you're within your rights to restrict them from going out, on the spot.

Talk to Your Teenager About False Impressions

Teenage boys and girls alike are often nervous and unsure about how to act on a date. Often they're worried that they're not interesting or cool enough, or that their date will lose interest and decide that they're stupid or boring. Unfortunately, many teens try to hide their insecurities by acting like someone they're not. They deliberately send a false impression to the opposite sex, an impression that they think is more attractive than who they really are. These false impressions are dangerous for several reasons.

Many teenage girls think they need to give guys the impression that they're sexy and seductive to get them interested. So they wear tight, skimpy clothing and use lots of sexual innuendo when they're talking to boys. This is an especially dangerous

---

How to Discuss the Importance of Honesty in Relationships

You'll need to alert your teenager to the pitfalls of deceit in relationships. Follow these suggestions to initiate productive discussions:

■ Emphasize that taking unfair advantage of someone through deceit is nothing to be proud of—and that you won't tolerate it.

■ Point out the consequences of dishonesty in relationships: people's feelings get hurt, trust is eroded, and reputations can be damaged.

■ How does your teen like to be treated by members of the opposite sex? Use that answer as a vehicle for a discussion about how he or she treats members of the opposite sex.

■ Talk about listening to your conscience. It should make you feel bad when you hurt someone's feelings, lie to them, or take advantage of them.

■ Ask your son or daughter how he or she would feel if they found out that their boyfriend or girlfriend was cheating on them.

■ Actions often speak louder than words, and tend to reveal a person's true feelings. Discuss with your teen ways that a boyfriend's or girlfriend's actions can demonstrate their true feelings, both for better and for worse.

impression to give, because boys often assume that sex is a given with such girls. In the movie *American Beauty*, Mena Suvari's character, Angela, acts very sophisticated and talks about sex in graphic terms. But her flirting and seductive attitude land her in a very real sexual encounter with her best friend's father, Lester, and she ends up tearfully asking him to stop, confessing that she is a virgin. In the movie, Lester treats her kindly and respectfully, but this is not always the case in real life. When girls give the impression that they're interested in sex and then don't follow through, guys can get angry. Some guys respond by spreading the word that the girl is a tease, while others respond by aggressively pushing for sex, assuming that she doesn't mean what she's saying. Many girls find themselves in dangerous situations they don't know how to control, and may even be forced into sex.

Girls who try too hard to act sexy are often afraid that no one will notice them if they act like themselves. They may also view boys as status symbols or prizes to be obtained rather than real people. Encourage your daughter to just be herself and to develop real relationships, even friendships, with boys, instead of playing games. It may not get her as much attention, but it will be well worth the wait to find someone who likes her for who she really is. And alert your daughter to the dangers of leading guys on by warning her of the potential negative and dangerous situations that can result.

SEX EDUCATION REVISITED

You'd think teenagers who are dating would have accurate information about sex. After all, their parents have probably discussed the basics with them, and they've taken sex education in school. However, their main source of information is often their peers. Many teens deny that sexual experimentation is risky and are convinced nothing bad can happen to them.

Make sure your children know the facts, including information about birth control, sexually transmitted diseases, and pregnancy. They should recognize all the potential consequences of sexual activity. Sometimes you can initiate a conversation matter-of-factly. You might say, "I guess you've heard a lot in school and on TV about AIDS. Do you understand how the HIV virus is contracted?" or "You probably know about birth control by now. Which method do you think is the safest?"

If he picks up on your overture, you can exchange views about responsible sexual behavior. And even if he doesn't follow your lead, you can still make your position clear. It's best to assume that your teenager isn't adequately informed. Tell him the facts straightforwardly and don't expect a response. There's no need to chastise him for his ignorance. If he challenges what you say, so much the better. Reply to his arguments as honestly as you can without passing judgment. However, don't read implications into your teenager's questions. For example, if she asks about a missed period, don't automatically assume she's worried that she's pregnant. If you jump to conclusions or start lecturing about irresponsible teens, you'll turn her off instantly. Instead, be calm, stick to the facts, take note of your child's concern, and make her comfortable with further dialogue. Following these guidelines makes it more likely that she'll come back to you if she needs you.

You should always emphasize the importance of behaving responsibly and being informed about issues of abstinence, birth control, STDs, and dating etiquette. Encourage your child to come to you with any concerns or questions he or she may have. To be prepared, keep abreast of what's going on in teenage circles and seek guidance when you need it. You'll find your pediatrician is happy to discuss any issues with you. And sometimes the pediatrician, family doctor, gynecologist, nurse, or physician's assistant can initiate a conversation with your child about a topic she's reluctant to talk with you about (like birth control, personal hygiene, or fears of pregnancy).

In summary, you want to strike a balance between censorship and overexposure when you talk to your teenager about sex. Withholding vital information and avoiding discussion don't reduce the likelihood of sexual activity. In fact, adolescents who grow up in repressive households where sex is a forbidden topic may be more likely to get into trouble with it, because they won't have been encouraged to establish a healthy attitude toward sex. On the other hand, excessive emphasis on sexual topics can be overstimulating. If you make frequent sexual references or jokes, suggest that you take relationships lightly, or walk around undressed, you may indirectly encourage inappropriate behavior in your teenagers.

When It's Time to Talk About Sex

It is important to learn to talk about sex with your teen comfortably. If you're actively involved in her life, you probably know who she's spending time with, where she's spending her time, and what's going on with various friendships and relationships. If you don't, you'll need to take a more active role and focus on the communication between you and your child.

Here are some suggestions to move your conversation along more comfortably:

- Don't interrogate them. Express an interest in what they're doing and the person they're spending time with.
- Share an experience with a member of the opposite sex from your own teenage years; it could be a friend, a lover, or someone in between.
- Discuss the stages two people go through when they find there's a mutual attraction. Examples include the initial thrill when two people connect, the decisions about what degree of involvement and type relationship both people want to have, and the decisions that have to be made about issues like seeing other people and the degree of sexual involvement.
- Tell them you don't want to be a worrier, but you'd be pleased to learn that they have values that they adhere to. And ask them to tell you a little about what they believe in.

- Make sure they are using birth control—ideally, condoms.
- Insist that you meet his significant friend, even if he insists that they're not dating and he's afraid you'll make a big deal. Assure him that you'll be cool and casual and won't say anything embarrassing, and that you just like knowing his friends, whether they're boys or girls.
- Assure them that they can always come to you when they have a problem.
- Make sure they're aware of the significant factors that contribute to a meaningful relationship. (We talked about these in the previous section.)
- Try to talk about dating and sex on a regular basis. Don't rely on a serious talk once a year (or only once, ever!).

If you create a safe climate for sharing, you'll be rewarded with a teenager who'll talk to you about what's on her mind. Don't expect her to tell you everything, but take comfort in the fact that she'll come to you when she needs you. And of course, remind her how much you care about her, again and again.

THE RIGHT TO PRIVACY AND OTHER BOUNDARIES

Certain matters pertaining to sex should be off-limits to parental prying. You don't have a right to know all the details of your children's sexual experiences, unless they're in an abusive or unhealthy relationship or may be pregnant or infected with a sexually transmitted disease. It's often difficult to tell when these occur, so you'll need to be a careful observer of your teens' behavior and moods. If they seem extremely secretive, depressed, despondent, or in physical discomfort, you'll certainly want to approach them with your concerns. Assuming you've consistently conveyed the message that they can come to you when they're in trouble, they'll be more likely to respond to your overtures. As in all other instances, trying to force teenagers to disclose personal information is a surefire way to lose their confidence.

Certain situations do require your immediate intervention. In the event that teens are in an abusive relationship, whether the abuse is physical or emotional, you'll have to help them stand up for themselves and take steps to ensure it won't happen again. If there's a persistent pattern of abuse, you should forbid them from seeing the person and inform his or her parents about what has transpired. If you suspect that your daughter is pregnant, you'll also need to approach her directly with your concerns. Try to do so in a caring way, so that she'll feel safe disclosing any problems she might have. Let her know that if she is pregnant, you still love her and you'll be there for her no matter what, and she'll have your help and support as you figure out the best way to handle it together. If she brushes off your concerns but you're convinced she's hiding something, make a doctor's appointment for her, and ensure that she keeps it. This is also the case if you suspect your teen has contracted an STD but is hiding it from you.

You must bite your tongue, however, about certain private subjects. You should certainly let your adolescent know that masturbation is perfectly normal, as are nocturnal emissions for boys. Generally speaking, what your teenagers do with their bodies is their business, not yours. This is also true of sexual fantasies, which are a private matter and should be respected as such. The fact is that sexual thoughts don't hurt anyone and are a natural part of growing up. So by all means voice this message—but keep it impersonal. Finally, when it's time for body talk, it's a bad idea to ask them about specific development, as many teens are very self-conscious about their changing bodies. It's okay to tell them about normal body development, just don't ask them for updates about what's going on.

There are a couple of other areas your child should not have access to. One is your own sex life. Teenagers don't want to hear about their parents' sexual activities and consider it a burden when they do. Even if parents are single and back on the dating scene, your teenager should not become your confidant for sex-charged stories.

Finally, pornography should be out of bounds. Yes, your teenager is probably pretty curious, and may really want to enjoy the wide range and variety of porn that's out there. But if he or she is under eighteen years of age, that makes it illegal. Pornography can appear in many forms, including movies, telephone conversations, magazines, and sites on the Internet. It's shockingly easy to obtain. There are video and magazine stores that don't ask for proof of age, pay-per-view options that just require a credit card, and 900 and 976 phone numbers listed in the backs of many major publications. And the Internet may be the easiest way of all to view porn. Parents have told me they've learned about their kids' activities in this area when they received phone bills of hundreds of dollars in charges for adult entertainment services. So make sure that you check your phone bills and credit card bills carefully and take a look at what your teens are doing on the computer (there are ways to print out lists of the Web sites most recently visited). If you learn that they're visiting adult Web sites, first explain to them why you don't want them doing it. If their behavior continues, contact your on-line service and put a block on these sites or phone numbers. If that's not possible, you may need to cancel their access to the Internet. You must take a stand whenever your children are exposed to information or activity that can harm them.

SPECIAL PROBLEMS WITH EARLY AND PROMISCUOUS SEXUAL ACTIVITY

Some young people go too far too soon. It's difficult to know exactly what your child is doing, but you should check out any suspicions you have. For example, if they're deeply involved with a member of the opposite sex and are spending nearly all their free time together in an unsupervised setting, or if you over-hear them talking to a friend about their sexual experiences, raise the issue with them.

Of course, your values come into play here, but I don't rec-ommend sexual intercourse or oral sex for any early adoles-cent. They're just not ready to take on the responsibility and implications of such actions. You have every right to be seri-ously concerned if this is happening to your child. It's impossi-ble to control what they do with their own bodies, but you should make your position crystal clear. And make certain that you provide adequate supervision and information for your teen.

Promiscuous teenagers are sexually active randomly and indiscreetly, without regard to possible consequences. Unfortunately, this is more common than we'd like to think. Naturally, most parents worry more about their daughters than their sons because they're at risk for pregnancy and because even in these modern times, the old double standard—it's okay for boys to be promiscuous but it's not okay for girls—still applies to some degree. Girls also run more of a risk of getting a nasty, damaging reputation as a slut or a ho; this can lead to their being rejected, ignored, or the butt of jokes. But boys can become every bit as promiscuous as girls—although the word is more rarely used to describe them—and the results can be as bad. Promiscuity could lead to your son impregnating a girl or spreading or catching a nasty disease. It could also lead to repu-tation problems and, as in the case of girls, usually signifies an underlying problem.

Promiscuous behavior is always a problem. At worst, indiscriminate sexual activity is dangerous, self-destructive, and unfulfilling. There is no healthy reason for teenagers to engage in promiscuous behavior, since any enjoyment and pleasure that it may bring is quite short-lived. But since they do, all too often, I'll explain why this happens and what you can do about it. Here are the primary reasons teens become promiscuous.

Feelings of Rejection

The promiscuous teen needs to be loved. She may feel rejected by her peers, shunned by the popular crowd, or ignored by her parents. This isolation leaves her feeling insecure and desperate to fit in and be liked. She wants someone to accept her, and because her self-esteem is low, she's fragile and easily manipulated. The result is a young person who compromises herself in a futile attempt to gain the favor of her peers.

This type of promiscuous teen views sex as a key to achieving intimacy, instead of an expression of a preexisting intimacy with dimensions like love, respect, and friendship. The promise of easy sex will always lure members of the opposite sex (though not necessarily its finest members), but rarely will it hold their attention once the deed is done. These teens are caught in a vicious cycle of emotional highs and lows. They feel sad and lonely, so they use the promise of sex to achieve a temporary intimacy with someone they usually don't know very well. This temporary intimacy and the pleasure they may derive from the sexual act makes them feel happy and worthy. Unfortunately, the attention and affection end once the deed is done, because there was only the illusion of intimacy, and they find themselves back in the same emotional lows of feeling unwanted and unworthy.

Both boys and girls can fit this pattern of behavior. One difference, though, is that girls are more likely to use sex as an attempt to establish genuine relationships with boys; they're crushed when these boys ignore them or make fun of them later. Boys who use sex to try to purge feelings of rejection and unworthiness are more likely to have one-night stands with few real emotional ties, because boys are less likely to seek personal validation through having a girlfriend.

Parents can unintentionally encourage promiscuous behavior through rejection. If you tell your daughter she looks like a tramp, she may be inclined to act like one. She'll say to herself: Well, since my parents already think I'm a tramp, it doesn't really matter what I do because they already have their minds made up. Since I can't change their thinking, I might as well do whatever I feel like doing. Thus, rejection and criticism make matters worse.

Peer Pressure

Teenage boys and girls can become promiscuous because of peer pressure. Both sexes have to deal with this pressure from their friends when they feel like "everybody's doing it." Guys often encourage one another to score whenever they can, and may give one of their friends who decides *not* to have sex a pretty hard time. They create an atmosphere where promiscuity is encouraged as a sign of masculinity and personal triumph. The type of peer pressure that girls get from their friends is usually a little different. Girls hear their friends talking about sex (although it's usually more accurate to say they're *bragging* about sex) and hear all about how great it is. Then they want to get in on the action too.

There are also teens who give in way too easily to pressure from the opposite sex. They often end up with the reputations for being sluts, and it's well known that they can be easily persuaded to have sex. They're easily swayed by pressure put on them, usually because they don't feel strongly enough about their own convictions. These teens, especially girls, are often persuaded to make really bad, reputation-damaging decisions.

Rebellion

Young people may use promiscuity as a way to rebel against their parents or their community. This often occurs in oppressive environments, where sex is viewed as sinful or evil and where teens are threatened with dire punishments (in this life and the next) if they engage in premarital sexual activity. So teens rebel against this authoritarian attitude by becoming sexually active. Think of the stereotypes of rebellious Catholic schoolgirls and the promiscuous preacher's daughter. Obviously stereotypes are not true of everyone—but there are plenty of young people who act out against the conservative religious values they feel they are forced to accept.

Other teens use promiscuous behavior as a way to get back at their parents because they know that sexual activity will make their parents' skin crawl. Finally, others rebel against parents whose discipline is too lax and whose values are lacking. In that instance, their promiscuity is a cry for help; they desperately want to push their parents to the point where they will step in and tell them to stop. They're rebelling because they want boundaries established.

Depression

Most promiscuous teens deny their feelings of sadness, but their actions announce it to the world. Depressed teenagers have poor self-esteem and are prone to self-destructive behavior. Sometimes this is the outgrowth of a long history of criticism, rejection, and failure, while at other times it is biologically based (it runs in the family) and seems less related to environmental factors. Although parents with no history of depression will sometimes be faced with a depressed child, there is usually an explanation for the disorder. An evaluation by a mental health professional will help you to determine the causes and chart a course of treatment. Situational factors can also play a role in depression. A young person who has experienced a major loss, parents' divorce, or serious illness is often susceptible to this disorder. Sometimes the feelings they experience are more than they can bear. These teens often show little concern for themselves and figure they deserve shabby treatment.

Sixteen-year-old Nora was an example of depression of long-standing origin. She'd been sexually promiscuous for more than a year with eight or nine different boys and seemed to float in and out of shallow relationships. Nora had a bad reputation at school, where it was widely known that boys went out with her for only one reason. She had few if any close friends and was strikingly detached from her family.

When I met Nora, she insisted she didn't care what people thought. "I do what I feel like," she told me defiantly. "I'm having a good time, so screw everybody else."

But her angry and indifferent façade quickly dissolved with more discussion. What emerged was a sad and lonely girl desperately searching for happiness and acceptance. Nora's alcoholic father and depressed mother had little time to spend with her, and most of their interaction with her revolved around their outrage over her behavior.

As I got to know Nora better, I realized she never felt like she fit in. She'd been a lonely, sad child with few friends and an unhappy home life. When she reached adolescence, her classmates started teasing her about her acne and boys ignored her, so she kept to herself. Nora carried around a great deal of anger that she couldn't express directly. Then suddenly she discovered sex. It happened the first time when she got drunk at a party and she went upstairs with a boy who was also drunk. This led to a string of meaningless sexual encounters that only made Nora feel worse.

Discussing this with Nora, I realized she didn't enjoy sex. In fact, she described herself as feeling empty. She lacked energy, was sad most of the time, and when she wasn't numb, she was despairing. She sensed that what she was doing was wrong, but felt she had no other options. As she bluntly put it, "My reputation really sucks. The kids in school call me a ho and they don't talk to me much. And to tell you the truth, my parents don't treat me much better. It really doesn't matter what I do."

Over time—and using the techniques described below—I was able to work with Nora and her parents to help her regain her self-esteem and take enough pride in herself that she ended her sexual promiscuity. But it was a long road back for Nora and for her parents as well, who learned that there were a number of things they could have done differently that would have helped their daughter avoid falling into the sexual promiscuity trap.

ADDRESSING PROMISCUITY

Dealing with a promiscuous teen can be devastating for a parent on so many different levels. You watch your child battle with low self-esteem, rejection, and self-hatred; their behavior hurts them and it hurts you too. Here are some of the ways to address promiscuity and help your child stop harmful behavior.

Talk to Them

You have to start to address sexually promiscuous behavior at home. Assuming that your children know you're aware of their sexual activities, try to express concern rather than criticism. Their behavior may be distasteful to you, but it's imperative that you let them know you love them. Recrimination, put-downs, and lectures will only alienate them further. They may not even be conscious of the relationship between their promiscuous behavior and their low self-esteem and unhappiness.

So try to put your insight to use. Keep in mind how sad they feel and how humiliated they may be by your discovery. Try to be supportive at all costs. Encourage them to be honest about their feelings. Hopefully they'll tell you what they're so angry and hurt about—perhaps parental criticism, peer rejection, a desire for attention or love, or resentment that you excessively control their behavior. If they share complaints, try not to be defensive; focus instead on working on a solution for the problem together. If they insist that you don't care about them and look down on things they do—even if you have good reason to feel this way—don't dismiss what they say. Listen actively and reflect back their concerns so you can help them feel understood. This is an important step toward reconciliation.

Set Limits and Stay Involved

You can't control everything your teen does, but you can certainly make it more difficult for him to run around sleeping with half the town. If he's being promiscuous, it means that he's got a lot of unsupervised time on his hands. Where is he engaging in all this sexual activity—at your house? in his car? at someone else's house? Try to deduce the answer so you can impose some supervision and restrict his behavior. If he's behaving promiscuously, don't let him have members of the opposite sex over at your house at all; who knows what's going on in the basement while you're making dinner! And use curfews and limits to curtail risky behavior. If there are lots of parties with alcohol or drugs involved in his promiscuous behavior, keep an eye and an ear out for these types of activities so you know what's going on. If he protests your restrictions, tell him that you know how he's been managing his unsupervised time and you don't approve. His independence is important, but if he's making poor decisions, he's not managing his independence effectively, and it's up to you to guide him toward the right choices.

Make Them Feel Special

When your teen goes out on dates, try to make her feel special before she leaves the house. Tell her how sweet, caring, attractive, and responsible she is, and remind her that you're proud of her. Express curiosity about where she's going and what she'll do when she gets there. Let her know that she should not settle for anything less than the best. Don't place undue importance on having dates or a boyfriend; after all, she's perfectly wonderful whether she's single or not! Make her self-esteem your first priority, and don't apologize for getting involved. Young people who feel valued are less likely to fall prey to negative influences. Working on the life skills I've discussed in Chapters 3, 4, and 5 will also help get them back on track.

Know When to Seek Help

Finally, know when to ask for outside assistance. If your child's promiscuous behavior has gotten out of hand, it may be more than you can handle. Contact your pediatrician, family doctor, gynecologist, guidance counselor, or a therapist for guidance and assistance on how to handle your current situation. Your child's pediatrician or gynecologist can help your teen to appreciate the risks she's taking and will encourage her to behave more responsibly. If you worry that your teen may be pregnant or carrying an STD, a physician can run any tests necessary. And a therapist or guidance counselor will help your teen to explore the factors that led to the promiscuous behavior pattern and attempt to address them directly.

DRINKING AND DRUGS

Substance abuse is a national concern for good reason. Dangerous and illegal substances like alcohol and marijuana have been responsible for family conflicts, school problems, health issues, bad decision making, and fatal car accidents. They're also associated in varying degrees with depression, sexual promiscuity, violence, and antisocial behavior. Depending on which substance you're talking about, your teenager will probably either tell you not to worry because everyone is doing it (alcohol, tobacco) or will assure you that no one he knows would ever use something like that (cocaine, meth, ecstasy). Forget your teen's attempts to dissuade you. Drug and alcohol use *is* a very real problem, no matter where you live or what your background is, and you must learn to deal with these issues.

From my point of view, teenage use of either alcohol or marijuana, the most frequently used drugs, is equally dangerous and illegal. That's my bottom line, no matter how unreasonable teenagers consider the laws against drugs and drinking. Here's what you're up against. In many teenage circles, drinking is socially acceptable. Some kids actually expect alcohol to be served at parties. This shouldn't surprise us, considering that the media are filled with images of drinking. The Absolut vodka book, calendar, and posters are all best-sellers, and a number of alcoholic products have been designed to appeal to young people. In a national survey, more young children recognized the Budweiser frogs than the president of the United States.

It would be wonderful if our children listened to us about drugs and alcohol. Unfortunately, giving them the facts about the dangers, along with a stern warning, is not enough. Many teens have tried illicit substances at least once. The main problem with this is that experimentation can lead to abuse. The combination of impulsive behavior, poor judgment, and lack of experience places many youth at risk. And substance abuse often coexists with other problems, which compound the difficulty of addressing it. Therefore, drinking or drug use should be addressed as soon as you perceive it to be a problem. But let's not get ahead of ourselves. There's a lot you can do to prevent alcohol and drug problems and deal with them at the first sign.

SUBSTANCES YOUR TEENAGER MIGHT ENCOUNTER

While I have included important facts about alcohol, tobacco, and marijuana, this book is not intended to be a resource for information about different substances. There are thousands of resources out there—books, magazine articles, brochures, news columns, TV reports, and information on the Internet. I have listed some resources that I find helpful in the Appendix of this book, and suggest that you make use of them if you have any questions, need information, or worry that your son or daughter is abusing a substance.

I will talk briefly, though, about what you need to worry about, and why. Please note that I am writing based on current trends and influences, and these do change over time. Sadly enough, it seems that as soon as one drug is on the decline, another surges up in popularity to take its place.

Alcohol

Alcohol is the number one substance of choice for thousands and thousands of teenagers. It's available at many parties and get-togethers, as well as in Mom and Dad's fridge or liquor cabinet. Many people view alcohol consumption as harmless fun, so while it can be a bit of a hassle for underage drinkers to find someone to make a run to the liquor store, finding the right someone isn't *too* difficult. Plus, some older teens have fake IDs that they can use to purchase alcohol.

As I mentioned, alcohol is viewed by many as a party drink whose worst consequence is a hangover the next day. What could be more fun than a night of keg stands and drinking games? Unfortunately, alcohol does have a deadlier side, one that teenage drinkers are not prepared for. First of all, many teenage drinkers don't understand their own body's ability to handle alcohol, so they overdo it. The focus at many high school parties is getting drunk; teens will brag that they want to get "wasted" or "f——d up." This means that they drink too much too fast, whether that means taking shot after shot of hard liquor, shotgunning or funneling beers, or just not knowing when to stop. For many teens, this leads to episodes of extreme drunkenness where they get out of control. They may get physically sick, vomiting uncontrollably, and it may take a day or two to recover. Their impaired decision-making abilities may lead them to start a fight, deliberately destroy property (like punching out windows), have unprotected or unwanted sex, or get behind the wheel of a car. Drunk driving kills so many people every year and it has received so much attention, yet teenagers persist in making this deadly mistake.

Worst of all, many teens who've consumed way too much alcohol go into a state of alcohol poisoning. The body is so overwhelmed by the level of alcohol it has received that the alcohol starts to act like a poison (which it is, in big enough quantities). Many alcohol-poisoned teens start by passing out, and their friends think they're just sleeping one off. Other teens often do not recognize or look for the signs of alcohol poisoning, like shallow breathing and a slowed pulse. Victims of alcohol poisoning can die if not taken to the hospital to have their stomachs pumped. The alcohol poisoning scenario has become one that's all too familiar to high school and college students.

There is also the danger of becoming dependent upon alcohol. I will discuss the reasons teens abuse alcohol in more detail later, but I will say now that if there is a history of alcoholism in your family, he or she will be much more prone to alcohol addiction than the average teenager. And a depressed, rebellious, or unhappy teen may use alcohol to try to self-medicate.

Tobacco

Depending on where you live and what your background is, smoking cigarettes is accepted or vilified. Many public places like restaurants, bars, and malls are cracking down on indoor smoking. At the same time, there are still plenty of smokers out there. And nearly all of them started during adolescence.

It's hard for many teens to understand how deadly smoking can be, because a few cigarettes probably won't hurt you. Besides, diseases like emphysema and lung cancer are for old people! And smoking seems like such a nice, social, enjoyable activity—you're hanging out with your friends, enjoying a little nicotine buzz. And even though few teens would admit it, many of them think it does look cool to smoke, and view smoking as a sign of maturity and sophistication.

Unfortunately, tobacco really does have a nasty side, one that may become apparent only after you've been smoking for years. Some of the drawbacks seem petty, like hideous-smelling clothes and hair and dry, leathery skin, but over time it can become quite unattractive. It causes shortness of breath and hurts the bronchial tubes of the lungs, so that smokers tend to be sicker more frequently and for a longer duration. Nicotine is also highly addictive, so while it's easy to ease into a smoking habit, quitting means fighting overwhelming urges and suffering from irritability, short temper, and increased hunger.

Finally, there are the diseases that tobacco causes. Teenagers are generally in the prime of their health and can't imagine anything really bad ever happening. Lung cancer, however, is very real and has been scientifically linked to smoking. It is one of the quickest and most painful forms of cancer, and there is absolutely no cure. It is tragic to watch someone die from lung cancer, mainly because in most cases it was brought on by smoking. Emphysema is also a horrible, crippling disease where you fight for every breath you take.

Marijuana

Even though it's hit a plateau, marijuana is probably the most popular illegal drug for teens. The debate to legalize it rages on, and the use of marijuana is championed by rappers, singers, actors, artists, and other public figures. There are even a few proven medical uses for marijuana. It's generally easy enough to obtain, and causes an enjoyable, peaceful buzz that many users enjoy. So what's wrong with it?

For one thing, marijuana decreases motivation. There are plenty of jokes about marijuana-smoking slackers, but the stereotype is rooted in reality; marijuana users don't want to do much of anything other than hang out and maybe eat that carton of ice cream. This is bad news if you're supposed to be, say, going to school, studying, or attending a sports practice. Though many can use it casually, it is addictive, and many users end up smoking several times a day, every day. And it really does hurt intelligence. Heavy marijuana smokers of many years are slow and sluggish, not just when they're high, but all the time. Finally, it is illegal.

Alcohol, tobacco, and marijuana are often called *gateway drugs* because serious drug users almost always begin with one of these three and then move on to something more hard-core. I will briefly discuss some of the harder drugs you may encounter, and a few disturbing drug trends.

Ecstasy

Ecstasy is on the rise everywhere, all over the country, especially among young drug users. It is a popular drug at parties, raves, and clubs because it produces a happy, ecstatic (hence the name) sensation by stimulating the brain to produce seratonin and dopamine. Many people, including members of the media, have dismissed ecstasy as being relatively harmless. Unfortunately, that's not the case. While ecstasy is working on your brain, it's also throwing off your body's electrolytes and causes water retention. Since it's usually taken in a social setting where there might be dancing or other physical activity, sweating and drinking a lot of water or liquids throws the body's balances off even further. If the body's sodium level gets too low, it can lead to seizures, brain damage, and even death. Because many users don't understand a lot about ecstasy, they don't know that it can be deadly.

Prescription Drugs

Many experts believe that our children—and people in general—are overmedicated, especially when it comes to behavior-altering drugs like antidepressants and ADD/ADHD inhibitors. Unfortunately, with all of these drugs floating around, there is a great potential for abuse. There is a black market among teenagers for drugs like Ritalin and Prozac, and unfortunately these drugs can be very dangerous when used inappropriately. There is also an abuse of diet drugs, which contain ephedrine (or similar compounds); they function like speed, stimulating the system and accelerating the heart. They can also be deadly, causing cardiovascular damage and even death. Finally, there are teens who, desperate to get drunk, will drink over-the-counter cough syrup. The terrible consequences of abusing prescription medications are too varied and numerous to get into here, but warn your children *not* to abuse prescription drugs, whether their own or someone else's.

Harder Drugs

As for other, more dangerous drugs, they tend to be concentrated in certain areas of the country and among specific ethnic and economic populations. A drug may be a big problem in your community but not have an impact anywhere else. For example, use of methamphetamines (crystal meth) is on the rise in many rural communities, especially in the western United States, but it is not really a problem in cities like New York. Cocaine is an expensive drug abused by the wealthy, whereas crack, a different form of cocaine, is very cheap and is abused by poorer members of the population. Other drugs that may plague your community are speed, heroin, PCP, LSD, nitrous oxide, and inhalants (like glue or paint thinner). I urge you to stay abreast of local trends; if you're not getting enough information from the news, contact the local high school, police station, or hospital.

WHY TEENAGERS USE— AND ABUSE—ALCOHOL AND OTHER DRUGS

To curb your children's substance use, you must understand it. Every one of today's adolescents has sat through countless lectures about the dangers of substance use from you, or in school classes and assemblies, the media, or DARE (Drug Abuse Resistance Education, a group with a strong middle school and high school presence). And every year thousands of older teens sign "prom promises" and other agreements vowing not to abuse substances. So with all this education and all these warnings, why are these dangerous substances still so appealing for teens?

There are several reasons youth gravitate toward substance use, usually beginning with alcohol, tobacco, and marijuana, and in some cases moving on to more dangerous drugs such as LSD, cocaine, ecstasy, heroin, and other potentially lethal mixtures.

Everybody's Doing It

Teenagers are astute observers, and they see *lots* of people using various substances. They see their parents and other adults drinking alcohol, smoking, and unfortunately, sometimes abusing other substances too. They look at TV and magazines and see hundreds of cool ads for alcohol and tobacco products. They see movies like *Studio 54* and *Coyote Ugly*, which glorify the substance-soaked nightlife of bars and clubs. And most important, they usually see a lot of other teenagers who enjoy alcohol, cigarettes, and other substances. How can it be wrong?

The teen social scene often revolves around drinking and smoking pot. That's what the word "party" means to most teenagers. Some parties, like family-sponsored birthday bashes and sweet sixteens, as well as cast parties and sport team parties, don't involve alcohol, but most "real" parties do. Sometimes friends urge one another to try a drink or smoke something, but it's just as common for teens to start using a substance because it's readily available and they observe all their friends enjoying it. Not only that, but it's a way to be social. One young man told me, "If I didn't drink, I wouldn't have anyone to hang out with." Teens see their friends enjoying themselves with various substances, and so they view it as acceptable. The flip side is that when their friends think that drinking is stupid or smoking pot is scary, they're much less likely to try it.

Escape and Self-Medication

Life is often difficult for teenagers. When they're unhappy and uncomfortable with themselves and have neither a healthy outlet for their frustration nor a trusted confidant, they may turn to chemicals for solace. Depending on what substance they're using, they may feel blissfully oblivious, wonderfully happy, or energized and confident. When they're given a chance to take something to make them feel better, many can't resist. "When I smoke up," one of my clients put it, "I can just forget about everything that's pressuring me."

After their initial exposure to a substance, teenagers start to believe it can ward off their painful feelings. It's a dangerous shortcut to solving problems, but what do they care? If their lives aren't going well, they figure they have nothing to lose. Of course, their problems don't vanish, and once the effects of the substance have worn off, they're left with the same problems as before, plus the low, depressed feelings that some substances leave you with. So these teens come back for even more of that substance. Before long, the substance takes on the role of a mood enhancer, an antidote to any unpleasant situation, and in many cases a crutch to deal with everyday life. As you'll see, any immediate benefits are short-lived.

Boredom and the Need for Excitement

I've already discussed boredom in Chapter 7 and noted its effect on a teenager's propensity for risk taking. Teens who can't tolerate being alone, have trouble keeping themselves occupied, and crave excitement are prime candidates for substance abuse. Not only do alcohol and marijuana give them something to do, but those substances help fill the internal void they feel. One boy's statement captures this sentiment. "When I'm stuck in my house with nothing to do," he said, "all I can think about is going out to party." Alcohol and drugs become false friends whose glittery promise of a good time is alluring to a bored adolescent. These false friends also help restless, bored, risk-taking teens to forget about troubles that they often face, like family conflicts, school failure, and peer rejection. Further, they provide a common ground for interacting with like-minded teens, a way to instantly bond with a group of kids. Soon the illicit substances define their existence and they spend increasing amounts of time seeking ways to get high.

Rebellion

What better way to express anger at your parents than doing something they tell you not to? Different rebellious teens choose different substances to use based on their personalities. I'm often struck by teenagers' lethal combination of despair and anger. Alcohol is the drug of choice for the angry teenager because it frees him to behave aggressively. One young man told me, "When we're drinking, the rest of the world can go to hell." Methamphetamines, or meth, also encourage aggressive, violent behavior, only it's far more dangerous and potent than alcohol. Marijuana, on the other hand, reduces aggression and is more of an avoidance drug. LSD and hallucinogens are also escape drugs, often used by young people who feel misunderstood and may long to escape to a more idealistic, kind world. Smoking cigarettes is a form of rebellion only if it's something that parents have specifically forbidden; they smoke to flaunt their independence and make their parents angry.

Instant Gratification

Drugs and alcohol work quickly. The initial effects feel really good (of course—why else would people use substances?). It's easy to get a nicotine buzz from a cigarette, or the warm, happy feelings that come with a few drinks. Who doesn't want an easy way to be happy? Young people do—especially unhappy young people who want to get rid of their bad feelings fast. Another teen told me, "When I get into a fight with my parents, I'm out the door. I just can't get stoned fast enough." It's a short-term shortcut to happiness. The problem is, again, that not only do any problems they were trying to avoid still exist once the happy feelings wear off, but most substances that lift you up high end up dropping you way low, so you're sadder than you were before you started. At the very least, you're back where you started emotionally, and that's not good enough for some teens.

Lack of Confidence

Many shy teenagers who lack confidence report that they'll do things under the influence of alcohol or drugs that they might not otherwise. One girl readily acknowledged this, saying, "I have to get drunk before going to a party. Otherwise, I wouldn't be able to talk to anyone." Of course, this is part of the appeal of drugs and alcohol even for relatively self-confident teens; you have the courage to dance if you're a bad dancer, or sing at the top of your lungs even if you have a terrible voice, or kiss the girl you're attracted to. And alcohol and other drugs tend not only to loosen your inhibitions but to alleviate social anxiety. Not only do you have something in common with the other people around you, but there's the mentality that "if I do anything or say anything stupid, everyone will just think I had too many drinks or smoked too much weed." For too many teens, substances become a crutch they rely on, and they don't feel comfortable in a social setting without them. This is the kind of confidence booster they can do without. Young people who feel bad about themselves are more susceptible to substance abuse, but the false sense of security alcohol and drugs give them is short-lived. And to make matters worse, substance abuse leads its users to make poor decisions that further undermine their self-confidence in the long run.

Misinformation

Perhaps the most avoidable cause of substance abuse is inaccurate information about drugs and alcohol. After all, there are so many statistics and facts readily available to teens! But nearly every teenager has friends who claim to be experts on various recreational substances, and they're happy to assure her that the risks are minimal. Several years ago, a young man told me his definition of a drinking problem was an alcoholic on skid row. Anything short of that, even vomiting, blackouts, and passing out, was no big deal. The same is true of ecstasy, "a totally harmless drug," marijuana—"It's not addictive and doesn't have any

Some Facts About Alcohol Use

Here are the proven facts about alcohol use, according to the American Council for Drug Education:

- A blood alcohol level of 0.08–0.10 defines you as legally drunk. This level is determined by the number of drinks consumed per hour measured against a person's weight.

- A 120-pound woman who has two drinks in an hour would have a blood alcohol level of 0.08, and that's legally drunk. A 160-pound man who has three drinks in an hour would have a blood alcohol level of 0.08, making him legally drunk.

- Poor judgment while using alcohol puts teens at risk for car accidents, falls, violence, and unplanned and unsafe sex.

- Most states have zero tolerance laws. That means that drivers under twenty-one with even a trace of alcohol on their breath will lose their driver's license. This is important for your teen to know.

- The amount of alcohol it takes to make you pass out is dangerously close to the amount it takes to kill you.

kind of negative side to it"—and any other substance. It's important for you to provide accurate information and correct misconceptions, not just about scary, hyped-up drugs like meth and heroin but about drugs like alcohol, tobacco, and marijuana, which most teens don't take very seriously.

Parents' Cues

Sometimes parents inadvertently encourage their children to use alcohol or other substances. Your condoning of occasional drinking, getting drunk yourselves, using illegal drugs, telling funny or entertaining personal stories that involve heavy drinking or drug use, or making light of the risks involved is called *enabling* in my line of work. This term refers to behavior that ignores or promotes an emerging problem with illicit substances. When you deny or minimize the seriousness of your teenager's actions, you're giving him subtle permission to continue.

The emotional climate in your home can also precipitate substance abuse. I've spoken about this earlier, in Chapters 2 and 3, so I'll just restate the most important points here. Inadequate parental involvement and lack of supervision put teenagers at risk. Poor family communication only worsens the problem. Teenagers who can't talk to their parents are more likely to feel isolated and unhappy, and these feelings lead them to seek chemical solutions to their problems. Finally, parents' relationships and behavior send powerful messages to their children about how to cope with problems. If they see you continually avoiding difficult issues, they'll probably do the same.

HOW TO TELL IF YOUR TEENAGER IS USING AN ILLICIT SUBSTANCE

Parents sometimes tell me they had no idea that their teenagers were drinking or using drugs. That's usually because they've been oblivious to the telltale hints all around them. Don't let this happen to you. Here are the signs you should be on the lookout for.

The Nose Knows

Your teenage son breezes into the house on a Saturday night after a night out with the guys. How do you know if he was drinking or smoking? Make a point of having a conversation with him—not a yelled conversation through various rooms and closed doors, but a real, face-to-face conversation. If your child has been drinking alcohol, smoking cigarettes, or smoking marijuana, the smell will be on his breath. Any smoke he's been around will also soak into his clothing and hair. That's not necessarily a sign of personal guilt, but if it's pot smoke you smell, you have the right to be alarmed; even if he wasn't smoking it himself, he was with peers who were. You should also be suspicious if your teen enters the house chomping on a fresh wad of spearmint gum or a handful of Altoids, or smelling of freshly applied lotion or perfume. He's probably trying to cover up a tell-tale odor.

Take a Closer Look

If your teenager is using or abusing an illegal substance, there's probably visual evidence to support it too. While you're chatting with her after she gets back from going out with her friends, take a close look. Pay attention to her eyes—they tend to reveal any substance use. If she's been smoking marijuana, her eyes will be red and heavy lidded, with constricted pupils. If she's been drinking alcohol, her pupils will be dilated, and she may have difficulty focusing on you. In addition, alcohol has the effect of giving a red, flushed color to the face and cheeks. There are also telltale signs of more serious drug use. Intravenous drug use leaves track marks, usually on the arms, but occasionally other places like the legs. Long sleeves in scorching hot summer weather may be an attempt to hide something. Snorting cocaine causes nosebleeds and eventually eats away at the septum inside the nose. Finally, if there are strange burns on her lips or fingers, she may be smoking a substance through a hot glass or metal pipe.

Mood Changes

Okay, the scenario is the same as above; it's Saturday night, and your son has just gotten back from a night out with his friends. How is he acting? Is he loud and obnoxious, or laughing hysterically at nothing? Is he unusually clumsy to the point where he's stumbling into furniture and walls, tripping over his own feet and knocking things over? Is he sullen, withdrawn, and unusually tired and slack-eyed for the hour of night? Does he look queasy and stumble into the bathroom? These are all signs that he could have just been using some kind of illegal substance:

alcohol, marijuana, or something else. You shouldn't read too much into a slight mood change after he gets home from being with his friends, but you should be on the lookout for unusual or extreme behavior.

You should also pay attention to your teenager's behavior over time. If your teenager has become silent, angry, withdrawn, and uncommunicative, and this has lasted for at least a few weeks, something else is going on. He may get angry if you try to reach out to him, and insist that you leave him alone, but you need to find out what's going on. While there are a number of reasons for a child to be moody, you should certainly consider the possibility that he has formed a habit of substance abuse.

Car Accidents

For many older teens, their cars are their lives. If you suspect your teenager has been using illicit substances recently, see if the car has any clues to offer. Maybe her driving is noticeably more reckless when she's coming home after being with her friends. She might whip into the driveway at eighty miles per hour, run over sections of lawn, hit things, or park carelessly. Or maybe there's a new dent in the front of the car and she claims she knows nothing about it. If you're suspicious, examine the inside of the car too; most teens are pretty sloppy about cleaning the inside of their car. Does it smell like marijuana smoke or alcohol fumes? Are there any bottles, pipes, bongs, or other drug paraphernalia rolling around on the floor or hidden in the glove box? If you find anything, challenge her on it immediately: be forthright, and tell her exactly what you've discovered and why you're concerned.

Deceit

Suddenly you find your normally honest child lying to you all the time. Her evening and weekend plans are starting to sound a little fishy; she's either vague about where she's going or her alibis don't work (she can't describe the movie she supposedly just saw; or the friend she's supposed to be out with just called looking for her). She says that parents will be at the parties she's going to but can't give you a phone number, and comes home acting intoxicated. She gets in way past her curfew or estimated time, and she's got a seemingly endless string of excuses to justify her behavior. Even if you find evidence of substance use—drunken or high behavior, a beer can or a marijuana rolling paper in her room—she's got someone or something else to place the blame on. When excuses fail, she'll respond to your inquiries and concern by telling you that it's none of your business. Something is wrong, and you need to figure out what she's really up to.

Decreased Motivation

Your child's grades start falling and there's no obvious reason for it. He gives you a weak explanation and assures you he can handle the situation, but he doesn't. He may be skipping school and spending less and less time on his homework. And he appears to be losing interest in other activities as well. You're getting calls from teachers, coaches, principals, all saying the same thing: that your teenager has been skipping his classes, activities, or practices, and when he's there he's not putting forth any effort. This could be a sign of a real substance abuse problem, where the desire to get drunk or high has taken top priority in his life.

Missing Alcohol, Cigarettes, Money, or Valuables

For the teen who's looking to get drunk or buy drugs, their parents' house can be a gold mine of resources. Nearly all parents keep some sort of alcohol in the house, whether it's six-packs of beer, a rack of wine bottles, or a cabinet featuring an assortment of liquor. Teens will start stealing this alcohol, hoping their parents won't miss it, or filling liquor bottles back up with water to bring them to the original level. If one or both of

Some Facts About Cigarette Smoking

Here are some proven facts about smoking, from the American Medical Association:

- Nine out of ten smokers began tobacco use during their childhood and teenage years.

- Nicotine is an addictive drug found in cigarettes.

- Every day in the United States, three thousand teens start to smoke; one thousand of them will die of a smoking-related disease someday.

- Chewing tobacco is not a safe alternative to smoking. Regular use can cause cancer of the cheek, gums, tongue, and throat.

Here are some suggestions for parents:

1. Don't wait for your child to smoke before you discuss tobacco use. Many kids begin trying cigarettes at eleven or twelve years of age.

2. Establish guidelines about smoking. Discuss your expectations and rules and let your child know what you'll do if he violates them.

3. Talk about the dangers of smoking, such as lung cancer and heart disease. Try to use examples of someone your teen knows who has died of a smoking-related illness.

4. Remind your teenager that smoking stains teeth and causes bad breath, yellow fingers, smelly hair and clothing, and premature wrinkles. It also affects athletic and sexual performance.

5. Even if you smoke, you can still express concern over your teen starting the habit. Talk about how hard it is to quit and share your regrets about starting.

their parents smokes cigarettes, they can always take some from the pack (or take the whole pack). If they need money to buy drugs, then they'll start going through their parents' wallets, stealing bills, or else will steal valuables like jewelry and heirlooms to pawn for money.

You should always keep track of the alcohol in the house. If you notice anything missing or your liquor tastes suspiciously watery, you should lock it up so your teen can't get to it. If your child is stealing cigarettes and you don't approve of him smoking, don't leave packs out where he can get to them. And in all these instances, particularly when money or valuables are being stolen, you need to confront him immediately. Let him know that

Tips to Help You Keep a Closer Eye on Your Teenager

1. Try to be in the house when he comes home in the evening. Make your child have a conversation with you before he goes to his room so you can look and smell for signs of alcohol or drug use.

2. If you're suspicious about your teens' activities, check with their friends' parents to find out what they know.

3. Let her know that you'll be spot-checking her for signs of drinking or marijuana use.

4. Be on the lookout for empty beer cans or bottles of alcohol that turn up in your trash. And if they do, make sure you question your teenager about them.

5. When your children tell you they're going to a party, find out where it is and make sure it's supervised. If it's not, don't allow them to go.

6. When they're at a party, have them phone in and talk to you briefly. This isn't foolproof, but it makes them think twice about getting drunk because they'll wonder if you can tell. They'll balk at the idea of calling, but you can make it a condition for going.

you're aware of what goes on and that you won't tolerate him stealing from you.

Cash Flow Problems

You know something is going on when your money starts disappearing. There are other money-related ways to detect this sort of problem too. Obviously, drugs and alcohol cost money, and even seemingly inexpensive substances add up over time. Your child may work a part-time job after school, but he's probably not earning much more than minimum wage. So if you find that he is increasingly concerned about getting more money but volunteers no explanation as to why, you should wonder what he's spending it on, especially if he doesn't turn up with any new clothes, CDs, or other material items. It may be that he's using his money—allowance, wages, handouts, whatever—to support his substance use. On the other hand, if he suddenly seems to have a whole lot more money for clothing, CDs, or other coveted items, way beyond what he reasonably should in his circumstances, consider that he could be dealing drugs. Under these circumstances, a room search may be justified (see Chapter 10).

Change in Friends

You notice that your teenager is hanging out with a different peer group. Sure, it's normal for teenagers to make new friends, but these friends worry you for some reason. Maybe they seem more immersed in stereotypical drug-user culture; they wear a lot of hemp products and pot-leaf shirts, or sport dreadlocks and lots of tie-dye. Maybe you've even met their new friends and suspected they were high or drunk when you were talking to them. Whatever the case, your teen will probably defend her new choice in friends, saying her old friends were boring or she outgrew them, and her new friends are more fun and understanding. But if you've got a feeling they're up to no good, keep your eyes and ears open, and go with your instincts.

WHAT TO DO IF YOUR CHILD IS USING ALCOHOL OR DRUGS

If you know for sure that your teenager is using alcohol or drugs, you need to take the following actions to deal with the problem.

Know Where You Stand

Think about your personal position on substance use. Are you willing to tolerate occasional responsible use, or do you insist on total abstinence? Let your child know your position and where you draw the line. But remember also that you're up against the fact that many teenagers consider their drinking or smoking marijuana reasonable, harmless fun. Remember too that teens' definition of casual use may be quite different from yours;

you might be talking about a few drinks total per month, while their definition might mean getting drunk only one night each weekend instead of both!

Let Your Child Know You're Concerned

Let's assume your teenager is overdoing his use of alcohol or drugs. Your initial overture to your child should be based on concern, not contempt. Don't tell him he's a loser, a waste, or a disgrace. This will only alienate him further. But do tell him about the changes you've noticed in his behavior and the reasons you're worried. And make it clear that you're not prepared to drop the issue until it's addressed. If he gets angry and defensive, don't take it personally. His reaction is intended to minimize the significance of the problem. Don't cover for him. If he's in trouble, let him experience the consequences. With or without his consent, go on to the next step.

Monitor Their Behavior

If you're trying to help your teenagers stay away from harmful substances, you'll need to keep a close watch on their activities. Let them know that you'll be doing this. In effect, you're saying to them, "I can no longer trust your word because you've been going behind my back and lying to me, so I'll need to be more actively involved with your life." This means you'll have to make some sacrifices. For starters, make sure you're awake when they get home, and check in with them before they go to bed. This will let you see whether they're clean and sober. They may not like this, but they'll get used to it.

Also, check with their friends' parents to find out what they know. Ask them how your teenager acts at their house. If these parents are also concerned about their own children, get together and plan how to restrict where and how the teens spend their time. Of course, you should tell your children you're doing this. The less room they have to manipulate, the better. Finally, randomly check to find out if they're where they've told you they would be. This might mean checking to see that their car is parked outside the friend's house where they're spending the night, or stopping by the movie theater or restaurant to make sure they're really there. This monitoring will really annoy your teenagers, but remind them that their past performance has led to this. Once they've regained your trust, you can stop such reconnaissance. And while you're checking up on them, be subtle and unobtrusive; they're already humiliated, so there's no point in adding insult to injury.

Use Drug Screens

Drug screens are particularly helpful for marijuana smokers. The active ingredient in marijuana, THC, stays in the bloodstream for up to thirty days. It can be detected through a urine test that can be done in your pediatrician's office or in a local laboratory that runs such tests (you can get a referral from your doctor). All you need to do is call them and arrange to have your teen's urine sample taken, and they'll have the laboratory results back in a few days. Of course, you should inform your child that you'll be doing a random drug screening to find out if she's getting high. Tell her that you can't trust her word anymore and don't want to argue about it. The test will tell the story, and then you can hold her accountable for her actions. In the event that your child refuses to take a drug screen, tell her that you'll assume she's using and proceed accordingly.

Teens often try to find a way to fool these tests. I've heard about kids drinking excessive amounts of water, spraying Lysol in their urine samples, or drinking herbal tea. The best way to ensure they don't try is to not give them advance notice of when they'll take the test. Watch them closely during the testing to make sure they don't try to swap their urine for a clean sample from a friend. To test for alcohol, some parents buy Breathalyzer tests. Requiring that children take such tests for alcohol, or even just threatening to do so when things are getting out of control, sends a no-nonsense message.

Search Their Rooms

I've advocated respecting your teenager's privacy throughout this book, but there are exceptions to this rule. You should tell your child that as long as you suspect drug or alcohol use, you reserve the right to search his room for incriminating evidence. If you find any drugs, drug paraphernalia, or empty beer cans or bottles, you'll take action. This can range from weekend restrictions to requiring him to attend a weekly drug prevention program. You'll need to find out the nature and extent of his problem before making this determination (we discussed how to do this in the previous section). If you're still unsure about the extent of his use (and it's often in question), have a drug counselor do a thorough evaluation.

Even the smell of the room can tell you something. Maybe she just likes incense and scented candles—there are plenty of teens, especially girls, who do—but it could also be to cover up a suspicious, drug-related smell. Excessive Lysol spraying is an even clearer giveaway. And don't overlook the obvious. If your teen's room is filled with alcohol and/or marijuana posters, it doesn't automatically mean they're using, but it means they've got some level of interest. Of course, it depends on the nature of their posters too. Budweiser posters featuring supermodels and the Absolut ads aren't worth worrying about too much, because their appeal transcends alcohol. But big pot leaves, lists of marijuana terms, issues of *High Times*, and posters of cool drinking games are a bit more of a clue that they may be involved with substances. If you think something's up, address it directly. Ask "Why do you have pictures of pot leaves up in your room?" or "Why is there always incense burning in there?" The more your child knows you're onto his ploys, the less likely he is to try to fool you.

Set Clear Limits

In no uncertain terms, tell your child you won't tolerate any further use of alcohol or marijuana. From now on you'll expect her to tell you where she's going, with whom, and when she'll be home. You should certainly restrict her privileges on Friday night and Saturday night, which are, I would say, the most likely times she'll be in a drug- or alcohol-related situation, like a party or informal get-together. You may also want to make her use her new free time to attend drug or alcohol education classes, or sit in on an AA meeting or group therapy session for drug abusers.

Your child may insist she doesn't have a problem with drinking and doesn't deserve to be restricted. This plays right into your hands. You can then ask her to prove she can stay sober or straight by abstaining for a specified time period. If she honors this contract, her privileges can be restored. If she doesn't, you'll have to decide what type of treatment program is best for her (see the Appendix for resources).

Never confront your teenager when she's drunk or stoned, because she won't be able to engage in a rational discussion. If you press the matter, you'll probably wind up in a meaningless argument that you'll both regret afterward. So please, wait until the morning or afternoon after, when you'll have a relatively alert, captive, and probably scared audience to discuss consequences.

Of course, when you define the bottom line, there's always the chance that your teenager will flagrantly disregard your limits. What if your child is adamant that you can't tell her what to do? If she refuses to be grounded or abide by rules you impose, ignore her threat. Just assume she hasn't said this and proceed accordingly. It may be that her protests are all talk—she's just venting her anger at you, and deep down she does respect your authority. But if she continues her illicit activity—in effect, daring you to try and stop her—you'll need to show her you mean business by moving to the next stage of severity.

If the drug problem is serious, consider using outside support to help you with this problem. This is a hard step for many parents to take, but you often need the support of others to take a stance against drug abuse. Dealing with a child who is a serious substance abuser is a terrible situation that can make home life a living hell—lies, broken promises, screaming fights, constant worry, or even violence—with no apparent way out. There are many resources in your community, including mental health clinics, self-help groups, and law enforcement agencies. They can direct you to more specific help and provide information about further options. Knowing that others are behind you can lighten your burden. The many other parents who have survived similar situations can be a great comfort as well as an invaluable resource.

There are times when teenagers run away from home because they feel trapped and see no way out of their situation. Their substance habit has become the most important thing in the world to them, and you're trying to get between them and their drug. When this occurs, you'll need to take immediate action. If they've run away from home for more than twenty-four hours, notify the police, who can often track down a runaway and bring her home. And when she returns, seek professional assistance immediately.

Make an appointment to see a mental health professional who specializes in substance abuse. And tell your child if she doesn't attend the appointment, you'll have to make important decisions about her future without her present. If your child still refuses to cooperate (and this is not unusual), you can contact the juvenile court system or inform his school that he has a serious drug problem and ask for their support. They'll advise you on the most prudent course of action. In an extreme situation (if, for instance, your child is deeply rooted in the addiction phase of alcohol or drug use), you'll need to consider placement in a residential drug treatment program. The problem is too great to handle on your own.

How to Get Your Teenager to Enter a Drug Treatment Program

Many teenagers who suffer from serious problems with substance abuse are in denial about their situation. Consequently, they see treatment as unnecessary and refuse to enter a rehabilitation program. Here are some suggestions to persuade them that they need assistance:

- Help them to see how the situation has worsened over the past few months. Point out any evidence that clearly exemplifies this: declining health, falling school grades, withdrawal from the family.

- Tell them that their privileges, like driving, allowance, and curfews, will be rescinded until they've begun to address their problems.

- Express your concern about them, and tell them that you can't sit idly by and watch them ruin their life.

- Explain that a treatment program is not a punishment. In fact, it's an opportunity for them to make a new start.

- Recruit the support of important others, like friends, relatives, teachers, and coaches, to persuade them to attend the program.

- Show them examples of people who are alcoholics or drug addicts who've refused to address their problem and have thrown their lives away. Or discuss former alcoholics and drug addicts who had to go through the same sort of programs to enjoy successful lives today.

- Tell them that if they refuse to attend the program, they may face more serious consequences, like a court appearance, school suspension, or mandatory placement in a facility outside the home.

A Family Faces a Drug Problem

At sixteen, David, a happy, outgoing, motivated teen, had really isolated himself from his family for the last several months. He spent much of his time in his room with the door locked and was very secretive about his activities, giving vague explanations when he went out with friends. His mostly-A grades had slipped down to a series of C's, and last week his football coach called, demanding to know why David had missed the last two practices. His parents sensed something was wrong and had tried to talk to him about it, but David always denied that anything was troubling him. Fortunately, his parents didn't buy this. They finally sat him down one evening for a serious discussion. When they asked if he was involved with drugs, he grew hostile and self-righteous. "You don't have any right to pry into my business," he told them.

His parents had wisely sought advice beforehand and were prepared to deal with the situation. They put it to him directly. "Look, David," they said, "we're really concerned about you. You're drifting away from us and from everything that matters to you. We're not going to argue about whether you're getting high or not. We want you to have a drug screen. That'll tell the story." At first David balked at the suggestion, but in the end he admitted using marijuana regularly. His parents contacted the community drug treatment program and arranged for him to attend regular group meetings.

At first David went to the treatment program to placate his parents, who to him seemed unreasonable and hysterical. But gradually David saw that he was dependent on marijuana both physically and socially and had to give it up completely, because it was taking a toll on the other aspects of his life. This meant finding some new friends and getting involved again with school. His teachers and coaches were willing to help him, and with some hard work he was doing well at school again. Unfortunately, it was harder to make a break with his friends; they were a tight-knit group of several years who had all drifted into smoking pot recently. However, he learned that it was easiest to resist the temptation of getting high when he kept his distance, and he made a few new friends who didn't use drugs. With the support of his group he was able to reconnect with his family and make a fresh start. During the rehabilitation period, his family made every effort to support him, demonstrated how much they loved him, and opened the door to a new relationship.

Not all stories progress so smoothly. Sometimes young people refuse to admit their problems and resist treatment. You can't always rescue them, despite your best efforts. Watching them get in deeper and deeper, you have to do some soul-searching. Are you prepared to let your teenagers self-destruct, or are you resolved to do what it takes to get help for them? Rest assured that you'll never regret taking a stand and insisting on help for your child.

WHY TEENAGERS ARE SUSCEPTIBLE TO TRENDS

Trends may seem like a pretty benign topic when compared to the serious problems of promiscuous sexual activity and alcohol and drug abuse. But teens who are overly susceptible to them may be demonstrating an overwhelming desire to follow the crowd and an inability to express their own personal taste and opinions. Some trends are even associated with a lack of concern for oneself and defiant behavior. And what about trends that are deliberately obscene or shocking? Parents of children who seem to slavishly follow these fads ask themselves what the significance is of a T-shirt slogan, extreme fashion choice, hair length, body piercing, or tattoos. Are these just window dressing, or are they signs of a greater, internal shift—signs that something wrong could be going on with your teenager?

Let's face it: there have been trends as long as there have been teenagers. Yes, many of us find it hard to accept our children's favorite music or clothing, but maybe we're forgetting that our grandparents and parents wrung their hands over Elvis Presley's gyrations and the Beatles' haircuts. Hippie children of the sixties deliberately grew long hair and wore bell-bottoms, tie-dyes, and flowers to distance themselves from the buttoned-down mainstream culture. But many parents think that today's counterparts have gone too far; flowers and love were one thing, but today's stars and styles are deliberately offensive and shocking. Elvis and the Beatles may have caused a ruckus in their day, but they look pretty benign compared to Eminem and Marilyn Manson.

The truth is that there's always some kind of trend that kids can adopt to shock the mainstream, whether it be fashion, music, or something else. In the 1920s it was jazz music, bobbed haircuts, and flapper clothing. In the 1950s it was rock 'n' roll, leather jackets, and greased-back hair. And in the late 1970s and early 1980s it was punk music, torn clothing, and brightly colored spiky hair. The adolescent years are typically a time of benign protest. Teens seem to take great pleasure in getting a rise out of their parents and enjoy the shock value of some of their antics. It's cool to stand out in some way—provided, of course, that their peers take notice.

Trends don't last forever, and not all teenagers fall prey to media hype and peer pressure. In fact, the more independent and self-assured they are, the less likely they are to fall victim to the latest trend or feel they need to shock. But like it or not, you'll have to cope with the impact of fads at one time or another. It'll help to think of music and fashion as a statement of individuality. These are vehicles for teenagers to differentiate themselves from their parents, and this can be healthy.

Teens get caught up in many crazes, but the most obvious ones have to do with the music they listen to and the way they look. It's up to you to distinguish between what's harmless and what could be dangerous.

Music

Music is the most distinctive, and possibly most annoying, sign of teenage identity. Every generation has music that makes parents shudder or scratch their heads, wondering how anyone can stand to listen to it. Even though rap and hip-hop have been around for about twenty years now, some parents still don't consider it to be music at all. Other parents feel the same way about punk rock and really heavy rock or metal. Because the lyrics accompanying such music often deal with sex, violence, drugs, anger, and anarchy, many people believe this music promotes negative and even dangerous values. But while you may be shocked by some of the messages you hear, it serves a purpose for today's youth: it lets them vent their anger and protest at adult and societal values they don't share.

Parents worry that song lyrics will encourage their children to commit acts of violence, engage in wild sex, even commit suicide. Every year or so, a different media story surfaces that blames a hideous act on a song or TV show. But if you've imparted your values and raised your children to be healthy, respectful, rational, nonviolent individuals, listening to current sounds in music won't destroy their moral fiber. If you're worried, feel free to listen to their music and tell them what you think about its lyrics. In fact, once you've made the effort to appreciate and understand the music your teen really cares about, you might end up in a really interesting and enlightening conversation. If you truly feel strongly about the music in your house, I would advise letting the "Parental Advisory" stickers on CDs guide your instincts. They were created in the 1980s so that parents could be alerted to any potentially offensive or upsetting music material.

Because teens use their music to express themselves, it may also give you a window into how they're feeling. If they've got gloom and doom on their stereos twenty-four hours a day, they may be feeling down and depressed about something, whether about themselves, a recent incident, or society in general. If their music is really angry and aggressive sounding, it could mean they have some anger and frustration that the music expresses for them. Finally, there are some bands that are stereotypically associated with drug use, like the Grateful Dead and Phish. Do *not* assume that taste in music is a sign of drug use. Just keep in mind that it is an expression of what's going on with your teenager— so it's good to familiarize yourself.

Clothing

Teenagers have been making their own fashion statements for many generations, and will for generations to come. Some kinds of dress are associated with rebellious youth, but these outfits reflect image more often than substance. Some teenagers wear all black, others choose army surplus clothing, and many avidly follow the latest fashions.

But choice of clothing is usually just an attempt to assert individuality and a harmless form of protest. It may be an assault on your personal taste, but it probably won't hurt anyone. If it's truly hideous, your child will figure it out sooner or later, and will probably laugh or cringe over it in years to come. You needn't make it a battleground unless it violates your child's school dress code, in which case you have no choice but to put your foot down. You may make an issue when clothing is highly inappropriate for a special occasion, like a wedding, funeral, church, or school concert. You should also make an issue out of clothing that is deliberately offensive, like T-shirts that feature racist, sexist, obscene, or violent material. And you should absolutely forbid any clothing that you know to be gang related. While the Crips and Bloods seem to be becoming national organizations, gang-related clothing styles are still often specific to each individual neighborhood. Know what to look for.

> Choice of clothing is usually just an attempt to assert individuality.

I would also recommend letting your child choose his or her own hairstyle. You may not like their dyed hair or partially shaved heads, but they don't hurt anyone. If you leave them alone, they'll probably change the style before you've figured out what to do about it. The only time that you should address hairstyle is when it is in violation of any school rules; these tend to apply mostly to boys, and tend to be regarding hair length or facial hair.

Just as with music, teens' appearances are a sign of what's going on within. A girl who slavishly follows the latest fashions and always worries about looking good may feel insecure or lack self-confidence. A boy who has dyed his hair bright blue, wears Doc Martens and mostly black clothing, enjoys T-shirts with deliberately provocative sayings, and sports several piercings may be rebelling against other people's expectations, either because he's been unable to live up to them or because he wants to be an individual. Another girl who worries about looking sexy enough and wears tight, provocative clothing and lots of make-up may worry about not being liked or noticed by boys. And a boy who wears wrinkled, unwashed clothes may not think his appearance matters because he doesn't think anyone cares what he looks like.

Tattoos and Body Piercing

This subject is somewhat more controversial. Although tattoos and body piercing are in vogue now, such alterations have a lasting effect. Many parents say they seem like self-mutilation and make their skin crawl. Tattooing and body piercing are very popular, possibly more common than you may think. A recent study found that one in ten college students had a tattoo, and half of them wanted to get one. The subjects of the survey came from all income levels and socioeconomic groups. And if that isn't enough, tattooing is the sixth-fastest-growing retail business in this country!

Most parents are concerned about body alterations, finding them either repulsive or dismayingly permanent. They think they're related to drug use. While there may be drug users with tattoos or piercings, neither body piercing nor tattoos should be viewed as a reliable indicator for drug use in teenagers. Experts on self-mutilation don't consider the body art fad pathological.

If your teenager is considering a tattoo or a body piercing against your very strong wishes, you have a few choices. One is that you can say you won't tolerate such changes under any circumstances. If your child respects you and fears the consequences, this may work, but remember that you can't control everything he does. If he's really determined, he'll find a way to do it. The law states that anyone under the age of eighteen requires parental consent if he wants to get a tattoo or piercing, but there are ways around this (especially piercing, which technically only requires a needle and a stud or ring). If he's already done it behind your back, you'll have to decide whether to ignore it or follow through with consequences, which may include removing the piercing

Potential Medical Complications of Tattoos and Body Piercings

Make sure your child is aware of all the possible things that can go wrong after a tattoo or body piercing. Here's a list of the most common complications:

1. The tongue swells tremendously when it's pierced. And a tongue piercing may result in slurred speech.

2. Dentists report that tongue studs can cause problems in the mouth such as chipped teeth.

3. A pierced navel can take up to twelve months to heal, and there's always a risk of infection.

4. The health risks of piercing include hepatitis B and tetanus, as well as skin reactions that can occur with red and yellow dyes.

5. An improperly placed piercing can cause nerve damage.

6. According to dermatologists, removing most tattoos takes several painful laser sessions and costs between $800 and $1,600.

stud or ring or going to a professional to have the tattoo lasered off, in addition to some form of punishment.

If your teenager expresses an interest in a tattoo or piercing, you can be honest about your disapproval, but I would recommend being willing to talk to him about it. If you're willing to work with him, ask him to wait at least a month before following through with his decision. Tattoos are very permanent, and what seems like a great idea to your teen today may seem pretty stupid tomorrow. I would especially recommend this for any teen thinking about tattooing a boyfriend or girlfriend's name, or a cool new cartoon character. Remind him that he's making a decision that he'll bear with him for the rest of his life; tattoo removal is expensive and often difficult. One teenager showed me the girlfriend's name he'd had tattooed on his arm, only to break up with her a few months later. His new girlfriend was insisting that he get rid of it, but where was he supposed to get the money?

Body piercings are less permanent because you can always take out the ring or stud, but stress to your teen that it does leave scars behind, which can be quite unattractive in some places (noses in particular). Besides, both procedures will cost money, so ask them to make sure they're positive about what they want before blowing their savings. One way to make sure they're ready for a real piercing or tattoo is to make a deal where they have to wear a temporary tattoo or faux piercing first. That way they'll get a more realistic sense of what the real deal will be like, and they might recognize and prevent any potentially bad or dumb decisions.

You should also ask your teen which body part he plans to get pierced or tattooed, because some areas are more high-profile than others. Pierced eyebrows and noses are very noticeable; tongues slightly less so, but some people are even more shocked when they do notice. Tattoos on ankles, biceps, and forearms will also be more noticeable than areas like the lower back. Remind your teen that some people make judgments, both positive and negative, based on tattoos and piercings, and to take that into account when they go to get theirs done.

Another topic to bring up is safety, and the risks involved. Because both procedures involve needles, there are serious risks of diseases and infection. Warn your child that if he really does decide to get a tattoo or piercing, he needs to go to a clean, reputable place where they carefully sterilize any needles involved. I recommend that you plan on accompanying him to make sure it's a decent place. And warn him that if he gets a serious infection from a piercing because he didn't follow directions and apply alcohol or hydrogen peroxide regularly, the ring or stud will be coming out.

A tattoo or piercing may be hard for you to accept, but if you work with your teen, you can help him avoid any dangerous or foolish decisions. Work with him to come to decisions that won't have negative repercussions for his appearance or for the relationship between the two of you.

Usually clothing, music, and body adornment don't cause trouble in and of themselves, and experimentation with appearance is a natural part of growing up. However, teenagers who gravitate toward extreme forms of self-expression may also be expressing their rebellious nature through other activities that aren't quite so discernible as a T-shirt or tattoo. Again, let your teenager's music, clothing, and general appearance serve as a reflection of what's going on inside his mind. If the picture they're showing you is one of an angry, depressed, or unhappy teen, then you should be aware that something more may be going on, whether it's substance abuse, sexual promiscuity, violent, illegal, or risk-taking behavior, or clinical depression. Each parent has to make an informed decision about what to tolerate in his or her child and where to draw the line. Always consider your teen's overall adjustment in such areas as school, family, and friends.

This chapter has dealt with several hotly contested issues—sex, drugs, and rock'n'roll! It will take time and patience for you to work out your own feelings about each of these issues and to work with your teen to get to a point where you can communicate honestly and effectively. The going may be rough for a while, but ultimately, any help you can provide your children will improve their lives and the quality of your relationship with them.

HELPING RESOLVE YOUR TEEN'S PROBLEMS WITH SCHOOL

"School is such a waste of time. It's like teachers are baby-sitting us until we're old enough to work."

"My teachers are all so out of touch. They're so boring and stupid."

"I'm skipping English today. I didn't finish reading the book, so I'll flunk the quiz if I go. That class sucks anyway."

"I hate every single person at this school. I can't wait to get out of here."

"These classes are so pointless. I'm never going to use any of this stuff in real life."

"Thank God it's Friday!"

School is an institution that teenagers love to hate. Yet most well-adjusted adolescents accept it as a necessary evil; even if they feel less than enthusiastic at times, they tolerate the academic regimen, do their homework, take their tests, and successfully complete their courses. Teens may complain that they're not getting anything out of school, but there's usually at least one subject that sparks their interest, lets them experience success, and gives them a glimpse of their role in life beyond high school. And students with definite plans for their future understand the importance of good grades, whether they plan to enter college, the military, or the workforce. School is every teenager's job, far more than any part-time after-school and weekend job. It consumes almost half of their waking hours each weekday and is also their major venue of socialization, the place they learn to relate to others and develop the skills necessary for success in the adult world. In time, most people come to look back on at least some of their school experiences fondly.

For teenagers in trouble, however, school is often a thoroughly unpleasant experience, an unfriendly environment that causes them anguish and frustration. Their school performance can taint their whole family's existence. You may know all too well how continual arguments over your child's attitude, grades, and homework create turmoil at home.

The majority of teenagers who get into trouble also do poorly in school. Falling school grades can be one of the earliest signals that a young person is at risk of other kinds of problems as well. According to the National Association for School Psychologists, the current high school dropout rate is between 15 and 30 percent, a sobering statistic. So if you're worried about your teenager's trouble with school, you're worried with good reason.

A teenager's school problems can stem from a wide variety of sources. So before you resort to extreme measures to solve them, you need to understand where the problems are coming from, so you can formulate a plan (with the help of the teachers and school personnel) to get your teenager back on track. This general sequence—which will be elaborated on in this chapter—will help you determine your course of action: First, consult the school to determine if your child has any learning or behavioral problems that interfere with his performance. Second, try to ally yourself with the school and collaborate to establish some type of motivational program. Third, implement a system to monitor your teenager's progress in this program. Finally, rule out the possibility of substance abuse and depression.

WHY THINGS GO WRONG AT SCHOOL

High school graduation is still, without question, the best ticket to a bright future. If your children need to be convinced of this fact, just have them talk to people who dropped out of high school. Most will say they wish their parents had pressed them more about studying or that they had taken school more seriously.

Young people with problems concerning school often come from families that value education and have parents who want the best for their children. Yet something seems to go wrong somewhere. Sadly, as their school experience deteriorates, so do other aspects of their lives. Unhappy, frustrated teenagers are prey to the variety of negative influences we've already explored—they give in to undesirable peer pressure; make dangerous, self-destructive choices; and fall into habits of substance abuse, vandalism, sexual promiscuity, or violence. This is why it's essential that you intervene quickly and decisively, with all the resources you can muster, if your child is having problems in school.

Let's take a look at some of the reasons for poor academic achievement:

Lack of Motivation

Perhaps the single greatest determinant of school problems is poor motivation. Unmotivated young people simply refuse to make any effort. Their parents know they can do better, but they just don't. This seems to be a relatively recent epidemic: "underachiever" has become a buzzword for this generation. But I believe that motivation, good or bad, is more complex than most people realize. It is the product of many factors, including family relationships, self-esteem, and social maturity.

Despite the fact that poor motivation is blamed for many school problems, its complex roots leave you at a loss as to how to handle it. Your teenagers' lack of effort causes many battles at home. You push them to try harder and they resist your pressure. You yell, threaten, bribe, and punish, all to no avail. If things have reached this point in your family, stop and take stock. What, exactly, is the nature of the problems that feed your child's poor motivation? Some difficulties are obvious, while others are subtle and complex. All of the following factors can contribute to lack of motivation, as well as leading to poor academic achievement on their own.

Learning Disabilities

Learning disabilities can severely impair a young person's education, causing frustration, apathy, and behavior problems if they're not addressed. The term "learning disabilities" has taken on a negative connotation by the uninformed because it has been confused with laziness and incorrectly labeled a permanent condition. Many parents strongly resist school recommendations to place their children in special education programs, fearing that this stigma will limit their future opportunities.

You should be aware that there are several types of deficiencies that can interfere with the learning process. They include problems of auditory and visual *perception*, the ability to take in information; *sequencing*, the ability to process information; and *memory*, the ability to recall information accurately.

Learning disabilities do not result from a lack of effort or intelligence, and there is some evidence to suggest that there may be a genetic component. This is not to suggest that they can't be overcome. The problem is that, more often than we would like to think, they are not recognized. Sometimes this happens because the deficits are very subtle, and sometimes because they're masked by behavior problems. In either case, learning disabilities should never be viewed as something to be ashamed of. Instead, think of them as a different style of learning that requires a different style of teaching.

You don't need to be an expert on learning disabilities, but you should be familiar with signs that suggest your child may have them. They may include:

- Poor word recognition
- Inability to distinguish between correct and incorrect word spellings, and poor spelling performance
- Illegible handwriting
- Trouble finding the correct or exact word (word retrieval problems)
- Poor short-term memory
- Special difficulty with written expression

- Poor organizational skills
- Frustration with seemingly routine school tasks, like copying down homework assignments, answering basic essay questions, and following class discussions
- Letter confusion, like mixing up *p* and *b*
- Writing letters backwards
- Difficulty with verbal expression
- Handwriting that is uneven, very crooked, or so big that it takes up too much room

It is important to note that acting out in class and getting in trouble can be a cover-up for not understanding how to do an assignment. In a child's mind, it is better to get a laugh and get in trouble than to be laughed at for not understanding what is happening in the class. Learning disabilities can therefore have a behavioral component as well.

If you suspect that your child has any of these deficiencies, contact your school guidance counselor. This person can arrange for a screening to determine if further testing is indicated, and if it is, refer your teenager to a psychoeducational diagnostician or a school psychologist. The expert will use specific tests to determine the nature of your child's learning deficits and can make recommendations for remedial measures and a more appropriate classroom setting for your child. Some kids and parents mistakenly believe that extra effort alone will be able to compensate for a disorder. This is not the case; you really must seek the professional help of a psychologist, learning specialist, or tutor with specialized training.

How to Talk to Your Child About Being Tested

If your teenager is doing poorly in school, it's likely that he's feeling frustrated and dejected. Consequently, he may be reluctant to take special tests because he perceives this as a humiliating experience. Here are eleven tips to gain his cooperation:

1. Frame the experience in a positive light. You could say, "We're really fortunate that your school has the resources to do testing and make helpful recommendations."

2. Tell him you understand that school must be frustrating for him and you're trying to do everything you can to help.

3. Explain that testing will help to identify his strengths and weaknesses and ultimately lead to better planning for his school curriculum.

4. Address the stigma of special education. Many young people feel that they will be labeled as deficient if they receive special assistance in school. Thus, they're reluctant to cooperate with any testing. You should point out that everyone learns differently and it's important to recognize one's individual learning style. Identifying that style enables educators to make certain accommodations that should make learning easier for the student.

5. Stress that there are no pass/fail grades on educational tests. The tests will indicate which areas of learning (for example, written expression, computational skills, and memory) the student can benefit from assistance in.

6. Emphasize that students who are targeted for special assistance are fortunate because they might not otherwise receive the help that they need.

7. Make sure that you don't express anger or put your teens down because they need to be tested.

8. Use examples of people they know who've been through special programs and derived benefits from them. If you can't find any examples, your school counselor will be happy to connect you with some of these students.

9. Tell your children you're proud of them for facing their learning difficulties.

10. Remind them that there are many times in life when we're required to take tests (like school tests, driver's permits, and tests on the job), and there's nothing wrong with it.

11. Ask him what Albert Einstein, Cher, and Olympic gold medal winner Bruce Jenner all have in common. (They all had learning disabilities.)

Your kids may not always tell you they're having problems learning. They may even deny it if you ask them about it directly. But if you observe them carefully and look over their work, you should be able to detect some of the clues. You can also check with their teachers to see if they've noticed your child having any difficulties completing class work or taking tests. Keep in mind that the subtle clues we've discussed may sometimes be overlooked, due to a variety of circumstances.

Attention Deficit Disorder and Attention Deficit Hyperactivity Disorder

Attention deficit disorder (ADD) or attention deficit hyperactivity disorder (ADHD) may accompany a documented learning disorder, or it may exist on its own, but if left untreated it generally has a negative effect on learning. The National Institute of Mental Health recently reported that about 3 to 5 percent of U.S. children have ADD/ADHD. This can markedly interfere with school performance and influence other aspects of a young person's life. The symptoms of the disorder are readily observable but can be confused with the temperament of a highly energetic and restless teenager. Therefore, a diagnosis should be based on both a thorough classroom observation and a review of the pertinent academic and behavior reports.

Signs of ADHD include:

- *Difficulty paying attention.* The teenager may not listen when you speak to him, or he may be easily distracted by external stimuli. He often has difficulty organizing tasks and activities. In school he may have trouble attending to details and make frequent careless errors. Further, he may often lose things or forget them.

- *Hyperactivity.* Hyperactive teenagers are fidgety. They often tap their hands or feet and leave their seats without permission. They may also talk excessively and have difficulty engaging in leisure activities quietly. They give the impression of always being restless or on the move. You may find these teenagers trying and exhausting at times.
- *Impulsiveness.* The impulsive young person often blurts out answers in class. He interrupts others when they're speaking and has trouble waiting his turn. We're never quite sure when or how he's going to react. At times his behavior may be embarrassing and difficult to manage. Bear in mind that this behavior is not intentional.

While many teenagers exhibit these behaviors occasionally, those with ADHD exhibit a pronounced pattern that has persisted for at least six months and to a degree that is not likely to change. There must be clear impairment in social, academic, or occupational functioning to meet the criteria for a diagnosis.

There are other symptoms of ADD/ADHD beyond those provided above, but if you consistently observe these behaviors in your child, you should seek help. Your pediatrician is a good place to start. She will review the behaviors of concern to you, collect data from your child's school, determine if ADD/ADHD is the correct diagnosis, and explain possible treatments. Provided that an accurate diagnosis is made, studies show that medication can be helpful in up to 75 percent of children and should be considered. The most common medications useful for treating ADD/ADHD are methylphenidate (Ritalin), dextroamphetamine (Dexedrine), Adderall, pemoline (Cylert), and most recently, methylphenedate HCl (Concerta). Be wary of fads and home remedies. The National Institute of Mental Health reports, for example, that there is no substantiated research to recommend nutrition as an appropriate treatment.

If you suspect your child has ADD/ADHD, first tell him your concerns about his behavior and say you want to help. Gently and nonjudgmentally, try to point out things he does that make his life and yours more difficult (perhaps he tunes out, loses things, behaves impulsively). Then explain that there are several ways to help him cope with his situation better, such as medication, school accommodations, and learning to compensate for his deficits. Many teenagers are familiar with this disorder and may be relieved to learn that there's an explanation for their difficulties. If they're reluctant to participate in an assessment, explore their concerns and reassure them that there's nothing to be embarrassed about. If possible, recruit the assistance of the school counselor or pediatrician to talk to them about this further.

Caution is always indicated in the diagnosis of this disorder. It is easy for those involved to jump to conclusions and seek a quick fix. I suggest that you look carefully at all possible explanations for your teenager's school restlessness and inattention. Other factors can strongly influence school performance, and you should consider each of them when trying to understand your child's issues.

Average Intellectual Potential

Some young people are of average or below average intelligence, at least when it comes to academics. It's simply a part of who they are, like the color of their eyes or their height or personality traits like patience or a quick temper. Of course, we all know stories of underachievers who really plug hard to keep up with the pack; movies like *Forrest Gump* and *Rudy* are so popular because people enjoy watching the likable underachiever triumph. And some real-life teens do excel because of their gargantuan efforts. But the majority of average- and below-average-intelligence youth who make a reasonable effort will still have trouble keeping pace with their more capable peers. If your child attends a competitive school with a rigorous curriculum, or if you're pushing him to take college prep courses that he's really struggling in, you may have to ask yourself if the shoe fits. We all want our children to achieve academically, but there's a limit to how far we can push. Teenagers who feel they're under excessive school pressure may abandon their efforts altogether because they feel they won't pay off.

If you're uncertain about your child's intellectual potential, contact the school counselor and review his standardized test results. Or if you choose, you can have him tested privately. If the results suggest that his achievement is consistent with his potential in the average range, the best advice for you is to accept your child just as he is and plan accordingly. If he's really struggling to get by, you may want to consider other alternatives, such as switching him to less accelerated classes or finding a less competitive school. Being an average student is certainly no stigma; both you and your child should keep that in mind. Parental pressure should be commensurate with the capabilities of the individual. Rather than pressuring your child to try harder, you might want to offer him praise and encouragement in what he does do well, whether it's inside or outside the classroom walls. After all, intelligence goes beyond academic success; instead of driving him to overcome his weaker areas, which are probably already quite frustrating, help him to discover and to succeed in his areas of strength. And if he's putting a lot of time and effort into his schoolwork, acknowledge and praise his efforts on a regular basis, even if his grades are less than stellar.

Difficulty with Authority

Many school problems involve neither learning disabilities nor attention deficit disorders—they have to do with attitude. Some teenagers can't tolerate adults telling them what to do, and that's exactly what teachers are to them: know-it-all adults who boss them around, order them to follow stupid rules, and yell and punish when they get angry. Since a school setting requires conformity and adherence to a routine, it can easily become a catalyst for misbehavior to youth who instinctively resist structure and refuse to comply with demands placed on them. These students' problems with authority take on an exaggerated significance and interfere with the learning process. Teens who are rigid, inflexible, strong-willed, and negative are likely to have difficulty with authority. Their posture is a reflection of their basic temperament, which is difficult to alter. A defiant attitude toward teachers may also stem from earlier childhood experiences; some teens have experienced humiliation and punishment at the hands of teachers and other adults, and now they're on the defense.

These teenagers often alienate people, especially adults. They strongly dislike the school regimen and go to great lengths to protest the rules. To them, a teacher is always wrong. These students challenge their teachers, show them no respect, and refuse to do what they say. They take issue with nearly all of what their teachers say to them, even if it's a routine classroom matter regarding homework or material they're studying. The unfortunate result is that they wind up in school detention and get suspended for their confrontational behavior. As you might imagine, they don't make for very compliant students. It's not that they can't learn; it's that they don't want to. Their combative attitude makes it very difficult to teach them because they treat school as another battle to be fought.

These teenagers may react this way to only one or two of their teachers. It could be that they're fine with teachers who are kind and patient and accommodating, but they have one or two teachers who have a teaching style that rubs them the wrong way. Unfortunately, these teens cannot adapt or get by within a system they dislike, so they lash out at these teachers, causing trouble for themselves. And even if there's only one teacher that they're clashing with, it can still negatively affect their school experience in many ways.

Teenagers who are allergic to authority resist learning for several reasons. First, they're extremely sensitive to criticism and feel that their teachers are trying to put them down or make them look stupid. Often they're unsure of themselves, but rather than acknowledge their shortcomings, they insist that they already know everything. Second, they consider themselves adults, so they are angered at the idea of another adult treating them without the respect they feel they deserve. Unfortunately, some teachers do rely on sarcasm, intimidation, and orders without explanations, and hypersensitive students get worked up because they feel their rights have been violated. Third, they tell themselves that school is a waste of time and rationalize that they have better things to do than learn useless information. And finally, they often have like-minded friends who reinforce their actions. These are the kids who laugh and snicker every time the defiant student makes a rude or insulting remark to a teacher. The result is a shut-down student who makes little or no effort.

Lack of a Realistic Future Vision

Almost all of the parents I see in my practice feel that not only high school, but college too, is a prerequisite for a successful life. They are devastated when their children seem uninterested in going or are unable to because of poor grades and behavioral problems. College was once an exclusive institution reserved for the wealthy elite. Now, the majority of graduating high school students in the United States are bound for some type of college after graduation—a four-year program, a two-year junior college program, or classes at a community college. Many desirable jobs require a college degree; while it's not always necessary to have a degree to succeed, it is a sound investment.

Yet many teens in academic trouble do not have a realistic vision for their own futures. They don't understand what it takes to get into college, or don't think they even need to bother with college. These teens often dream of bright, successful futures but have no clue about what it realistically takes to get there. Many frustrated students dream of becoming rock stars, or actors, or professional athletes, all high-paying jobs that don't require a college degree, but they don't realize what a small percentage of the population actually succeeds in these fields. Others don't even have a solid plan, assuming that they'll find a good enough job with little to no real effort. To top it off, these high school students often have little to no idea of what things like rent and car insurance and even supermarket trips really cost.

If you feel strongly about college and your teen doesn't want to go, try pointing out the practical side of a college education, not just the intellectual and cultural rewards. Talk about all the different jobs that require a college degree, particularly those in her field of interest. Ask her what things she would like to have as an adult; she'll probably mention a car, a home, nice clothes, the ability to travel. Discuss what those things realistically cost. Then give her an idea of what people in various professions make per year; there's a big difference between the salaries of lawyers, computer specialists, and businesspeople compared to salesclerks, workers in fast food restaurants, or struggling actors and musicians. She may be surprised by what she hears. If she insists she'd be happy in a blue-collar job or that she feels very strongly about not going to college, that's fine, but make sure she understands the opportunities she's passing up by forgoing college. Of course, your child can always bring up an exception to the rule; just make sure you've given her a dose of reality so she knows how unusual these exceptions are.

Peer Rejection

This is also an important reason that many students do badly in school. All high schools have a pecking order, and sometimes it's cruel. Once you're singled out as a loser or an oddball, you're a target. Constant antagonism can make life miserable for an ostracized teenager. This antagonism can come in the form of public humiliation, or threats of violence, or even the decision of the majority to ignore a particular student. And sometimes teachers inadvertently reinforce their hurt feelings by singling them out for ridicule. Because this harassment takes place within the walls of school, these unhappy teens come to reject the institution itself.

School then becomes the target for these teens' anger and frustration. Some respond by isolating themselves, drifting further and further away from school life. They want to distance themselves from the pain school has caused them so they drift through their classes like ghosts, not speaking up or doing their homework or even showing up unless they have to. Other victims of peer rejection respond by lashing out at their school. All too often, alienated, troubled teenagers are responsible for random acts of violence in our schools, including incidents where students have opened fire on their classmates with the intent to kill. Some have actually said they wanted to get back at other students who treated them with contempt.

Certain teenagers run a greater risk of being rejected by their peers than others. Usually it's those who act or appear a little different from their conformity-conscious peers. It can be the way they dress (being unaware of what's in fashion or unable to afford the popular styles, or following their own distinctive preferences instead), their social awkwardness (like being shy or making inappropriate remarks), or their divergent interests (collecting butterflies, wearing thrift shop clothing, listening to esoteric music, or promoting an unpopular cause). You can tell your child is having problems in school when she makes negative comments about her peers, such as, "They're all stuck-up," or, "They're not worth getting to know." She's probably feeling lonely and rejected but may refuse to talk about her experiences. Often there's a lot of anger and sadness that accompanies these feelings about school. And of course, you should encourage your teenagers to talk about them.

Excessive Family Stress

There are times when family situations exert a great deal of pressure on teenagers. Marital problems, financial problems, a death or serious illness, or an alcoholic or abusive parent can greatly affect a young person's emotional well-being. If the accompanying stress is more than she can bear, the unfortunate outcome may be impaired school performance—poor attendance, preoccupation or distractibility in class, and minimal effort in academic subjects.

Some parents try to hide or minimize their problems in the hope that they won't affect their children. But that's not usually possible. Family problems have a way of spilling over into other aspects of life, and if they're excessively stressful, they can even poison and damage school performance. So rather than turn your back on an unhappy family situation, I urge you to face up to the problems. If you can solve them on your own, that's commendable. But often the best course of action is to seek the assistance of a mental health professional who will help you identify the causes of stress, formulate a plan for change, and support you through the process. You'll be doing yourselves and your children a favor.

Poor Self-Esteem

Poor self-esteem is another reason that teenagers do badly in school. This is certainly the case if it comes from experiences of disappointment or failure within the classroom. But sometimes poor self-esteem stems from nonacademic sources: ongoing criticisms by peers and parents, the experience of failure in a different aspect of life (like friendship or dating), and a negative, depressed outlook on life. As a result of their frustration with and disappointment in themselves, they conclude that there's no point trying and abandon their efforts. School becomes yet another reminder that they can't meet people's expectations.

These teenagers think very negatively. Because they're convinced that they're worthless and have such a pessimistic view of themselves and life in general, they give up easily and find it difficult to imagine that things could be different. Most of them are able to do much better than their grades indicate, but they steadfastly cling to their conviction that they're failures. Unless something happens to turn that belief around, it's likely to become a self-fulfilling prophecy.

Substance Abuse

I've explored substance abuse previously, but it should be included among the major impediments to school achievement. Teenagers who regularly drink or get high lack the wherewithal to attend class regularly and sustain their academic efforts. Despite what they would have you believe, the substances they abuse reduce their motivation and impair their concentration. As they get deeper into drugs or alcohol, their daily life revolves around using their substance of choice; matters like school and grades take a backseat to questions like, "When am I going to get drunk next?" and, "Where can I score some more pot so I can get high again?" This either keeps them away from school, leads them to attend school while under the influence, or brings them into their various classes tired, unprepared, and uninterested.

Students who are caught up in a cycle of substance abuse increasingly withdraw from "distractions" like school and find friends who share the same priorities, in which school figures pretty low on the list. Since their energy level is consumed by their substance abuse, they're unable to study or sustain any school effort. These teenagers convince themselves that getting high lends meaning to their lives, yet they abandon everything that was ever meaningful to them before they discovered drugs or alcohol. Their time is increasingly spent under the influence, indulging in the impulses that come along with a particular substance, whether it means wasting money on thoughtless purchases, an act of violence, a random sexual encounter, a meandering, pointless conversation about philosophy or the virtues of drugs, or simply excessive amounts of sleep. It's a downward spiral with little room for escape—until they're confronted regarding their behavior and placed in a substance abuse treatment program.

Negative Peer Influence

Negative peer influence may be the most powerful factor in a child's neglect of school. Sometimes it's hard to say just who's

How to Tell If Your Teen Is Neglecting School

■ He often "forgets" to bring home his books and insists that he has no homework every night. He tells you, "You can ask my friend John who's in my class if you don't believe me."

■ Her weeknight activities never seem school-related—instead they revolve around phone calls, visits with friends, TV shows. None of her stories that take place in school have anything to do with academics.

■ He insists that he studies, but you never see him doing it. And if you ask to see his work, he accuses you of treating him like a baby.

■ Her report card shows several unexcused absences. When you question her, she insists that the school was mistaken.

■ He's spending more and more time with dropouts and other teens who do poorly in school.

■ She's working at a part-time job and is devoting all of her energy toward her job instead of toward her schoolwork. She says she's looking forward to when she can work there full-time and make more money. Or she plans to follow in the footsteps of older friends or acquaintances who hold menial jobs without prestige or good pay.

■ He stays up until the wee hours of the morning talking on the phone, watching TV, or fooling around on the Internet.

■ Her teachers or school counselors have expressed concern about her deteriorating performance.

■ He cites unrealistic stories of success—professional athletes or singers or models who make loads of money without having succeeded in school. (To which you can respond that John Lithgow, Tommy Lee Jones, Mira Sorvino, and Conan O'Brien all went to Harvard, Lisa Kudrow and Meryl Streep went to Vassar, and David Duchovny went to Princeton.)

Trust your observations and your instincts. If several of these signs are present, follow the suggestions ahead on addressing school problems.

influencing whom. Is your teen so bored and disaffected with school that she's seeking out friends who feel the same? Or are her friends turning away from school for other reasons, and influencing her to do the same? No matter which came first, one thing is certain: birds of a feather do flock together. Teens who are turned off by school tend to hang out together, cut classes, find risky ways to create excitement, and validate one another's rejection of education. They come up with a host of rationalizations to justify their poor performance, even though they know on some level that they're making a mistake that will have long-term consequences. Friends take on an exaggerated significance for these adolescents; often friends are all they have.

Groups of friends who reject school encourage one another to seek ways to beat the system. They devise schemes to get themselves out of school (like sneaking out at lunchtime, forging notes, calling the school pretending to be a friend's parents). Further, they look for shortcuts to circumvent studying for exams (getting the tests in advance or cutting the exam and taking a makeup test) and conjure up elaborate excuses for their failure to complete assignments. Some shut down completely and refuse to do any work. Of course, their friends egg them on, laugh approvingly at their obnoxious behavior, and view their actions as a badge of courage. Since their parents and the school strongly disapprove of their actions, they become increasingly reliant on one another for support.

A young man once explained to me that he chose his friends, all low achievers with poor academic records, because they were the only ones who understood him. He and his friends spent most of their time wandering from house to house and mall to mall. I asked this young man what his group talked about and he said succinctly, "Not much of anything." He and his friends all scoffed at the importance of school and assured one another that they'd make a good living when they were older, despite the fact that most of them were failing the majority of their classes and lacked any direction.

HOW POOR ACHIEVERS SEE SCHOOL

We've reviewed the main factors that interfere with school involvement and achievement. Before giving you some ways to help resolve these issues, I'd like to share a few of the complaints I've heard from school-averse teenagers. They raise a number of important points that will help you identify and respond to similar feelings in your child.

"School is a waste of time—they don't teach you anything relevant there." This may be the most common excuse a teenager gives for poor school performance. He fails to make a connection between what he's learning in school and his future. Whether or not he's struggling with the academic concepts themselves, he's clearly losing interest, and as he puts in less time and effort, his grades will plummet. I think of this statement of disinterest as a veiled plea for help. The young person is telling us that he finds school uninteresting and doesn't feel he's deriving any benefit from it. The message implies, though, that if he saw a purpose and a meaning to his classes, he would apply himself. Take this complaint seriously and find a way to convince him of the benefits of education. He needs to establish a meaningful connection with someone on the school staff (a guidance counselor or teacher he likes and can relate to) who can take him under their wing, help him make the connections between school and "the real world," and lend meaning to his school experience. He may also benefit from talking with someone in a career he aspires to, someone who can tell this young person the exact ways that his education helped him get where he is today.

"The teachers in my school are all dumb (or boring or critical)." We hear this complaint from young people who feel they're not treated very well in class. They often have stories about teachers putting them down, failing to help them when they ask for it, or teaching in a dull, dry manner that involves lots of dittos and busywork. Teenagers like this may simply not respond well to conventional teaching approaches. Another possibility is that teenagers are placed in classes that are too easy for them and they need a challenge. And be alert to the possibility of ADD/ADHD or learning disabilities (discussed earlier in the chapter) in students who often complain about their teachers. If they are unable to keep up with their classes, they may blame their teachers for not being able to make them understand, rather than acknowledging their own shortcomings. It's certainly much easier to blame someone else than to examine what's going on inside yourself. In any case, these teenagers need individual attention. It's admittedly a little hard to come by in today's crowded public high schools, but many teachers are willing to make some extra time, and these teenagers benefit greatly from a meaningful connection with an interested teacher.

"You'll see—I'll do better next marking period."

Famous last words. This promise usually isn't kept, and that's because the teenager who makes it is avoiding responsibility. Why wait until the next marking period to start studying and doing assignments? The time is now.

Accountability is the issue. If your child tells you something like this, make sure you hold her to it. If the marking period is almost over and she's failing, it's not unreasonable to wait a few days for a fresh start. Otherwise, remind her that delaying her efforts will only make the problem worse— because she'll have even more work to make up during the next marking period.

If you see that she's still not making an effort, confront her by saying something along these lines: "You're the one who insisted you'd do better when the next marking period began. Now we're two weeks into it, and you're still not making an effort. What's the point of making that statement if you don't mean it? And furthermore, how can anyone take your word seriously if you don't take yourself seriously? How about showing us and yourself that your word is good? It would make us happy to see you take charge of your own life. And remember, we'll try to help you in any way we can."

It's hard for your teenager to argue when you remind her that it's her credibility at stake. So try to get her to say what she's planning to do and then hold her accountable to herself, rather than you. After all, that's what you want your teenagers to do: assume increased responsibility for their own behavior.

"School is the only thing my parents care about."

This is a very powerful statement and shouldn't be taken lightly. Teenagers who truly believe it usually feel estranged from their families. They're convinced that their parents don't care about them as unique individuals but are interested only in their academic accomplishments. As a result, they fail in school to protest their parents' emphasis on academic achievement. If you hear this complaint from your child, ask yourself if it's legitimate.

Stop and think about your teenager for a minute. Do you know what he's really interested in? For example, if he plays the guitar, have you ever really listened to him play a song? Or if she's an artist, do you regularly ask to see her portfolio? These overtures are very powerful; be certain to make them. If your child feels you're genuinely interested in everything he does, he'll be more inclined to please you, knowing that you're happy to see him happy.

If you have been holding your teenager to a standard of academic success that he is either not interested in or not capable of, it's time to rethink your strategy. You want your child to succeed, but pushing him until he turns against you isn't the way to do it. If your set of standards and expectations for your teenager's school experience is wildly different from his own, then it's time to sit down and figure out some sort of compromise. You may think you're doing him a favor by pushing him hard, but if it's too much, no one is going to benefit.

On the other hand, if you feel there's no legitimacy to your child's complaints, you'll need to ask yourself why he's making the accusation that you care only about his grades. It's possible that it's his rationalization for poor school performance or that he truly misunderstands your concern about him. In this case, you'll want to remind him that you're concerned about many aspects of his life. And make certain that your daily conversations aren't excessively focused on school.

SCHOOL PROBLEMS YOU'RE LIKELY TO FACE

Now that we've heard some teenagers' complaints, let's see how their attitudes affect everyday life. Imagine how you would feel if every time the telephone rang, you worried that it was the school calling with another problem your child had caused. Some parents go through this almost every day. In this section, I'll review some of the challenges you may face as the parent of a teen with school difficulties and offer some advice.

No Homework Today, Honest!

Say you have a junior in high school who insists every day that her teachers aren't giving her any homework assignments. This is not likely. The average high school student gets two or three hours of homework every day, even if it's a long-term assignment like finishing a novel by a certain date or reviewing for a test at the end of the week. What are you to do in this situation?

First, there's not much point in arguing. Just let your daughter know that what she says is hard to believe. Then tell her that you're going to call the school to put your mind at rest. After all, there's no point in hassling her when her teachers can easily answer your questions. So speak to each of them, and ask about what's going on in their classes. They'll be happy to tell you how much homework they're giving and will let you know if your child is turning in her assignments.

Once you get accurate information from the school, deal with your child accordingly. Assuming she's not doing her homework, set up a system of checks with the teacher so you can track her performance. Have your child carry a homework sheet to and from school; it will list the assignment each day (if there isn't one, the teacher will say so) and require the teacher's signature. If your child fails to bring the sheet home, she'll be expected to do work at home, whether or not there's an assignment. And by the way, when it comes to her word against the teacher's, trust the teacher's. Teachers have no reason to lie to you, but your child does. Your teenager will hate having to use a homework sheet; she'll probably complain that you're treating her like a baby and that no one else has to do anything so stupid. Therefore, you might want to motivate her by agreeing that after a certain time period (between a week and a month, depending on how badly her homework habits are slipping), if she has turned in all her assignments and been responsible about the homework sheet, you won't need to use it anymore. By then she should have learned two things: good homework habits, and the fact that she won't be able to pull the wool over your eyes.

Homework is one of the major battlegrounds between parents and students with school problems. The children avoid it like the plague, while the parents are determined to force their teens to fulfill their obligations. But whose responsibility is it, anyway? In one of the next sections, I'll discuss a number of ways you can set limits and enforce consequences for negligence about school. But always begin by asking yourself what gets in the way of your children doing their homework. It could be any of the possibilities we've explored in this chapter: poor motivation, substance abuse, learning problems, disenchantment with education. Once you've learned what's interfering with your teenager's completing assignments, you'll be ready to take action.

While you must take a firm stand on homework, you must also be careful not to get too involved with it. I have known a number of parents who actually do assignments for their children. They sit down with the books, force the teenagers to sit next to them, and then do the work themselves, while the incredulous students watch with a smile! Obviously, this serves no useful purpose other than to make the parents feel better. The fact is that your child is going to school, not you.

The Missing Report Card

Another opportunity for deceit is the report card. Some teenagers insist they never got one, even though everyone else in their class did, or that it disappeared in the mail. Rather than argue the point, you should simply insist that your child produce the report card, and if she won't or can't (having destroyed or defaced it), have the school send a replacement to your business address or pick it up yourself. Obviously, this kind of violation of trust requires punishment and a talk about honesty and the importance of facing consequences. Let your teen know that you'll always respect her more for showing you a bad report card than none at all. The same holds for the young person who changes the grades on her report card. If there's any cause for suspicion, you have every right to check up on her. Ask yourself why your child tried to deceive you in the first place. Was she ashamed of her grades or afraid of your reaction? If either of these is true, then both of you need to talk and work together to resolve this situation.

There is a quality of desperation to this kind of ploy. Teenagers who resort to such measures can't face up to their failures. Their judgment is weakened by their anger and poor self-esteem. On some level, they actually believe their little ruse will work.

Cutting Class and Truancy

Avoiding school is another way teenagers try to beat their academic blues. Having convinced themselves that school is a waste of time, they either sneak out partway through the day or never show up in the first place. They usually look for like-minded peers to accompany them in their escapades. The problem is that before they know it, they've gotten themselves in so deep that they can't be bailed out. There are only so many days of school students can miss before they're suspended or expelled. And many schools have guidelines specifying how many unexcused absences are allowed before the student is automatically failed for the marking period. Once an academically troubled student has failed all his classes, it will be even less likely that he'll make the effort needed to earn good grades in the next marking period.

Refusing to Go Back to School

Teenagers who've gotten into fights or bad situations at school often feel so humiliated that they don't want to return and deal with the other people involved. Sometimes these feelings are justified, but they may also use this as an excuse to get out of school for a few days. Even if you sympathize with them, don't let them skip school. Instead, talk with your teenagers about their anger and fear and reassure them that you'll back them up in any way you can. Emphasize that everyone makes mistakes sometimes and it's important that we face up to them. But reiterate that avoiding school is an unacceptable solution. The longer the young person stays out, the more difficult it is to get him back.

Disruptive Behavior

I've saved this category for last because it often overlaps with the others. Notes from the teacher, calls from the principal, disapproving looks from other parents because your child behaved badly in class—these are the times that try parents' souls. There is a wide range and variety of disruptive behavior; it can be something as minor as making a wisecrack or vulgar noise or taking someone's pencil during class. It can also mean more serious offenses like swearing or yelling at a teacher during an altercation, defacing school property, starting a fight, or setting off a fire alarm. Offenses like these result in calls from the teacher or principal, detention, probation, or suspension.

It's up to you to decipher the message the disruptive teenager is trying to send. Teenagers assume the role of class clown or provocateur for different reasons, but the one thing all troublemakers have in common is that in some fundamental way they feel like they don't really belong at their school. Your son may be trying to make his presence known, or he may be bored with the academic routine, or he may have trouble controlling impulsive and inappropriate behavior. He may be rebelling against students or teachers that he doesn't like, or he may be craving attention and has decided that negative attention is better than none at all. Disruptive behavior is a symptom of something serious going on with your teenager, and you need to diagnose his real problem before you can cure him (and his school) of his inappropriate actions.

TALKING ABOUT SCHOOL PROBLEMS

You must be prepared to deal with difficulties like these quickly, efficiently, and directly. It's best to raise school issues with your teenager in a caring, unthreatening, and forthright way, without accusing him or playing the martyr. This is not easy, considering the strong emotions that are involved in school-related issues. Even if you want to break his neck, try to keep calm. Talking to your teenager will help. Here are some suggestions that will make this easier.

Analyze How You Feel About School Yourself

Perhaps the best way to approach your teenager's failure to meet school obligations and expectations is to evaluate your own beliefs. How much do you value education? If you feel strongly that it's important, then you should make it a priority in your child rearing, but not to the exclusion of everything else. If you don't think much of higher learning, could your own attitude be negatively affecting your child?

Next, how much do you think you should push your children to learn? Do you really want to engage in a life-and-death struggle over schoolwork? You might win the battle and lose the war; that is, your child may comply reluctantly with your demands but end up resenting you greatly. Or do you believe in a laissez-faire approach, where you'll let your teenager make her own decisions and learn from them herself, even if it means failing in school?

Obviously, your attitude toward education will affect how you deal with your teenager's misconduct at school. You want to convey to your children the importance and worth of an education. But it's important to bear in mind that you can't always impose your values on your children. The older your teenager, the more he'll need to discover the value of education for himself. Hopefully he'll get pleasure out of learning and will realize that a good education is the best ticket for a bright future. If this isn't the case, share your disappointment with him, and alert him to the drawbacks of dropping out: lower income potential, lost opportunities, and future regrets. Arrange for your child to talk with some people who've had second thoughts about their choices, and let him draw his own conclusions.

Understand How Your Child Feels About School Failure

If you're going to have an effective dialogue and set up good communication habits with your teenager about school-related matters, you need to understand how she feels about school. It's safe to assume that if your child is facing school problems, she's feeling embarrassed, ashamed, guilty, and pretty low on herself. On top of that, she may feel angry, frustrated, apathetic, or rebellious, depending on the source of her school troubles. Remember that school failure often has many causes. Once you understand what's really going on with her, you can cut through any of her defense mechanisms, like excuses, lies, or passing the blame onto teachers, other kids in her class, or even you. Since your child is unlikely to tell you directly, you'll need to consider each of the possibilities we've discussed earlier in the chapter. Somehow you must get to the bottom of it and figure out what to do together.

Don't Approach Your Child About School Problems with Criticism or Threats

You may have learned about your teen's difficulties at school directly from her, or the school may have informed you. Either way, pay attention to the issue immediately. This is another situation in which you don't want to come on too strong. If you blow up or become critical or threatening, your behavior may obscure the important points you're trying to make. Your child feels bad enough about her predicament and may withdraw further if she feels she's being attacked. You need to emphasize that everyone makes mistakes and the most important thing is to learn from them and make a stronger effort in the future.

I'm not saying you shouldn't challenge your teenagers' school difficulties. You should absolutely hold your teenagers accountable for their actions. What I'm saying is that you should also show some empathy for their plight. Think about how humiliating it is to feel like a failure while you watch your classmates enjoying and succeeding in school. And remember that your child probably feels trapped in his situation, with no way out. So when you discuss these issues with him, express concern and curiosity about what's wrong, and convey your intention to stand by them throughout the ordeal. You want to avoid making it a contest of wills—their determination to avoid the issue and yours to face it.

One approach is to ask your teenager what he plans to do about his school problems. It's not unreasonable to expect him to take some responsibility. If he has a viable plan, support his efforts in every way possible. On the other hand, if he's at a loss for a solution, make some suggestions and ask if he'd like you to intervene on his behalf with the teacher or principal. The worst that can happen is that he'll flatly refuse to make an effort to improve the situation. In that case, you'll have to assume that he's turning the responsibility over to you to do whatever is necessary.

ADDRESSING SCHOOL PROBLEMS

Although you want your children to take some responsibility for their difficulties in school, you must also be proactive. I don't advocate the laissez-faire approach to school problems,

Some Approaches to School Problems

Before you seize the initiative in resolving school problems, ask your child what he's prepared to do about his school situation. Following are several suggestions to consider:

■ Remind your teenager you'd prefer that he take action on his situation, so that you don't have to. This approach conveys respect and affords the possibility of generating some goodwill. If he does take action, tell him that you're proud of him.

■ Ask your teenager if she's willing to approach her teacher to get suggestions about how to raise her grade. She may be embarrassed or reluctant, but emphasize that the teacher will probably be receptive to her overture, and that even if the teacher doesn't respond to her gesture, she's no worse off than she is now.

■ Ask him what he thinks will happen if he ignores the situation. If he says, "I don't know," or, "I don't care," review with him the consequences of school failure.

■ Offer to get a tutor to help with her weakest subjects. You can hire a professional tutor, visit a learning center, or recruit the help of a good student in a higher grade.

■ Remind her if she fails her classes and doesn't want to repeat the year, summer school will be necessary. Ask her if she's prepared to sacrifice her summer vacation to attend school every morning.

■ Ask him how he feels about his current school—if he were offered the option of switching to a local charter, magnet, alternative, private, or parochial school, would he want to go to one of the different schools, or would he prefer to stay at his current school? If he says he likes his current school, then help him to figure out what he can do to stay there. If he says he strongly feels that he would like to switch to a different school, then seriously consider a transfer and look into other school options together.

■ If there's a serious problem with truancy, make sure your child understands the consequences if it continues. Those might include expulsion, a court appearance, or placement in a special program (see Chapter 11).

because students are often in over their heads and need your help. After you have talked with your teenager about his school problems, he may refuse to make any effort, or he may make promises to do better that he doesn't want to (or know how to) keep. If a few weeks have gone by and you don't notice any changes or improvements, it's time for you to get involved. Follow these suggestions to address your child's school problems when they're more than he can handle on his own.

Contact the School Counselor

This is probably the best place to start. By the time the teenager reaches junior high, at least five teachers are involved in his education. You'll have a hard time reaching all of them and finding a convenient time for conferences. The school counselor, however, is there for just this kind of consultation. You can start by calling to discuss your child's situation. She'll probably be happy to check on his grades and gather information from his various teachers and will then get back to you to discuss what she's learned.

If your child's teachers express concern at this point, request a meeting with the counselor and the teachers of classes in which he's having problems. These professionals will ordinarily be happy to accommodate you, but bear in mind that they are quite busy. They often have responsibility for several hundred students. Don't be too demanding or critical of the system, or your request for a conference may wind up at the bottom of a pile in the counseling office.

I recommend involving your teenagers in these school conferences. If you don't, they may get the impression that you're conspiring behind their backs. Furthermore, when your child feels a part of the solution and not only the problem, he's more apt to comply with the recommendations the counselor makes.

During the conference, you'll want to find out all you can about how your child is doing in class. The counselor will probably invite your teenager to share her perspective on her problems. This gives the teachers the opportunity to hear about what's wrong and try to be responsive. Be sure to ask about your child's behavior, attitude, and attendance, not only his grades. With this information, you can all work together to formulate a game plan. Whether your teenager's problem is attendance, poor grades, or disruptive behavior, this plan will have to address the root of the problem. Everyone should send the student the same powerful message: "We're concerned about you and want to help."

Formulating a Plan to Address Specific School Problems

Following are the ingredients for implementing a plan to address three major problem areas in school:

ATTENDANCE PROBLEMS

1. Talk to your child about the possible causes for his truancy from school. These include negative peer pressure, feeling turned off to the school system, and believing that there's no chance of passing his classes.

2. Seek incentives and leverage to encourage his regular attendance at school. Think about possible rewards and consequences that are likely to be effective.

3. Monitor his activities carefully. Insist that your child tell you what he's doing. Check with his friends' parents about what they're up to, and check up on him every now and then to verify his whereabouts. He won't like this at all, but you should let him know that your lack of trust in him is one of the consequences of the irresponsibility and deceit he displayed by skipping school.

4. Establish a contact person in the school (usually it's the guidance counselor) whom he'll check in with each day and meet with when needed. Hopefully, he'll develop a supportive relationship with this person.

5. Make sure that you receive a daily report on his school attendance. If the school fails to provide one, call the counselor yourself and ask for feedback. And ask to be notified immediately if he misses any of his classes.

POOR GRADES

1. Make sure you've explored each of the possible causes for school problems discussed in the first section of this chapter.

2. Seek incentives to motivate greater school effort. Discuss possible rewards your child could earn contingent upon improved grades. And set up a system that defines how she earns those rewards (for example, if her average is C or better, she gets $50 to spend on clothing or CDs).

3. Arrange for a tutor, whether it's a successful student, a teacher, or a specialist in the subject.

4. Try to match your child with teachers who relate well to underachievers and inspire learning (you'll need to speak with the school counselor about this).

5. Try to create the opportunity for a fresh start. This will be discussed in detail in the next section.

DISRUPTIVE BEHAVIOR

1. Consider why your teenager is behaving disruptively (seeking attention? ADD/ADHD? anger at a teacher or classmates? avoiding failure or embarrassment?) and address the issue.

2. Ask his teacher to help you and your teenager come up with techniques to manage his disruptive behavior (like assigning him a seat away from anyone who eggs on his bad behavior, excusing him from class briefly if he needs to compose himself, or giving him a position of prestige and responsibility within the classroom or school).

3. Encourage his friends to exert positive peer pressure to get him to behave more appropriately in class and to give him positive reinforcement when he does.

4. Impose meaningful consequences for violations of classroom expectations. For example, your child will forfeit specific privileges at home if the school contacts you about his behavior.

5. Set up a record sheet for teachers to track her behavior in the classroom. And make sure it gets sent home each day.

Seek Incentives and Leverage

You, the counselor, and the teachers will need to collectively find a way to exert pressure on the student. For the moment, I'll concentrate on incentives related to school. There's always going to be a level of work associated with classes that's not fun. Sometimes an incentive that's more immediate and tangible than grades can help motivate reluctant or uninterested students. There are several possibilities. If your teenager is already involved in school activities like sports, clubs, or band, you can make his continued participation contingent on his efforts to do better work or behave better in class. If he's turned off by school, you can use driving privileges, curfew, allowance, and other factors as leverage to bargain for an improved performance.

You can also set up incentives for good grades on tests, good classroom behavior, regular school attendance, and improved report card grades. These incentives don't have to be major to work. Some rewards you might offer would be the CD of their choice, dinner at their favorite restaurant or fast food joint, a gift certificate to their favorite store, increased privileges, or even money. You can also work with their teachers and school counselor to set up rewards within the classroom. Even a word of praise, a cute sticker on a good homework assignment, a little extra free time, or an unexpected class privilege can make the classroom experience a much nicer one for the struggling student.

Some people are against incentives and rewards for academic achievement. They believe that a good education and good grades should be their own rewards, and that if doing well in school only becomes a way to earn cash or presents or privileges, then these students are missing the purpose of education. I can understand this perspective, and agree that teenagers should all recognize the value and importance of an education. However, many teenagers who are experiencing serious school problems benefit from a more tangible, immediate reward than the far-off rewards of a diploma, a good job, or a college acceptance. They don't like school and don't experience anything positive in the classroom, so it's hard to think of its rewards in such abstract terms. But these students are motivated by immediate gratification and are willing to make the effort to obtain it. Hopefully, once they're in the habit of succeeding and doing well, a positive academic attitude will persist even without tangible incentives.

Look for Additional Support

Increased pressure on your troubled teenager, whether from the school or the courts, is not always the answer. Some schools offer what are called peer support programs. These can be especially helpful to alienated young people who are lost in the system. Peer support programs recruit other students to help a floundering young person get back on track. Many teenagers find these programs face-saving, since they would rather deal with someone their own age than an adult authority figure. Be sure to ask your school counselor if such a program is available. If not, the school may be able to recruit someone to fill the role.

Peer companions help troubled students get through the school day. They may actually escort them to school to make sure they get there on time. Then the companions accompany them to class and help with their work when needed. If problem students get into hassles with teachers, their partners will intervene on their behalf. After school, peers are available to help with homework assignments. Needless to say, this type of support requires a team effort by the school, the peer helpers, and the floundering teenager.

The goal of peer support is to make the lost student feel a part of the school. And ultimately, the new connection will expand his social horizon, and may even develop into a genuine friendship. Everyone has something to gain in this situation: the student eases back into the school routine without suffering through humiliating punishments, and the peer companion receives either class credit or special recognition. Peer support programs go to great lengths to help marginal students feel important. They're not considered a stigma but are presented as innovative dropout prevention initiatives. Surprisingly, most teenagers accept this type of assistance willingly.

Make Tomorrow a New Day

Sometimes teenagers get trapped in a bad situation. They may be failing school and have abandoned hope for passing the year, or they may get into trouble so often that they spend most of their time in detention. Under these circumstances, they have little incentive to make an effort to do better: the prospect is too daunting. If your child is at this stage, confer with the school to find a way to give him hope. I urge parents of such teens to take the attitude that tomorrow is a new day. Tell your child that he can make a fresh start. It's never too late to salvage something of the school year.

There are several ways to accomplish this. First, the school can allow the student to drop classes that he's failing. He can either take incompletes or repeat the courses in summer school. In place of those classes, he can pick up a study hall to help him pass other courses, or can finish the year in a more remedial class in that subject. This is a serious decision, but I don't see much point for a student to sit in a class he can't follow or has no hope of passing; it's boring at best and humiliating at worst. When these teenagers are presented with an alternative, they may be able to shift gears and get involved again with their studies.

Another way to help your teenager get back on track is to let him take a work-study class or internship. While it will be less academically oriented, such a class can increase a student's motivation because it's connected to the real world. Some teenagers do much better in a subject when they learn it on the job. They have to comply with a specific set of expectations and a boss who will enforce them. Although some parents are reluctant to consider this alternative, look at it as a means to an end. Your goal, after all, is to get your child interested in school again.

Explore Ways to Make the School User Friendly

The fact is that some teenagers don't take to rote learning. They don't complete their assignments, and they have trouble focusing on class lectures. They do much better in a hands-on learning situation.

For example, if they're studying history, they might go to visit a Civil War battlefield or graveyard. If they're studying Spanish, they could make an excursion to a Latino community to observe the culture firsthand, including eating at a local restaurant. For science, they can go on a nature walk or to an amusement park to see how the rides operate on basic principles of physics. These experiences teach them visually and experientially and are usually more interesting and more fun than learning from a textbook. Certain teachers are more inclined than others to engage their students in this type of activity. Matching students who have motivational problems with such teachers should be the school's job, but you should get involved to ask that your children be placed in such classes. These teachers' approach to education often works for students with motivational problems.

If you're resourceful, you can find opportunities for experiential learning outside of school as well. There are probably outdoor adventure groups in your area, sponsored by churches, clubs, community organizations, scouts, and independent groups. You can learn about them through your school, area resource directory, or one of the referral services listed in the Appendix. Those groups and others explore the countryside, go on archaeological digs, visit historical sites, and seek highly stimulating and challenging (but not dangerous) situations. They're a nice way to spark your child's interest in learning and help her to make some new friends in the process.

DEALING WITH SCHOOL PROBLEMS AT HOME

Another dimension of teenagers' problems with school occurs at home. Many teenagers avoid doing their homework and fail to study properly, if at all. They tell you to leave them alone and insist that school is going well. If they are doing well at school, they deserve to be rewarded with your trust. But if they're doing poorly at school, you should keep a close watch on their activities, so that you can exert helpful pressure when necessary. In this section, I'll review what you can do at home to help your child with school problems. It won't always be easy, but if you persist, you'll be rewarded with change.

Tracking Poor School Performance

Teenagers need to know they can't fool their parents. Once you've met with school personnel, establish a system to get feedback on your child's performance. This is especially important because it bridges the gap between school and home.

There are several ways to create this bridge, but the simplest is a feedback sheet that travels to and from school with your child. Ask teachers to fill out the form daily. Typically, the checklist will include categories that reflect the student's efforts, such as assignments completed, behavior, attendance, and participation. If you like, you can include a section for the teachers' comments. At the end of each class, the student gives the form to the

Ten Tips for Helping Your Children with Schoolwork

1. Ask yourself if you and your child get along well enough to work together. If you don't, you'll need to improve your communication with your child before you sit down together.

2. When you're ready, choose an agreed-upon time and specify how long you'll be helping him. You might start with fifteen minutes and increase the time if you both feel it's going well.

3. Approach the situation with a friendly attitude. Remember, you're on the same team and the goal is improved performance. That means no put-downs, criticism, or long lectures.

4. Don't teach your child more than the assignment calls for. Many teenagers complain that their parents turn their tutoring sessions into a discourse on their class. It's a turnoff for them and discourages future interactions on the subject matter.

5. If your child tells you his teacher just wants the answer and he doesn't have to show how he got it, accept it for the moment. But make sure to follow up afterward and find out exactly how the teacher wants the assignment done.

6. If the going gets tough, take a break. Each of you should do something relaxing and unrelated to the assignment for at least fifteen minutes before you return to the task at hand.

7. Ask your teens for feedback on how you're doing as a tutor. And listen carefully to what they tell you. If they insist that you're impatient or harsh, try to soften your approach.

8. If you don't understand the subject matter, admit it and seek other options (ask an older sibling for help or call another parent). Don't make your child sit there while you try to figure out the assignment. You can do that on your time, not theirs.

9. Praise your child liberally for any accomplishments, however small. For example, say, "That's great, you've got the hang of it now," or, "I can see you're really working hard at this."

10. After your child learns to work independently, let her know that you'll make yourself available when she needs you.

teacher, who signs and returns it. The student then takes the form home to show it to his parents and gets their signature.

Some teens will always try to beat the system, of course. They may forge signatures, claim their teacher forgot to sign the form, or say they left it at school. Close these loopholes in advance by telling your child that the sheet is her responsibility, not the teacher's. If she doesn't bring it home, you'll treat it the same way as you would a poor report. In the next section, I talk about the range of consequences you can apply.

Study Time and Homework Revisited

Perhaps your greatest challenge is to develop a viable system for your child to study at home. If she hasn't been doing her work on her own, you'll need to establish some enforceable guidelines. Start by asking the school how much time they think students should devote to studying each day. As young people reach the higher grades, these demands will increase.

At first, you may have to be patient. If your demands are excessive, your child may be unable to meet them. This serves no purpose; you'll wind up feeling frustrated and your child will give up. Consequently, it's better to begin with lower expectations and raise them gradually as your child adapts to studying again. Keep in mind that change is difficult. If bad habits have existed for a while, it will take work and patience to modify them.

As you begin this shift back to a regular study routine, set a time frame. In other words, ask your teenager whether she'd like to do her homework right after school or after dinner. Then hold her to her choice. Even if she doesn't have any homework on a given day, insist that she spend an hour or two reading or doing something else that's constructive, like watching an educational television program or researching a topic on the Internet or even reviewing subjects that will appear again on a final exam. This will help establish the routine and reduce the likelihood that she'll avoid her studies.

Don't leave floundering students to their own resources in the beginning. You're better off assuming that they need your assistance. So provide some well-intentioned direction and make it clear that you'll be actively involved for a while. There will be plenty of time to grant some leeway after your teens learn to adhere to the schedule you've agreed on. And by the way, check on them periodically. Teenagers don't like this, but struggling students usually need it for a while. Don't overdo it, but make sure they know you're keeping an eye on them. This will be difficult if you're at work in the after-school hours. You can call home, but you won't know if they're really studying. Consider instituting some kind of honor system, or simply ask to see the work they've done when you get home. Of course, eventually their grades will speak for themselves. If they're doing what they're supposed to, you should note some improvement over the next month or so. Don't hesitate to contact your teens' teacher by note, phone, or e-mail and request feedback on their efforts.

A Word About Distractions

I'm often asked whether parents should allow teenagers to listen to the radio or watch television while they're studying. Many children claim the noise doesn't bother them, but the decibel level alone makes you wonder how they can concentrate. As far as I can tell, teenagers have a much greater tolerance for noise than adults do. Many of them can probably listen to the radio and do their work at the same time. Some actually find loud music soothing.

Television is an entirely different story. Watching and listening at the same time is just too much stimulation—even for teenagers. You're better off forbidding them to watch television while they study. If they refuse to listen, you may have to remove the television altogether. The same goes for other distractions. Inform your child that the computer is to be used only for schoolwork because computer games can be an even greater distraction than television. Again, you will have to decide where to draw the line.

CONSTRUCTIVE CONSEQUENCES

Meaningful consequences are essential to motivating behavior and interrupting the cycle of failure. You can't force young people to like school. At best, you can make sure they attend and make some effort, in the hope that they'll come to see the value of an education. I don't believe you should give your children a choice about going to school if they're under seventeen. Consistent with the theme of this chapter, you should do everything you can to ensure that they take their education seriously. The implications of abandoning it are too far-reaching to leave the decision up to someone with so little experience. This means you'll have to hang tough and do what you can to guide your child toward a good education.

I spoke earlier about using leverage and incentives to motivate your teenager to academic success. This is one aspect of constructive consequences, which incorporate not only rewards but restrictions, privileges, and punishment as well. Constructive consequences mean more than special one-time deals meant to motivate poor students. One of the most important things you can do is to establish a logical and consistent connection between your teenager's effort and the privileges he gets— or loses.

Making Consequences Matter

Consequences should serve a useful purpose. That is, they should not hurt your teenager but should point him in the right direction. Random punishment can make your teenager feel you're punishing him without considering his feelings, and he'll be even more likely to rebel. Be consistent.

Begin by limiting your consequences to activities that can interfere with schoolwork. This is easily justified and more likely to have an impact. For example, the telephone, television, and stereo are not necessities, but privileges your teenager should earn. Let him know that the consequence of his poor school performance will be the removal of one or all of these entertainments. If he doesn't demonstrate any improved attitude or effort toward school, remove these privileges until he shows some improvement. Conversely, if he really makes a demonstrable effort that's rewarded with good grades or positive teacher reports, he will have earned back the privilege of these enjoyments. I'm less enthusiastic about withdrawing teenagers from activities that might serve a useful purpose, such as volunteer work or a constructive hobby. Such punishments can deprive students of meaning in their lives and lead them to give up hope.

When Your Consequences Are Challenged

If your teenager's poor school performance isn't affected by the loss of TV, telephone, or stereo privileges, the situation calls for stronger measures and more serious consequences. I suggest curfew restrictions or a reduction in allowance, and you can restrict their car use if they're old enough to drive. What is important is that they see the relationship between taking responsibility and earning privileges. It's not that you don't want them to have freedom; it's just that you expect them to be ready for it. School is one of the major proving grounds of maturity, and it's where teens can earn back their privileges and personal freedom.

There will be times when your consequences are met with outrage, anger, and refusal to comply. Your furious teenager tells you that she's going to break her new curfew, make all the calls she wants, or even run away from home. Even if you're tempted to argue with them, your best course is nonresponse. In my career, I've heard a great many threats from teenagers, but most of them have been empty. Your teen will probably rant and rave, stew awhile, and eventually accept her punishment. I'm sure you're familiar with this sequence. In the unlikely event that your children make good on their threats and do something extreme, you should be prepared to deal with emergencies like damage to your home, physical assault, or running away. And if you stay the course, you'll find that your child's behavior will eventually become manageable again.

Acknowledge Effort with Positive Consequences

While you need to implement meaningful consequences for irresponsible behavior, you also need to create consequences for positive efforts and responsible behavior. As I've said before, praise and contingent reinforcement are powerful agents of change. But just as with consequences for bad behavior, the consequences for good behavior will also need to be consistent.

The key is to have realistic expectations. If your child is failing her classes, first ask for C's and then gradually raise your expectations. You'll be much better off rewarding small steps than setting long-term goals. I've heard many stories of parents offering their children $50 for each A. At first teenagers are very excited about this, but they rapidly lose interest as they realize the hard work ahead of them.

A sensible way to approach this is to break down goals into smaller parts. For example, you might tell your child that each week he attends school regularly, he'll earn a slight increase in his privileges. Even better, connect weekly rewards to feedback from the tracking sheet I discussed earlier in this chapter. Specify the rewards beforehand so that there will be no room for argument. Some possible rewards are a larger allowance, tickets to a special event, or increased use of the family car. Don't worry if you can't think of any good ideas for rewards; your teenager will be happy to help you.

A warning about rewards for good behavior: you need to make sure that you keep your promises, or else your children will quickly figure out that your offered rewards are meaningless and they won't see any point in trying to do better. If you're offering a specific reward as a consequence of good school performance, you may want to consider a signed contract. The contract can serve as a reminder and incentive for your teenager, and there won't be any confusion about the deal. If there are witnesses to the contract, all the better.

ALTERNATIVE ARRANGEMENTS

There are several other options to consider when you're dealing with school problems. I encourage you to give some thought to each of these in order to determine whether they could be useful to your child. Some of the options will probably make you uncomfortable, but bear in mind that the end sometimes justifies the means. Before you make any decisions, take into account your teenager's age, level of maturity, and motivation. Since there are no firm guidelines for the right route to follow, I'll discuss the pros and cons of each of the options.

The Part-Time Job

Work has always been associated with building good character and preparing a young person for an adult role in life. Jobs teach responsibility and can help teach teens how to manage money. Many working teenagers also feel more independent. Nonetheless, many parents are torn between whether or not their teenagers should be encouraged, or even permitted, to take part-time jobs after school or on weekends. Some parents think their children should devote their attention to school and avoid distractions. Others feel that the advantages of working greatly outweigh the disadvantages.

Fortunately, research has been done on how jobs affect school performance. The results show that young people who work fewer than fifteen hours a week seem to fare well, but those who work more than that appear to do worse academically, having less energy to devote to their studies and less time to be involved with their school. Though there are exceptions, on the average their grades are not as good as those of their nonworking peers.

I like to think of a job as a privilege. Ideally, we allow our children to work because they can handle other aspects of their lives reasonably well. If they already feel overwhelmed by responsibilities, a job will not help to ease this feeling; it will like-

Case Example: Averting School Crisis

Here's an example of how a school worked with parents to solve a long-standing problem.

Chip was a fifteen-year-old ninth-grader who was failing several of his classes. His parents had contacted the school twice about this and had been assured the problem was being addressed. However, Chip kept skipping school and failed to show up for a meeting with his counselor. It was not until he allegedly pulled a fire alarm that the school administration took action. They suspended him for a week and notified his parents that they had to attend a conference before their son could return.

Chip refused to go back to school. He claimed that several teachers had it in for him and were blaming him unfairly for the fire alarm stunt. His parents were angry as they sat in the principal's office waiting for the conference to start. Several questions went through their minds: Why hadn't the school arranged a conference sooner? And why had it taken a crisis like this to get their attention? They felt the system had failed them.

The principal began the conference on an apologetic note. He acknowledged that the school was remiss in not calling the parents in sooner. "But that doesn't justify your son's actions," he added sternly. Since Chip had refused to attend the meeting, his parents could only assert his innocence secondhand.

Because of the seriousness of the matter, the school counselor, the psychologist, and several of Chip's teachers had been asked to attend the conference. As they reviewed Chip's school performance, many claimed he was unmotivated and lost in class. None felt there was any evidence of learning disabilities. His teachers described Chip as a quiet kid who wasn't a troublemaker. No one in the room seemed to know him, really. Even his parents admitted they found it hard to talk to him, but they said they didn't believe he was the kind of kid who would pull a fire alarm. He'd never done anything to jeopardize other people's safety before, and after all, the school's information was just hearsay.

It turned out that the school had been informed of Chip's action by one of his peers. The principal listened carefully

ly only increase it. Teenagers who ask to work usually want to earn more spending money or to save for something they want. Sometimes they want a job because it will get them out of the house more or because they don't care about school. This only underscores the importance of finding out why your teenager wants to go to work.

Provided that their reasons for working are legitimate, I don't as Chip's school record was reviewed. He reiterated the seriousness of the infraction, but allowed for the possibility that Chip may not have been responsible. Nonetheless, he felt, something had to be done to set an example for the other students. Chip's parents told him that their son had other difficulties as well and repeated their plea for the school's help. They assured the principal that they would cooperate in any way they could. They just didn't think suspension would help their son.

At this point, the school psychologist jumped in. "Maybe we can turn this into a positive situation for everyone," he suggested. "We need some kind of consequence, but I don't see any reason why it can't be constructive. Since Chip has been floundering in school, I think we can use this to get him involved again. What if we make his return to school contingent on doing some kind of service for us? He can work as an aide in the counselor's office and help out a day or two a week at the after-school program we sponsor. As for the classroom, we can move his seat to the front so the teachers can keep a closer eye on him. He'll have a harder

time slipping through the cracks that way. Then we'll ask the teachers to report back to me. I can keep his parents informed of his progress."

Chip's parents were quite receptive to this suggestion, as they felt the school was finally taking an active role. The principal also thought the idea was worth a try and agreed to support it. That left the issue of Chip's cooperation. Since he wasn't present at the meeting, his parents would approach him at home with the idea. His guilt or innocence was no longer the issue. Now they could tell him that there was a solution to the problem.

Although Chip was stubborn in his refusal to go back to school, he eventually agreed to return after some coaxing from his parents. They assured him that he would start with a clean slate. They also set up a reward system that would allow him to work toward earning the new electric guitar he desperately wanted. The issue of suspension was resolved, and a viable plan was in place. The parents and the school were communicating, and this paved the way for Chip to return successfully to school.

believe you should try to control the money your children earn. It's one thing to help them save, but a very different thing to tell them what they can spend money on. Doing so is a surefire way to start an argument. There's an exception to this laissez-faire policy about spending money. If you suspect that your child is using his money to buy alcohol or drugs or to participate in another illicit activity, you'll have to watch closely how he spends his money or forbid him from working at all. When it comes to the number of hours your teenager works, you should not allow him to take on more than he can handle. Sometimes employers place excessive demands on high school students, demanding they work late hours on school nights or on weekends before exam time. I've heard stories of teens kept after midnight on weeknights to wait tables at a restaurant or finish inventory at a retail store. Your child may have a hard time saying no, so it's up to you to make sure his employer respects your rules. Certain professions are more respectful of a teenager's real priorities than others.

Some parents open a joint banking account with their teenager so that they can monitor the flow of cash. The teenager retains the prerogative to make withdrawals, but the parent has the final say. Certain teenagers will balk at this agreement, insisting that it restricts their independence. But it's a reasonable compromise between unbridled freedom and total parental control. And besides, most banks require an adult signature on an account. You can usually sell your teenager on this idea, touting the value of saving and the interest earned on the account. If that's not enough, you can propose to match his savings by making a deposit of your own into his account, say $20 for every $100 he earns.

A part-time job may also be useful for teenagers who do poorly in school because they're not academically oriented. They may enjoy working with their hands, dealing with people, or being outdoors instead. In this case, why not allow them to get a job doing something that sparks their interest? They may meet others who are going to school and working with a particular goal in mind. Often this increases their motivation to at least finish high school so that they can earn more money. If there is any downside, it's the risk that they may drop out of school because they enjoy their work so much. That may be a chance you have to take. Without motivation, they're not likely to succeed at school or in life. But keep in mind, if your child is doing something she loves and is acting responsibly, you should be content. After all, if she's safe, happy, and feels like she belongs, she'll probably turn out just fine.

Alternatives to an Academic High School Diploma

Many parents ask me whether they should allow their teenagers to drop out of school when they reach seventeen or eighteen before they graduate from high school. This is an especially difficult decision if their children are capable of doing better. While I don't generally encourage this option, there are times when children just need a break, usually when they're failing courses and are resistant to school. Night school might be a possibility either immediately or for the future, particularly if students are willing to work toward a GED. You can learn about such programs by contacting your child's high school guidance counselor. Other teenagers may propose the idea of getting a job by day *and* taking classes at night. You might want to consider the alternative of a vocational school in this case. Vocational training gives the teenager a useful skill that can lead to employment. The vocational setting combines the discipline of work with the fundamentals of education, and it may motivate your teenager to stay in school.

If this option is not available and your teenager is adamant about dropping out, you may need to go along with his wishes. I've known a number of students who dropped out and then returned of their own volition a year or two later. Not surprisingly, their motivation was much improved by their experience. There's nothing like a year or two on your own to show you how tough the world can be for someone without qualifications.

Sometimes a pattern of truancy persists despite your best efforts. If you're convinced that you've tried everything and you need more powerful leverage, you always have the option of notifying the truant officer (or probation officer if your child's on court probation). Of course, you would take this recourse only if the student is cutting school frequently and violating the laws of the jurisdiction. It's a last resort and should never be taken lightly. You'll need to do some real soul-searching to be certain you're prepared to live with the consequences, which I'll specify shortly.

If indeed you're ready to forge ahead, I suggest you warn your child beforehand that you're considering this action. Sometimes he'll think twice about what he's doing when he knows there's a bottom line. And if you notice any sign of change, you can avoid taking such a drastic step.

Even if he's not on probation, you can talk to someone from the juvenile court to learn how to involve them. If you do, your teenager's difficulties will become a legal matter, and the battle will shift from the school to the courtroom. This extreme approach makes teenagers angry, but they take it seriously. By resorting to the law you're holding them accountable to a higher authority. But remember, there are future repercussions when you involve the legal system in your situation. You'll be giving the court jurisdiction over your child's well-being, and the case will become a matter of public record.

I'm happy to say that many school problems can be successfully addressed when parents are actively involved. The process can be slow and arduous, but if you take the right steps and you're determined to see it through, your teenagers will gradually begin to improve. They may not become academic superstars, and in fact, some will choose a course that may differ drastically from your aspirations for them. While education is of paramount importance, ultimately it's your children's happiness and well-being that is crucial.

DEALING WITH DEFIANCE AND ANTISOCIAL BEHAVIOR

"I know she's dealing drugs, but she denies it. I think it's getting worse, too."

"We fight constantly. Last night he punched a hole in the wall, then disappeared. We don't even know where he is."

"She keeps telling me she's going to change, but she never does. I'm afraid she's going to end up in jail, or dead."

S ome teenagers move beyond borderline troubled into a more unacceptable realm. They regularly defy authority and violate the norms of society. They avoid responsibility and take extreme risks because they "just feel like it." They show little insight into their behavior and, worst of all, no remorse or compassion for their victims. They may be vandalizing property, lying, stealing, behaving aggressively, or becoming involved in gang-related activities. Problems like these may seem unsolvable, but there are ways of dealing with them—and preventing further damage.

THE UNMANAGEABLE TEENAGER

Antisocial youth are chronically dishonest and often aggressive. Some are caught and taken to account for their misdemeanors. Others manage to get away with them. To complicate matters, problem behaviors usually come in packages; a young person engaged in one kind of antisocial behavior is likely to be involved in others. This makes it more difficult to detect the extent of illicit activity. Rule-breaking teenagers keep breaking rules because they're convinced that they're above the law. Even if your teenager gets into trouble only occasionally, you should be equipped to deal with the misbehavior I'll describe in this chapter.

We've already looked at factors that can propel young people into trouble. They may be angry and estranged in reaction to feelings of rejection. They're determined to broadcast their grievances and their independence from authority. Some were difficult to manage from early childhood and continue to play out their rebellion. Others get involved with illicit substances and wind up prisoners of their addictions. Typically, they have low self-esteem and poor self-control. They don't relate appropriately to their peers or to adults, and they're usually failing in school.

These are problems that you can't ignore. If your teen's behavior isn't challenged, it will continue unabated. Eventually he'll have trouble holding jobs and establishing strong relationships. You probably couldn't ignore these problems even if you wanted to. Children who rebel to an extreme extent make you angry, keep you awake at night, and corrode the fabric of your family. Life with these teenagers is a daily ordeal. In and out of trouble, they leave you feeling you can't leave them alone for a minute. The worst of it is that they show so little desire to change. They say they don't care what happens to them. You hardly know them anymore (and may wish you didn't).

Unfortunately, these teenagers' misbehavior becomes part of their identity. They take pride in their anger and flaunt their disregard for authority. Under the surface, they feel unhappy and confused, but few people would ever know this. They believe they're above the rules and are always on the defensive. Because the world seems a hostile place to them, they think their antagonism is fully justified. Naturally, they can't admit to being wrong.

It is heartbreaking to live with one of these unmanageable teenagers. Parenting becomes a torment; your child wears you down and leaves you feeling like a failure. No

Does Your Child Have a Conduct Disorder?

A conduct disorder is a serious psychiatric disturbance that involves a repetitive pattern of behavior in which the basic rights of others are violated. Be on the lookout for these signs in your teenager:

- Bullies, threatens, or intimidates others

- Often initiates physical fights

- Has used a weapon that can cause serious physical harm to others

- Has been physically cruel to animals

- Has stolen items of value

- Has forced someone into sexual activity

- Has deliberately set fires

- Has deliberately destroyed others' property

- Often lies to get what he wants

- Often stays out at night despite parental prohibitions

- Has run away from home overnight

- Is often truant from school

If your teenager displays repetitive problems with aggression, deceit, theft, and serious violations of rules, you'll need all the help you can get. Read this chapter carefully and seek professional assistance if your efforts are unsuccessful.

matter what you do, he continues to defy your authority and break your rules. The simplest of requests—"Would you please take out the trash?"—becomes a war of wills. His promises don't mean much, and almost everything he does upsets you. But if you find yourself on the verge of giving up, remember that you're not alone and that there are actions you can take to bring some workable resolution to the situation.

TALKING TO TEENAGERS IN TROUBLE

Teenagers who've gotten into trouble prefer not to talk about it, at least not with their parents. They may brag about their exploits to their friends, but at home they're masters of deceit and denial. This behavior works directly against your goal of getting them to face their wrongdoing and change their ways.

All the principles of good communication apply when you're trying to get through to callous and oppositional teenagers: listen carefully, don't be judgmental, and encourage them to express their feelings openly. However, you'll need some special strategies with these youth. Some will be obvious, but others may surprise you.

Control Your Anger

You have every right to be enraged if your child gets into trouble over and over again. You may be at your wits' end. But realize that your lecturing and screaming won't accomplish their intended purpose. In fact, the harsher and more critical you are, the more your child will tune out or strike back.

So first, calm down. Practice a composed approach with your spouse or a trusted friend beforehand. If you're really fuming, do something to relax before you confront your child. You'll be much more likely to say what you mean and to say it convincingly.

Here are some suggestions to help you accomplish this:

1. Remind yourself that he's the child and you're the adult. And make certain that you act accordingly; be calm, direct, and resolute.

2. Take a deep breath and hold it for a few seconds. Then exhale slowly and feel yourself relaxing. If necessary, repeat the exercise.

3. Count backwards from ten slowly. As you focus on each number, try to think of your ten favorite movies, one at a time.

4. Close your eyes and imagine yourself in a pleasant, serene setting. Think, for instance, about lying on the beach and feeling the warm sun shining down on you.

5. Talk to yourself. Make positive statements to keep calm. You can say: "I'm not going to let her get to me, I know I can control myself," or, "I've been through this before."

6. Ask your partner to help you calm down. They can encourage you to keep your composure and to wait a few minutes before approaching your teen. Or have them give you a quick massage.

7. Do something you enjoy to distract yourself from the heat of the moment. Listen to a favorite CD, eat your favorite dessert, or visit your favorite Web site.

8. Try to remember a time when your parent screamed at you or harshly criticized you. Did it make you feel angry, hurt, or rejected? If so, ask yourself if that's how you want to make your child feel.

You should experiment with each of these techniques to find which works best for you. After you've done so, resolve to use it the next time you're upset. With practice, you'll find that you're able to calm yourself when you need to.

In the following dialogue, a mother was initially infuriated to learn that her son had been suspended from school for the second time. But since she had several hours to calm down before the boy came home, she went jogging and took a long, hot bath. Then she called her husband's office to discuss the issue with him. By the time her son arrived, she'd thought out how to handle the situation.

Mother: Sal, I guess you know the principal called this morning to tell me you'd been suspended again.

Sal: So, I'll just be home for two days.

Mother: Well, I'm really upset. I don't feel like you take this seriously.

Sal: He started the fight, Mom.

Mother: That's beside the point. This is the second time you've been sent home.

Sal: I didn't think the teacher would make that big a deal of it. Besides, it was outside the school. And if he hadn't seen us, I would never have been suspended.

Mother: That attitude makes me angry. But I'm tired of yelling at you.

Sal: Then don't yell.

Mother: This situation has gone too far. You seem to have very little respect for the rights of others. I'm taking away your car keys for the next month, and there will be no allowance. During that time, I want you to think long and hard about what you've done. When your punishment is over, we'll sit down and talk about it again, and I'll expect you to explain why your actions were wrong.

Sal: Mom, you're overreacting. Don't get bent out of shape. It won't happen again.

Mother: I'm not overreacting. In fact, I think I'm letting you off pretty easy. If there are any more incidents this year, you're not going to use the car until school is over.

Sal: No way. You're such a bitch.

Mother: Sal, I don't have anything else to say to you.

If Sal's mother hadn't cooled down before talking to him, she probably wouldn't have been able to keep her composure. She was really angry with him and his attempt to brush off the problem. But she stuck to her guns and imposed a reasonable punishment. Finally, and this takes practice and discipline, she ended the discussion when it was no longer productive.

Don't Ask Them Why They Get into Trouble

Your natural inclination when your child gets into a sticky situation is to collar him, look him in the eye, and ask how he could have done something so stupid. If you do this, don't expect much of an answer. He'll say, "I don't know," ignore you, or lose his temper. Frankly, if he knew the answer, he probably wouldn't have done what he's in trouble for in the first place. If you really want him to learn something from the confrontation, you'll need to find a less provocative way to broach the subject.

The following suggestions will help you discuss such incidents with your teens.

Show curiosity and concern. When your child gets in trouble, your first response should reflect your concern, not your anger or criticism. An expression of concern is helpful because it doesn't put your teenager on the defensive and it offers the opportunity for discussion. You might say: "I was shocked to learn what happened. It upset me a great deal and I can't understand what made you do this." If it's a repeated offense, by all means express your frustration and disappointment; and make it clear that you'll do what you must to get the situation straightened out.

A Productive Conversation About Shoplifting

In this conversation, a father shows his curiosity and concern about his daughter's actions:

Father: Maria, I just found out you were caught shoplifting at the mall yesterday. I was shocked to hear it.

Maria: I'm sorry, Dad. It was really stupid.

Father: I can't imagine what you were thinking at the time.

Maria: I don't know. It was sort of impulsive. We were just standing at this watch stand looking at one of the watches, and all of a sudden Diana says, "Let's just take it." And before I knew it, we were running away.

Father: And of course you got caught.

Maria: Yeah. It served us right.

Father: And now you're banned from the mall for six months.

Maria: Yeah.

Father: Well, I guess you've learned things the hard way.

Maria: Yeah. And Diana's mother won't let us hang out together anymore.

Father: All this happened because you didn't stop to think about what could happen.

Maria: I guess so.

Notice that the father never actually asks his daughter anything. He expresses his concern and encourages her to talk about what happened. This is a difficult but enormously useful way to approach wrongdoing on your teenager's part. Without asking directly, Maria's father learns that she knows her impulsiveness has gotten her into trouble and that she's sorry and understands she's saddled with the natural consequences of her actions. He could impose further restrictions at this point, but even if he doesn't, the conversation has been constructive. Of course, Maria's story resembles that of a typical adolescent who gets in trouble once and learns from the experience. But her father's approach applies to more seriously troubled teens as well.

Speculate about their motives. It's a good idea to express your hunch about why your child got in trouble. But don't be insulting when you do so. When properly executed, this approach helps to establish the basis for further conversation. Sometimes you'll touch on a theme that resonates with your child and he'll pick up on it. For example, you can say, "I guess you felt you needed to prove yourself to your friends." When John's father made this comment to his son after he got caught tagging a public building, John responded, "Yeah, I was afraid what my friends would think if I didn't go along with them. They'd probably laugh at me and call me a chicken." His father was then in a position to discuss the pressure to be accepted that his son felt. Another illustrative speculative comment from Mary's mother: "I guess you stole the blouse from the store because you felt that was the only way you could get what you wanted." And Mary's response to her mother's comment was, "Well, you spend most of our money on your own clothing." Clearly, Mary was angry at her mother, and they needed to spend considerable time talking about Mary's feelings.

Ask them to tell you what happened. It's important to give your child a chance to talk before you take the offensive. Try saying, "I'd like to hear your view of the events before I jump to any conclusions." If he shares his perspective, you can openly discuss his actions, trying to help him learn from the experience. If he's indifferent and insists that he doesn't care—or he's defiant and refuses to talk with you—give him some time to think about the incident and get back to you. Should his attitude remain unchanged, you'll need to impose an appropriate consequence and explain why you're doing so.

Find Out What They Think

Sometimes you're so frustrated and angry you don't know what to do next. I see no reason why you can't share this feeling with your teenagers. Letting them know you're at the end of your rope may open their eyes and help them understand why you're considering serious disciplinary measures. Say the words straight out: "We can't go on like this anymore. If you have any ideas, we'll be happy to listen to them." If your children don't say anything or reply, "I don't know," you can assume that they need you to decide what to do. But sometimes they'll surprise you with an interesting answer.

Once in a family conference in my office, a boy proposed that his parents send him away to boarding school or let him live with relatives in another state. He recognized that he was trapped and was seeking a way out. "There's just too much pressure here," he said. "I can't break away from my friends; I feel like I've dug myself into a hole. We don't get along at home and we spend most of our time fighting. I really want to make a fresh start." His parents took his request seriously and helped him consider ways out of his situation.

Enlist Their Help

Another way to get your teenagers' cooperation is to tell them you need their assistance. Remember that most young people find it easier to give help than to accept it. Consequently, by soliciting their advice, you make it possible for them to save face while making some changes.

Follow this sequence of steps to recruit your child's help:

1. Reiterate the dilemma or problem situation that your child is facing. Try to do this without being judgmental.

2. Tell your teenager that you don't want to take action without his input.

3. Ask your child if she has any ideas about how to proceed. If she gives you a brief answer, encourage her to expand on it. If she says, "I don't know," first ask if she'd like your help. And finally, if she expresses no ideas and doesn't want your help, tell her that you may have to proceed without her. And then ask if that's what she prefers.

4. Assuming that your child has given you a suggestion, work together to refine it. And stick with the task until you can agree that the plan is worth a try.

5. To whatever extent possible, implement the plan jointly. At the conclusion of the process, thank your teenager for his help.

Here's how the father of Tom, one of my clients, put these suggestions to good use. He'd been alerted by his son's school that the boy was failing the year. Rather than reprimand Tom, he sought his counsel. Tom's father told his son he didn't know what to tell the administrator. "I know you don't want to repeat the tenth grade," he said, "so I need your help with this. We've got to come up with a way to convince Mr. Lewis that you're going to make an effort. If you can tell me what you're willing to do to bring up your grades, at least I'll have somewhere to start."

Tom resisted at first, but when his father reminded him that he couldn't deal with the school without his input, he came around. He suggested that he could be held accountable for his attendance and raise his F's to passing grades by the end of the quarter. "That would help," said his father, "but how would it convince the school you're serious about turning over a new leaf? You've got to give me more to go on."

Tom thought about it some more and eventually came up with the basis of a contract. He would agree to make more of an effort if the school would hold off on its decision to keep him back. If his grades didn't improve, he'd accept the school's recommendation of retention and go to summer school. At this point, Tom's father felt he had a reasonable proposal for the counselor. He thanked Tom for his help and promised to let him know as soon as he had an answer from the school.

In effect, Tom was helping himself by helping his father. By coming up with an idea for a contract, he was taking responsibility for his failure and saving face. He and his father avoided an argument between them by working together to solve the problem.

While not all interactions between a worried parent and a teenager in trouble will be this clear-cut, this situation illustrates how you can make your child part of the solution to his problems. The important point about this discussion is that Tom's father tried to find out what his son wanted and how to help him get it. This way Tom had a stake in the outcome beyond pleasing his parents or the school authorities. He challenged himself to keep up his end of a deal that he had engineered.

Find Out What They Really Want

Young people who are unsure of themselves may not respond as agreeably as Tom did. As you know, teens are famous for saying, "Just leave me alone." Since you can't do that when they're continually in trouble, tell them what they can do to get you off their backs. Here are some tips to help you to do this:

1. Tell your child you're not sure what she really wants, and make it clear that you'd like to know what it is.

2. Encourage your child to be as specific as possible.

3. After she tells you what she wants, let her know if her request is realistic. If it is, tell her exactly what you'd like her to do and how long you'd like her to do it for, in order to give her what she wants. If her request is unrealistic, don't attack it; instead, encourage her to ask for something that's within the realm of possibility.

4. If she equivocates, stand firm and encourage her to try to think about what she wants. Sometimes her actions will give you a clue. For example, your child might spend most of her time with younger friends. This could suggest that she's uncomfortable with her peers and is uncertain or afraid of her future.

5. End the conversation on a positive note.

Here's an illustration of this process in action.

Parents: We don't know what you want anymore.

Nell: I want you to trust me. If you'd stop bugging me, everything would be fine.

Parents: But you're still drinking on the weekends and you're barely getting C's.

Nell: That's what I mean, you get on me about everything.

Parents: And you expect us to leave you alone, with the way things are going!

Nell: You've never even given me a chance!

Parents: Well, we laid off for a few weeks, but nothing changed.

Nell: Yeah, right! Your laying off is what most people consider nagging.

Parents: All right. Do you really want to prove yourself once and for all?

Nell: Whatever!

Parents: Well do you?

Nell: Okay. Sure.

Parents: Fine. Here you go. You can stick to a curfew and make sure you come home sober on the weekend. And we'd like to see some improvement in school.

Nell: And what would I get?

Parents: You would get what you're asking for. If you keep your word, we won't have to check up on you anymore.

Nell: How long would I have to do this for?

Parents: We think two months would be fair.

Nell: That long?

Parents: Yes. That's what it would take to convince us.

Nell: I don't know.

Parents: Well, you're the one who said you wanted us off your case. Now we've given you a way to get what you want. How about it?

Nell: All right, I guess I'll try.

Nell's parents began by asking what their daughter really wanted. She answered them directly but was skeptical about getting it. They persisted and challenged her to prove her point. They told her she could have her wish if she was willing to meet certain conditions. After some discussion, they reached an agreement giving her the chance for a fresh start.

Talk About What Toughness Means

Some young people won't budge an inch when they feel cornered. They'll neither ask for help nor offer it and don't in fact know what they want. They confuse their pose of stubbornness, indifference, and opposition with being tough, which they consider a valuable trait. Try not to make the same mistake they do by confusing your anger and inflexibility with taking a courageous stand. You don't want to send your child the message that you're forever locked in combat.

I believe we should define "toughness" in a way that may be different from what our children usually mean by the term; we should, instead, use the word to mean a combination of pride, willpower, and independence of thought. Helping someone in danger is an act of bravery, but so is saying no to someone who's pressuring you, admitting you're wrong about something, and accepting the consequences of your own actions. With teens, stress these other types of strength, which I prefer to equate with courage. Here's how one parent talked to his son about what it means to be tough.

Father: Norm, several people told me you've gotten a reputation as one of the toughest kids in tenth grade. Do you like that?

Norm: Yeah, I don't take s—t from anyone.

Father: And that's what makes you tough.

Norm: I guess so.

Father: You've been in three fights that I know of this year.

Norm: Yeah. And I won them all.

Father: Aren't your friends always around when you're fighting?

Norm: Yeah, but what's that supposed to mean?

Father: Well, they cheer you on, right?

Norm: Sure, they're my buddies.

Father: And what would they do if you decided not to fight?

Norm: Probably call me a wimp.

Father: Even if they thought you'd get in trouble for fighting?

Norm: I guess so.

Father: Well, you've just told me you were tough, but you say you wouldn't avoid a fight because you're afraid of what your friends might think. Maybe you're not really that tough after all. Your friends sure have a lot of influence over you.

Norm: No one tells me what to do. And most kids are scared of me.

Father: Well, I don't think that's anything to be proud of.

Norm: Dad, you don't get it. My reputation is important.

Father: You mean you want everyone to think you're tough.

Norm: Yeah. That's what really matters.

Father: You know, there are other things that matter too.

Norm: Like what?

Father: That you have some willpower. That you could stay out of a fight and still hold your head up high. Or that you didn't worry so much about what your friends think. Those things are important.

Norm: Well, I could do them if I wanted to, but I don't know . . .

Father: I'd love to see you give it a try. That's what I'd call real courage.

Norm: I'll think about it.

Father: That's fair enough. And if you decide to go for it, I'll help you in any way I can.

Norm: Okay, Dad, I get it.

This is an interesting conversation because Norm hears not his father's disapproval but his interest in him. He's challenged on his interpretation of toughness and offered another way of looking at it. At first he has trouble getting the point, but his father doesn't give up. By the end of the conversation, Norm has agreed to give the matter further thought. He knows what his father values and knows he has confidence in him and will support his efforts to change. Of course, one conversation won't change a teenager's outlook, but it's important that you don't buy into your child's defiance and give up.

Challenge Their Excuses

The problem with most teenagers in trouble is that they display little wish to change. Worse yet, they rarely play it straight with their parents. Deceit, manipulation, and rationalization seem to be their preferred mode of interaction. You have to challenge these ploys. Since I've already addressed how to talk to your defiant teenager, I'll confine this section to challenging the excuses they make.

If your child plays down the seriousness of her actions, call her to account. If she brushes off unexcused school absences, for instance, you might say, "Wait; you're trying to tell me this is no big deal. You know the school policy. After four unexcused absences, you automatically fail the class. Are you willing to throw away this whole term?"

You'll often be able to spot the inconsistencies in your teenager's excuses. One girl came home an hour past her curfew and told her parents that she'd tried to call but the line was busy. The next day she changed her story, saying she hadn't had enough change to call from the restaurant's phone booth. Her parents said, "Last night you told us one thing, and today you're telling us another. How can you expect us to believe you?"

HOW TO MANAGE THEIR DIFFICULT BEHAVIOR

I've given you several suggestions for talking constructively with teenagers at risk of getting into trouble. At the very least, you want to encourage their feedback, ask for their cooperation, and challenge inconsistencies in their words and actions. But sometimes teenagers are too angry and noncompliant for these strategies to work. You should be prepared to deal with such behavior in the heat of the moment, with a measured but firm response. In this section, I'll talk about how and when to intervene when your child is defiant and aggressive.

It's Not What You Say, But How You Say It

Throughout this book, I've advised you to be positive, direct, and consistent with your teenager if you want to convey your message clearly and encourage him to respond. However, your best intentions can fail when your child is determined not to comply. You get angry and he responds by escalating the argument. You want to head off this kind of impasse before it overshadows your real aim of communication. To do this, say things in a way that expects your teenager's cooperation, without directly imposing your control.

For example, if you say, "You'd better stay home and study tonight," your teenager might ask, "Why?" or, "What happens if I don't?" He takes your comment as a challenge and instinctively opposes it. Alternatively, you could say, "The house should be quiet tonight. Maybe it would be a good time for you to study," or, "You said you wanted to pass that test tomorrow. Is there any-

How to Keep an Angry Teenager Talking

Try these suggestions to keep your teen focused when the conversation heats up:

1. Encourage him to tell you why he's so angry, and then reflect his feelings back to him. For example, if your son screams at you for being too strict, you can say: "You really feel we're unfair, don't you?" He's likely to say "Yeah" and continue talking.

2. Challenge your teenager to stay around and talk, rather than taking the easy way out and fleeing the situation.

3. Tell your child: "If you leave now, I'll never know what you really feel."

4. Don't be provocative by saying, "That's stupid," or, "You're obnoxious." Instead say: "I'm not really sure what you mean by that; you've got to tell me more."

5. Don't stoop to her level (for example, arguing about something ridiculous). Two hotheads are worse than one.

6. Remind your teenager that his best chance of being involved in the resolution of the problem is to stay around and talk. If he doesn't, you'll assume he's leaving the decision up to you.

7. Ask thought-provoking questions to try to get them to stop and think. For instance, try saying, "What do you think I'll do if you leave (keep this up, etc.)?"

8. Use humor. For example, you could say: "You look like me when you get angry," or, "This situation is ridiculous; it's like something from *The Godfather* (*Saturday Night Live, The Three Stooges*, etc.)."

thing I can do to help?" This kind of statement is more likely to get a positive response. But if your teen still brushes you off, you'll need to find other ways to motivate his behavior.

If you tell your child it hurts you when you have to force her to study, she might well turn around and ask, "Then why are you doing it?" Trying to make these teenagers feel guilty doesn't work very well. So in general, be forthright, impersonal, and non-authoritarian in your approach. This is likely to encourage your teenager's compliance, and more important, it sets a good example. After all, you don't want your child to cooperate just because he's being coerced. If you lay down conditions because you're forced into a corner by your unruly child, you're showing him that it's legitimate to do things out of desperation, not because you feel it's in your best interests. Also, it's hard for your teenager to fight with you when you're clearly not in the mood.

Keep Them Talking

Sometimes you can almost see the steam rising from your teenager when she starts getting angry. From experience, you know she'll blow up any minute. When you notice this happening, what's your best bet? I suggest you calm her down before trying to negotiate with her. You'll find that talking is incompatible with temper outbursts. Keep her talking when you're dealing with a hotly contested issue. She'll demand an immediate answer or expect you to lay down the law immediately, but don't give in. Insist on continuing the discussion, and her fury may subside.

Examine Your Options

It's always a good idea to consider your options before responding to a demanding teenager. Ask yourself what kind of response would be most helpful. For example, if he's yelling and screaming, would it be best to ignore him, support him, or challenge him?

Let's say you choose to ignore her; that is, you refuse to get sucked into her tirade. She might stop ranting and raving, realizing there's nothing to gain. On the other hand, if she can't let go, you're better off reflecting her angry feelings. Say, for example, "I understand how angry you are and I know how badly you want to go, but we can't continue our discussion when you're like this. So calm down a little and then tell me when you're ready to talk about it more." This can help, but remember that the teenager may not be able to pull back at this point. If she's worked up, you'll need to challenge her inappropriate behavior. Be direct and say, "I'm not going to discuss the matter when you're acting like this. I've told you before that I won't tolerate verbal abuse. Either you leave the room or I will. After you've calmed down, you can let me know if you still want to talk about it."

Obviously, these approaches presuppose that the teenager has some capacity for self-restraint. If not, you'll want to take the following advice about how to deal with a crisis. Always begin with the least intrusive response. If you can ignore the behavior, do so. If that doesn't work, change the subject or redirect the discussion. Whenever possible, remain friendly and keep your voice calm. One upset family member is enough. There's little to gain by adding to the mess.

WHEN THE GOING GETS TOUGHER

As I've said, sometimes you'll be convinced there's no way out. Your teenager may be so upset that he can't think clearly or flat out refuses to do what you ask. We all dread these moments and should be prepared to deal with them. The best approach, of course, is prevention. Tell your teen in advance what will happen if things get out of hand. Include your definition of misbehavior and its likely consequences. You could say, "When we're talking about a problem and you start screaming or threatening, you lose your chance to influence me. That could mean you'll have to stay home for the weekend."

Avert a Blowup

Certain teenagers feel compelled to test their parents when they don't know what to expect from them. If this is true of your child, give her a chance to ask questions and satisfy herself that your behavior will be predictable. She should know that you'll remove yourself from the situation or call for reinforcements. But let's not get ahead of ourselves.

When your teenager pushes you, first ask her if she has the self-control to sit down, take a break, and stop raising her voice.

If she doesn't respond, tell her what her options are and ask which one she prefers: "Either I can leave the room or you can. Which would help you more?" If she's unable or unwilling to choose, assume that she wants you to make the decision for her. Hopefully, things will settle down after that.

When They Lose Control

Unfortunately, teenagers sometimes lose control. They may scream irrationally, say hurtful things, or become physically aggressive. Needless to say, this is scary and upsetting for both you and your children. You're at a loss as to what to do, and they're unable to manage their rage. Although your instinct is to try to subdue your child during an outburst, the more you try to do so, the more he escalates the situation. So where does that leave you?

First, remember to challenge your teenager respectfully: don't put him down, and avoid backing him up against the wall. The trick is to offer face-saving alternatives such as taking a break or working out a compromise. The way you say things is equally important because the angry, irrational teenager is likely to misinterpret your words and respond accordingly. To see what I mean, let's look at a heated confrontation with a teenager who is about to explode.

Kevin and his father are in the middle of a huge argument about Kevin's new tattoo, with his mother and sister within earshot. As tempers flare, his father calls him a loser and says he's throwing away his life. He says this out of frustration and doesn't intend it as a rejection, but Kevin hears the statement otherwise. He feels his father disapproves of everything he does. In retaliation, he accuses his father of being rigid and judgmental.

As the altercation continues, his father approaches Kevin physically, determined not to back down. Although he's afraid, Kevin stands his ground. He picks up a poker from the fireplace and threatens to strike his father if he comes any closer. His father angrily tells him to put the poker down or else. Backed up against the wall with no way out, Kevin furiously throws the poker across the room, breaking a glass coffee table.

There's no need to give any more details of this unfortunate showdown. Both father and son let the situation get out of hand. Neither is able to back down, and the result hurts both of them. This outcome could have been prevented. They both should have tried to control their tempers better. If Kevin's father had stuck to the issue at hand, his son's tattoo, the argument might not have escalated so quickly. Further, he put his son down when he called him a loser. As he moved toward him menacingly in the midst of this challenge, Kevin's instinctive response was to look for a weapon, whether for protection or intimidation.

> The more you try to subdue your child during an outburst, the more he escalates the situation.

The father's next mistake was to threaten Kevin so he'd put the poker down. Unfortunately, this only made him furious. The crisis could have been avoided at this point if the father had said, "Wait a minute. Things are getting out of hand here. As soon as you put the poker down, we can figure out what to do next." This would have been less of a challenge and might have given Kevin time to think so he could do something to save face.

If that hadn't worked, the mother could have stepped in. Sometimes a new person on the scene can defuse a tense situation. She could have told her husband or her son to leave so she could speak to one of them alone. Or she could have asked one to accompany her to another room. This would have provided a cooling-off period to regain composure.

Once Kevin lost control, it was impossible to reason with him. His parents might have attempted to restrain him, but that could have been dangerous. Or they could have left the scene and hoped he would eventually settle down, but that could have meant further damage to their home. In that situation, the best they could have done would have been to wait it out and hold their son responsible for any destruction. As the old saying goes,

"You break it, you buy it." Maybe if Kevin had known that in advance, he would have thought before throwing the poker.

Kevin's story may sound a little extreme to readers who have never witnessed physical violence in their families. But things like this do happen with troubled teenagers, and parents should be prepared in advance. When push comes to shove, you need to keep your composure and refrain from any type of threat or insult that may cause the situation to escalate. If need be, back off, or offer your child options to do the same. You can't win with an irrational teenager. But you can make certain he knows that you won't play his game. And that will reduce the likelihood of a future recurrence.

DEALING WITH DEFIANCE

I've talked about extremes of antisocial behavior in general, but now I want to address the specifics of defiance. At this juncture, I'd like to discuss two of the most difficult types of teenagers and give you some guidance on how to deal with them. Forewarned, you'll be able to step in before things get too far.

The Volatile Teenager

This young person blows up without warning but doesn't do it intentionally. Her feelings bruise easily and she's difficult to reason with. Often her outlook is rigid and she sees the world in black-and-white. Sometimes she's spiteful and vindictive as well. She may seem to constantly have a chip on her shoulder. Her poor self-control and hot temper lead her into frequent conflicts. Not surprisingly, she's difficult to manage at home and at school.

If your child fits this description, learn to anticipate her outbursts. Carefully monitor her behavior for signs that she's losing control: a tense posture, a flushed face, pacing the floor. When she starts getting agitated, help her stop in her tracks and think for a moment. You should follow the suggestions in the box earlier in

How to Get Your Teen to Agree to an Evaluation

Some teenagers resist evaluations because they don't want to be blamed for the family's problems; others are fearful that an examiner will think they're crazy. And of course, many resist just because their parents want the evaluation. Here's how you can enlist their cooperation.

■ Tell them that you've met with a psychiatrist (or psychologist, social worker, or other mental health professional) to review the family situation. And now that they've heard the parents' side of the story, they'd like to hear your child's side. Many young people find this invitation enticing because they want the professional to know how difficult their parents are.

■ Acknowledge that you're unhappy with the family situation and tell them you assume that they feel the same way. Then ask if they're willing to do their part by helping themselves and their family. And make it clear that you're ready and willing to be a part of the process.

■ Express your concern about them, calling attention to their recent moods and behavior (for example,

being angry, sad, defiant). Then suggest that there are experts who can help them to feel better and thus make their life easier (not to mention your own).

■ Ask them to meet with a psychologist once. And leave it up to the therapist to enlist their cooperation. Most therapists are well prepared for the initial resistance that teenagers present.

■ If it becomes necessary, insist on an evaluation as a condition for driving the car, getting an allowance, or receiving other privileges.

■ Recruit support from sources outside the family. For example, the teen's school can require an evaluation as a condition for remaining enrolled.

this chapter on how to keep an angry teenager talking. It won't be easy because she can't put off gratification and always wants an immediate answer. But if you've told her in advance that you refuse to make spur-of-the-moment decisions, you can reduce the intensity of her demands.

You can also help this kind of teenager practice anger control during his calmer moments. Encourage him to count to ten, take deep breaths, or think about something pleasant to relax him. Tell him he can use these techniques whenever he feels himself getting angry. Finally, don't forget to compliment him whenever you see him showing self-control. You want him to know that his efforts are recognized.

You'll also have to help him learn how to let go of an argument. A volatile teenager always wants to have the last word. Even after a battle is over, he storms out and continues screaming when you're out of earshot. But don't let him suck you in. When he acts provocatively, point it out and remind him that there will be no discussion when he's in that state of mind. Then take a break from the argument and resume a civilized conversation when he's more composed.

If your teenager flies into rages with seemingly little provocation and you can't do anything to change this, have him evaluated by a mental health professional. A small but significant percentage of these youth have rage and mood disorders and their actions are outside their conscious control. The signs are striking: abrupt mood shifts, excitability, thoughts that are racing, irrational behavior, or withdrawal from the family and increasing isolation that leaves parents wondering who these children really are.

Teens like this may make light of their moodiness, but they feel bad about not being able to control it. If the pattern has persisted for some time, it can color all aspects of their lives, and you should be seriously concerned. No one wants to think their child has psychological problems, and sometimes parents write off this behavior as a stage of adolescence that will pass. But it won't. You should know that psychotherapy and medication can help regulate these emotional states, especially if they are chemically based.

The following suggestions will assist you as you try to help your teens learn to express anger directly:

1. Make sure that you express your own feelings directly. If you're angry with your child, don't tune her out; tell her why you're angry and be specific. For example, say, "I'm angry with you because you did not clean your room this weekend, and you promised me that you would."

2. Stress the importance of expressing feelings directly. Tell your kids that you're not a mind reader; the only way that you'll know what they're feeling is if they tell you.

3. Don't buy into their passive-aggressive actions. If your child does something annoying, don't just yell at him. Point out what he did, and discuss why he did it. For example, say: "You just came down to dinner ten minutes late, and that's inconsiderate. Were you angry that we wouldn't let your friend come over after dinner?"

4. Encourage your children to role-play the direct expression of angry feelings. Teach them to express their anger with words, not indirect actions. For example, if they're angry because you didn't let them go to a rock concert, rather than intentionally ignoring their chores, they can tell you why they're upset.

5. When their actions are indirect, speak for them. For example, if your teenager annoys his sister, you might speculate: "I guess you feel we're easier on your sister than we are on you." If he agrees (and they often do), you can discuss his feelings further.

The Rule Breaker

Defiant teenagers continually violate rules. They may not actually break the law, but their actions can lead to antisocial behavior. Eventually they convince themselves that they can get away with these things and begin to up the ante. Examples of their rule breaking are curfew violations and smoking in the house. They do these things intentionally and don't want to be told what to do.

The challenge with these teenagers is to set and enforce limits. The disobedient teenager will wear you down with excuses and resistance to authority. He believes the problem is with the rules, not with him. This puts you in a difficult position because he sees you as standing between him and his freedom.

To help your rule-breaking teen improve, you must establish

a connection between his behavior and its consequences. This means showing him you won't tolerate his infractions and are prepared to take whatever action is necessary. At the same time, you need to remind him that you care about him and want the best for him. This is no easy task when you're angry.

Several years ago I worked with a sixteen-year-old named Gloria and her family. Gloria refused to obey her parents' rules. She stayed out past her curfew and hung out with an unsavory group of older friends. Despite this, she got by in school and had no substance abuse problems. She was quick to point this out in her defense whenever her parents challenged her behavior. Gloria's excuse for any misbehavior was that her parents were too restrictive: if they would just leave her alone, she'd show them she could handle her life. The basic problem was that she wanted complete freedom but wasn't prepared to take responsibility for it, which was precisely what her parents asked of her. They expected her to be home by curfew and imposed stringent consequences for rule violations. In response, Gloria sneaked out of the house late at night, only to get caught and face further restrictions.

Steps for When Your Teen Refuses to Follow Your Rules

1. Try to understand the purpose of their protest (for example, a wish to be more independent, rebelling against authority, or following a negative peer group).

2. Establish the connection between freedom and responsibility: the message you want to convey is that the more responsibly they behave, the more freedom they earn.

3. Tell your child that you care about her—even when she's obnoxious, defiant, or on the run.

4. Focus on improving family communication and learning to negotiate fairly.

5. Seek activities that the whole family can enjoy.

6. Define the bottom line. Tell your child what you will do if the defiance continues, and make sure you follow through on your intentions. Examples include seeking professional counseling, notifying the appropriate authorities, or making a change in the environment.

This standoff continued for several months, until Gloria began staying out all night on weekends, coming home exhausted and disheveled in the morning. This caused quite a disturbance in the family, and no one found it easy to communicate with anyone else. After one major blowup, Gloria ran away for several days. Her parents finally tracked her down at an older boy's apartment, and Gloria informed them that she wasn't going to come home. That was the last straw for her parents, who decided to seek help and do anything necessary to ensure her safe return to the family.

When they consulted the local mental health clinic, they got a rude awakening. First of all, they were told they were responsible for Gloria's health and well-being because she was only sixteen. Second, they learned that the boy she was staying with was committing a criminal offense, contributing to the delinquency of a minor. Finally, they were advised to get her home first and ask questions later.

This last was easier said than done, but Gloria's parents were determined to see the situation through. They called their daughter and told her they expected her home the next evening. There would be no discussion until she was back in their house. If she disregarded their instructions, they would contact the police, report her as a runaway, and press charges against the boy. This put the ball squarely in her court.

Gloria hung up the phone angrily and didn't call her parents back until the next day. Then she simply asked them to pick her up and hung up. During the ride home, she was quiet and seemed exhausted. When they arrived at home, her parents told her to go take a nap and said they'd meet after dinner to discuss the situation.

When that time came, they told Gloria how intolerable the family situation had become. She sat crying quietly while she listened. They said they loved her and wanted her to stay at home but couldn't stand by and watch her life go downhill. They told her they'd arranged a meeting with a family counselor to set the conditions for her to stay at home; this meant that curfews and family rules would be clear and strictly enforced. "What's my choice?" Gloria asked. "You don't have one right now," her parents responded. "We'll have to wait and see how things work out."

Family counseling didn't go smoothly at first. Gloria was angry about how her parents treated her, complaining that they set rules arbitrarily and held her to an extremely high standard. Worse yet, she felt they had never been available when she needed them.

"So I found people who appreciated me more," she told me. "And I'm happier when I'm away from the house."

Her parents had a different perspective. They thought Gloria had always been difficult to manage, disrespectful, and headstrong. Despite their best efforts, her rebelliousness increased as she got older. Now they were at the end of their rope.

I emphasized that since the family could no longer talk to one another, they needed to work on communication before establishing new guidelines. They had to learn to solve their problems without fighting and to spend quality time together. So we searched for some things they could all enjoy. I told Gloria that if she went along with the program, she could gradually regain her freedom, but if she didn't, we would have to explore alternative placements for her. Living on her own was not an option at her age.

The counseling continued for about six months. There were arguments and tense moments, but the family stuck with it. They listened to one another's complaints and tried to address them. Eventually they negotiated a new set of rules for Gloria, agreeing to restore her privileges if she spent time with different friends.

Gloria's case illustrates what a family may have to go through to restore order. A teenager who leaves home risks substance abuse, sexual misadventure, and involvement in other illicit activities. The first order of business is to ensure her safety and open the channels of communication with her family.

If your teenager leaves home, you may have to settle for conversations on the telephone. If so, send the message that you want her back as soon as possible. If she ran away because the home situation was intolerable, your family must work on this right away. On the other hand, if she thrives on taking risks and left home in search of excitement, she probably won't return until she's apprehended.

When your teen finally comes home, I strongly urge you to seek family counseling. You'll need to work on your family's communication, her impulsive behavior, and her difficulty accepting limits. This type of teenager needs frequent supervision because she can't be trusted and her judgment is poor. Further, you'll have to address the negative peer pressure that fuels runaway situations. If all else fails, she'll need more restrictive alternatives—a detention center, group home, wilderness program, or residential treatment center—before she's sent home. I'll be talking more about these options in the next chapter.

DEALING WITH ANTISOCIAL BEHAVIOR

Nothing is more humiliating for a parent than seeing a child show flagrant disregard for social standards. Imagine how it feels to get a phone call saying your child has been picked up by the police and is being charged with a felony or misdemeanor. That's where the pattern of defiance, resistance to authority, and rule breaking can lead.

In this section, I'll explore several types of antisocial behavior. After explaining why teenagers fall into each category, I'll tell you how to deal with them. You are your children's most important lifeline, and there are preventive actions you can take.

Aggression

By aggressive behavior I don't mean minor temper tantrums but physical attacks on other people. Teenagers often blame their aggressiveness on someone else, saying, for example, "I hit him because he was going to hit me first." After instances of aggressive behavior, they show little remorse or motivation to change. These

Talking About Anger Rather Than Acting It Out

Here are some suggestions for how to convince your teenager that talking about anger is more effective than acting it out:

- Point out that people shy away from those who have hot tempers.

- Tell them that others take you more seriously when you state your concerns in a calm and assertive fashion.

- Compliment them whenever they express their anger appropriately.

- Ask them whether they prefer that you scream at them or talk to them rationally. They'll get the point.

- Tell them you won't deal with them when they're angry and irrational, but you'll always be willing to listen when they approach you in a reasonable fashion.

- Use examples of people who have expressed their anger appropriately and dealt effectively with others (someone, for instance, who protests unfair treatment or working conditions).

- When you get angry, model the behavior that you'd like your children to display. Remain composed, be direct, and stay focused on the topic at hand.

- Show your children the consequences people face as a result of poor anger management (for example, violence leads to incarceration, poor sportsmanship leads to ejections from games, and inappropriate behavior toward colleagues leads to job loss).

kids are difficult to manage because they express themselves in actions rather than words. Your goal is to reverse that pattern.

Aggressive behavior usually shows up when a child is young. In his childhood and preteen years, he typically relies on physical force to express his demands, lacking self-confidence and self-control. Combined with excessive sensitivity and accumulated feelings of rejection, it's a recipe for trouble. People who spend time around these teens say they carry around a lot of anger and can't express it appropriately. One antagonistic young man told me nonchalantly, "I'm just a fight looking for a place to happen."

Aggressive teenagers are deficient in the life skills of socializing with others, showing compassion, and using solid judgment. You'll recognize this personality from earlier parts of this book.

These kids need help in most of these areas, but I'll concentrate here on their aggressive behavior and suggestions for dealing with it.

Don't fight fire with fire. It should be obvious that when you try to strong-arm your kids, it usually backfires. Domination alone—that is, physical punishment or other forms of coercion—doesn't work very well. Over the years, I've seen a number of parents and their teenage children, especially fathers and sons, come to blows, and they always regret it afterward. For one thing, violence begets violence. For another, teenagers won't admit defeat—it means humiliation for them. Even if you force them into submission, they'll pay you back later by pushing around younger siblings or someone else weaker or by getting into trouble that may be worse than the initial conflict. Rather than responding to violence with violence, it's better to exercise restraint and try to settle them down.

Think about the reasons for their aggression. Ask yourself why your child acts the way she does. Perhaps she feels everyone is against her and she has to be on her guard. Or she may not know how to interact with other people (or keep them at a safe distance) except through bravado. Some young people behave aggressively because they feel that's the only way they can get what they want. And finally, there are those who never learned to manage their aggression and control their impulses.

Deal with the underlying anger. Most troubled teenagers are very angry. They don't always express it directly, but they will when provoked. To help them cope with their anger, encourage them to use words instead of actions. Tell them they may have a right to be angry, but they have no right to be aggressive. Convince them that telling people what's bothering them will be just as effective as showing them with an angry outburst. You'll have to spend some time working on this, but it can be done.

Sometimes teenagers have good reason to be angry over the way they've been treated or the raw deal they believe they've gotten in life. Many of them feel like failures. They need someone trustworthy to confide in, an adult who can help them see themselves more objectively. If you can fill this role, terrific. If not, you can enlist the help of counselors, Big Brothers and Big Sisters, peer helpers, and other positive role models and mentors.

Help them change their self-perception. Teenagers act according to how they see themselves. To change their antisocial behavior, you have to help them change their self-perception. This may take ingenuity and energy, but it's worth the effort. Many aggressive youth feel their behavior is part of their identity. They think people expect them to behave the way they do. To alter this self-defeating view, give them opportunities to channel their aggressive energy appropriately and take on a more positive role.

For example, ask a bully to protect a younger child who is teased by other children. This will gain him respect in a more appropriate way, casting him in the role of a helper instead of a troublemaker. As others begin to see him in a different light, they can let go of their old image of him. The goal is to help the aggressive youth feel that he belongs, thereby weakening his anger and helping him to let go of his tough guy image. This change in image sets the stage for a reduction in his antisocial behavior.

Another option is to get your aggressive teen into a sport or some other physical activity. This gives him an outlet for his aggressive energy and an opportunity to gain further acceptance. One potential problem is that some teens aren't well coordinated, so they may get frustrated easily and give up. In that case, you have to come up with a noncompetitive activity like weightlifting or running that doesn't require quick or coordinated moves.

Improve their relationship skills. Aggressive youth assume they can't get what they want without bravado, demands, and intimidation. They have to learn basic social skills like making requests, asserting themselves appropriately, and voicing complaints. They'll need to practice and practice these skills, and first they have to be motivated to do so. This means you'll have to convince them of their importance, a theme I've stressed throughout the book.

Take their actions seriously. Aggressive behavior is rarely justified except in self-defense. Therefore, you must hold your children accountable for it. Don't wait for something serious to happen; call them on even minor acts of aggression like kicking a wall, roughing up a pet, or saying something provocative. If they do something more serious, make them apologize and listen to their victim's feelings. Without question, they should know there are consequences for their actions. Ideally, these will be constructive rather than punitive. You want your teenagers to learn something useful from their misbehavior.

If you're the target of your teenager's aggression, you'll need to take immediate and powerful action. No parent should be the recipient of verbal or physical abuse from his child. But make sure also that you don't retaliate. Instead, make a clear statement that you won't tolerate that type of aggressive behavior and remind them of the consequences if it continues. These can include restriction of privileges, grounding, and loss of allowance. And if the aggressive behavior continues, you should seek professional assistance to determine the proper course of action.

Vandalism

Although many antisocial behaviors occur in clusters, you should know how to deal with each of them. Vandalism is a broad category that includes setting fires, destroying property, and writing graffiti on walls (kids call this "tagging"). Often it begins with minor offenses and progresses in time to more serious ones.

Teenagers have different reasons for doing these things. Some do it only once for fun, with no harm intended, and feel bad when it goes wrong or gets out of hand. These are often typical teenagers who've experienced a lapse of judgment and can learn from their experience. Others are malicious and vindictive, planning their actions in advance to get back at other people. The most worrying group thinks it's exciting to flirt with danger. These teens are often very troubled and need help.

Regardless of how serious the behavior, teenagers who get involved in vandalism must be dealt with swiftly and decisively.

Not too long ago a teenager I worked with was picked up for vandalism and disorderly conduct. He and his friends were driving around and knocking down mailboxes with a sledgehammer. They'd been drinking and thought it was great fun. Of course, the owners of the mailboxes didn't feel the same way, and the boys wound up in court. The judge put them on probation and made them go to alcohol awareness classes. Their day in court scared them into never having a brush with the law again.

If your child is involved with an incident of vandalism, take the following actions.

Find out what else is going on. Many teenagers commit acts of vandalism under the influence of alcohol or drugs. Some are sorry afterward, but many think it's amusing. It's important to find out if your child has a drinking or drug problem that predisposes him to reckless behavior. If so, be prepared to deal with these problems too.

Other kids simply go along with the crowd. Destruction of property goes against their better judgment, but they're unable to say no to their friends. These teenagers need to be challenged on their foolishness; they're paying the price for someone else's distorted view of fun. If they can't remove themselves from a compromising situation, they shouldn't be allowed to hang out with the negative influences. All the guidelines for dealing with peer pressure apply here; you'll find them in Chapter 7.

Finally, some teenagers have an ax to grind. They're convinced they've been wronged and feel justified in getting revenge. They take a rigid and inflexible view of events. And you'll have a hard time convincing them that their actions were unjustified. If their vandalism is specifically directed, you must make them deal directly with the injured party and realize there are better ways to express their anger. These teenagers are filled with hostility and lack compassion for others. Look back at Chapter 6 for ways to generate empathic feelings in this group.

Challenge their explanations. Don't let your teenager get away with the excuse that he was just having fun or didn't mean any harm by committing an act of vandalism. Vandalism is not cool and is not harmless mischief. It often has serious repercussions. Perpetrators can be picked up by the police and required to face charges for their wrongdoing. And their fate will be determined in a hearing by a judge. So if your child isn't taking responsibility for his behavior, make sure he does. Ask him how he'd feel if it was his window that was broken or his car that was damaged or defaced. Never give the message that you condone this type of behavior.

Arrange for constructive consequences. If by some chance your teenager has gotten away with destructive behavior, you must arrange for a consequence that can serve as a learning experience. For example, if he's defaced school property, make him repay the damage with some type of service—cleaning the cafeteria, whitewashing dirty walls, or acting as a janitorial assistant for a few weeks. The school will be happy to accommodate this. Even if he has already been suspended from school, you can make him do constructive things around the house, like raking the leaves or cleaning out the garage. Under no circumstances should his suspension be construed as a vacation from school.

Lying

Lying often accompanies other illicit actions like theft, substance abuse, and rule violation. Most people tell a little white lie now and then, but some teenagers make an occupation of it. These are the ones we should be really concerned about. Some people play down the significance of dishonesty, but it's your job to insist that your teens acknowledge and understand the value of truth telling.

Some youth can't bear to take responsibility for their behavior. They want to look good at all costs, so rather than face up to what they've done, they make up stories to cover their tracks. Even if these stories are preposterous, they stick to their guns. A problem with lying is that one lie leads to another. If a teenager lies about his grades once, he'll have to keep covering his tracks as the term winds down, and this will eventually catch up with him. To break this cycle, he needs alternatives to lying about his wrongdoing.

If your child has a problem with honesty, here are some suggestions to help you deal with the problem.

Talk to your teenager about lying. Yelling and screaming won't help. You must be genuinely curious about why your child lies to you and try to put that knowledge to use. For example, if she's desperate for your approval and fears your rejection, you might want to reconsider your standards. You'll recognize this pattern when your teenager overreacts to criticism and says you're impossible to please. But don't expect her to express her needs directly. Most teenagers hate to beg for their parents' approval and would rather go without it than acknowledge their desire. No child should be saddled with the burden that she can never please her parents. It's far better to ask less of her and get something in return than to ask for too much and get nothing.

On the other hand, if she lies to protest against your values, you should discuss her thoughts and try to reconcile your differences. If you can't, you'll need to decide if it's a battle worth fighting. A young person shouldn't have to hide what she believes in, but if she's contemptuous of society's rules, you'll need to challenge her. Ask your teenager why she feels she's above the law.

Talk to your child about the importance of honesty. Tell her that people trust you more when you're honest; that honesty is a highly respected trait that requires courage and independence of thought; that when people lie, they're often sorry afterward because lying erodes goodwill and interferes with important relationships. Also point out that most liars usually get caught in their lies, with some very embarrassing and possibly destructive results. Rather than simply punishing her dishonesty, encourage her to think before she makes up a story. She should ask herself, What will probably happen if I lie about this?

Consider granting immunity. Some young people get caught in a web of lies and can't get out. You can sometimes help them out by offering them a chance to clear the record. Tell them that if they tell the truth, there will be no immediate consequences. This way you can have a productive conversation about why they lied and they can get a fresh start. Your children should know that you can forgive and forget, but they should also know that they'll have to conduct themselves differently in the future and that if they don't, they'll be held accountable.

Create opportunities for honesty and reward it. Let your teenagers know that you're keeping an eye on them and intend to put them to the test. But first, tell them why their past performance has made you suspicious of them. Remind them that you want to trust them, but before you can, you'll be watching them more closely. And this means sometimes you'll be testing them to gauge their honesty. They may complain about your actions, but remind them that trust evolves from consistent performance, not a series of demands. For example, leave money lying on the kitchen table, and watch what they do. Or stay up late to see what time they get home, and ask them the next morning when they came in. If they're honest with you, tell them you're proud of them and appreciate their efforts. If they lie, challenge them with the facts.

Practice what you preach. Don't underestimate the impact of your own behavior. If you insist on honesty, avoid doing little things that imply it's okay to be dishonest, like asking your child to tell someone calling that you're not home or fudging your child's age to get a lower ticket price. If you're determined to stop your child's lying, don't give him any ammunition to justify it. He'll be sure to remind you of your hypocrisy.

Stealing

Theft is another antisocial act that makes parents shudder. They can't understand how their children could steal after having been raised with such different values.

The reasons teenagers steal are complex. Some take things because they think it's the only way they can get them, while others simply find excitement in getting away with something that's forbidden.

How to Know When Your Child Is Stealing

■ He shows up with a new possession and insists that his friend gave it to him. Sometimes he'll tell you that he found it. (Kids do lend one another things, but if it happens a lot, question it.)

■ She grows defensive anytime you inquire about her personal belongings.

■ You notice that things around the house (like money, clothing, or other items of value) disappear with no apparent explanation.

■ You overhear him talking with a friend on the phone, and he's bragging about his stealing exploits.

■ She seems very secretive and sneaky at times.

■ He admires his friends who "get away with stuff."

■ When you tell her you're suspicious that she's taken something, she turns it around and accuses you of blaming her for everything.

■ Other people report that items have disappeared from their house when your child was there. Of course, he denies it vehemently, but the situation has occurred before.

The more consistently these signs occur, the greater the likelihood that your child is stealing. If the evidence is strong, challenge them on their actions.

One young woman described to me the thrill she got from shoplifting. "I love that feeling of tension I get just before I steal something," she said. "I know I could get caught and that makes it like an adventure. And then, I pull it off. Afterward, there's this enormous sense of relief. It's almost like getting high." A surprising number of young people report a similar feeling.

Stealing can also be addictive: every time the teenager gets away with it, he's more likely to do it again. If his peers are involved, they may encourage him in his antisocial activity. So, parents, be on the alert. You'll have to take a firm stand when you first find out this is happening.

One teenager I knew learned a powerful lesson when he was caught stealing from his parents. Don thought he was pretty slick, for he'd taken his mother's credit card several times to charge clothing and CDs. Somehow he managed to get away with it, but as is often the case, his luck eventually ran out. One month his mother received a credit card bill for over $1,000 in charges. Confused, she reviewed that bill and several previous ones and soon realized what Don was up to. She and her husband had gone through a number of troubling incidents with him before and decided it was high time to get help.

After they'd been referred to me, Mr. and Mrs. Allen sat in my office, discouraged and uncertain about what to do next. They were loving parents, but they'd tried everything and lost hope. Don seemed to do as he pleased without caring about anyone else.

I cut right to the chase. "Are you both prepared to do anything you can to break this pattern?" They answered in unison that they were. "These problems have been going on for almost a year now. You'll need to challenge him on what he's done. You must tell him that you won't tolerate stealing and impose stringent consequences. I suggest you restrict his free time, dock his allowance, and require him to do chores around the house to fulfill his debt. Then tell him that if he takes your credit card again, you'll notify the police and press charges. And this will probably mean a court appearance."

Both parents were silent for a couple of minutes, and then Mrs. Allen spoke. "I don't know if we could do that, Dr. Bernstein. After all, we love our son and wouldn't want to put him through that ordeal. I don't know what he would think."

"Well, hopefully it won't be necessary," I responded, "but I want you to be prepared, just in case. Don really needs to take this matter seriously. And you've tried lectures, restrictions, and pleas in the past. So how about giving Don a chance to cease his illicit behavior, and if he doesn't, proceed with the plan? I understand that it's difficult for you, but this really is the right way to handle the situation," I continued. "Otherwise, Don will continue with this sort of behavior."

Mr. and Mrs. Allen finally agreed to my suggestion.

After a month had elapsed, they sadly told me that Don took their credit card again and ran up another large tab. "Well, he's had his chance," I said. "Now I think it's time to proceed with the contingency measure. I don't believe that waiting any longer will serve your son well. He has broken the agreement, and you need to send him a powerful message to interrupt this cycle of stealing. Believe me, I wouldn't recommend this drastic action unless I thought it was necessary."

Again, they were at a loss for words. Mr. Allen broke the silence. "If you really think it'll work, we'll try it," he said quietly. I asked them to give me a call later in the week and let me know what happened.

I heard from Mrs. Allen a few days later. She calmly related that they had told Don that they were pressing charges. Don had called his mother a bitch, said he never wanted to see her again, and stormed out of the house. She was terrified, but half an hour later he was back home, begging her not to go through with it. He told her how much he loved her and swore he would never do it again. She almost caved in, but her husband convinced her to follow my advice. Mrs. Allen told me that the last couple of days had actually been pleasant, despite the fact that they were going through with pressing charges.

Perhaps this story sounds harsh to you, but these parents really had no choice. Their son was involved in a cycle of antisocial behavior that they couldn't break. When they informed the authorities, they were saying to their son, in effect, "This is the bottom line. We will no longer tolerate this type of behavior and you will have to face the consequences."

In this case, the young man went on to do much better afterward. He was anxious about his court appearance and watched his behavior until that time. The judge placed him on probation for one year, on condition that he attend school regularly and participate in therapy. Because Don was accountable to a higher authority, he had an additional incentive to not fall back into antisocial behavior.

Fortunately, it's not always necessary to go to this extreme. To prevent such a crisis, I recommend some basic guidelines to parents dealing with their teenager stealing.

Presume she's guilty. When your child does something wrong once, it's natural to let her off with a stern warning. But if she does it again and again, you have to buckle down. Let her know that if anything suspicious happens, she'll be presumed guilty. This means that if something disappears in the house or the school calls about a problem, she'll be held accountable. You'll certainly listen to her side of the story, but she must understand that her track record is working against her. As she realizes that you're not going to debate her innocence every time a crisis arises, she'll start thinking twice about her actions.

Impose meaningful consequences. Stealing has natural consequences for teens—such as causing them to be suspended from school, banned from a store, or face court charges—that should discourage them from doing it more than once. However, you may need to add consequences of your own. If you come across stolen property or get wind of a theft through another source, insist that your child return what he's taken. He'll find this humiliating, but he will have learned a valuable lesson. Have him take the stolen item back personally and apologize to the person he took it from. If for some reason this is impossible (say the store has closed, or is in a town where you were on vacation), you can still have him write a letter of apology.

At the very least, you should confiscate any merchandise that was illegally obtained. Your teenager may tell you that a friend gave it to him as a gift or lent it to him, but don't believe that for a minute. Call the friend's parents and ask if their child ever owned the item. If the answer is no, you'll have to deal with both lying and stealing.

Enforce the law. You have every right to object to your home being used as a clearinghouse for stolen merchandise or illicit drugs. Make this very clear to your teenager, because you are legally responsible for her actions. Let her know that you are deeply concerned about her and fear for her safety and well-being. Then impose consequences for her actions and put her on notice that you expect her to discontinue the illicit behavior immediately. Further, you have no intention of violating the law or harboring her as a fugitive. She may try to tell you that what she's doing won't affect you, but that's ridiculous. Emphasize the seriousness of her actions and reiterate that you will do whatever is necessary to prevent her from breaking the law again. If the problem continues, seek professional assistance, and take the necessary action to rectify the situation. As I discussed in Don's case, that means notifying the authorities when all else fails.

Tell him how stealing makes you feel. The natural response to the news that your child is a thief is anger and disappointment. He'll be able to see that easily, but you need to go further. Tell him that you're hurt and feel he's violated your trust; that his actions will influence his privileges and make you watch him more closely in the future; and that you'll do this because you care about him, not because you want to pay him back for the pain he's caused you. Let him know he'll have many fences to mend when he engages in antisocial behavior.

Gang-Related Activities

Gang members are a growing problem in our nation. They have proliferated everywhere—small cities and towns as well as big cities like New York and L.A., whose gang problems have been well documented, have been affected. All parents want to think that their children would never associate with such a group, but it can happen. Some gangs are tightly organized, nationally syndicated, and involved in criminal activity, but many of them are confined to a single neighborhood and content with mischief and aggressive behavior.

You should become familiar with signs that suggest your child is involved with a gang. If he usually wears a certain "uniform" (a particular bandanna, a specific color, a distinctive hairstyle), or has tattoos or jewelry of a gang-related nature, he may be conforming to a group norm that comes from a gang. Maybe he hangs out in a pool hall or a neighborhood that a particular gang considers its turf. Teens who associate with gangs are very susceptible to peer influence. Many of them are lonely, angry, and bitter, having felt isolated from their families and rejected by their peers. Gang members frequently tell me they feel a sense of power and security for the first time when they're with their companions. Finally, they feel like they belong to something important.

The gang offers teenagers like this a place to feel they belong, but at a price: they're expected to conform to the group's norms and sacrifice their individuality. Unfortunately, it's difficult, even dangerous, for kids to get out of a gang once they've joined, and because members have few meaningful connections outside the group, they're very difficult for parents to reach.

If you suspect your child is involved in gang-related activity, I suggest you contact your local police precinct and ask for their gang officer or gang unit. These experts have considerable information on what's going on in your area and can give you advice about where to turn. They can also tell you the specifics of gangs in your area, like clothing, speech, and behavior. In some areas of the country there are also parent support groups that work toward weakening gang involvement. Your local police precinct or school resource officer can direct you to them. Further, in the Appendix, you'll find specific resources that provide further information to help you to deal with your child's gang involvement.

Generally, the first thing to do is to get your child away from the gang. Some families have actually relocated to accomplish this, but at the very least you'll have to exert considerable pressure to get

Signs of Possible Gang Involvement

■ Wearing clothes or hairstyles that conform to a group norm

■ Spending a lot of time in a location with a gang presence

■ Admitting having friends who are gang members

■ Wearing ornamental jewelry or sporting new tattoos with cryptic designs

■ Exhibiting a desperate need for companionship

■ Being unwilling to invite peers home

■ Possessing cash or jewelry that you don't know the source of, and they won't explain your child to associate with more desirable peers. You'll need all the support you can get. In the next chapter you'll find more extreme measures you can take when your child has gone too far.

PUTTING IT ALL TOGETHER

It's important to remember that a child who has gotten into trouble doesn't have to stay in trouble. Each chapter in this book tries to help you understand the roots of deviant behaviors and to begin chipping away at them. You will also have to confront your teenagers' specific offenses. This will require monitoring their behavior, setting limits, ensuring their infractions have meaningful consequences, and showing that you care about them. Perhaps most important, you'll need to give them alternatives to their misbehavior.

To capture this process at work, I'd like to tell you about the ordeal of one family that managed, by following some sensible advice, to weather the storm of a defiant, antisocial teenager and ultimately turn things around.

Alvin was a sixteen-year-old in a great deal of trouble. He was truant from school, had failing grades, and spent most of his time with peers of whom his parents did not approve. This had been going on for almost two years. Alvin also drank every weekend and got into fights because of his combative attitude. Twice he'd been picked up by the police for disorderly conduct. After a court appearance, he was placed on probation for six months. That's when he was referred to me.

As I sat in my office with Alvin's family, I wondered how I could help them. His parents were angry and dejected, while he was blasé about his predicament. Since he was there against his wishes, he indicated that he felt no need to cooperate. The court had ordered him to get treatment, and he was just going along for the ride.

Alvin's mother lamented that she and her husband didn't know what to do with their son. His father nodded in affirmation, while Alvin sat there grinning. I immediately asked the parents why they thought their son was smiling.

"Because he gets away with everything, that's why," his mother replied.

"Would you agree with that?" I asked Alvin.

"Well, sort of, but they're always trying to punish me."

"What else would you expect?" I asked him.

Alvin launched into the usual teen monologue about wanting to be left alone. When he'd finished, I reminded his parents that they had to take charge of the situation. "He's basically doing as he pleases," I said. "He's drinking, getting into fights, and using your home as a crash pad. You just can't continue like this."

Alvin shot me a dirty look. His mother jumped in, assuring me that things hadn't always been this way. I asked Alvin if he agreed with that. Sure enough, he also felt that things had once been much better at home.

"Why?" I asked.

"Well, me and Dad did fun stuff, and we all got along better," he answered.

"It sounds like all of you miss the good old days," I responded, and they agreed. At that point, we resolved to try to improve the situation.

First was Alvin's defiance and antisocial behavior. Initially his parents were skeptical about the expediency of setting limits because such attempts had failed in the past. Alvin had told them, after all, that they couldn't tell him what to do. With my support, however, they established a curfew and resolved to hold the line if Alvin violated it. Their position was that if he didn't comply with their rules, he'd lose his driving privileges. Further, if he continued his old behavior, they would send him away to a special school.

The next problem was Alvin's fighting and infringing on the rights of others. On this issue his parents told their son they didn't understand why he had to be so aggressive if he was so tough. After all, if people respected him, they wouldn't bug him all the time as he said they did. His parents said they expected him to stay out of fights and protect himself only in self-defense.

If he initiated any fights, he'd be violating their agreement and would jeopardize his chances of staying in the same school and remaining at home. Also, since his misbehavior seemed to be related to his drinking, he would have to attend alcohol education classes. This was one of the terms of his probation and could be enforced.

Third came the issue of Alvin's choice of friends. His parents realized this was the hardest aspect of his life for them to control, so they invited his two closest friends to the house for a talk. They told the friends that Alvin was in serious trouble, on the verge of being sent away from home, and he needed all the help he could get. If they were really concerned about him, as they insisted they were, they'd need to help him stay away from alcohol and fighting. Alvin sat quietly through this discussion, smiling when his friends said they'd do anything to help their man. Believe it or not, that was exactly what they did.

Fourth came Alvin's academic problems. His parents knew they couldn't force him to do well in school or enlist his friends' help to improve his grades. Instead, they asked him what he wanted to do with his life. After all, he was old enough to have some say in his future. They told him they'd be willing to listen to any ideas he had. Alvin gave this some thought and decided he wanted to try a vocational curriculum. He felt he couldn't handle his academic subjects and would have a better shot at graduating if he did something he enjoyed. This was hard for his parents to accept, since they had college degrees and wanted the same for him. But they agreed to let him follow his own interests and allowed him to make the change.

Last but not least came the issue of family relationships, which had soured over the past few years. Alvin was convinced that his parents preferred his sister to him, and this feeling made him reject their overtures and avoid his family altogether. Fortunately, his parents learned to choose their battles, relieving some of the pressure on Alvin. His father began reaching out to him. He got two tickets to a football game and invited his son. The two stuck mostly to sports talk and eating the stadium food,

How to Know When Your Efforts Are Paying Off

Your rate of progress often depends on the severity of the problems. If your teenager is minimally defiant or antisocial and your family functions reasonably well, you may observe marked change in a month or two. Conversely, if the pattern of misbehavior is well established and has eroded the fabric of your family, you'll need to be more patient. Expect anywhere from six months to a year before order is restored in your family and your child begins to redefine his life. Following are ten signs that suggest your teenager is coming around:

1. Her judgment has improved considerably. She knows right from wrong and her actions reflect this.

2. He displays some empathy for the feelings of others and thinks twice before hurting another person. If he does something wrong, he expresses remorse afterward.

3. She attends school regularly and shows some effort.

4. His choice of friends is better. He no longer seeks out troublemaking peers and can steer away from trouble.

5. Family relationships are improved. You can talk to one another without arguing and spend some quality family time together.

6. She doesn't seem angry all the time. She's more responsive to your feedback and seems to be on a more even keel.

7. He accepts the rules you set and talks to you when he feels they are unfair.

8. She believes that she is a decent, lovable person and expresses positive feelings toward significant others.

9. He acknowledges his past problems and has some understanding of what he did wrong and why he did it.

10. She appears to have goals and is beginning to give some thought to the future.

Don't expect all these signs to be readily apparent in your children. They'll emerge gradually, and in random order. You'll have some gratifying moments, but more often it will be business as usual for your teenagers and they'll be too absorbed in their own lives to notice that things have changed. But that doesn't mean you can't point it out. And be prepared: you may have a setback every now and then (they'll break a rule or lose their temper), but your teenager will quickly rebound. Finally, most important are your feelings about the family situation, so trust them. If you feel satisfied with your child's progress and there's no evidence to the contrary, your situation is probably well in hand.

so the excursion went well. Several weeks later, the father proposed a camping trip. They had gone camping when Alvin was younger, and both had fond memories of those outings. Alvin asked to take a friend along so he wouldn't be bored, but his father was afraid that would defeat the purpose of spending time together as a family. After some discussion, they agreed that Alvin could invite a friend and his father. That way the boys would have each other's companionship and also be with their parents. This, too, came off well, and tension began to ease up at home. Alvin began talking more, and his parents listened. They didn't always like what they heard, but they understood it was important to reconnect with their son.

Life gradually returned to normal. The family had dinner together several times a week, sharing the events of their lives and trying not to judge one another. Alvin was comfortable in his vocational program and attended school regularly. He remained headstrong, but no longer broke rules or hurt people. Although he still needed to sustain his effort, his self-esteem had improved. Perhaps most important, the scene of battle had shifted: he was grappling not with his parents but with what he wanted to do with his life.

A year after they'd started counseling, this family was a little wiser and a great deal happier. They still had some work to do, of course, but they were equipped to finish the journey on their own.

Stories like Alvin's are not unusual. With the proper guidance and determination, you too can write a happy ending to your ordeal with a defiant or antisocial teenager. If things have unfortunately gone too far for these strategies to work, you'll find relief in the next chapter.

DESPERATE TIMES, DRASTIC MEASURES

There may come a time when you need to recognize that your teenager's self-destructive behavior is beyond your control. If she's trapped in a downward spiral of defiance, school failure, substance abuse, or antisocial behavior, you're going to have to take drastic measures.

Let's say you've followed all the suggestions in this book so far to no avail. You've challenged your teenager's behavior, set limits, tried to repair your family relationships, perhaps considered or tried a change of schools. If none of these strategies has worked, you'll have to resign yourself to a series of increasingly stringent measures. These will require some familiarity with community resources and a willingness to follow the advice of experts. No one expects you to do this alone. Your challenge is to find enough leverage to exert on your unmanageable teenager to bring her around.

In this chapter I'll help you determine how serious your situation really is and, if it is really serious, to present some last-ditch efforts worth considering to get your child back on track. If you're among the unfortunate few parents who've been driven to this extreme, I'll guide you through the maze of treatment alternatives, and at the end of the book I'll give you a list of contacts to help you get your child into the program you've chosen.

IS YOUR SITUATION OUT OF CONTROL?

Have you reached the point at which your teenager does whatever she pleases? Does she ignore your rules, abuse illegal drugs, and hang out with undesirable peers? Perhaps no punishment seems to have an effect on her. She seems unfazed by her legal or school difficulties and shows no desire to change. Even her school has told you that they can't manage her anymore. Since nothing you've tried seems to work, you've reached the point at which you're ready to give up. You make rules; she breaks them. You punish her; she ignores it. Everyone tells you she's out of control, and you don't know where to turn. You're backed up against the wall and feel your situation has become impossible. Is any relief in sight?

Fortunately, many out-of-control teenagers can be saved. But first they have to understand that their parents mean business. Convincing them of that may be difficult if they've been getting away with their offenses for a long time.

Consider each of these factors to determine if your situation has reached the point at which drastic measures are necessary:

- Your child does what he pleases, when he pleases, without regard to the limits you have set for him.
- Your child repeatedly gets into serious trouble (like stealing, vandalism, fighting, substance abuse) and refuses to take it seriously.
- You believe—and competent professionals confirm your concerns—that your child is in serious danger because of her actions.
- His continued pattern of defiance and antisocial behavior is destroying your family life.
- The school has told you that they can no longer keep her there, and you can't find an appropriate educational setting for her.
- You've followed the suggestions in this book, but his behavior continues to deteriorate.
- She no longer complies with any type of authority (like a teacher, boss, coach, or family members) and has been in repeated conflicts with others.
- His behavior has become violent, self-destructive, or dangerously impulsive (including such actions as experimenting with dangerous drugs and violating the rights of others), and you fear for his safety or the safety of others.
- She regularly associates with a gang, cult, or other destructive group and has lost all contact with her family.
- The established behavior patterns have continued for at least several months.

OPTIONS FOR HELP BEFORE CONSIDERING REMOVAL FROM THE HOME

Somehow, you have to show your child that you're prepared to do whatever's necessary to get him back on track. The most extreme measure available to you is to remove your child to a place outside the home. However, you have a number of options before you consider this. As you might imagine, there is no magic approach that will work for everyone. You may need to try several things in the hope that one will have an impact. Remember that the problems you're facing took a long time to develop and won't go away overnight.

I suggest you begin by sitting down for a heartfelt discussion with your teenager and telling him that you can't allow his behavior to control your life anymore. Be explicit about the stress he's causing the family, reiterate the risks he's taking, and express your serious concern for him. Then let him know what options you're considering. There's no need for secrecy at this point. He'll probably get angry, show little interest in your suggestions, or refuse to go anywhere. But just because he responds negatively doesn't mean you have to follow suit.

You cannot waver at this point, so think through decisions carefully before you make them, and then follow through. None of the following suggestions is easy but I have seen them work. At the same time as you try one or more of these ideas, you must make every effort to send your teen the powerful message that you're not giving up on him.

Professional Help

If the situation with your child has gotten out of hand, you should arrange to see a mental health professional. Many psychologists, social workers, and psychiatrists are equipped to deal with troubled teenagers. Those experts will assess your situation and recommend a course of action that will probably include therapy for both child and family. There are a couple of ways for your child to get help. Some teenagers fare better in the safety of a one-on-one therapy relationship, while others need the feedback and positive peer pressure they get in group therapy. In conjunction with either of these modes of therapy for your child, it is nearly always also advisable for you, and in some cases the troubled teen's siblings as well, to participate actively in some family therapy.

Convincing Your Teen to Attend the First Meeting with a Therapist

1. Ask his school counselor, coach, employer, or favorite teacher or relative to encourage him to try at least one session.

2. Tell her that a therapist may be sympathetic to her point of view and could help to improve her family situation.

3. Explain that his meeting with a therapist will be treated as confidential and nothing he says in that setting will be held against him in any way. Further, the meeting is an opportunity to freely express what's on his mind.

4. Tell her that if the therapist feels she has no problems or that you're the one who needs help, you'll promise to leave her alone.

5. Schedule the meeting at a desirable time to him. For instance, if your child dislikes math class, tell him you'll get him excused from that class to attend the therapy appointment.

6. Offer her a temporary reprieve from restriction if she attends the appointment. If she's not restricted, offer her an additional privilege for the weekend, like attending a concert or extending her curfew for one night.

A seasoned professional will work with all aspects of your teenager's life, including his family, school, and community. Make sure the person you choose has specific experience with teenage behavior problems and, at the very least, can help you set limits and help your child with self-control, deficiencies in empathy and morals, and poor self-esteem. You can learn more about qualified professionals in your area by consulting your child's school, your family physician, or a mental health referral service. You'll find additional resources in the Appendix of this book.

When you contact a psychologist, ask whether they have a flexible treatment approach and connections with community resources. This is especially important because most teens in trouble have great difficulty with an authoritarian approach to counseling. You'll also want to make certain they can advise you about other resources if your situation calls for such additional support as special programs, court-related resources, or community service opportunities. Don't expect them to know everything, but they should be able to point you in the right direction.

How to Know When You've Run Out of Alternatives

Before taking drastic action, ask yourself if any of these situations applies to you:

1. Your family is in immediate danger because of your child's behavior. For example, he has a history of violence and has hurt family members, or his reckless, careless behavior has put himself and other family members in danger.

2. You've reached a point at which you feel your teenager's problems are destroying the fabric of your family (her actions are affecting your other children, your marriage).

3. Your teenager has grown so depressed that she can no longer function in school or at home. She's abandoned all efforts and you're gravely concerned about the possibility of suicide.

4. Your child is out of control. He refuses to abide by any of your rules, regularly engages in dangerous behavior, doesn't attend school, and cannot be physically restrained.

5. You've tried counseling and special programs, and they've been unsuccessful.

6. Competent professionals (school, mental health, and medical) assure you that your child needs a more restrictive and therapeutic living environment to alter his self-destructive behavior patterns (like substance abuse, truancy, and violating the law).

If these situations apply to you, you'll have to consider more stringent measures to get your teenager back on track. In Chapter 11 you'll learn more about each of the possible alternative placements.

At the very least, the person you contact should be willing to give you a few minutes on the telephone to determine if your child is an appropriate client for her. You shouldn't plan on telling her your life story and don't expect her to be able to give you advice on the spot. But it's perfectly legitimate to ask if she's licensed or board-certified in her discipline and if she's had experience working with behavior-disordered teenagers. If she refuses to answer you on the phone, move on to someone else.

Many parents wonder how they're going to get their teenagers to agree to visit a therapist once they've made an appointment. Most young people will insist they don't have problems and refuse to attend the session. In that case, make the appointment and inform your child that you're going with or without him. If he's not there for the first meeting, the therapist will give you some ideas about how to get him there later.

In fact, I usually meet with parents alone first. At that meeting I ask them to go home and tell their child that I've heard the parents' side of the story and now want to hear hers. After all, I suggest to the teen, I also need to find out what her parents are doing wrong. Most teenagers will come in at least once to tell me their gripes and I can take things from there. If this doesn't work, I'll recommend that their parents encourage her with privileges or special activities, or set consequences for noncompliance. Together, the parents and I can usually make the teenager an offer she can't refuse.

Withdrawal of Domestic Supports

Think about how much your teenagers take for granted. They expect you to prepare their meals, do their laundry, give them money, and drive them around. One first step to try if your child has been totally uncooperative is to inform her that from now on she'll have to do some or all of these things for herself. Present this shift in responsibility not as a punishment, but as an exercise of your own rights. If she won't comply with any of your requests, I see no reason that you have to with hers.

The next time your son asks for a ride to the mall, for example, tell him you're too busy. If he balks at your reluctance, remind him that you've grown tired of catering to his whims when you get nothing in return. Or if she isn't home by dinner, don't hold up your meal; in fact, make sure that the family eats without her and don't save her any leftovers. Let her know that she's on her own for making up the meal when she gets home. I'm not suggesting that these actions will single-handedly turn things around, but they will send a powerful message to your recalcitrant child: "We're not treating you like an equal family member because you don't act like one." Of course, you'll want to accompany this with continual reminders to your child that you do want him back in the family.

A much more extreme measure to take if your teenager

chronically violates her curfew is to forewarn her that you'll be locking the door from the inside. This prevents her late-night access to your home and forces her to stay elsewhere. At first she may think it's cool, but she'll soon grow weary of spending time on the street, sleeping in the backseat of a car, or floating from house to house. And if she runs out of money, she'll soon start thinking about where her next meal is going to come from. Some kids may consider this an adventure, but many more will miss the creature comforts of home. This approach won't work for everyone, but it does establish a bottom line. Some parents have actually installed alarm systems to prevent their children from sneaking in or out at night. Although these measures seem extreme, you should keep them in mind after you've exhausted less dramatic alternatives.

School Authorities and Employers

The more pressure you can exert on your teenager from various sources, the better. If he's involved in a school activity or has a job, tap authority figures there for leverage. For example, if he's drinking a lot and behaving dangerously, it makes sense to inform his place of work of his problem. Tell him of your intention in advance, and be prepared for him to get angry and object that it's none of his employer's business. If you say you'll leave it up to the employer to decide how to handle the matter, he'll start to take you more seriously and may even use the occasion as a motivation to change his behavior.

The same principle can work if your teenager plays on a sports team. Contact the coach and ask for help in holding your child accountable for her actions. If the coach suspends her from the team, she'll have to meet certain conditions to be reinstated. You'll have to weigh decisions such as these against the risks of taking away what little your child has that's meaningful. But often, if you don't strike first, your teenager will eventually self-destruct—getting herself fired or thrown off her team. I think it's a gamble worth taking, especially if the authority figure reinforces your message that your child must address her problems.

Special Programs

An hour or two a week of therapy is not always enough. Fortunately, most school systems offer a range of options for troubled teenagers who have problems at school as well as at home. These vary from special classes to day programs that deal with emotional and behavioral problems. Your child will have to be assessed for his eligibility for such services and it may take several months to work your way through the system, but getting into such programs will be worth the effort.

The community mental health system and the private sector also have day treatment centers. Costs vary greatly, so make careful inquiries before committing yourself. If your child is placed in such a program, you can expect a comprehensive approach to treatment that includes groups, special classes, drug prevention sessions, and various activity therapies, all under close supervision. Such programs, needless to say, are only for teenagers who can still be managed at home.

The Courts

I once counseled parents who decided to press charges against their son for repeatedly destroying property in their home. He was placed on court probation and was forced to take his actions seriously and learn better self-control. The thought of turning a child in is difficult for many parents to accept. But if your teenager is violating the law and can't be stopped, you may not have a choice. You can give him notice that you're considering this and then back up your words. When the time comes, remind him that he's had his chance to improve his behavior before but nothing has worked.

The courts do not normally like to get involved in family issues except in serious cases, but they may be able to help you. If your teenager is summoned to juvenile court, the judge may place him on probation, send him to a detention center, or even order him into treatment, during which time his case will be monitored. Having to sweat out the uncertainty, not knowing what the consequences of his actions will be, can serve as a deterrent to your teenager to future wrongdoing.

If you can't bring yourself to do this, take your child to visit a courtroom or detention center. There he'll at least get an idea of what can happen to teenagers in his situation. As you might imagine, many judges have little compassion for chronic offenders and dole out harsh sentences. More than likely, your teenager will see frightened and remorseful kids who've crossed the line. Interestingly, many teenagers agree to make this kind of a visit out of curiosity or to avoid having further consequences imposed. They rarely like what they see.

One more option is a crime prevention program offered through some law enforcement agencies. Some of these programs introduce young people to reformed adult criminals who have served time and learned a hard lesson in the process. They'll talk to them about their time in prison, explain how and why they eventually came to regret their crimes, and talk about how they gradually transformed their lives. This can be a powerful experience, and in some cases will discourage teenagers from following in the adult criminals' footsteps. You can get further information about these programs by contacting your local juvenile court, police, or the National Criminal Justice Referral Service (see Appendix for details). The video *Scared Straight* demonstrates this method of crime deterrence in action and is worth watching.

Distant Relatives

A final option is sending your teenager to live with a relative in a distant city. The catch is that you have to find someone to take him, but if you can, such a move would at least remove your child from his undesirable peer group and give him a fresh start. He can enroll in a new school and adopt a new image if he chooses. Sometimes, freeing teenagers from their familiar contacts can create the opportunity for change. Though life with relatives far away is in most cases better than no change at all, it must be accompanied by treatment.

WHEN PLACEMENT OUTSIDE THE HOME IS WARRANTED

Although I'm no advocate of excessively stern parenting, I believe sometimes parents tolerate too much from teenagers and there's a point when something has to give. This usually means the teenager will have to leave the home. Of course, this is a last resort. Fewer than 10 percent of the cases I've ever dealt with have called for such an extreme decision. If placement is inevitable, don't present it as a punishment. It's probably your last hope for getting your out-of-control teenager—and the rest of your family—back on track.

If the criteria below apply to your situation and your other efforts have failed, you'll want to consider some of the placements I discuss later in this chapter.

You've Tried Everything Else

If you can honestly say you've exhausted all other options, placement may be justified. Don't wait for an emergency to take action. In the long run, you'll thank yourself for having the courage to act.

Before you consider removing your teenager from your home, make sure you've taken each of these ten steps:

1. Asked yourself if your actions are an attempt to retaliate, rather than a consideration of your child's best interests.

2. Tried to set reasonable limits and consistently enforce them.

3. Told your child that you've reached the end of your rope and are considering other alternatives.

4. Sought professional assistance (individual, group, or family counseling) and stuck with it for at least several months.

5. Consulted with the school counselor about your child's difficulties.

6. Considered whether there's any basis for court involvement (for example, your teenager is selling drugs or engaging in anti-social behavior).

7. Had an adequate assessment of your child's difficulties that led to a recommendation for residential placement.

8. Followed the suggestions offered in previous chapters of this book with no success.

9. Explored all possible options short of placement outside the home, including school transfer, day treatment programs, and drug rehabilitation services.

10. Considered the implications of sending your child away (she'll feel angry, betrayed, and rejected, and you may feel guilty) versus the consequences of keeping her at home (further family stress and the risk of harm to your child or others).

Your Teenager Is Destroying Your Family

If the problems with your child are changing the complexion of your family life, ask yourself how much more you're willing to tolerate. If you argue with him constantly, worry most of the time, and fear for your family's safety or happiness, things have gone too far. Further, you need to put your foot down if your teenager is engaged in repeated illicit activity or is using your home as a storage place for drugs, stolen merchandise, or other suspicious items.

If your situation has deteriorated to the point of violence at home, you'll definitely need to consider a major change. Physical confrontations between parents and children are not only dangerous but destructive of other family relationships. Of course, outside placement is justified only if the teen has shown a regular pattern of intolerable behavior. Teenagers often insist that their parents should leave, not them, but that's unrealistic.

Your Teenager Wants to Leave Home

If your child asks to be sent away to a boarding school or treatment facility, take her request seriously. Teenagers whose lives are painful or who feel entrenched in their defiant and antisocial patterns may need to get away for a while. I'm not talking about the young person who wants to go live at a friend's house or get an apartment of her own—this is usually avoidance of problems rather than a plea for help—but one who is desperately looking for help. You should be certain to heed this warning.

Experts Have Recommended Placement

When you realize you can't handle your troubled teen alone and seek the advice of school personnel, mental health professionals, or juvenile court workers, these experts may recommend placement if they're convinced all other options have been exhausted. They take these matters quite seriously. Sometimes parents are so distressed that they lose their objectivity. Professionals can point you in the right direction and support you throughout the process.

Your Teenager Can't Be Separated from His Negative Peer Group

Sometimes the attraction of your child's peer group is so strong that you can't separate him from it. He probably depends exclusively on his friends for approval and is easily influenced by their negative attitudes and dangerous routines. The group may be involved with substance abuse or antisocial behavior, and its power over him may be so strong that he feels like a prisoner. It's obvious that he's unhappy, no matter what he says. If all your efforts to wean your child away from such influences have failed, an enforced separation may be your only hope. This generally means sending him to a facility away from home.

Your Teenager Shows No Remorse, No Fear, and No Wish to Change

This scenario is perhaps the scariest of all. Hard-core teenagers—those who are callous, distant, and self-absorbed—are difficult to work with because there's no way to reach them. They're set in their ways, contemptuous of society's rules, unconcerned about their family, indifferent to sympathy, and immune to punishment. These are usually the teens who are involved in the most serious offenses. I'm sorry to say that mental health professionals have the least success with this group, and many wind up in juvenile correctional facilities. Fortunately, they represent only a small percentage of teenagers in trouble. Their harsh and uncaring behavior is often of long-standing origin, and only intensive, long-term rehabilitation can have any impact on them. The sooner this process begins, the better.

Questions to Ask Admissions Officers at Treatment Facilities

Many facilities will send you an information packet prior to accepting your child. Make sure you read through it carefully and try to answer each of these questions.

1. Do they work with teenagers who have problems similar to your child's?

2. Do they have any statistics available on their success rates with students/patients similar to your child?

3. Will they accept teenagers who have drug problems accompanying their other problems?

4. Are there any violent youth in their program?

5. How long is the average length of stay?

6. What is the average cost per month?

7. Will health insurance cover any portion of your child's stay there? If not, are there any other options for funding?

8. What types of therapy will your child receive in their facility, and how often?

9. What is the physical layout of their facility? How many acres of land does it rest on?

10. Are there adequate recreational facilities and opportunities for residents to face physical challenges (rope climbing, hiking, outdoor adventures)?

11. Do they have an accredited school on the premises?

12. What is the level of the living conditions there? Spartan? Plush?

13. Do they have any problems with patients/students running away from their facility? And what security measures do they have to ensure their safety?

14. Is there a medical person (preferably a psychiatrist) on staff?

15. To what extent does the program involve the child's family in the treatment process?

16. What is their treatment philosophy?

17. What is their policy regarding visitation and patients/students going home for vacations, holidays, weekends?

18. Will they help the family to plan for their child's future after discharge from the facility? (This question is especially important because many young people return from treatment to the same environment they were in before admission.)

If you find that the admissions officer downplays the significance of your questions or gives you consistently vague answers, I suggest you look elsewhere.

QUESTIONS PARENTS ASK ABOUT PLACEMENT

You should ask as many questions as you can about the treatment facilities and program at the treatment centers you are considering. Speak to an admissions counselor at each of the facilities directly to discuss your situation, and consult with your psychologist or family therapist before making a final decision.

Over the years, I've been asked a number of questions by concerned parents faced with the decision of arranging a placement for their teenager. These are the most common.

Will My Child Ever Grow Out of This?

Some teenagers will, but unfortunately, most will get worse unless someone intervenes. On rare occasions, young people improve spontaneously. One way in which this improvement can happen is if they fall in love with someone outside their undesirable peer group and the boyfriend or girlfriend has strong family values and a sense of decency. This is an interesting situation. If the troubled teenager can't sell the other person on his way of life, he has to make a difficult choice between the superficial but safe friendship of undesirable peers or the comfort of a close relationship. If the new relationship prevails, he's exposed to a different kind of relationship, one based on trust rather than exploitation, and suddenly finds himself enjoying a life without trouble.

Spontaneous improvement can also result from a young person hooking up with a powerful role model such as a teacher, coach, employer, or Big Brother or Big Sister. This person can motivate him to raise his aspirations and emulate more responsible behavior. Through an identification with the mentor's work, values, or interests, the teenager moves away from the undesirable peers and finds more meaning in his life. It's a wonderful solution to a complex problem, but unfortunately it's still too rare. In the Appendix you'll find resources for connecting your child with a positive influence.

All things considered, the best way out of a problem is to take decisive action and not to simply wait for things to change. Look for and find the right placement for your child, and then fully commit yourself to the course of action you've chosen.

When You Put Kids Who've Been in Trouble Together, Won't They Just Get Worse?

This is a perfectly reasonable question. Many parents doubt that placing their child in a treatment facility will help because of the negative influence of the other teenagers there. I suppose that, in the best of all possible worlds, we'd keep our children away from anyone who's had problems and make sure they spend all their time with desirable peers. Unfortunately, this is not realistic.

Although special schools and treatment programs do group troubled kids together, it's much more likely your teenager will benefit from the lessons of others than pick up bad traits. Usually there's a powerful esprit de corps in these programs because they spend considerable time mobilizing positive peer pressure. So all things considered, some type of rehabilitative setting is still your best bet if your child is out of control. If you still have doubts and you're considering only a school change, keep in mind that defiant youth usually get themselves thrown out of the academically oriented private schools. That's why your best option is to choose a facility that's equipped to deal with serious behavior problems.

What Are the Success Rates of These Programs?

To be honest, it's hard to collect data on the effectiveness of treatment programs. Many claim high success rates but have little research to back them up. You'll usually get a lot of anecdotal evidence; that is, you'll be told about other parents who had a successful experience with the facility. You can call them directly and ask any questions you might have about the similarity of their teens' problems and yours.

But as you will see shortly, there are many different types of programs, and parents usually base their decision on the needs of their teenager, unless costs are the main factor. The effectiveness of the programs will thus vary with the nature and extent of the young person's difficulties. The answer to this question also depends on how you define success—as improvement, or complete change? For example, teens in correctional institutions have a 75 percent recidivism rate following their discharge, which is very discouraging. On the other hand, better than 50 percent of teens placed in residential facilities show at least some improvement. I can assure you that almost anyone in serious trouble will be better off being removed from the situation he's in, assuming everything else has been tried first.

Will Our Teenagers Ever Forgive Us for Putting Them There?

Now that you've resolved to forge ahead, you may have to deal with guilt. If you're one of the many parents who worry about a child's reaction to placement, you can rest easy. Your teenager will protest, complain, and insist he won't go, no matter what you say. But his bark is usually worse than his bite. If you've done your homework in advance, there's a good chance he'll go along with it when the time comes. I'll tell you more about how to get him there later in the chapter.

For the moment, keep this thought in mind. On some level, most troubled teenagers know they need help. They may go to treatment centers kicking and screaming, but their anger is usually short-lived. Upon their arrival, they'll meet other teenagers who are in the same situation. They'll show the newcomers the ropes and tell them how to make the most of it.

Staff members at these institutions are also skilled in dealing with resistance. They'll get your child involved in the program as quickly as possible and define the issues he needs to work on. By the time most teenagers get out, they've accepted the need for treatment. Usually they can't wait to get home and, once there, acknowledge the extent of their problems in retrospect. So don't feel guilty if you need to send your child to a residential program, as you're taking the first important step in turning her life around. Someday, she might even thank you.

Won't They Just Run Away If They Don't Want to Be There?

This is a point well taken. Many teens in trouble can get themselves thrown out of a situation they don't like. If they can't, they may consider other ways to escape. Even the best of programs are faced with an occasional resident taking off, but this is the exception rather than the rule.

When a teenager is considered an escape risk, staff will watch him very closely. This is especially true for newcomers. Most treatment centers have a high staff-patient ratio and provide close supervision. If teenagers do run away, they're usually located quickly and returned to the facility. Typically they lose all their privileges until they can prove they can be trusted again.

TYPES OF PROGRAMS

We've looked at some of the issues relating to placement outside the home. Now we'll look at the options. First, you should know that there are over a thousand facilities across the nation that deal with troubled young adults. Costs, nature of treatment, and length of stay vary widely. Some are private and others are publicly funded. Here is an overview of the various types of programs and how they differ.

Psychiatric Facilities

Historically, psychiatric facilities, like psychiatric hospitals and residential treatment centers, have furnished the lion's share of treatment for young people in trouble. They are usually the most traditional programs available. They should be accredited and staffed by a full complement of mental health professionals. You can expect treatment to include individual, group, and family therapy. Many of these programs have self-contained schools and comprehensive therapeutic recreational activities.

Until about the 1980s, hospitalization for as long as six months in these facilities was covered by insurance. However, with the advent of managed care, the average length of stay dwindled to under a week. Very little can be accomplished with a behavior-disordered teenager in such a short time. These hospitals are therefore now used for emergency situations such as extreme violence, suicide attempts, severe drug problems, and emotional breakdowns.

Residential treatment centers keep teenagers for a longer period, from a few months to a year. They're similar to psychiatric hospitals but offer treatment that is by definition longer and more in-depth. These programs rely heavily on the impact of the therapeutic community—the staff and other residents—to motivate the young person to change. The patients spend twenty-four hours a day together under close supervision. Their interactions with others, their schooling, and their family relationships are closely scrutinized. Often their behavior is governed by a privilege system that allows them more freedom as they demonstrate more responsibility. Usually the programs involve intensive psychotherapy based on an individualized treatment plan.

Residential treatment centers treat various psychiatric disorders. While they will accept youth with serious behavior problems, most do not specialize in this. Before ruling them out, however, remember that many teenagers in trouble have other problems as well. These may include substance abuse, depression, and mood disorders. If your child fits into one of these categories, the comprehensive services available may be appropriate for him. Investigate the program closely before considering it for your child and have him thoroughly evaluated prior to admission. You can arrange for this through a public mental health clinic or a mental health professional in private practice. And if necessary, some facilities will do their own assessment when the patient arrives.

Group Homes

Many jurisdictions fund group homes in the community for teenagers who can't be controlled by their parents. These are generally staffed around the clock by mental health counselors. Residential advisers sometimes live in and assume full responsibility for the teenagers under their care. A young person stays there seven days a week but usually goes to school in the community. Contact with the family is limited during the stay.

The nature of the counseling provided in group homes is less intensive than that in psychiatric facilities. Residents may attend therapy outside of the group home, escorted by staff members. These homes emphasize learning to get along with others and following the house rules. They can't keep teenagers there against their will, so they rely heavily on external pressure from social services or the legal system.

Placements in these homes are limited because of scarce public funding. Such residences frequently accept teenagers who have already completed other treatment programs. However, they expect the young person's behavior to be manageable and ask that he willingly agree to be there. Waiting lists are often long. But this shouldn't deter you from looking into them if they seem appropriate for your child.

Boarding Schools

I'm including boarding schools in this list because some parents are more comfortable trying this stigma-free option first. But don't expect boarding schools to provide treatment for your child. They're in the business of education, not remediation. At best, they provide a change of scenery, smaller classes, and a new peer group. But trouble-prone youth can also find like-minded peers there and find their way into problems. So don't count on a boarding school to single-handedly turn your child around.

Boarding schools are useful for teenagers who want to be there. They can be helpful in a situation in which a young person is having mild family conflicts and expresses a wish to change. And sometimes they're used to get a teenager away from negative peer influence, although there's no guarantee that will happen. Of course, the young person must be prepared for an academically rigorous curriculum and accept the (usually stringent) school rules.

Therapeutic Boarding Schools

Therapeutic boarding schools fill the gap between boarding schools and residential treatment centers. They are highly structured programs, often in a rural setting, that combine classroom education with an emphasis on emotional growth. While they offer a full educational curriculum, they do not stress competition and will help the individual student achieve success. Almost all of these schools expect their students to spend a minimum of one to two years there. Typically they have a counseling component that includes individual or group work. They focus on helping teens build self-esteem, be more responsible, and develop a value system. Many of these programs offer addiction education as part of the curriculum.

Therapeutic boarding schools accept students who are troubled, have a history of school failure, and are unresponsive to their parents' direction. Often the students have had counseling prior to admission. Such schools will consider those who are defiant and school-averse and have experimented with drugs. They usually steer away from teens with more serious psychiatric problems (mental breakdowns, violence, drug addictions, serious depression, suicidal behavior). The schools rely heavily on positive peer pressure and helping students learn to overcome environmental challenges. They report reasonably high success rates. Not surprisingly, their tuition rates are quite high (averaging $5,000 a month); but some offer financial aid.

Military Schools

Military schools are highly structured boarding schools based on the type of discipline found in the military. They have no formal association with the military. Parents have been threatening their rebellious children with military school for decades. Many have actually sent them there, hoping to keep them out of trouble, but the results have been mixed.

First of all, the majority of these schools are not equipped to provide the type of assistance that these youth need. They were never intended to be a dumping ground for defiant and antisocial young people. What they do offer is considerable structure and a strict regimen. Unfortunately, not all young people are willing to accept this discipline.

Another problem is that many unruly teenagers get thrown out of military school, leaving their parents unsure where to turn next. So think carefully about this option. If your child is determined to get expelled, he almost certainly will. On the other hand, some teenagers take these programs quite seriously. Despite their objections, they actually want and need discipline, which is exactly what they'll get there. You'll know your child fits the bill for these programs if he has responded well to authority figures in the past. Young people who've shown an interest in the military and want to be away from home will usually benefit from these programs.

Generally speaking, however, I wouldn't recommend military school for adolescents with multiple problems. The emphasis on discipline is too great, and the attention given to behavioral difficulties too small. Teenagers with such problems need a more comprehensive approach to help them. You should also consider that the better-quality military schools carefully screen their applicants and may not consider teenagers who are sent there against their will. This policy often rules out a significant percentage of troubled kids we've been discussing.

Boot Camps

These programs are modeled on military boot camps and are a relatively recent phenomenon. Boot camps are part of the juvenile justice system, and a teenager can be placed there only by the court, so parents may have little say in the process. Recently a few private, for-profit boot camps have sprung up across the nation, but usually they don't serve teens with histories of mental illness.

Treatment in boot camps varies from facility to facility, though they typically emphasize military-style discipline, physical conditioning, and hard labor. The emphasis in these programs is on respecting authority and conforming to rules. "Inmates," as they are called, usually spend about three months there. Although there have been dramatic anecdotal claims of striking successes (featured, for example, on daytime talk shows), the long-term effectiveness of these programs has not been demonstrated to date.

I don't recommend boot camps for most circumstances. There is some evidence, however, that they can be useful for youth who are placed there early in their cycle of offending. If they'll tolerate the regimen, fine, but there's always the risk of altercations with staff and occasionally physical injury. As I've stated throughout the book, punishment is generally not an effective approach with youth who have serious behavior problems. So make sure you inquire about the auxiliary therapeutic services before placing a child there on your own.

Wilderness Programs

If there is any trend in the therapeutic field, it's toward an increase in the use of these programs, which now serve a large number of youth who've been in trouble. The wilderness treatment model combines a hands-on, outdoors education with a therapeutic experience. Typically, participants are placed in a secluded setting lacking the usual creature comforts. With the assistance of counselors, they're expected to master the natural environment through a sequence of increasingly difficult challenges. These might include rappelling, rock climbing, hiking, camping, and whitewater rafting. The theory is that in the absence of an authority to challenge them, and away from the distractions at home, young people will be forced to focus on their own issues and develop their own resources.

Wilderness programs rely heavily on group pressure to accomplish their objectives. Participants must learn to count on one another to overcome obstacles. Their experiences are designed to promote selflessness and responsibility. Proponents of the wilderness model claim that it cultivates feelings of competence and mastery. Although it seems best suited for the action-oriented, it's not necessary to have outdoor skills to benefit.

The length of stay in a wilderness program varies from several days to one year. Don't expect any overnight miracles; teenagers with serious behavioral disturbances usually need at least six months. Wilderness programs are more cost-effective than psychiatric facilities, and their success rates are at least as impressive. They work well for kids who've had an ongoing history of behavior problems that are not accompanied by serious psychiatric problems like depression, mood disorders, and thought disorders. Consequently, I recommend that you give this option serious consideration if all else has failed.

Detention Centers

I hesitate to include these in the category of treatment alternatives, but they are a reality for some. Detention centers are municipal and state facilities that house youngsters who've been in trouble with the legal system, often having committed criminal acts punishable by law. Typically, teenagers are placed in these centers by a judge. The length of stay ranges from a few days to a few months. Family visits are usually restricted to only a few hours once or twice a week.

The quality of life in these centers leaves much to be desired. They're not intended to be pleasant. Little rehabilitation is offered in most of the programs, although some are more progressive than others. Inmates spend much of the day in small, secured rooms with few if any distractions. I suppose the goal is to teach the young person a hard lesson. Occasionally that happens. But unfortunately, a thirty-day stint in detention is rarely sufficient to turn a young person's life around. Their experience after discharge often determines their fate. If they return to their previous adverse influences and fail to receive further assistance, they're at great risk for further trouble.

Correctional Institutions

Teens are sentenced to these programs, which are the longer-term extension of detention centers, through the court system and are not discharged until they complete their term. The conditions are as spartan as in detention centers, but many correctional institutions offer opportunities for continued education and other constructive involvement. The quality of treatment varies greatly from institution to institution, so it's difficult to describe a typical program. At the least, you can expect a maximum security facility with almost constant supervision. I have yet to meet a teenager who enjoyed the experience.

If your child is sentenced to a correctional institution, you'll find that family visits are extremely restricted. In some facilities they're limited to once a month. The statistics on youth placed in correctional institutions are sobering. Within a year of discharge, over 50 percent of them will be in trouble again.

COST CONSIDERATIONS

A wide range of services, then, is available, but even if you find a program suited to your child, you'll still have to get him admitted and pay for the high cost of treatment. How will you pay, and will anyone help?

Private psychiatric facilities are by far the most expensive of the treatment alternatives. It's not unusual to hear of hospital costs approaching a thousand dollars a day. Sometimes health insurance will cover the treatment, but only for a brief stay. Unless you have health insurance, you'll likely find these programs out of reach. State facilities are usually more affordable, sometimes even free, but the quality of treatment may be inferior.

Wilderness programs are more cost-effective. You can expect a tab of several thousand dollars a month for placement there. Insurance companies rarely cover these costs, because these programs are not considered psychiatric. This is unfortunate because they offer a viable alternative to expensive traditional care. Don't let this discourage you, however. You can find other sources of funding, which I'll discuss shortly.

Finally, military schools compete with other boarding schools for the tuition dollar. You'll be totally on your own here because no funding source is willing to pay for them. Military school is usually less expensive than a wilderness program, but as I said earlier, helpful only under certain circumstances.

How will you pay for treatment in these facilities? Some parents are able to cover the costs on their own, but they are in the minority. If you're worried about not being able to afford any of these programs, first bear in mind that admissions officers are usually savvy fund-raisers. They'll be happy to help you explore sources of financial assistance, and sometimes they'll be willing to reduce their fees.

Public funds are available, but eligibility requirements are very strict. Most schools, for example, have a budget to serve the needs of special students. If your school system can't meet your child's educational needs because of a learning disability, emotional or psychological disorder, or some other reason, the county is required to pay for an appropriate placement. Your child will have to be declared eligible for funding, and this will take some time. Usually the school must be satisfied that all other possibilities have been ruled out and that the problems are school related as well as behavioral. This means that teenagers are typically placed in day programs before being considered for residential settings.

Other types of county and state funding are also available under certain circumstances, which usually involve the court system. Most judges have the discretion to order children into residential treatment and to make funds available for them. Such rulings are infrequent because the courts have to make certain that other options have been exhausted. This could mean placement in a detention center first. Teenage candidates for this kind of funding usually have a long history of antisocial behavior and are considered risks to other people. Consequently they are more likely to be sentenced to a correctional institution.

The final funding possibility is available to parents who've relinquished custody of their teenager, either voluntarily, because the young person is out of control, or as a result of a court mandate, because they've been found to be unfit parents. In the latter case, the county or state assumes legal responsibility and provides funding for whatever services are needed. This doesn't happen very often either.

As much as I hate to say it, sometimes no funding is obtainable. This can put you in a terrible position. You know your child badly needs a change, but your hands are tied. And if your child's aware of this, he may push the limits even further, convinced that there's nothing you can do to him. If your teenager is eighteen, you might consider throwing him out of the house to live on his own. It's absolutely a last resort, but you have to consider the safety and well-being of your whole family. If you're convinced that your child is a destructive force and you've warned him that you'll throw him out if his actions continue, then go ahead if you can live with yourself. There are no guarantees that this will help him, and the situation may worsen before it gets better. But sometimes the real world can teach a teenager some valuable lessons. He might realize that home wasn't such a bad place after all, and ask to return.

Over the years, I've worked with several teenagers who were shocked by their parents' throwing them out of the house. At first they were thrilled to be on their own, but gradually the harsh realities set in. With a menial job (if they were able to get that), little money, substandard housing, and inadequate support systems, they floundered and grew increasingly unhappy. Within several months, they approached their parents and asked for another chance. In each case, their parents regained some leverage. They were able to establish the conditions for their child's return, thereby restoring some order to the family. Of course, some teenagers never come home and manage to get by on their own. But for every successful story I've heard, there have been a great deal more failures. Many teenagers stay out on their own and get into even more serious trouble. So think long and hard before you consider the "tough love" option.

GETTING YOUR TEENAGER TO ENTER A PROGRAM

Let's assume your child has been accepted in a residential program and the funding is taken care of. Now you face the challenge of persuading her to go. Not surprisingly, many teenagers do not go willingly into these programs. They're well aware that they'll have to leave their home and their friends for at least several months. If they've been uncooperative before, it's unrealistic to expect them to acquiesce without at least some protest.

As I said earlier, you should prepare your child for this step gradually. Ideally, you've been telling her that you've considered residential placement because of her extreme behavior. You've also given her the chance to participate in choosing a program. On some level, most teenagers in serious trouble know they're out of control and drastic measures are called for, even though they wouldn't ask for help directly. She may feel compelled to fight the decision but feel secretly relieved. If you're prepared for this and remember that her dramatic resistance will pass, you should be able to weather the storm.

I have known of parents who have planted information about residential programs around the house. They have left the brochures in a conspicuous place. One mother stamped CONFIDENTIAL: FOR PARENTS ONLY on a piece of literature to ensure that her daughter would pick it up and read it.

You may be able to visit a facility with your child before sending him there. This can serve two purposes. First, it shows him what he's in for, dispels any misconceptions he might have, and paves the way for a smoother transition. Second, it can scare him into making an effort to change. His fear of leaving home may prevail over his defiance. Either way, this type of excursion is almost always useful. In the event that your child refuses to accompany you, you can remind him that he's giving up his say in the decision. For some teenagers, such a visit is an eye-opener.

There are times, however, when teenagers' resistance is extreme. Have a plan in mind if your teenager threatens to run away or kill himself rather than be sent away. Don't overreact to his intimidation, but that doesn't mean you should take the threats lightly. If your teenager is impulsive and prone to self-destructive behavior, he may escalate the situation in an attempt to manipulate you. But if he's not backing up his words with actions, you're better off not responding to them. This is certainly

Alternative Programs for Teens in Trouble

Type of Facility	Referral	Length of Stay
Psychiatric hospital	Self, mental health professional, agency	Under a week
Residential treatment center	Self, school, agency, court, mental health professional	Few months to a year
Group home	Social services or legal system	Open
Boarding school	Self	School terms
Military school	Self; usually voluntary	School terms
Boot camp	Juvenile justice system	Average of 3 months
Wilderness program	Self, school system, mental health professional	Several days to one year
Detention center	Legal system	A few days to few months
Correctional institution	Courts	Set terms
Therapeutic boarding schools	Self or educational placement specialist	6 months to two years

Treatment	Characteristics	Cost
Individual, group, and family therapy	Full complement of mental health professionals; schools; therapeutic recreation	Up to $1,000/day; insurance coverage for brief stay; state facilities more expensive
Intense psychotherapy for psychiatric disorders	24-hour supervision	Possible county and state funding
Mental health counselors	7 days a week; school outside; limited contact with family; limited placements for family members; long waiting lists	Public funding
None	Varies	Tuition from $10,000 to $50,000 per year
Little attention to behavioral difficulties	Structure; strict regimen	Less expensive than wilderness program; tuition responsibility of family
Not for youth with history of mental illness	Military-style discipline; secluded; spartan	Public funding
Experiential one year education and therapy through outdoor activity	Secluded; spartan	$3,000 to $6,000 per month
Little treatment option	Small, secured rooms; few distractions	Public funding
Some education, other activities	Maximum security, constant supervision	Public funding
Education, counseling, positive peer pressure	Some security, moderate supervision	$35,000 to $70,000 per year

not the time to argue with your child. It's best to give him some time to settle down and then bring up the issue again. If your child runs away, notify the police after he's been gone for more than twenty-four hours. And if he actually attempts to hurt himself, head right for the emergency room of your local hospital. Your child needs immediate medical and psychiatric attention. Don't try to make your own judgment of how serious the situation is. You can't afford to be wrong on this one.

If she remains adamant about her refusal to attend a program, you'll need to arrange for her to be taken to the facility with or without her consent. Don't get into a physical struggle with your child. Either recruit support from friends and family or hire someone to do the job. Many programs will help you hire an agency that specializes in coming to your home and firmly but safely transporting your teenager to the facility. Once she's there, she'll have plenty of time to get over her anger about the placement.

In some instances there is a genuine risk of the teenager running away or otherwise disappearing when the time comes for her to leave. In that case, you may need to catch her off guard. That means packing her bags in advance and, without warning, telling her that it's time to leave. If you've planned the situation in advance and have others available to provide physical support if necessary, it will usually go smoothly. Your teenager will quickly realize that she has no choice: she'll either have to go willingly or be forcibly taken.

A FINAL WORD

The message in this book should be clear by now: you have the power to influence your child's behavior. If you're resolved to do so, take heart. You'll make a significant contribution to your own family life by raising a secure and confident teenager who can steer away from trouble. Be actively involved in your teenagers' lives, recognize their accomplishments, and hold them accountable for their failure to abide by the rules. If you see trouble brewing, take action right away. Many teens are unwilling to ask for help until they hit rock bottom, but you shouldn't wait for that to happen before you act.

Parenting a teenager is difficult and demanding. Sometimes you can't believe that things could ever turn out well—that the adoring child you raised will ever emerge from the ugly cocoon of adolescence in the shape of a mature, intelligent, caring adult. That part takes faith.

APPENDIX

Resources for Parents of Teens in Trouble

Al-Anon/Al-ateen Family Group Headquarters

Information and referral to self-help programs.
Telephone: (800) 344-2666
Address: 1600 Corporate Landing Parkway,
    Virginia Beach, VA 23454-5617
Web site: www.al-anon.al-ateen.org
E-mail: wso@al-anon.org

American Psychiatric Association

Information pamphlets and referrals to a
    psychiatrist in your area.
Telephone: (202) 682-6000
Address: 1400 K Street NW, Washington, DC 20005
Web site: www.psych.org

Association for Experiential Education

Directory of wilderness programs throughout the country.
    Publications and jobs clearinghouse for teenagers and
    adults.
Telephone: (303) 440-8844
Address: 2305 Canyon Blvd. #100, Boulder, CO 80302
Web site: www.aee.org

Big Brothers/Big Sisters of America

Adult volunteers who serve as friends and companions to
    children from single-parent families and at-risk youth.
Telephone: (215) 567-7000
Address: 230 N. 13th Street, Philadelphia, PA 19107
Web site: www.bbbsa.org
E-mail: national@bbbsa.org

Boys Town USA Hotline

Crisis intervention, resources, and referrals, as well as
residential placement for youth in trouble.
Telephone: (800) 448-3000
Address: 13940 Gutowski Road, Boys Town, NE 68010
Web site: www.Boystown.org
E-mail: Hotline@Boystown.org

The Brown Schools

National information and referral service; network of
psychiatric residential treatment facilities.
Telephone: (800) 531-5305
Address: The Brown Schools Call Center, P.O. Box 4008, Austin,
TX 78765
Web site: www.brownschools.com

Center for Disease Control/Office on Smoking and Health

Publications and information on smoking, tobacco, and health.
Telephone: (800) 232-1311
Address: P.O. Box 6003, Rockville, MD 20849-6003
Web site: www.cdc.gov/tobacco

Center for Substance Abuse Treatment (CSAT)

Referrals for substance abuse treatment in your area. Free
information and pamphlets.
Telephone: (800) 662-HELP
Address: National Clearinghouse for Alcohol and Drug
Information, 11426-28 Rockville Pike, Rockville, MD
20817-2345
Web site: www.health.org
E-mail: info@health.org

Child Help USA (Hotline)

Listening and referral service for parents who feel they're in
danger of abusing their children. Provides additional
resources and general information.

Telephone: (800) 4A-Child
Address: Child Help USA, 15757 N. 78th Street,
   Scottsdale, AZ 85260
Web site: www.childhelpUSA.org

Children with Attention Deficit Disorders (CHADD)
Information, brochures, and membership information.
Telephone: (800) 233-4050
Address: 8181 Professional Place, Landover, MD 20785
Web site: www.chadd.org

Drug Abuse Resistance Organization (DARE)
Brochures, information, referrals to hot lines.
Telephone: (800) 223-DARE
Address: P.O. Box 2090, Los Angeles, CA 90051
Web site: www.dare.com

Gang Resistance Education and Training (GREAT)
Information about programs to prevent gang
   involvement.
Telephone: (800) 726-7070
Address: Great Program, 800 K Street NW,
   Washington, DC 20091
Web site: www.atf.treas.gov/great/great.htm

Independent Educational Consultants Association (IECA)
Referrals and free directory of educational consultants.
Telephone: (703) 591-4850
Address: 3251 Old Lee Highway #510, Fairfax, VA 22030
Web site: www.iecaonline.com

Learning Disabilities Association of America
Information and referrals.
Telephone: (888) 300-6710
Address: 4156 Library Road, Pittsburgh, PA 15234
Web site: www.ldanatl.org

National Association of Therapeutic Schools and Programs (NATSAP)
Information, referrals, and directory of therapeutic boarding
    schools and programs.
Telephone: (912) 447-8404
Address: 409 East 48 Street, Savannah, GA 31405
Web site: www.natsap.org

National Council on Alcoholism and Drug Dependence
Information, resources, and referrals.
Telephone: (800) NCA-CALL
Address: 12 West 21 Street, 7th Floor, New York, NY 10017
Web site: www.ncadd.org

National Criminal Justice Referral Service
Information about programs within the juvenile justice system
    (boot camps, correctional institutions, and other services).
    Referrals to appropriate services.
Telephone: (800) 638-8736
Address: NCJRS, 9015 Junction Drive,
    Annapolis Junction, MD 20701
Web site: www.ncjrs.org

**National Institute of Mental Health (NIMH)/Public Information
Office**
Information, brochures on mental illness, descriptions of
    ongoing research programs.
Telephone: (301) 443-4513
Address: 5600 Fishers Lane, Rockville, MD 20857
Web site: www.nimh.nih.gov

National Register of Health Service Providers in Psychology
Information and referrals to psychologists throughout
    the country.
Telephone: (202) 783-7663
Address: 1120 G Street NW, Suite 330, Washington, DC 20005
Web site: www.nationalregister.org

National Runaway Switchboard
Crisis intervention for youth and families through a national network.
Telephone: (800) 621-4000
Web site: www.nrscrisisline.org
E-mail: info@nrscrisisline.org

National Sexually Transmitted Disease Hotline
Information, referrals, and free brochures.
Telephone: (800) 227-8922
Address: American Social Help Association, P.O. Box 13827, Research Triangle Park, NC 27709
Web site: www.ashastd.org

New Cult Awareness Network
Information and referrals for assistance with cult-involved teens.
Telephone: (773) 267-7777
Address: 1680 N. Vine Street #415, Los Angeles, CA 90028
Web site: www.cultawarenessnetwork.org

Tough Love
Support groups for families in trouble. Highly structured behavior modification approach.
Telephone: (800) 333-1069
Address: Tough Love, P.O. Box 1069, Doylestown, PA 18901
Web site: www.toughlove.org
E-mail: Tlove@netcarrier.com

Woodbury Reports
Information on struggling teens, referrals, newsletter.
Telephone: (208) 267-5550
Address: P.O. Box 1107, Bonners Ferry, ID 83805
Web site: www.strugglingteens.com

INDEX

N

O

P